INTRODUCTION TO SPEECH COMMUNICATION

WILLIAM J. SEILER
The University of Nebraska

SCOTT, FORESMAN/LITTLE, BROWN COLLEGE DIVISION
SCOTT, FORESMAN AND COMPANY
Glenview, Illinois • Boston • London

Library of Congress Cataloging-in-Publication Data

Seiler, William J.
  Introduction to speech communication.

  Includes bibliographies and index.
  1. Oral communication.   I. Title.
P95.S45   1987   001.54'2   87-16676
ISBN 0-673-18573-7
    123456RRC929190898887

Credits

Cover photos: (ctr) Sarah Putnam/Picture Cube; (lr) © Susan Lapides 1986/Design Conceptions.   Photos on p. 1:
(l) Richard Kalvar/Magnum; (r) Owen Franken/Stock Boston.   Photo on p. 5: Joseph A. Dichello, Jr.   Figure on p. 8:
From "Schematic Model of the Essential Components of Communication" by William D. Brooks. Reprinted by
permission of author.   Figure on p. 20: From *Communication in Business and Professional Organizations* by William Seiler,
E. Scott Baudhuin, and L. David Schuelke. Copyright © 1982 by Random House, Inc. Reprinted by permission.   Photo
on p. 39: Elizabeth Crews.   Box on p. 50: From "English Language, It's Like, You Know, Truly Tubular" by Rick
Horowitz, *Chicago Tribune*, November 23, 1986. Copyright © 1986 by Rick Horowitz. Reprinted by permission of the
author.   Box on p. 52: From "Programmed Loose Lips Think Slips" by Keay Davidson. Reprinted by permission of The
San Francisco Examiner.   Photo on p. 66: Pat Coffey/Picture Cube.   Photo on p. 78: Margaret Thompson/Picture Cube.
Photo on p. 82: Richard Kalvar/Magnum.   Box on p. 101: "Quiz #1" from *Your Personal Listening Profile*. Prepared by Dr.
Lyman K. Steil, President of Communication Development, Inc., St. Paul, Minnesota, for the Sperry Corporation.
Reprinted with permission of Dr. Steil and Unisys Corporation.   Photo on p. 103: Jean-Claude Lejeune/Stock Boston.
Photo on p. 105: Arnold Ogden/University of Colorado Information Service.   Photo on p. 106: Stacy Pick/Stock Boston.
Photos on p. 121: (l) Jerry Brandt/Stock Boston; (r) Elizabeth Crews.   Box on p. 124: From "Wickless Finds Speech Class
Was Valuable Lifetime Lesson" by Bob Reeves, *The Lincoln Star*, April 21, 1987. Reprinted by permission of The Lincoln
Star.   Photo on p. 125: Jeffry W. Myers/Stock Boston.   Photo on p. 129: Elizabeth Crews.   Figure on p. 174: From
"Baseball Pay: DHs a hit" by Hal Bodley, *USA Today*, January 10, 1986. Copyright © 1986 USA Today. Reprinted with
permission.   Photo on p. 213: Susan Lapides/Design Conceptions.   Photo on p. 218: Brent Jones.   Figure on p. 230:
(bottom) From "Yankees at top of salary scale; Mariners last," *USA Today*, January 10, 1986. Copyright © 1986, USA
Today. Excerpted with permission.   Figure on p. 231: From "Number of farmers fell sharply in 1985," *USA Today*,
January 10, 1986. Copyright © 1986 by USA Today. Reprinted by permission.   Figures on p. 232: From *Statistics for
Business and Economics* by Heinz Kohler, p. 78. Copyright © 1985 Scott, Foresman and Company.   Photo on p. 266:
Richard Younker.   Photo on p. 282: The Museum of Modern Art/Film Stills Archives.   Photos on p. 289: (l) Richard
Kalvar/Magnum; (r) Steve & Mary Skjold Photographs.   Box on p. 291: From "Teens" by Beth Winship, *Detroit Free
Press*, December 29, 1980. Copyright © 1980 by The Los Angeles Times Syndicate. Reprinted by permission.   Photo on
p. 292: Steve & Mary Skjold Photographs.   Box on p. 296: Adapted from *The Interpersonal Underworld* by William C.
Schutz. Copyright © 1958 by William C. Schutz. Reprinted by permission of Science and Behavior Books.   Box on
p. 304: "A Model of Interactive Stages" from *Interpersonal Communication and Human Relationships* by Mark L. Knapp,
p. 33. Copyright © 1984 by Allyn and Bacon, Inc. Reprinted by permission.   Box on p. 305: From "Small Talk," *Chicago
Tribune*, February 26, 1987. Copyright © 1987 Chicago Tribune Company, all rights reserved, used with permission.
Figure on p. 306: "The Johari Window" from *Group Processes: An Introduction to Group Dynamics* by J. Luft, 2/E, p. 10.
Copyright © 1963 by Joseph Luft. Reprinted by permission of Mayfield Publishing Company.   Figure on p. 307:
"Laboratory Objectives" from *Group Processes: An Introduction to Group Dynamics* by J. Luft, 2/E, p. 13. Copyright © 1963
by Joseph Luft. Reprinted by permission of Mayfield Publishing Company.   Photo on p. 317: Dennis Budd Gray/Stock
Boston.   Box on p. 319: "PTA Candidate Forum Slated" from *The Lincoln Star*, April 18, 1987. Reprinted by permisson of
The Lincoln Star.   Photo on p. 324: Richard Kalvar/Magnum.   Appendix on pages 331–332: From *Principles of Speech
Communication*, 9th edition, by Douglas Ehninger, Bruce E. Gronbeck, and Alan H. Monroe, pp. 286–287. Copyright ©
1984 by Scott, Foresman and Company.   Photo on p. 335: Richard Wood/Picture Cube.   Photo on p. 360: James H.
Pickerell.

Preface

This book is designed to help all who wish to improve their understanding and skill in communicating with others. But, more specifically, it is designed for college students who are taking an introductory speech communication course to learn about communication principles, public speaking, and interpersonal and group communication. With this audience in mind, I have drawn on over twenty years of my experience working with students and colleagues, both as a teacher and as the director of a beginning course in speech communication, to create a book that will help students develop practical communication skills that will serve them throughout their lives.

Goal

The goal of this book is *to provide students with a comprehensive, practical, readable, enjoyable, and, most important, intellectually sound vehicle to learn about communication.* As a result, this book is readily adaptable to the teaching styles of experienced teachers, who will be able to complement its content with their personal knowledge, and beginning instructors, who will be assisted by its thoroughness, examples, and pedagogy.

Features

Effectiveness in speech communication is an acquired skill. Although natural speaking ability is an asset, any person's capabilities in communication can be developed and improved through (1) an understanding of communicative theories and principles, (2) training in its basic principles, and (3) practice. This book meets students' needs in all three areas by providing:

- Simply stated and specific learning objectives at the beginning of each chapter.
- Thorough and systematic explanations of basic principles.

- Clear, concrete, student-oriented examples, photos, cartoons, and other visual materials that support and expand on key concepts.
- Thought-provoking **Think About It** boxes and **Mini-Exercises** that encourage students' active involvement throughout each chapter.
- Review boxes that highlight key information.
- Lists of down-to-earth hints and guidelines that help students transform theory into practice.
- Thorough, end-of-chapter summaries that review key terms and concepts.
- Chapter-by-chapter glossaries of key terms plus a complete glossary at the end of the book.
- Discussion questions at the end of each chapter.
- Chapter lists of suggested readings to provide students with scholarly and contemporary resource materials.

Introduction to Speech Communication includes a number of pedagogical devices to help students learn about speech communication. Each principle, idea, or concept is systematically explained and illustrated with clear, relevant examples from students' actual experiences both on and off campus. when appropriate, examples of my personal experiences as a teacher, colleague, student, husband, and parent are also included. And there are contemporary cartoons, photos, tables, and figures to illustrate concepts and principles visually.

At the beginning of each chapter is a list of learning objectives that direct students' attention to important ideas, concepts, and principles. Boxed sections labeled **Think About It** ask students to reflect on what they have read or to relate their reading to situations they are likely to encounter when communicating with others. In addition, each chapter includes boxed sections called **Mini-Exercises** whose purpose is to encourage students to experiment with significant ideas, principles, or skills by putting them to work.

A particularly useful element of this text is its many **Review Boxes,** which summarize important ideas, principles, and skills to help students better understand and remember what they have read. To aid students further, all key terms and concepts are printed in boldface and are defined immediately upon their first appearance in the text and at the end of each chapter in a section labeled **Key Terms.** And for handy reference, all key terms and concepts, along with their definitions, are repeated in a glossary at the end of the book.

Also aimed at helping students review and assimilate target information are the extensive and thorough chapter summaries. By including both an overview of the chapter's important information and a review of all its key terms and concepts, each summary helps students construct individual facts into a total and cohesive picture.

The two final sections of each chapter are also noteworthy. **Discussion**

Starters are though-provoking questions about the information presented in the chapter. These questions are intended to provoke discussions that will raise students' awareness of how the information they are learning in the classroom applies to their everyday lives. And the section entitled **Additional Readings** lists scholarly and contemporary materials that will give students a deeper understanding or another perspective of the ideas presented in each chapter.

ORGANIZATION

This book is organized not only to present the range of topics required in every introductory college speech communication course, but also to meet the time and instructional demands of one of the most important courses in the college curriculum. With this dual goal in mind, the chapters are arranged to provide a practical and workable approach to teaching the fundamentals of speech communication. **Part I: The Foundations of Communication** provides the necessary background and basic principles for all communication. **Part II: Public Communication** helps students to develop their speaking skills as they learn to select a topic, analyze an audience, gather and use supporting and clarifying materials, organize and outline speech material, deliver a speech with confidence, and effectively inform and persuade an audience. And **Part III: Interpersonal Communication** includes information about communication in relationships, small groups, and interviews.

Public communication skills are taught early because I believe that they are fundamental to all levels of communication. All communication is goal-oriented. Therefore, in order to communicate effectively throughout life, whether socially or on the job, in dyads, in small groups, or before an audience, a person must be able to communicate with confidence, support and clarify his or her thoughts, organize information, analyze those with whom he or she is communicating, and inform and persuade effectively. Moreover, in life after school, students will discover that purposive, career-related communication relies more on the preparedness underlying public communication than it does on the empathy and self-disclosure found at the heart of interpersonal communication.

This sequence of presentation is also based on the recognition that students in an introductory speech communication course must master a great deal of basic information before they give a speech, yet, due to time constraints, they need to begin preparing and presenting speeches as early in the term as possible. Introducing public speaking skills first provides a more even balance between speech presentations and other activities and alleviates the tendency to focus on speechmaking exclusively at the end of the term.

Considerable demands are placed on the introductory communication course, and as a result, there is a wide variety of ways to teach the course—emphasis on interpersonal communication, emphasis on public speaking, equal emphasis on all types of communication. To meet these differing needs, each chapter is completely self-contained so that an instructor can easily arrange the sequence to meet the demands of his or her specific teaching situation. Further, a section of the *Instructor's Manual* is devoted to suggestions for using this book to achieve the desired course focus. The book is also planned to meet the needs of those who use the Personalized System of Instruction (PSI) and organize their courses to meet specific learning objectives.

THE STUDY GUIDE

The study guide is designed to supplement *Introduction to Speech Communication* and to help students learn more efficiently and effectively. It is a set of objectives, questions, exercises, and self-testing questions, which, if mastered, will give students a thorough understanding of speech communication. Completing the study guide accurately will help students to learn the fundamentals of speech communication, their implications, and their applications. It can also be used in courses that use PSI.

THE INSTRUCTOR'S MANUAL

The instructor's manual was written to provide nuts-and-bolts information about designing and developing a fundamental speech communication course and to suggest methods for improving instruction. Of course, it would be presumptuous of me to pretend to know what each individual instructor needs or wants. But it is my hope that the manual will make the book more useful to instructors and students alike. The manual includes four sections:

- **Section I** presents suggestions for organizing the basic course in speech communication. Included is a checklist for managing and designing the beginning course in speech communication, my view on using the book, and sample class schedules.
- **Section II** provides classroom exercises and assignments to be used in conjunction with **Introduction to Speech Communication.** There are a variety of exercises, including both the classic ones and some that other instructors and I have developed for the basic speech course. There is a list of resources for additional activities and a film list. Finally, there are specific sample-performance and other assignments. Each performance assignment is presented with a complete description, a rationale, procedures for implementation, and suggestions for evaluating the results.
- **Section III** is a complete test-item file, including multiple-choice, true-false, and short-answer questions. Each item is directly related to the learning objectives, and answers are provided along with the page numbers of their sources. A computer-based test file is also available to those who adopt the text.

- **Section IV** discusses the use of PSI for teaching the basic speech communication course. It includes all the basics for setting up such a program. The PSI method has been in successful use for over seven years at the University of Nebraska and for over five years at the University of South Dakota.

ACKNOWLEDGMENTS

Numerous people have contributed to this book. There are first and foremost, the students who have shared their time and learning experiences with me, the instructors who patiently taught me about communication and life, the colleagues who have shared their expertise with me, the many graduate students who have worked in our basic speech course over the past fifteen years, and the hundreds of undergraduate assistants and assistant supervisory instructors who have worked in our Personalized System of Instruction basic speech communication course during the past seven years.

I owe a great deal to Robert J. Kibler for never saying "never" and for instilling in me a desire to do my very best, whatever the task. I am most indebted to Gus Friedrich for his continued support and his willingness to allow me to introduce the Personalized System of Instruction at the University of Nebraska. There are, in addition, many people who worked beyond any reasonable expectation to improve our basic course and who deserve special mention: Marilyn Fuss-Reineck, Sandi Hanisko, George Lawson, Diana Prentice, Melissa Beall, Arlie Daniel, Vicki Nogel, Charles Wilbanks, Drew McGukin, Ruth Kay, Kate Joeckel, Dave Dunning, Bill Mullen, Debra Japp, Olga Davis, and Esther Yook.

The publishing of any book requires people dedicated to quality, and this book is no exception. I am extremely thankful to June Rugg, who edited the first and second drafts of the manuscript, to Cynthia Fostle, who edited the third and fourth drafts of the manuscript—she was simply outstanding as well as a joy to work with, and, finally, to Barbara Muller, who believed in the manuscript from the very first day we talked about it.

Special thanks and love to my children, Dana and Dionne, for being the two neatest kids in the whole world, and to my wife, Kathi, for allowing me to have the freedom necessary to work on a project of this magnitude. They made it all worthwhile!

Finally, I would like to thank the following persons who participated in the review process: Philip M. Backlund, Central Washington University; Allan R. Broadhurst, Cape Cod Community College; Skip Eno, University of Texas at San Antonio; Mary C. Forestieri, Lane Community College; Marc E. Routhier, Frostburg State College; and Kathie A. Webster, Northwest Missouri State University. Their comments and suggestions were invaluable and I appreciate their honesty and expertise.

Sincerely,

Bill Seiler

SPECIAL NOTE TO THE INSTRUCTOR

Instructors who are interested in adopting the PSI method should request the appropriate ancillary materials that accompany this book, namely, an Instructor's Manual, an Instructor Assistant's Manual, and a Student's Study Guide. In addition, there is a test bank and a computer program to generate random test items. Videotapes on the use of competency-based evaluation of student speeches and other aspects of using the PSI method are also available from the author. You will need to provide a blank VHS or beta tape. Please send videotape requests to Bill Seiler, Department of Speech Communication, University of Nebraska, Lincoln, NE 68588-0329. If you should need any other additional information please feel free to call the author at 402-472-6922.

CONTENTS

PART II

PUBLIC COMMUNICATION

CHAPTER 6

GETTING STARTED: TOPIC SELECTION AND AUDIENCE ANALYSIS

CHAPTER 7

GATHERING AND USING INFORMATION

CHAPTER 14

PARTICIPATING IN SMALL GROUPS   *333*

CHAPTER 15

INTERVIEWING   *352*

FOUNDATIONS OF COMMUNICATION

CHAPTER 1

Human Communication

LEARNING OBJECTIVES

After studying this chapter, you should be able to:

1. Explain what speech communication is and what it involves.

2. Demonstrate the importance of having effective oral communication skills by citing examples from history and the business world.

3. Describe the functions and interrelationships of the seven essential components of communication.

4. Use the four fundamental principles of communication to illustrate the complex nature of communication.

5. Identify five common misconceptions about communication and tell why they are incorrect.

Although we are all by our very nature communicative beings, we are not automatically effective or proficient communicators. Think about people you know who have been successful in their family, social, and professional relationships, and ask yourself why they excelled. Of course, you can name many factors, but the ability to communicate effectively almost always plays a key role. Communication is a crucial skill, and yet most of us do very little, if any, thinking about it. Can you communicate effectively with others? Even if you answer yes to this question, you probably will have to admit that there is always room for improvement. Improving on anything we do— and particularly improving our communication abilities—requires ambition, hard work, and an appropriate learning environment. This book cannot be a substitute for those basic requirements, but it can serve as a foundation and a catalyst for developing your communication effectiveness. Its goal is to supply you with the essential information you need to become a more effective communicator than you are now.

To begin this process, the first chapter presents the necessary underlying principles of effective communication in everyday life. In particular, we examine speech communication, the importance of effective communication, and what communication is and is not—its essential components, principles, and misconceptions.

KATHI: What's happening?

BILL: Not much. . . . How you doin' in your classes?

KATHI: Okay! I really like them, especially my literature class.

BILL: You're lucky. I have speech this semester.

KATHI: Oh!

BILL: So far, I hate it! My teacher is requiring three speeches, two written papers—one paper can be on anything related to speech communication and the other is based on a small-group assignment—plus two tests and a final exam.

KATHI: I had speech last semester and it really helped me. At first I was afraid because I didn't have very much confidence, but it was worth it! I feel much more confident now and I learned a lot of useful information. I thought all we would do is give speeches, but we didn't. We studied all kinds of things—perception, language, nonverbal communication, listening, speech giving, interpersonal and small group communication, and interviewing. It turned out to be one of the best classes for me.

BILL: We'll see, but so far I . . . .

SPEECH COMMUNICATION

Just mentioning the words *speech communication* evokes a range of interpretations and reactions among individuals. No matter how you may feel about speech communication, you would find it hard to deny that the ability to communicate effectively and efficiently with others is one of the most important skills a person can possess in our society.

THINK ABOUT IT

What is speech communication?
Why does the mention of speech communication bring fear to
    some people?

People who underestimate the value of speech communication usually do so because they don't understand exactly what it is. They think that it is merely giving speeches, but the following definition, developed by the Association for Communication Administrators, shows that speech communication is much more than that:

> **Speech communication** is a humanistic and scientific field of study, research, and application. Its focus is upon how, why, and with what effects people communicate through spoken language and associated nonverbal messages. Just as political scientists are concerned with political behavior and economists with economic behavior, the student of speech communication is concerned with communicative behavior.[1]

According to this definition, speech communication involves a broad range of behaviors, and it occurs in a variety of situations: private and public, business and social, home and school, informal and formal. These diverse situations are all brought together by one common thread—the spoken word.

To learn to be an effective communicator requires personal involvement. Thus, in this course, you will study and apply the principles of speech communication as it occurs within and among individuals, groups, organizations, and societies. In the process, you will learn about the nature of human communication, listening, public speaking, interpersonal communication, small group communication, and interviewing.

THE IMPORTANCE OF EFFECTIVE COMMUNICATION

To understand why speech communication is so important, just examine the impact it has on all of us. Stop and think. How does communication affect you personally? How does it affect your family, friends, education, job, community, country, and our world? Communication is what distin-

guishes us as human beings—not religion, race, politics, culture, education, or gender. In addition, it helps determine our success in all aspects of life.

Communication Shapes History

Although the significant impact of written communication cannot be denied, oral communication has had broader and more profound effects on a greater number of people. The success of the great leaders of the present century has been generally attributed to their ability to speak effectively. Consider, for example, the well-honed speaking skills of Winston Churchill, Franklin D. Roosevelt, Golda Meir, John F. Kennedy, Martin Luther King, Jr., Barbara Jordan, Billy Graham, Bella Abzug, and Pope John Paul II.

Karl Marx's *Communist Manifesto*, as a written document, influenced large numbers of individuals, but it was the oral communication of Marx's writings that affected the masses and eventually spread the philosophy of Communism throughout the world. Adolf Hitler's *Mein Kampf*, as a written document, records his struggle to attain power, but it was Hitler's oratory that established his political dominance during the 1930s and 1940s and enabled him to build the world's most powerful military machine. It was also oral communication that provided the bases and means for democracy and, for that matter, all political systems to exist.

Communication Shapes Careers

Even though many of us have little or no aspirations to be national or international leaders, we should aspire to be the best communicators possible. Ample evidence supports the impact effective communication has on career success. In a study of 84 personnel officers from major companies throughout the United States, 85 percent indicated that communication skills in comparison to other abilities are "very important," and 95 percent indicated that when they hire someone, it is because of good communication skills.[2]

MINI-EXERCISE

Interview someone in a career of your choice. Ask the following:

1. What forms of communication are most likely to be used by people in your career field?
2. What specific communication skills are required by people entering your career field?
3. How important to success in your career is effective communication?

Another survey asked 217 public leaders to rank the following six curriculums—physical sciences, biological sciences, social sciences, communication skills, specialized or technical skills, and humanities—based on skills a college student should possess to obtain an executive position. Of those surveyed, 45 percent ranked communication skills the highest, and 95 percent ranked communication skills within the top three.[3]

Chief executives of 55 different companies ranging in size from 8 to 7000 employees were asked to rank the most troublesome communication situations, to rate how well or how poorly their managers and supervisors communicated, and to list how many times certain kinds of communication were used by managers, supervisors, and other employees. The results suggest that listening to employees, motivating people, giving directions, delegating authority, group problem-solving, handling grievances, engaging in one-to-one conferences, using the grapevine, giving formal presentations, assuming conference leadership, and negotiating and bargaining all presented troublesome areas of communication.[4]

A review of 25 studies, designed to examine important communication skills that students will need in their career fields, found that listening, writing, oral reporting, motivating/persuading, interpersonal skills, informational interviewing, and small group problem-solving are the communication skills most often required and important for success.[5] All of these communication competencies are discussed either directly or indirectly throughout this book.

Despite what many may think, communicating effectively is not easy and does not occur by chance. It takes time, energy, desire, instruction, and practice—the same basic requirements needed to be successful in anything.

WHAT IS COMMUNICATION?

A review of speech communication textbooks quickly shows the lack of a universally accepted definition of communication. Definitions can be long and complex, or brief and simple, and they may take the view of the initiator, the receiver, or both. Our purpose is not to argue whether one definition is better than another, but rather to provide a common starting point and meaning for understanding communication. For these reasons we will define **communication** as the process by which verbal and nonverbal symbols are sent, received, and given meaning. Each term in this definition will be explained in more detail throughout the book.

Communication is a complex and multifaceted phenomenon. On the surface, communication appears to be just the sending and receiving of messages, but if it were this simple we would have no misunderstandings or difficulties in communicating with one another. Actually, to understand the true nature of communication, we must know its essential components and principles, and avoid some common misconceptions.

THE ESSENTIAL COMPONENTS OF COMMUNICATION

Stop and think of the way you might list and describe the components of communication. What would you include? Your response could be very simplistic—listing and describing, for example, only a speaker, a message, and a listener. Or your answer could be very technical and complex, listing and describing the components of computer language. Although there may be no all-inclusive or best way to list and describe the components of communication, you can begin to better understand the nature of this process if you are familiar with seven of its most basic elements. The most often listed and described components of the communication system are:

1. Source
2. Message
3. Channel
4. Receiver
5. Feedback
6. Environment
7. Noise

The model in Figure 1.1 helps to illustrate the relationship among the essential components of communication.

Figure 1.1

Schematic Model of the Essential Components of Communication

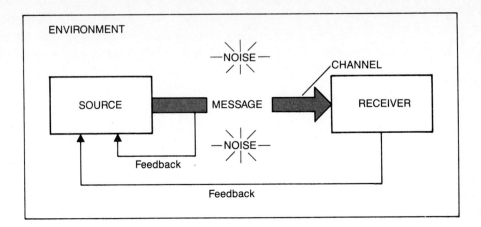

Source

The **source** is the creator of messages; the prime function of the communication source, therefore, is to initiate messages. Because communication usually involves more than one person, there is always the potential for more than one source of communication to exist at a time. Both the teacher and the students in a classroom, for example, can function as sources, sending messages simultaneously to one another—teacher to students, students to teacher, and students to students.

In communication, a source has four roles: to determine the meaning of what is to be communicated, to encode the meaning into a message, to send the message, and to perceive and react to a listener's response to a message.

Determining Meanings.   A source has an infinite number of decisions to make in creating a message. The first is to determine the meaning of what is to be sent. The meanings of some communication messages are relatively simple, but others can be extremely complex and difficult. For example, telling someone about a high grade you received on a recent speech entails making a decision about the meaning you wish to convey: Do you want the other person to know how you felt—that this was the highest grade you've ever gotten on a speech—or merely that you got a high grade? And do you want the person to know the details about what you did to get the high grade?

The precommunication meaning is partially controlled by the source's ability to think and process information. The way information is processed internally and the decision about what is to be communicated determine the source's meaning for a message. For example, when we act as a communication source, we must transfer our feelings, thoughts, and experiences into language so that we can communicate them to others. Because we are all individuals, we have varying experiences and varying levels of ability and willingness to express our thoughts and feelings in words. These factors contribute to how each of us determines the meaning of a message that we intend to send.

Effective communication simply means that a message is received as intended by its creator. It does not automatically mean that the communicator's purpose is virtuous. For example, if one person persuades another to do something morally wrong, the communication is effective but not virtuous. Deliberate lying can certainly achieve a person's goal, but a lack of ethics should not be condoned merely because someone communicates effectively. A receiver of messages cannot be passive. Each of us, whether a sender or a receiver, must be responsible for communication that is accurate, honest, and within the norms of society.

Encoding. Once a source has chosen a meaning, he or she **encodes** it. In other words, a source mentally changes the thoughts or feelings into words, sounds, and physical expressions, which make up the eventual message that is to be sent.

Sending. The source then sends the message, which involves his or her ability to communicate overtly—that is, to use voice and body to accurately communicate the intended meaning. For example, if your internal meaning is to tell the other person how excited you were to receive a high grade on your speech, then you must translate your feelings and thoughts into actions by verbalizing and illustrating how you are feeling and thinking.

Reacting. Finally, a source must be prepared to interpret a receiver's response to the message. A source's perception of a receiver's response in most communication situations is simultaneous. For example, the persons you are telling about the high grade you received on your speech will be sending out messages (such as smiles) nods of the head, eye contact) to indicate both their attention and their reaction to what you are telling them. If your perception of their communication is positive, you will probably continue to tell more about your high grade.

Message

A **message** is the stimulus that is produced by the source. It, consists of such stimuli as words, grammar, organization, appearance, body movement, voice, personality, self-concept, style, environment, and noise. Any stimulus that affects a receiver is a message, whether it is intended or not. Hence, the teacher whose words tell a student that everything appears to be fine, but whose face shows deep concern, might be communicating more to the student than intended, even if the concern on the teacher's face has nothing to do with the student.

Remember, communication is a process that is constantly changing. Thus, each message that is created differs from all other messages. Even if the same message were created over and over, it would be different because messages cannot be repeated or received in exactly the same way. To illustrate this, imagine reading the headline "The World Has Been Invaded by Small Green People!" in a comic book and then in your local newspaper. Although the words might be the same, the messages would be quite different.

Channel

A **channel** is the route by which messages flow between sources and receivers. The usual communication channels are light waves and sound waves—that is, we see and hear one another. The means by which light and sound waves travel, however, may differ. For example, when two people are talking face to face, light and sound waves in the air serve as the channels. If a letter is sent from one person to another person, the light waves serve as the channel, but the paper, the writing itself, and the postal system that delivers the letter serve as the means by which the message is conveyed. Books, films, videotapes, television sets, computers, radios, magazines, newspapers, and pictures are all means by which messages may be conveyed; nevertheless, light and sound waves are the primary channels that allow the messages to be sent and received.

We also receive communication by smelling, touching, and tasting. We sometimes take these senses for granted, but imagine walking into a bakery and not being able to smell the aroma or taste the flavors. All you have to do is hug someone you care about to recognize how important touch is as a means of communicating. All five of our senses, therefore, allow communication to exist.

Receiver

A **receiver,** who can be a single individual or many individuals, analyzes and interprets messages, both intended and unintended. You can simultaneously be a receiver of communication messages and a source. As you listen to others' messages, you react with your body and facial expression; and the others, while sending their messages, are receiving the information conveyed by your physical reactions.

Like the source, a receiver has several roles: (1) to receive (listen, see, touch, smell, or taste) the message, (2) to attend to the message, (3) to interpret and analyze the message, (4) to store and recall the message, and (5) to respond to the source, channel, environment, noise, and message.

Receiving.   A receiver must be an able and willing participant or communication will be difficult at best. Willingness to receive a message does not guarantee an accurate interpretation, however. It means merely that a person is open to a communication message and will attend to it.

Attending. Receivers also have a responsibility to attend to messages intended for them. This is not easy, because many stimuli are begging for a receiver's attention at one time. Effective receivers must learn to concentrate on specific stimuli and to eliminate extraneous stimuli (noise) that can interfere with the reception and interpretation of a message. This ability takes effort but can be learned.

Interpreting and Analyzing. The receiver must not only attend to messages but also interpret and analyze them. Accurate interpretation requires an ability to understand an intended meaning. This process of translating a message into thoughts and feelings that were communicated is called **decoding.** On the surface decoding may seem rather easy, but because messages consist of symbols and signs that are transmitted through a channel, the possibility of a misunderstanding always exists. For example, if I say to you as we stand together by an open door, "Please close the door," the message is simple and leaves little room for misunderstanding; but is the intention of the message clear? Why did I tell you to close the door when I could have closed it myself? The intention might be clearer if my hands are full of books. But assume that I have nothing in my hands and that you see no reason why I cannot close the door myself. In that case, there are a number of possible intended messages. For instance, I might be lazy and using you to do something that is work for me, or I might be exerting my authority to see if you will close the door when I tell you to do so. Thus, although there is only one basic meaning to the sentence "Please close the door," when the intention of the sender is taken into account, the message might take on different interpretations.

It is a sender's responsibility to clearly convey the intention of a message, unless he or she deliberately intends to be unclear. But it is still a receiver's responsibility to determine the intention and meaning of the sender's message.

The receiver must analyze and evaluate each message. For example: Does the message mean what the receiver thinks it means? Is the message ethical? Is the received message the one that was intended? Many other questions need to be considered to ensure clear and accurate understanding, and the process of analyzing and evaluating these questions and their answers will vary from source to source, message to message, situation to situation, and receiver to receiver. Despite this complexity, a receiver is responsible for making sure the received message is the one intended and that it is valid and reliable.

Storing and Recalling. Storing and recalling messages is too complex a topic to be fully discussed in this book. Suffice it to say, however, that the ability to store messages varies from individual to individual. Let's assume, for example, that your roommate asks you to pick up some groceries on your way back from class. Every individual may not store and recall this message in the same way. Those of us who are poor at remembering such messages may need to write it down. Other people may use a key word to help them store and recall a list. For example, if you needed to buy hamburger, eggs, lettuce, and pop at the grocery store and wanted a simple way to recall those items, you might use the word *HELP:*

> *H* = hamburger
> *E* = eggs
> *L* = lettuce
> *P* = pop

Our ability to store and recall information is similar to a computer's, except that a computer is a machine that cannot think for itself. Computers store vast amounts of information and never forget, although they can be turned off or the information they are storing can be destroyed. Humans can also store vast amounts of information but we can forget what has been stored.

Responding. The final role of the receiver is to respond to the communication source. Your response to a message may be simply a nod of the head or a comment indicating that the message was received and understood or that more information is needed. Such a response makes the receiver a source of information for the sender. A receiver's failure to react or respond is also considered a response and is thus a message that may be received and interpreted.

Mini-Exercise

Ask a friend to listen carefully as you read the following story aloud. Use a monotone voice and do not vary your speaking rate.

> Homer Garrison, a school teacher, unexpectedly inherited $60,000. He decided that he would invest his money in a restaurant.
>
> He spent $18,000 for a down payment on an old house in his hometown of Greenwood. He did not want a showplace—just a nice family-style restaurant. He used the rest of the money to purchase equipment and to convert the house. Soon his restaurant became the talk of the small town.

When you have finished, ask your listener to repeat the story. How much detail did the person remember? Why did the person remember some things and forget others? What could you as a speaker do to help the listener to recall the information? What could the listener do to improve his or her memory?

Feedback

Another component in the communication process is **feedback,** the response to a message that a receiver sends back to a source. Feedback thus enables a sender to determine whether the communication has been received and understood as intended. If the purpose of communication is to share meaning accurately, to influence others, and to respond to others' needs, then some means of correcting faulty messages, misconceptions, missed meanings, and incorrect responses is necessary.

Feedback is a natural extension of effective receiving. Receivers have the responsibility of listening, attaching meaning to the messages they receive, and determining if the messages have been accurately received as intended. The next logical step is to provide responses (feedback) that let the sender know that the message was received and understood. It is then up to the sender to decide if the feedback provides enough information to judge whether the receiver accurately interpreted the message. Thus, you could say that feedback serves as a kind of control mechanism in the communication process.

Unfortunately, we too often fail to monitor our own communication and—more important—others' reactions to it. By not monitoring our communication and the responses of others, we may be misunderstood or may not be heard by others. To imagine the consequences, consider what would happen to the temperature in a room if the heater and the thermostat acted independently of each other.

Feedback is an essential component of the communication process, because it is not only a corrective device, but also a means by which we learn about ourselves. It allows us to function better by adjusting to others and to our surroundings. Feedback from others helps us to assess ourselves, to understand how others see us, to form perceptions of ourselves, and to determine our personalities and individual needs. Most of us need to be perceived as worthwhile and significant. If you doubt this, give a compliment to someone and then watch and listen to his or her reactions. Giving feedback to others is just as important as receiving it, because it makes the communication process more personal.

Feedback has other advantages. A classic study found that when feedback is increased, the reception of information becomes more accurate.[6] The experiment required students to construct geometric patterns that were described by a teacher under these conditions: (1) zero feedback—the teacher's back was turned to the students and they were not allowed to ask questions or make noise; (2) visible audience—the students could see the teacher's face, but again, could not ask questions; (3) limited verbal—the students were allowed to ask the teacher questions, but the teacher could only respond with yes or no; (4) free feedback—all channels of communication were open with no limits placed on the questions asked of the teacher. Two important findings from this study were that:

1. as the amount of feedback increases, so does the accuracy of communication;
2. as the amount of feedback increases, so does the confidence about performance.

The Costs of Feedback. To enhance accuracy and confidence in communication, we must provide and monitor feedback. This takes time and effort and entails potential and actual costs. For example, the classic study on feedback shows that the time used for gaining accuracy and creating confidence can be costly in terms of getting things done. A free feedback condition takes much longer—anywhere from three to ten times longer—than the zero feedback condition. Time, if wasted or used excessively to get a message across, can be as costly as mistakes.

On the other hand, the extra time may be well spent. A large manufacturing company, after making changes in its production process, found that many misunderstandings occurred, which resulted in breakdowns in the system and low worker morale. After the production managers increased the opportunity for feedback, there were fewer misunderstandings, thus fewer breakdowns, and more satisfaction among workers. In this situation, the additional time spent on increased opportunity for feedback paid off.

Besides requiring time, increased feedback may entail costs at a personal level. When you request feedback, you may find that the responses you receive diminish your self-concept—that is, if you receive negative feedback, you may be apt to take it too personally. For instance, if someone tells you that you don't look good in the clothes you're wearing, you may feel hurt. You can probably recall situations in your own life in which feedback seemed too threatening or expensive to justify. At times, preventing or ignoring feedback might be easier than running the risk of negative reactions.

Positive Versus Negative Feedback. Although most of us would rather receive positive feedback, negative feedback—if given and taken in the right perspective—can be helpful and equally as productive. For example, if your professor says, "Your term paper was very interesting but you had several spelling errors," her feedback is both positive and negative. She hopes that you will consider her comments as constructive and thus be more careful in your future writing. On the other hand, if your professor says, "This is the worst paper I've ever read—you sure have a lot to learn," her feedback is belittling and potentially destructive. That kind of feedback may destroy your confidence and perhaps even make you want to quit. Feedback, like all messages, should be carefully chosen and treated as an important aspect of the communication process.

Environment

The **environment** is both the psychological and the physical surroundings in which communication occurs. Often referred to as the atmosphere of the communication, it encompasses the attitudes, feelings, perceptions, and relationships of the communicators as well as the characteristics of the location in which communication takes place. For example, communication that takes place indoors is affected not only by the relationship of the communicators but also by the size, color, arrangement, decorations, and temperature of the room. Hence, both the perceptions that communicators have of the physical setting and their attitudes toward each other determine the environment.

The environment affects the nature and quality of the communication. For example, it is much easier to carry on an intimate conversation in a private, quiet, and comfortable surrounding than in a public, noisy, and uncomfortable setting, and most of us find it easier to communicate with someone we know than with someone we do not know. Some environments appear to foster communication, while others seem to inhibit it. Consider these contrasting environments:

> The room is clean, painted light blue, and has quiet music playing in the background. Two people, seated in soft, comfortable chairs, are facing each other, smiling, and one is gently touching the other. They show genuine concern for each other. Their communication is open and caring.

> The room is dirty, painted dark brown, and has loud music playing in the background. Two people, seated ten feet apart on folding chairs, are staring at each other. They show little respect or concern for each other. Their communication is guarded.

Comparing the two environments helps to reveal the attitudes, the kind of relationship, and the communicative feelings of the individuals. Both effective and ineffective communication are, in part, the results of their environments. Effective communication can occur anywhere and under most circumstances, but pleasing, comfortable environments along with open, trusting relationships are more likely to produce positive exchanges.

How Environment Affects Communication. The characteristics of communication environments are usually discussed in terms of opposites— supportive-defensive, open-closed, confident-uncertain, accepting-rejecting, trusting-suspicious, orderly-chaotic, or friendly-unfriendly. Climates that are supportive and positive tend to enhance communication. A study of the characteristics of supportive versus defensive climates in business and industrial organizations revealed that people in defensive climates frequently believed they were being evaluated, manipulated, and subjected to criticism and too many rules and procedures.[7] The defensive climate seemed indifferent and cold, with people talking down to one another. The supportive climate encouraged more openness, trust, and confidence. People were more involved with one another and were more likely to seek out the causes of difficulties rather than rely on rules.

In a supportive climate people describe events and behaviors, while in a defensive climate people judge them. Furthermore, in a supportive climate people show **empathy** toward one another by either intellectually identifying with or vicariously experiencing the feelings, thoughts, and attitudes of others. In contrast, people in a defensive climate are neutral—they show no outward concern or feelings for one another. For example, in a supportive climate comments like the following are apt to be heard: "Dave, you really spoke well during the first part of your speech. It had a lot of good examples and was clearly organized. The last part didn't seem to have as many examples as the first, but your delivery had good vocal variety throughout." In a defensive climate, similar thoughts may be expressed in words like these: "Dave, the first part of your speech was OK and the last part was not very good. You sure didn't do very well." What we say and how we react to others help to determine the environment in which communication takes place. People who are always talked down to, evaluated, or governed by strict rules will tend to become distant and thus less open in their communication.

Noise

Anything that distorts, interferes with, or changes the meaning of an intended message is called **noise.** It is included in our model because it is present, to one degree or another, in every communication environment.

Noise can be physical, such as the slamming of the door, the blasting of a stereo, or the shouting of playing children, but it can also be psychological. For example, the thoughts going through a person's mind that interfere with the reception or creation of a message and the distraction caused by an object's sudden and unexpected movement are also forms of noise. Think about ways a person who speaks in a loud voice to get someone's attention may create both physical and psychological noise. If the receiver perceives the loudness as anger, the loud voice creates not only a distraction but also a distortion of what was actually intended. If the receiver responds accordingly, the sender may be quite surprised.

THINK ABOUT IT

In what way would the following things function as noise?

1. Chewing gum
2. A hot, sticky room
3. Shyness
4. A cold
5. A personal bias
6. Sunglasses
7. The playing of a stereo
8. An inappropriate choice of words

Essentially, noise is anything that reduces the clarity, accuracy, meaning, understanding, or retention of a message. This may include a speaker's annoying vocal habits or physical movements, the temperature of a room, inadequate lighting, a seating arrangement, the movements and sounds of others, listeners' inattentiveness or lack of motivation, perceptual inaccuracies, and physical hearing impairments. Such kinds of noise, either alone or in combination, distort or reduce the effectiveness of communication.

PRINCIPLES OF COMMUNICATION

Communication is a complex and multifaceted phenomenon. On the surface, communication appears to be just the sending and receiving of messages, but if it were this simple we would have no misunderstandings or difficulties in communicating with one another. Actually, to appreciate the true nature of communication it is important to understand four fundamental principles: (1) communication is a **process,** (2) communication is **systemic,** (3) communication is both **interactional** and **transactional,** and (4) communication can be **intentional** or **unintentional.**

Communication Is a Process

Communication is considered to be a **process** because it is a continuous series of actions, having no beginning or end, that is constantly changing.[8] It is not a thing that you can grab onto and hold in your hand to examine or dissect. It is more like the weather, which is made up of a variety of complex variables and changes constantly.[9] Sometimes the weather is warm, sunny, and dry, and at other times it is cold, cloudy, and wet. The weather reflects a variety of complex interrelationships that can never be duplicated the same way. The interrelationships among such variables as high and low pressure systems, the position of the earth, ocean currents, and a whole host of other factors determine the weather that we experience on any given day.

Communication also involves a variety of complex interrelationships that can never be duplicated in exactly the same way. The interrelationships among people, environments, skills, attitudes, status, experiences, and feelings all determine communication at any given moment. Think about a relationship you developed with someone recently. How did it occur? It may have happened by chance (striking up a conversation with someone you met while walking to class), or it may have been a prearranged meeting (a blind date set up by your roommate). No two relationships are developed in the same way, nor is the communication that allows them to occur the same. And like the weather, some relationships are warm and others cold.

Communication by itself may seem insignificant, but when you view it as an everchanging process, its importance becomes overwhelming. Whether it be a speech or a single word, communication can effect change. Saying something that you wish you hadn't said is an excellent example of this principle. No matter how hard you try to take back your comment, you can't. It has made its impact and has, in all likelihood, affected your relationship with another person in some way. The change may not be immediate or significant, but it does take place as a result of your communication.

Furthermore, all events that occur in your life are eventually related to some act of communication. The communication and the changes may not have a clearly identifiable beginning or end, but they do occur. For example, someone might say that communication in this course began the moment you stepped into the classroom, but the reason you came was to learn, and you probably made that decision before you even registered. Although specific situations may have definite beginnings and endings, the events leading to them and the resulting effects might not. If you were to stop reading this book, it would not be the end of its effect on you. You would carry away some new information, or at least a general impression, whether positive or negative. If you can accept the idea that communication is a process, you will view events and relationships around you as constantly changing and continuous.

Communication Is a System

Simply stated, a **system** is a combination of parts interdependently acting to form a whole. The human body is an excellent example of a systematic process. If something is not functioning correctly, there is a physical or psychological reaction—some response usually occurs either to correct what has gone wrong or to warn that something is going wrong. All parts of the body, therefore, are interdependent and work together as parts of one complex system.

In a similar sense, the communication process is systematic in that communication occurs only when the necessary components interact and affect one another. As discussed earlier, the essential components of communication are a source, a message, a channel, a receiver, feedback, an environment, and noise. The elimination or malfunction of any one of these components would prevent communication from occurring or make it less effective.

Communication Is Both Interactional and Transactional

The interactional and transactional aspects of communication are closely related and should be considered together. **Interaction** is an exchange of communication in which, similar to playing catch, communicators take turns sending and receiving messages. For example, someone throws a ball. The other person catches it and then throws it back. Each throw and each catch is a separate action.

It is unlikely that face-to-face communication would occur as a series of distinctly separate actions. Thus, the term **transaction** is used to extend the concept of interaction one step further to view communication as a *simultaneous, sharing* event. That is, the persons involved in the communication process share in the encoding and decoding at the same time. For example, when teachers communicate to their students, they not only send information, but also receive information simultaneously. The teacher and students are therefore sending and receiving messages at the same time. This does not necessarily mean that they are talking at the same time; it does mean, however, that two-way communication is taking place. Your handshake communicates a message that the other person interprets at the same time that you are receiving and interpreting the message in the handshake that you are receiving. In addition, you both are simultaneously receiving feedback about your own message from the handshake you are giving.

Without simultaneous sharing, face-to-face communication would be impossible, or at the very least extremely limited—like sending a letter to someone and never receiving a response. In face-to-face communication, each person affects the other and shares in the process *simultaneously*. Thus, communication transaction can be seen as the simultaneous exchange by which we share our reality with others.

Communication Can Be Intentional or Unintentional

Communication can occur whether it is intended or not. Generally, when one person communicates with another, he or she intends that specific messages with specific purposes and meanings be received. But often, as we all know too well, the message sent is not the one received. A message may mean one thing to the person who sends it and another to the person who receives it. Misunderstanding occurs when a person cannot create a clear and concise message; his or her idea might not be received as intended. If a person is able to express an idea clearly and concisely but the receiver doesn't listen to it or doesn't interpret it correctly, the message will be ineffective.

Intentional communication is a message that is purposely sent to a specific receiver. **Unintentional communication** is a message that was not intended to be sent or was not intended for the individual who received it. Based on intent or the lack of intent, four possible communication situations can occur, as shown in Figure 1.2. If communication always occurred under ideal circumstances, we would have the situation depicted by number 1 in the figure. In this case, a person intends to send a message to another person, who wishes to receive it. This situation does not guarantee that effective communication will occur, however. It merely means that the persons involved in the communication are willing participants. A community leader, for example, may present information on a new pollution control law intending to have news reporters write feature stories about it. The reporters cover the presentation because it is their job, but their stories, when printed, may or may not reflect the politician's message. Remember, the mere intent to send and receive messages does not mean effectiveness; it only means a desire to be involved in the communication process.

Figure 1.2

Intentional-
Unintentional
Communication

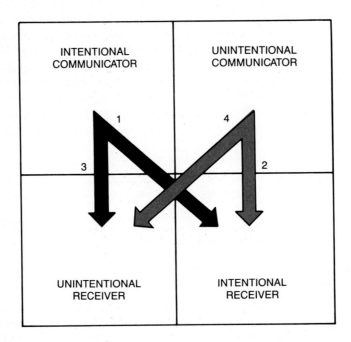

Arrow number 2 indicates a situation in which a person unintentionally communicates something to someone who is intentionally trying to receive a message or messages. This situation arises every time someone reads more into a communication than was intended by the source. For example, when a student in a quiet classroom gets up to sharpen a pencil, the eyes of the other students immediately focus on the moving student, who may have no specific intention of communicating anything. The mere movement, however, provides an opportunity for many messages to be received by the observers. If the pencil-sharpening student is attractive, many different messages might be created unintentionally but received intentionally. For instance, one observer may believe that the moving student is trying to flirt with her, another may think that he's trying to call attention to his attractiveness, while the instructor may perceive that he is trying to disrupt the others' concentration. The problem here should be obvious. Despite the student's lack of intention to communicate anything, others have read meaning into his movement. In one way or another, he may have to contend with the others' interpretations.

Arrow number 3 illustrates the opposite situation. Here the source intends to send a message but the person for whom the message is intended is not consciously or intentionally receiving it. Such a situation arises when a parent tries to communicate to a child who intentionally does not want to hear. It also happens in the classroom when students daydream while the instructor is lecturing.

The fourth arrow in the figure shows that communication can be unintentional for both the source and the receiver and can occur without anyone intentionally sending or receiving a message. Communication that is not intended, or that is at least not consciously sent and received, is usually nonverbal. For example, the clothing a person wears might not be intended to communicate any specific message, and persons observing the clothing might not intentionally or consciously receive any message about it, but they do see it. Thus, communication occurs even though neither the sender nor the receiver has any intention of communicating.

THINK ABOUT IT

In your opinion, are the following statements true or false? Justify your answers.

1. Communication can solve all of our problems.
2. The more we communicate, the better.
3. Communication can break down.
4. Meanings are in words.
5. Communication is a natural ability.

MISCONCEPTIONS ABOUT COMMUNICATION

Several misconceptions keep many of us from examining *our own* communication more closely.[10] Notice the emphasis on *our own!* Most of us who have problems communicating tend to look for the fault in places other than ourselves. Here are some of the most common myths that interfere with people improving their own communication skills.

Communication Can Solve All of Our Problems

The first misconception lies in the notion that communication has the magical power to solve all of our problems. However, as stated earlier, the act of communicating with others does not carry any guarantees. Obviously, without communication we cannot solve our problems, but sometimes communication can also create problems. In this regard, a personal experience comes to mind. During an annual review of a colleague, I remarked that the student evaluations in one of his courses were rather negative. He immediately launched into a long and bitter defense of his teaching ability, telling me, in no uncertain terms, that I was unfair because I was looking only at his poor evaluations and not at his good ones. What I thought was a simple descriptive statement created a significant problem between us.

Communication can help to eliminate or reduce our problems but it is not a panacea. Communicating does not make a difference: what is communicated does.

The More We Communicate, the Better

Most of us assume that the more we communicate, the better off we will be. Within limits, people who communicate a great deal are often perceived to be more friendly, competent, and powerful, and to have more leadership potential than those who do not. However, *quantity* of communication is not the same as *quality.* In the discussion I had with my colleague about his poor teacher evaluations, the more we communicated, the more we disagreed with one another and the more negative our discussion became. Hence, as with the first misconception, it isn't the act or the amount of communication, but the content of communication that makes the difference.

Communication Can Break Down

"We just had a communication breakdown." How often have you heard this statement? Whenever a misunderstanding arises between people, the conclusion is likely to be that their communication broke down. You can probably think of international, national, local, and personal circumstances in which this expression was used as the excuse for failure, but in reality, communication does not break down—the people using it do. Communi-

cation is neither good nor bad: it is a tool used to convey meaning. Like any tool, it can be used correctly or incorrectly, effectively or ineffectively, efficiently or inefficiently. For example, a hammer by itself is neither good nor bad: the user makes it useful or not. Hitting my finger instead of the nail does not make the hammer a bad tool—it just makes me an ineffective user. The more we understand about communication and its use, the better communicators we can become.

Meanings Are in Words

If this statement is true, why do we have so much trouble understanding one another? If I tell you that I don't feel very well, what does that mean to you? That I am sick? That I have a cold? That I have an upset stomach? That my feelings have been hurt? It could mean any number of things, for, without context, my statement is not all that clear. However, if I tell you that I have a cold and I don't feel very well, would that be clear? Well, at least it would narrow the choices a little. Confusion may arise because the statement "I don't feel very well" is relative—that is, it may not mean the same thing to you that it does to me. For example, you may seldom get a cold, but when you do it is a bad one. On the other hand, because I get colds all the time and have hay fever, my not feeling well means merely that I have a stuffy nose and a sinus headache. Thus, *meanings are in people and not in the words we use.*

The notion that words contain meanings is probably the most serious misconception of all. Words only have meaning when we give them meaning. "No two people share the same meanings for all words, because no two people completely share the same background and experiences."[11] Thus, the meaning of a word cannot be separated from the person using it. For you to know how I feel when I say that I don't feel very well, you have to know me and how much I suffer from colds and hay fever.

Communication Is a Natural Ability

Many people believe that because we are born with the physical characteristics needed to communicate, communication must be a natural ability. This simply is not true. The ability to communicate, like almost everything we do, is learned. Most of us were born with the physical ability to tie our shoes, but we still had to learn how the strings go together. Similarly, most of us were born with the ability to see, but that does not make us effective readers. Reading requires knowledge of the alphabet, the acquisition of vocabulary, and practice.

The ability to communicate requires not only that we be physically capable but also that we understand how human communication works and that we have an opportunity to use that knowledge. This book is designed to help you understand human communication and thus to make a better communicator.

SUMMARY

Speech communication is much more than giving speeches. It is a humanistic and scientific field of study that focuses on how, why, and with what effects people communicate using spoken language and associated nonverbal messages.

Communicating effectively is important in shaping our history and careers. And beyond exchanging mere meanings, effective communication involves ethical considerations. This means that each of us, whether senders or receivers, must be responsible for what is communicated.

Communication is defined as the process by which verbal and nonverbal symbols are sent, received, and given meaning. There are seven components of communication: the source, the message, the channel, the receiver, feedback, the environment, and noise. Each is an integral part of effective communication. The *source encodes* thoughts or feelings into words that become the *message*, or stimulus. The *channel* is the route that allows messages to flow between source and receiver. The *receiver*, after obtaining the message, *decodes* it into thoughts and feelings. The receiver then gives the sender *feedback*, which indicates his or her reaction to the message. Feedback can be either positive or negative. Although it takes time and effort to provide and receive feedback, the result is usually more effective communication.

The *environment* is the physical and psychological climate in which communication occurs. Climates can be described as supportive, in which case the communicators show *empathy* toward one another, or they can be defensive, in which case the participants show no outward mutual concern.

Noise is always present to one degree or another in all communication. It is anything that distorts, interferes with, or changes the meaning of a message.

Communication is described as both a *process* and a *system*—a process because it is dynamic, continuous, and has no specific beginning or end, and a system because, for communication to occur, all of its elements must work interdependently. In addition to being both a process and a system, communication is also both *interactional* and *transactional,* and *intentional* and *unintentional.* Interaction and transaction are closely related; both explain how communication is exchanged—interaction is an exchange of communication in which communicators take turns sending and receiving messages, while transaction is the simultaneous sending and receiving of messages. Communication can occur whether it is intended or not. Under the best of circumstances, the intended message reaches the intended receiver. But it is not unusual to communicate an unintended message or to reach an unintended receiver.

Some common misconceptions keep many of us from examining and improving our own communication. For example, we should not expect communication to solve all of our problems, and we should recognize that when used improperly, communication can create more problems than it solves. We cannot hope to improve relationships or solve problems by merely increasing our quantity of communication. In fact, more communication may mean more confusion and more misunderstandings. We must also recognize that problems stem from communicators—not from communication. Communication is only a tool, and, as such, is neither good nor bad. It is how we use communication that makes it either effective or ineffective.

KEY TERMS

Channel: the route by which messages flow between sources and receivers, such as light waves and sound waves.

Communication: the process by which verbal and nonverbal symbols are sent, received, and given meaning.

Decoding: the process of translating a message into the thoughts or feelings that were communicated.

Empathy: intellectual identification with, or vicarious experiencing of, the feelings, thoughts, and attitudes of another person.

Encoding: the process by which the source mentally changes thoughts or feelings into words, sounds, and physical expressions that make up the eventual message to be sent.

Environment: both the psychological and the physical surroundings in which communication occurs; it encompasses the attitudes, feelings, perceptions, and relationships of the communicators as well as the characteristics of the location in which communication takes place.

Feedback: the response to a message that the receiver sends to the source.

Intentional Communication: a message that is purposely sent to a specific receiver.

Interaction: an exchange of communication in which communicators take turns sending and receiving messages.

Message: the stimulus that is produced by the source.

Noise: anything that distorts, interferes with, or changes the meaning of an intended message.

Process: a continuous series of actions that is constantly changing, with no beginning or end.

Receiver: the individual who analyzes and interprets the message.

Source: the creator of messages.

Speech Communication: a humanistic and scientific field of study, research, and application. Its focus is upon how, why, and with what effects people communicate through spoken language and associated nonverbal messages.

System: a combination of parts interdependently acting to form a whole.

Transaction: an exchange of communication between people that is a simultaneous, shared event; that is, both encoding and decoding go on at the same time.

Unintentional Communication: a message that is not intended to be sent or is not intended for the person who receives it.

DISCUSSION STARTERS

1. If someone asked you to define speech communication, what would you tell them?

2. What current national leader do you believe to be the most effective oral communicator? Why?

3. When is oral communication effective?

4. Why is effective oral communication so important in our society?

5. Which careers can you name that require effective communication skills?

6. In what way does understanding the components of the communication process help us to be more effective communicators?

7. Who is responsible for effective oral communication—the source or the receiver? Why?

8. Why is feedback so important to the communication process?

9. Drawing on your own experiences, describe how feedback can be both a motivator and an inhibitor of behavior.

10. Why should we as communicators be concerned about the environment in which our communication occurs?

11. How is communication both a process and a system?

12. How does interaction differ from transaction? Why do you think there is controversy among scholars about these two terms?

13. Why are there no meanings in words?

14. Which misconception about communication do you think can cause us the most difficulty when communicating with others?

FURTHER READINGS

Arnold, Carroll C., ed. *Studies in Rhetoric/Communication*. Columbia, S. C.: University of South Carolina Press, 1987.

Campbell, Karlyn Kohrs. *The Rhetorical Act*. Belmont, Calif.: Wadsworth, Inc., 1982.

Dance, F. E. *Human Communication Theory: Comparative Essays*. New York: Harper & Row, Publishers, Inc., 1982.

Howell, William S. *The Empathic Communicator.* Belmont, Calif.: Wadsworth, Inc., 1982.

Naisbitt, John. *Megatrends: Ten New Directions Transforming Our Lives.* New York: Warner Books, Inc., 1984.

Steward, John, ed. *Bridges Not Walls: A Book About Interpersonal Communication.* 4th ed. New York: Random House, Inc., 1986.

Thompkins, Phillip K. *Communication as Action: An Introduction to Rhetoric and Communication.* Wadsworth Publishing Co., 1983.

Williams, Frederick. *The New Communications.* Belmont, Calif.: Wadsworth, Inc., 1984.

NOTES

1. "Communication Careers" (brochure), (Falls Church, Va.: Association for Communication Administrators, 1981).
2. Belohlov, J., P. Popp, and M. Porte, "Communication: A View from the Inside of Business," *Journal of Business Communication,* 11 (1974): 53–59.
3. 1963 Public Leaders' Conference—State of Washington, (Unpublished Report).
4. Hanna, M., "Speech Communication Training Needs in the Business Community," *Central States Speech Journal* 29 (1978): 163–179.
5. Di Salvo, V. S., "A Summary of Current Research Identifying Communication Skills in Various Organizations," *Communication Education* 29 (1980): 283–290.
6. Leavitt, H. J., and R. Mueller, "Some Effects of Feedback on Communication," *Human Relations* 4 (1951): 401–410.
7. Gibb, J., "Defensive Communication," *Journal of Communication* 11 (1961): 141–148.
8. Berlo, D. K., *The Process of Communication,* (New York: Holt, Rinehart and Winston, 1960), p. 23.
9. Masterson, John T., Steven A. Beebe, and Norman H. Watson, *Speech Communication Theory and Practice,* (New York: Holt, Rinehart and Winston, 1983), pp. 6–7.
10. The misconceptions described here are for the most part taken from James McCroskey, and Lawrence R. Wheeless, *Introduction to Human Communication,* (Boston: Allyn & Bacon, Inc., 1976).
11. McCroskey and Wheeless, p. 9.

CHAPTER 2

Perception and Self in Human Communication

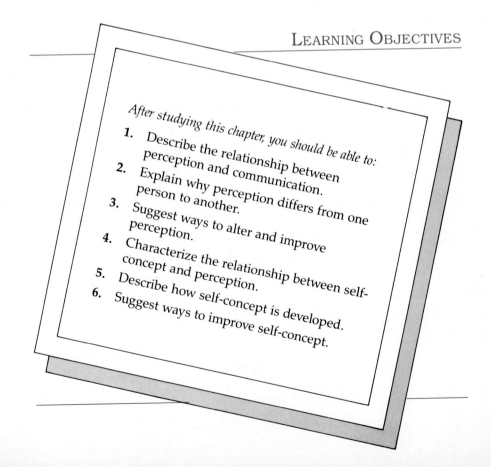

LEARNING OBJECTIVES

After studying this chapter, you should be able to:

1. Describe the relationship between perception and communication.
2. Explain why perception differs from one person to another.
3. Suggest ways to alter and improve perception.
4. Characterize the relationship between self-concept and perception.
5. Describe how self-concept is developed.
6. Suggest ways to improve self-concept.

Perception lies at the heart of communication. What we perceive allows us to understand ourselves, others, objects, and events around us. Perception gives meanings to our experiences, and it is these meanings that we communicate to others. In addition, the ability to perceive stimuli creates the differences in what individuals see, hear, smell, taste, and feel. The *meanings we give to our experiences are in us and not in the experiences themselves.* When we share our perceptions, communication occurs. For this reason, no two people can have identical meanings for the same words, messages, or experiences. **Communication is indeed personal!** In this chapter we focus on perception and self as they relate to communication with others.

"Did you see what I saw?"
"Did you hear what I heard?"
"I thought you said . . . ."
"I didn't say that at all."

"I am so shy."
"I don't think you are."

"Mary is beautiful."
"I don't think she's so neat."

"Gee, that perfume smells good."
"It does?"

"Officer, the blue Trans Am over there caused the accident."
"No, it was the red Chevy van."
"No, it was the green Firebird."

PERCEPTION AND ITS RELATIONSHIP TO COMMUNICATION

All of the preceding remarks are based on **perception**—the process of sensing, selecting, organizing, interpreting, and evaluating information in order to give it personal meaning. Our perceptions make events, people, ideas, and things become real to us, but what is perceived by one person is not always perceived by another in the same way. Individual experiences are not identical, making perception, like communication, complex and multifaceted.

The Perception Process

Much of what we know about perception and the way we perceive events, objects, and people seems to center around how we select, organize, and interpret information.

Selection. In many respects we view the world around us as if we are looking through a television camera. It is impossible to attend to, perceive, retain, and give meaning to every stimulus we encounter so we narrow our focus. A **stimulus** incites or quickens action, feeling, or thought. Although the eye can see millions of bits of data, or stimuli, at one time, the mind can process only a small fraction of those stimuli. As a result, we must use selection to give meaning to specific events, objects, situations, and people. **Selection** is the sorting of one stimulus from another. We select persons to talk to, books to read, television shows to watch, music to listen to, words to speak, objects to look at, movies to attend, meaning to give to communication, and so on.

There are two kinds of selectivity: selective attention and selective retention. To respond appropriately to a given situation, we must constantly select and attend to important stimuli and ignore the others. The process of focusing on specific stimuli while ignoring or downplaying other stimuli is called **selective attention.** This task is sometimes easier said than done. Paying attention to something usually requires that we decide to make the effort and concentrate, but sometimes our attention may be distracted. For example, a book dropped in a quiet classroom, a loud sneeze, a siren, a baby's cry, a call for help, an odor, or a movement can distract our attention from the original stimuli. Continuing to attend to the original stimuli eventually requires some deliberate effort—that is, selective attention. Similarly, when we converse with someone in a crowded lounge with loud music playing in the background, we focus on each other's words and ignore the other sounds. This process of blocking out all extraneous stimuli to concentrate on the other person is another instance of selective attention. To make sense out of the multitude of stimuli that surrounds us, we learn to focus our senses on a few stimuli at a time.

THINK ABOUT IT

How does selectivity affect your communication?
In what ways has selectivity created a barrier between you and
   others?
Why are selective attention and selective retention necessary for
   you to communicate effectively?

Because we cannot possibly remember all the stimuli we encounter, we also selectively retain information. **Selective retention** occurs when we process, store, and retrieve information that we have already selected, organized, and interpreted. Research shows that we often remember information that is in agreement with our views. By the same token, we also selectively forget information. After choosing and perceiving stimuli, we retain only part of them. How many times, for example, have you listened to someone tell you how to do a task, and later, after thinking that you had done everything, found that you have done only a portion of it? Chances are that you had retained the pleasant parts of the task and had forgotten the not-so-pleasant parts. Sometimes we do forget deliberately but even that is selective. Selectivity plays an important role in what, why, and how we communicate.

Figure 2.1

An Example of Figure and Ground: A Vase or Twins?

Organization. The categorizing of stimuli in our environment in order to make sense of them, known as **organization,** plays a very important role in how we perceive events, objects, and people. Probably the most common way to organize stimuli is to distinguish between figure and ground. **Figure and ground organization** is the ordering of perceptions so that some stimuli are in focus and others become the background. Examine Figure 2.1. You may see a vase, but you may see what appears to be two faces. People who see a vase identify the middle of the drawing as the figure and the sides, or dark area, as the ground. The opposite is true for those who see the two faces.[1]

Closure is another way to organize the stimuli around us. Most of us do not like to leave things unfinished or incomplete and tend to fill in the missing pieces. This completion process is called **closure.** Figure 2.2 shows three disconnected lines that most of us would identify as a triangle rather than just three lines. Filling in the blank spaces helps us to categorize, label, and make sense of the things we see and hear.

Figure 2.2

An Example of Closure: A Triangle or Straight Lines?

Two additional approaches to organizing stimuli are proximity and similarity. **Proximity,** or nearness, is simply the grouping of two or more things because they appear to be either physically or psychologically close to one another. Figure 2.3 illustrates proximity by showing a series of lines that may be interpreted as either nine separate lines or three groups of three lines each. Proximity assumes that because several objects appear together, they are basically the same. This, of course, is not always true. For example, just because several people come from the same town or city does not make them alike in all respects.

Figure 2.3

An Example of Proximity: Three Groups of Lines or Nine Separate Lines?

Similarity is the grouping of elements that resemble one another in size, shape, color, or other traits. For example, persons who like baseball might believe that others who enjoy baseball resemble them in other ways as well. Thus, if someone likes both baseball and opera, she might assume that other baseball fans will also like opera.

Organizing the stimuli around us affects how we communicate with others. It determines what we say, to whom we say it, and how and why we say it.

Interpretation. Our interpretations of the stimuli around us depend on our past experiences. **Interpretation** is the assigning of meaning to stimuli. The more familiar you are with objects, events, and people, the less ambiguous are your interpretations of them. For example, when you first arrived on campus, you probably either had help or consulted a map in order to locate various buildings and classrooms. Your perception of campus locations, if you were like most new university or college students, was a bit unclear. With each passing day, however, you probably found it much easier to get around and probably even discovered shortcuts from one place to another. In similar ways, all of our experiences provide contexts that help us to make sense of the world around us.

While past experiences become a basis for our interpretation of stimuli, we must be careful not to let these experiences interfere with our ability to find fresh meanings in new happenings. For example, your having had one easygoing and compatible roommate does not automatically mean that your next roommate will be the same. The experience of having had a good roommate only provides you with a yardstick against which to compare future roommates and is by no means a guarantee of the type of roommate you will have next. It is important to recognize that sometimes our past experiences can create blinders and thus produce inaccurate perceptions.

Perceptual Differences

The differences in our perceptions occur because we are all psychologically and physically different from one another, and our past experiences are not identical, even if we have participated in the same events. We often perceive events differently when we are feeling stress or strong emotions as depression, loneliness, love, anger, or hate. Our unique experiences determine what we perceive; how we interpret, evaluate, and organize our perceptions; and what actions we might take in response to them.

A person's weight, height, body shape, strength, and ability to use his or her five senses account for perceptual differences too. For example, a visually impaired person experiences the world in ways that a sighted person finds difficult to comprehend or even imagine.

Short persons sometimes perceive events differently from the way tall persons do. For example, two young boys were walking to a neighborhood store when two older boys threatened them with a knife and demanded their money. Afterward, the police asked the victims to describe their assailants. One boy gave the robbers' heights as about 5'6" and 5'10" and estimated their ages to be about 16 and 20. The other boy described them as about 5'10" and 6'2" and guessed their ages to be about 20 and 27. The reason for the discrepancy in their descriptions was that one of the victims was only six years old and a little over four feet tall, while the other was nine years old and five feet tall. Of course, the smaller boy perceived the robbers as much taller and older.[2]

The cartoon in Figure 2.4 depicts much the same situation. Whose perception is right? This kind of situation has probably happened to each of us. Our perceptions usually change with experience; it is very difficult for us to see a situation through someone else's eyes—even if we were once in the very same position. Our experiences can help us solve problems or see things more clearly, but they can also limit our view of events and people, hinder us in solving problems, and create barriers to effective communication.

Figure 2.4

Perception and Experience

Mini-Exercise

To gain a better understanding of perceptual differences, try one or more of the following:

1. Blindfold yourself and attempt to walk around a room.
2. Turn off the sound on your television set and watch only the picture.
3. Spend a day in a wheelchair.

You will soon discover that these self-imposed conditions will force you to change your perceptions to adjust to your limitations. This does not mean that your new perceptions are better or worse, however—only that they are different.

Perceptual Set. When a past experience limits us to a fixed, predetermined view of events, objects, and people, we are using a **perceptual set.**[3] Perceptual sets affect the way we process information by allowing our past experiences to control our expectations and thus what we perceive. It is not unusual for many of us to view things as unchanging once we have become experienced with them. To illustrate this concept, quickly read the statements inside each of the triangles in Figure 2.5. Look again. Did you notice two *a*'s or *the*'s in the statements the first time you read them? If you didn't, you are not alone. Most people don't notice these extra words for several

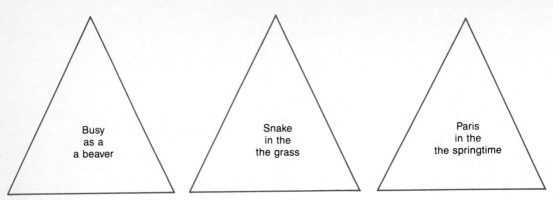

Figure 2.5
Perceptual Set

reasons: (1) the statements are very familiar and common; (2) most of us have learned to read groups of words rather than each individual word; (3) the words are placed in an unusual setting—inside the triangles; and (4) some of us may be conditioned to ignore what we think are typographical errors.

MINI-EXERCISE

Use a sheet of paper to cover the number listed below. Move the paper slowly downward to reveal one number at a time and total the numbers aloud as they appear. Say, for example, "One thousand, two thousand, two thousand twenty," and so on.[4]

```
1000
1000
  20
1000
  40
1000
  30
1000
  10
```

What did you get for a total? 6000? 6100? 5010? 6010? If you did you are wrong! The correct total is 5100. How is it possible to have obtained anything other than 5100? The error is probably because of perceptual set, unless you are poor at adding numbers. Since grade school you have been taught to add one column at a time and carry the remainder to the next column, but this time you were asked to move the paper down the numbers, which changed your perception and may have led you to obtain an incorrect total.

Frozen Evaluation.   Our tendency to look at events, things, or people as if they never change, and to ignore any change that may have taken place is called **frozen evaluation.**[5] Many of us, for one reason or another, refuse to accept change in others, particularly when we have lost trust in them. We become accustomed to seeing things that are familiar to us in certain ways and we assume that they will always remain the same. For example, prison officials would probably find it difficult to believe that a repeat offender serving a life sentence would ever be completely rehabilitated.

THINK ABOUT IT

1. How do perceptual sets and frozen evaluations differ?.
2. Cite some frozen evaluations that you have made recently.
3. What can you do to help yourself avoid using perceptual sets and making frozen evaluations?

The Positive Side of Perceptual Sets and Frozen Evaluations.   Perceptual sets and frozen evaluations do not always limit or hinder us. Sometimes they actually help to make our decisions more efficient. For example, people who first try solving a Rubik's cube generally become quite frustrated and may even give up until they discover the correct steps to completing the cube. With every successful experience, finding the correct solution becomes easier for people because of their growing perception of how the cube is solved.

We could not make sense of the world around us without perceptual sets and frozen evaluations. They provide us with expectations of how things, events, or people should be, and they enable us to compare our expectations with the reality of the moment and respond accordingly. The key is to avoid assuming that perceptual sets and frozen evaluations will always be accurate.

Cultural Background.   Cultural heritage also leads to experiences that contribute to the perceptual differences that influence how we communicate. Two students—one from a small town in Nebraska (population 135) and the other from a large city in Illinois (population over 1.5 million)—were discussing the city of Lincoln (population 175,000), where the University of Nebraska is located. The student from the small town saw Lincoln as huge and almost overwhelming, while the other student saw it as a quaint small town. Their cultural backgrounds were vastly different, which influenced their perceptions of small and large towns.

Some cultural differences in perception are so deeply rooted that they are reflected in the language. The Navaho Indian language, for example, has words for white, red, and yellow but none for gray, brown, blue, or green. The language does, however, have two terms that correspond to black—one denoting the black of darkness and the other the black of such objects as coal. The Navaho vocabulary reflects the fact that the culture divides the color spectrum differently from others. This does not imply that the Navahos are incapable of making color distinctions or that they suffer from some form of color blindness. It only means that their vocabulary does not take certain color differences into account. In their culture there is little or no need to make further distinctions. Think of how this lack of color differentiation would affect the way they view the world around them.

Culture not only influences our own perceptions; it also influences others' perceptions of us. Probably one of the most startling examples of cultural and ethnic differences is illustrated by John Howard Griffin in his book *Black Like Me*.[6] Griffin, a white man, decided to cross into the black culture and, after a series of medical treatments to darken his skin color, traveled into the South during the early 1960s. This was a transitional period when the U.S. was moving toward more equality to blacks, but there was still widespread discrimination, particularly in the South. Griffin discovered that others' perceptions of him as a black man differed entirely from their perceptions of him as a white man. For example, many whites saw him as lazy, oversexed, uneducated, and burdensome to society, and many blacks saw him as they saw themselves—poor, persecuted, defrauded, feared, and detested. Griffin was the same man he had always been—a well-educated, outgoing writer. The only difference was the color of his skin. Yet whites as well as blacks communicated with him in vastly changed ways.

People from differing backgrounds or locations may not see things in the same way, but their perceptions are neither right nor wrong. They merely represent the ways these people have learned to view the world around them. Thus, the more we know about other cultures, the better we should understand other people and the more effective our communication should become.

Altering Perception

Because we tend to take our perceptions for granted, most of us accept things at face value and fail to look beneath the surface. If we look at our personal experiences, though, we can begin to recognize and identify the misperceptions that create problems for us.

Because of many factors involved in perception and the complexity of the perception process, there are no simple rules to follow to improve our perceptions. Nonetheless, we can do several things to help ourselves.

First, we must recognize the role of the perceiver for what it is—a highly active role. To be active perceivers, we must be willing to seek out as much information as possible about a given person, subject, event, or situation. The more information we obtain, the deeper our understanding and the more accurate our perceptions will be.

A second way of improving our perceptions is to get as close as possible to the person, subject, event, or situation being assessed. Although making judgments from a distance can also be valuable, we also need to acknowledge the potential disadvantages that may arise. Each of us has been impressed by a person from a distance, only to change our opinion dramatically upon closer contact. Becoming closer to other people and situations often enables us to form more accurate opinions. Of course, being too close to a subject or situation can also color our perceptions. In such cases, past experiences and strong feelings can impair our judgments. Consequently, to improve our perceptions, we must be aware of how proximity to people, events, and situations can affect us, and we must adjust our perceptions accordingly.

Third, we can improve our perceptions by recognizing the uniqueness of our own frame of reference. We must remember that our view of things may be only one of many views. Each of us has a unique window to the world as well as a unique system of understanding and storing things. Some of us make judgments about people based on appearance, while others base their judgments on ability, income, education, or other factors. The variety of approaches means that all of us operate on different systems and it would be wrong to assume that one system is better than another.

As communicators we need to be aware of the role that perceptions and selectivity play in our communication, take others' perceptions into account, and avoid the tendency to assume too much about what we perceive.

MINI-EXERCISE

Get someone, preferably a friend, to join you in this exercise. First, each of you should privately write brief responses to the following questions. Your answers should address appearance, personality, and intelligence.

1. How do you see yourself?
2. How do you believe the other person sees you?
3. How do you see the other person?

Then, share your responses with each other and discuss them. How do your perceptions of yourself and the other person affect communication?

SELF-CONCEPT AND ITS RELATIONSHIP TO COMMUNICATION

Who are you? How would you describe yourself? Would you say that you are outgoing, an effective speaker, a good listener, well organized, a good writer, happy, responsible, lovable, attractive, warm, sensitive, caring, tall, thin, intelligent, interesting? Or would you choose other adjectives? No matter what terms you would use, the next logical question might be: What makes you think those terms describe the real you? Our **self-concept** is what we perceive ourselves to be—our mental picture of our physical, social, and psychological self. The messages that we communicate, intentionally or unintentionally, relate directly to the way we feel about and view ourselves. Who and what we perceive ourselves to be influences how we present ourselves to others.

Self-concept, the collection of views we have about ourselves, is determined by our experiences and communication with others, and the roles and values we have selected for ourselves. It can also be viewed as our perception of ourselves as we believe others perceive us. Self-concept consists of two components: our **self-image**—the mental picture we have of ourselves, or the person whom we perceive ourselves to be—and our **self-esteem**—our feelings and attitudes toward ourselves.

What and how we communicate with others and the reactions of others toward us help develop our self-concept and ultimately our self-image and self-esteem.

Self-Concept as a Process

In Chapter 1, we described communication as a process because it has no beginning or end and is constantly changing. For the same reasons, self-concept is also a process. Our self-perceptions and the perceptions others have of us differ from time to time, from situation to situation, and from person to person. For example, your view of yourself depends a great deal on how you feel about yourself at any given time. If you had recently received a high grade on a speech, you would probably feel good about yourself, especially about your effectiveness and confidence as a speaker. In contrast, your view of yourself might be different if you had received a low grade. In addition, the perception you have of yourself in class is probably different from the one you have of yourself at work, at church, or at home.

The notion that self-concept is a process is perfectly illustrated by the film *The Eye of the Beholder*, which depicts how others view a character named Jerrard and how he views himself.[7] The maître d´ at a restaurant perceives Jerrard as a very smooth lady's man; his mother sees him as a good boy but thoughtless and unpredictable; the cab driver thinks he is a real hoodlum; the owner of the building where Jerrard has his art studio sees him as a lunatic; the cleaning lady sees him as a monster and murderer; and Jerrard believes himself to be a creative idealist who loves his work. The question the film raises is: Who, really, is Jerrard? Is he the person whom others perceive him to be, or is he the person he perceives himself to be? In reality, Jerrard may not be any of the persons described in the film, including his own description of himself. The perceptions, however, whether accurate or inaccurate, become Jerrard the person as seen through the "eye of the beholder." Jerrard's self-concept consists of his and others' perceptions and is determined by the beliefs he holds about those perceptions.

The Development of Self-Concept

As children, our first communication involves the sensing of our environment, which includes all the sights, sounds, tastes, and odors that surround us. We learn about ourselves as others touch and speak to us; their responses to us help to determine how we view ourselves. Parental communication, both verbal and nonverbal, generally has an extremely strong impact on the initial development of our self-concept. As we expand our environment and relationships, the communication of others may reinforce or alter our perceptions of self.

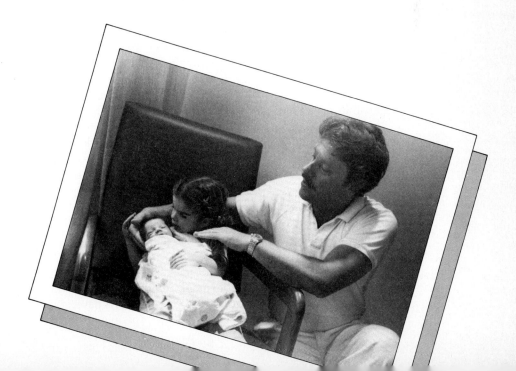

THINK ABOUT IT

"No one can make you feel inferior without your consent."
Eleanor Roosevelt

Our self-concept, which develops through an extremely complex process, usually consists of many images that we place on a continuum from negative to positive. There is no way to predict which image will dominate, because our view of ourselves is a composite of all the self-images that interact within our mind at any given moment. Our self-concept is affected not only by how we look at ourselves, but also by how we look at others, how others look at us, and how we think others see us. In effect, our self-concept is based on both past and present experiences, which affect how we will see ourselves in the future.

Values.   Our self-concept is determined by the values, attitudes, and beliefs we possess, by how we attribute these qualities to others, and by how they attribute them to us. Broad-based, relatively long-lasting ideals that guide our behavior are called **values.** They can generally be classified into broad categories, such as aesthetic, religious, humanitarian, intellectual, and material.

Each category determines our behavior as well as our communication, and is reflected in our self-concept. For example, if material things are important to us, we tend to judge ourselves by what we possess or don't possess. A desire to have the finer things of life is not unusual, at least not in our society, but the strength of this desire can greatly affect our behavior. Possessions can become so important for some people that they ignore other concerns to accomplish their needs. They may pursue higher incomes at the expense of job satisfaction, family life, leisure time, and personal health.

Attitudes.   Evaluative dispositions, feelings, or positions about oneself, another, an event, an idea, or a thing are called **attitudes.** A student expresses a winning attitude by stating "I can do it!" Our attitudes help to determine our self-concept, but unlike values, they are generally more narrowly defined. In addition, the relationship between values and attitudes is very close because our values are reflected in our attitudes. For example, your attitude might be that the federal government is spending too much money on defense, especially at the expense of social programs. Your attitude says something about your value system, which in turn determines who you are and what you communicate.

Beliefs.   Closely related to attitudes are beliefs. **Beliefs** are our convictions or confidence in the truth of something that is not based on absolute proof. They are a person's perception of reality. We have, for example, beliefs about history, religion, school, events, people, and ourselves. We say:

"Space exploration is helpful to humanity," "God is good to us," "Speech class is important," "We will win the Orange Bowl game," "I know Sally loves me," or "I am going to get a high grade on my next speech." Each of these statements and hundreds of similar statements that we make daily could begin with "I believe," or "There is good evidence that."

Our beliefs, like our attitudes and values, have a hierarchy of importance—that is, some are much more important than others. Our most important beliefs, such as those about religion, education, and family life, do not change very easily, but our less important beliefs, such as that it is going to rain today, or that we will win tonight's game, are only momentary.

It is extremely difficult to completely distinguish among values, attitudes, and beliefs because they are often interrelated. Consider, for example, the close relationship among the following three statements:

Value (ideal): People should love one another.
Attitude (feeling or position): Love is good.
Belief (conviction): Love is important in our lives.

Attitudes differ from beliefs in that attitudes include an evaluation of whether someone or something is good or bad. Beliefs, in turn, reflect the perception of whether something is true or false. Attitudes and beliefs are usually short-term expressions of values. Your attitudes and beliefs about love may change as a result of your experiences, but the value you place on love endures.

VALUES, ATTITUDES, AND BELIEFS

	Definition	*Example*
Values	Broad-based ideals that are relatively long lasting	Everyone should have an education.
Attitudes	Evaluative dispositions, feelings, or positions about ourselves, other persons, an event, an idea, or a thing	Our educational system, as it operates today, is too costly.
Beliefs	Convictions or confidence in the truth of something that lacks absolute proof	Even though it has its faults, our educational system is the best in the world.

The Hierarchy of Self-Concept

Like the beliefs we hold, the components of our self-concept may be organized into a hierarchy, as shown in Figure 2.6. At the highest level is our general self-concept, a set of beliefs we hold about ourselves. These beliefs are well established and relatively difficult to change or modify. At

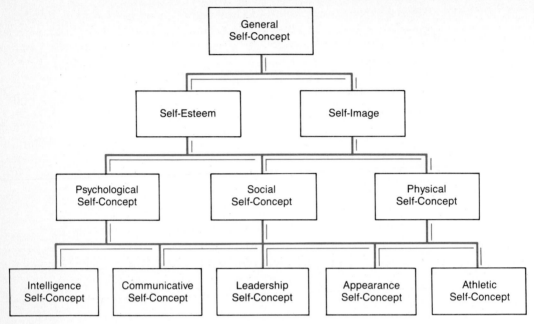

Figure 2.6
*Hierarchy of
Self-Concept*

the next lower level are the principal components of self-concept—self-esteem and self-image. The next level down consists of the elements that form our self-esteem and self-image—psychological self-concept, social self-concept, and physical self-concept. On the lowest level are specific aspects of self-concept; such as intelligence self-concept, communicative self-concept, leadership self-concept, appearance self-concept, and athletic self-concept. The further we travel down the hierarchy, the more specific the elements become and the more susceptible the elements are to change.

Self-Fulfilling Prophecy

In addition to values, attitudes, and beliefs, expectations help to determine how we behave, who we eventually become, and what we communicate to ourselves and others. Our own expectations and those of others can influence our perceptions and behavior.

Expectations help to create the conditions that lead us to act in predicted ways. A **self-fulfilling prophecy** is the way we carry out our expectations.

We are more likely to succeed if we believe that we have the potential for success. It follows that we are more likely to fail if we believe ourselves to be failures. For example, students sometimes believe that they aren't good at speaking before groups. These students often do poorly on their public speaking assignments. Their expectation of not succeeding usually becomes reality and negatively affects their self-concept. The pattern of failure that they set for themselves becomes difficult to break. Thus, to some extent, our expectations for ourselves and others are based on past behavior.

THINK ABOUT IT

"Show me a thoroughly satisfied man and I will show you a failure."

Thomas Edison

Improving Our Self-Concept

Changing our self-concept is not easy, nor is there any magic formula to help us be anything but ourselves. We must usually begin with a concentrated effort to change our behavior. Sometimes, though, dramatic events may force us to alter our behavior and thus create a new self-concept. For example, couples who have just gotten married or have just had their first child often drastically change their perspective of themselves and adjust by making striking changes in their behavior.

To alter our self-concept, we must try to get to know ourselves. Once we understand more about ourselves and our feelings, we must take a positive attitude toward our strengths and begin to improve upon our weaknesses.

The first big step in creating a positive self-concept is to really want to improve yourself. A defeatist attitude diminishes anyone's chances for improvement.

To develop a positive concept of yourself, you must believe that you can succeed. That is, you must make self-fulfilling prophecy work in your favor. Of course, just thinking about success won't necessarily make you successful—you must take action. Anytime you act, you run the risk of failure, but the primary difference between successful people and defeatists stems from how they handle failure. Successful people learn from failure and realize that they should avoid similar situations in the future. When you understand your shortcomings, learn how to deal with them, and believe that you can succeed, you will begin to see yourself in a more positive light.

A positive self-concept exists because we want it to exist. We must recognize that the people around us are basically no different from us and that we all share some of the same insecurities.

Here are several specific things you can do to help improve your self-concept:

1. *Decide what it is that you would like to change about yourself.* In order to begin the process of improvement, you must know specifically what needs changing. Describe, as accurately as you can, what you are unhappy about or what you don't like about yourself.

2. *Describe why you feel the way you do about yourself.* Is your problem brought on by yourself or by others? Many students, for example, do not really want to be in college. They are there because either their parents or their friends put pressure on them. Although they'd rather be doing something else, they are afraid to take a stand. Before they can begin to feel better about themselves, they must recognize why they are unhappy and who is contributing to their problem. You may feel that you are not capable of earning good grades in a certain subject or that you are too shy to make friends easily. Ask yourself why you feel that way. Are you living out a self-fulfilling prophecy?

3. *Decide that you are going to do something to change your feelings about yourself.* If you can describe your problem, you can almost always find a solution—that is, if you want to find one. If you are unhappy about your appearance—make plans to change it. If you feel inadequate about meeting people, plan some ways to build your confidence. Nothing will ever change unless you decide to change it yourself.

4. *Set goals for yourself.* You must be reasonable in setting your goals. You may be able to change some things overnight, but other things may require long-term effort. For example, you may decide that you are going to improve your grades by studying for several hours every night. You can begin your new study schedule immediately, but actually raising your grades may take much longer.

Sometimes a problem becomes more manageable if it is solved step by step. For example, you may feel hesitant to visit your professor in his or her office. Why not start by speaking briefly with your professor before or after class? You might begin by asking a question about your coursework. Once you begin to feel more comfortable, ask for an appointment or stop in to visit during office hours. If you pursue such visits, you will gradually gain more confidence in yourself.

5. *Associate with people who will support and help you.* Try to surround yourself with upbeat people whom you like and trust. That will make it much easier to discuss your problems and ask for support. When others know what you are trying to do, they can help. Of course, you must choose your friends carefully and give them specific suggestions about ways they can be of service. It is much easier to make behavioral changes if there are others around to offer support.

SUMMARY

Perception—the process of sensing, selecting, organizing, and evaluating information in order to give it personal meaning—lies at the heart of the communication process. Our perceptions of events, people, ideas, and things become our reality.

Much of what we know about the perception process centers around how we select, organize, and interpret information. *Selection* is the sorting of one *stimulus* from another. We use two kinds of selection—*selective attention* and *selective retention*—to focus on important stimuli and ignore or downplay other stimuli.

Organization is the categorizing of stimuli so that we can make sense of them. *Figure and ground, closure, proximity,* and *similarity* are all ways in which we organize our perceptions.

Interpretation is the assigning of meaning to stimuli. The meanings we choose are usually based on our past experiences. We must, therefore, take care that our past experiences do not create blinders that distort our perceptions.

Differences in people's perceptions result from each individual's state of mind, physiological makeup, and past experiences. People tend to believe that their own perception of the world is the only correct one. This, of course, is unrealistic. Actually, because perception is so subjective, one person's perception of a situation is no more correct than another's.

Two common phenomena that can distort our perceptions of reality are perceptual sets and frozen evaluations. A *perceptual set* is a fixed, predetermined view of people, things, or events based on past experience, while a *frozen evaluation* is the tendency to look on people, things, and events as if they never change. In addition, our perceptions are sometimes limited by our cultural background. People from differing cultures do not always see things in the same way. To improve our communication, therefore, we must constantly remember that perceptions, by themselves, are neither right nor wrong—they merely reflect how we have learned to view the world and ourselves.

Our perceptions of our physical, social, and psychological selves are our *self-concepts.* Self-concept consists of our *self-image*—the mental pictures we have of ourselves—and our *self-esteem*—our feelings and attitudes toward ourselves. Our self-concepts are affected by the communication we receive about ourselves and flow on a continuum from negative to positive. Self-concepts are affected not only by how we look at ourselves, but also by how we look at others, how others look at us, and how we think others see us. Like communication, self-concept is a process that has no beginning or end and is continuously changing. Self-perception and other people's perceptions of us change from time to time, from situation to situation, and from person to person.

Our self-concept is based on our values, attitudes, and beliefs. *Values* are broad-based ideals that are relatively stable over time; *attitudes* are evaluative dispositions or feelings that relate to ourselves, others, events, or things; and *beliefs* are convictions about the truth of something.

The components of self-concept may be organized into a hierarchy. The lower in the hierarchy a particular component of our self-concept exists, the easier it is to change.

Expectations also influence our self-concept. Our expectations can become *self-fulfilling prophecies* that determine how we behave, who we eventually become, and what we communicate to ourselves and others.

Although it is not easy to alter our self-concept, we can achieve some progress through hard work and a desire to improve. The specific steps we can take to help ourselves are: (1) decide what we want to change, (2) describe why we feel the way we do, (3) decide that we are going to do something to change, (4) set goals for ourselves, and (5) surround ourselves with people who are supportive. To have a positive self-image is to believe that we are and will be successful.

KEY TERMS

Attitudes: an evaluative disposition, feeling, or position about a person, event, idea, or thing.

Belief: a conviction or confidence in the truth of something that is not based on absolute proof.

Closure: the filling in of details by a perceiver so that whatever is perceived appears to be complete.

Figure and Ground Organization: the ordering of perceptions so that some stimuli are in focus and others become the background.

Frozen Evaluation: the tendency to look at events, things, or people as if they never change and to ignore any change that may have taken place.

Interpretation: the assigning of meaning to stimuli.

Organization: the categorizing of stimuli in our environment in order to make sense of them.

Perception: the process of sensing, selecting, organizing, interpreting, and evaluating information in order to give it personal meaning.

Perceptual Set: a fixed, predetermined view of events, things, or people based on past experiences.

Proximity: the grouping of stimuli perceived to be either physically or psychologically close to one another.

Selection: the sorting of one stimulus from another.

Selective Attention: the process of focusing on specific stimuli while ignoring or downplaying other stimuli.

Selective Retention: the processing, storage, and retrieval of information that we have already selected, organized, and interpreted.

Self-Concept: a person's mental picture of his or her physical, social, and psychological self.

Self-Esteem: our feelings and attitudes toward ourselves.

Self-Fulfilling Prophecy: the carrying out of expectations.

Self-Image: the mental picture we have of ourselves or the person we perceive ourselves to be.

Similarity: the grouping of elements that resemble one another in size, shape, color, or other traits.

Stimulus: something that incites or quickens action, feeling, or thought.

Value: a broad-based, relatively long-lasting ideal that guides our behavior.

DISCUSSION
STARTERS

1. How can an understanding of perception make you a more effective communicator?

2. What role does selectivity play in our communication?

3. Why do people from differing backgrounds see things in differing ways? Cite an example from your personal experience.

4. How can perceptual sets and frozen evaluations interfere with communication? How can they aid communication?

5. How does a person's self-concept affect his or her communication? Give both a positive and a negative example of this phenomenon.

6. How is our self-concept determined?

7. How do our expectations influence our self-concept and ultimately our communication? How have your expectations helped or hindered you?

8. What can a person do to alter his or her self-concept?

9. How can we help to change another person's self-concept?

10. In reviewing this chapter, what is the most important thing you learned about communication, perception, and self? Why?

FURTHER READINGS

Adler, R. B. *Confidence in Communication: A Guide to Assertive and Social Skills.* New York: Holt, Rinehart and Winston, 1977.

Barnlund, D. C. "Toward a Meaning Centered Philosophy of Communication." *Journal of Communication* 12, (1962):198–202.

Bower, S. A., and G. H. Bower. *Asserting Yourself: A Practical Guide for Positive Change.* Reading, Mass.: Addison-Wesley Publishing Co., Inc., 1976.

Carney, C. G., and S. L. McMahon. *Exploring Contemporary Male/Female Roles.* La Jolla, Calif.: University Associates, Inc., 1977.

Carr, Jacquelyn B. *Communication with Myself: A Journal.* Dubuque, Iowa: Wm. C. Brown Group, 1984.

Civikly, J. M. *Contexts of Communication.* New York: Holt, Rinehart and Winston, 1981.

Dance, F. E. X. *Human Communication Theory: Comparative Essays.* New York: Harper & Row Publishers, Inc., 1980.

Dance, F. E. X., and C. E. Larson. *The Function of Human Communication: A Theoretical Approach.* New York: Holt, Rinehart and Winston, 1976.

Dyer, W. W. *Pulling Your Own Strings.* New York: Avon Books, 1977.

Dyer, W. W. *The Sky's the Limit.* New York: Simon & Schuster, Inc., 1980.

Dyer, W. W. *Your Erroneous Zones.* New York: Funk & Wagnalls, Inc., 1976.

Fersterheim, H., and J. Baer. *Stop Running Scared!* New York: Rawson-Wade Publishers, Inc., 1977.

Goffman, E. *The Presentation of Self in Everyday Life.* Garden City, N.Y.: Doubleday & Co., Inc., 1959.

Goldhaber, Gerald M., and Marylynn B. Goldhaber. *Transactional Analysis: Principles and Applications.* Boston: Allyn & Bacon, Inc., 1976.

Hamachek, Don E. *Encounters with the Self.* 2nd ed. New York: Holt, Rinehart and Winston, 1978.

Laing, R. D., H. Phillipson, and A. R. Lee. *Interpersonal Perception: A Theory and a Method of Research.* New York: Harper & Row Publishers, Inc., 1966.

Lair, J. *I Ain't Much Baby, But I'm All I've Got.* New York: Doubleday & Co., Inc., 1972.

Mortensen, C. D. "Communication Postulates." In *Messages,* 2nd ed., Jean Civikly, ed. New York: Random House, Inc., 1977.

Prather, H. *Notes to Myself.* Moab, Utah: Real People Press, 1970.

Rubin, Z. "The Rise and Fall of First Impressions." In *Interpersonal Communication in Action,* 2nd ed., B. R. Patton and K. Griffin, eds. New York: Harper & Row Publishers, Inc., 1977; pp. 149–167.

Smith, M. J. *When I Say No, I Feel Guilty.* New York: Dial Press, 1975.

Smith, R. G. *Speech Communication Theory and Models.* New York: Harper & Row Publishers, Inc., 1970.

Waltzlawick, P., J. Beavin, and D. Jackson. *Pragmatics of Human Communication.* New York: W. W. Norton & Co., Inc., 1967.

Weinhold, B., and L. Elliott. *Transpersonal Communication: How to Establish Contact with Yourself and Others.* Englewood Cliffs, N.J.: Prentice-Hall—Spectrum Books, 1978.

Wylie, R. C. *The Self-Concept.* 2 vols. Lincoln, Nebr.: University of Nebraska Press, 1974.

Zimbardo, P. G. *Shyness: What It Is and What to Do About It.* Reading, Mass.: Addison-Wesley Publishing Co., Inc., 1977.

NOTES

1. The organization of our perception and the separating of the figure from the ground and vice versa is often referred to as *gestalt*.

2. Pearson, J., and P. Nelson, *Understanding and Sharing: An Introduction to Speech Communication*, 3rd ed. (Dubuque, Iowa: Wm. C. Brown Group, 1985), p. 27.

3. Haney, W. V., *Communication and Organizational Behavior: Text and Cases*, 3rd ed. (Homewood, Ill.: Richard D. Irwin, Inc., 1973), pp. 389–408.

4. Wenburg, J., and W. Wilmot, *The Personal Communication Process*, (New York: John Wiley & Sons, Inc., 1973), p. 115. The "Counting Game" was adapted by Wenburg and Wilmot from an exercise used in AID Communication Seminars, Michigan State University.

5. Haney, W. V., pp. 391–392.

6. Griffin, J. H., *Black Like Me,* (New York: Signet Books, 1960).

7. *The Eye of the Beholder* was produced in 1955 by BNA Communications Inc., 9401 Decoverly Hall Rd., Rockville, MD 20850.

CHAPTER 3

Verbal Communication

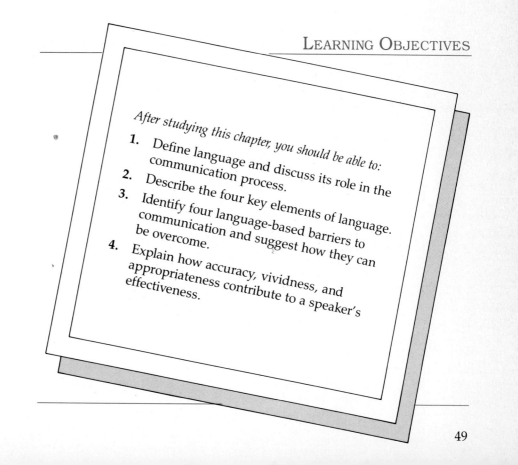

After studying this chapter, you should be able to:

1. Define language and discuss its role in the communication process.
2. Describe the four key elements of language.
3. Identify four language-based barriers to communication and suggest how they can be overcome.
4. Explain how accuracy, vividness, and appropriateness contribute to a speaker's effectiveness.

As you learned in Chapter 1, our ability to communicate allows us to be human, to be individuals, and to be personal. However, while it is our ability to communicate that distinguishes us from other creatures and from each other, it is language that allows us to communicate in the first place.

For two individuals to communicate, they must speak the same language. This is not as easy as it sounds. As we know from Chapter 2, each person's perceptions are different, so no two individuals can have identical meanings for the same words, messages, and experiences. These perceptual differences are reflected in our use of language—in what we say and how we interpret what others say to us. Thus, language is highly personal, and it is this personal language that we use to translate our thoughts, feelings, and experiences into messages that have meaning for us and that we hope will have meaning for others.

Election update: "California voters approve referendum making English the state's 'official language.'"

Like, I don't even know where to start, you know? Melissa and I are at the mall the other day, you know, and here comes Krissie, and she goes, "It passed! It passed!" Like, you know, we know what she's talking about.

So anyway, Melissa goes, "What passed?" and Krissie goes, "The referendum!" And I look at Melissa and Melissa looks at me, and we both, like, crack up, you know? And we go, "What referendum?"

So Krissie goes, "The English language referendum! They voted for it!"

So she tells us about this referendum that was on the California ballot to make English the official language. I'm wrapped about the whole thing—like who cares, you know?

Krissie looks at me like I'm a total jel, you know? Then she goes, "What language do you speak, Tamara?"

I go, "English."

Then she goes, "And what's California's official language going to be?"

And I go, "English."

Then she goes, "And who speaks 'official languages'?"

And I go, "Politicians?"

"Who else?"

"TEACHERS?!!"

She goes, "Fer sure."

"Gag me with a spoon! You mean, every one of those geeks at school will be, you know, talking just the way we do?"

So now Melissa and I are thinking of learning Chinese.

Bummer.

Adapted from Rick Horowitz, "English language, it's like, you know, truly tubular," *Chicago Tribune*, November 23, 1986, Section 5, p. 3.

To ensure that others will understand us, we must try to use the same language they use. Our meanings must be as close to their meanings as possible. This is desirable whether we are speaking to a close friend, a stranger, a potential employer, or a group. Whatever the situation, our use of language determines our success as communicators.

Because language is so important to communication, we will learn how to use language more effectively. First, we will examine what language is. Then we will discuss some common barriers to effective language use and how we can overcome them.

THE IMPORTANCE OF LANGUAGE

Created by humans, **language** is a structured system of signs, sounds, gestures, or marks that are used and understood to express ideas and feelings among people within a community or nation, within the same geographical area, or within the same cultural tradition. Without language there would be little or no human communication as we now know it. Can you imagine what it would be like not to read a book, listen to the radio, talk on the telephone, or simply tell someone what you think or feel? Language is a powerful tool! As a tool, language is neither good nor bad, and it is only as effective and efficient as the person or persons using it.

THINK ABOUT IT

According to the cliché, "Sticks and stones will break my bones, but names will never hurt me." Of course, in reality, being called names does hurt. Why?

The Power of Language

We depend not only on our own experiences for information, but also on those of our neighbors, friends, and relatives. Because we have language and are able to communicate, we are not limited to just our own personal experiences and knowledge. For example, because we have language, we can learn by talking with others, taking courses, watching television, and reading newspapers, magazines, and books. Language allows us to progress, to cooperate, to create and resolve conflicts, and to be human.

Our use of language is so powerful that it can prevent wars or start them, create friends or enemies, and change our behavior or the behavior of others. Yet, most of us take language for granted and ignore its potential effects. We regard language as a "mere matter of words," forgetting that words have the power to affect our mind, feelings, thoughts, will, actions, and being.

Successful communicators respect language and have learned how to use it. A mispronounced word, a grammatically incorrect statement, a misused term, or the repetition of such meaningless utterances as *you know, uh, like,* and *really* can quickly reduce a speaker's effectiveness. Other barriers to successful use of language are discussed in more detail later in this chapter.

Mini-Exercise

Consider the following segments from a recent article about how thought might influence what we say:

> We're constantly at war with our tongues. Who hasn't tried to say something, then startled himself by saying something else?
>
> And who hasn't occasionally wondered if a verbal gaffe is more than a mere mistake, a faint signal from our subconscious, perhaps a reminder of long-suppressed feelings and desires?
>
> Many psychologists regard slips as "information processing" errors, brief breakdowns in the neural machinery that controls speech.
>
> But many also follow Sigmund Freud's belief that slips are clues to a person's most intimate and repressed feelings.
>
> Researcher Bernard J. Baars, seeking to assess Freud's ideas in the lab, developed a technique to induce volunteers to commit slips and another to affect the content of the slips by changing the context of the experiment.
>
> Barr tries to "prime" a volunteer to think about a particular subject. The goal is to see how the "priming" will affect the content of the slips.
>
> In one experiment, male subjects were divided into three groups. The first was run by an attractive female experimenter, who volunteered to dress in a sexually spectacular fashion; the second group was told they might receive an electric shock during the experiment, and shown some impressive-looking equipment (no shock was given); and the third group received neither of these treatments.
>
> The results were dramatic. Subjects were given different word pairs such as "lice legs" and "shad bok."
>
> When exposed to the lovely female experimenter, they were more than twice as likely to mess up "lice legs" by saying "nice legs."
>
> When threatened with a shock, they more than doubled their rate of saying "bad shock" instead of "shad bok."

Why do you think this happened? Have similar things happened to you? Explain.

Adapted from Keay Davidson, "Programmed loose lips think slips," *Chicago Tribune,* December 21, 1986, Section 5, p. 7.

Language and Thought

The misuse of language is, therefore, more than the mere misuse of words. Misused language also affects our ability to think. Thought and language, according to most scholars, are inseparable. But which comes first? As with the proverbial dilemma of the chicken and the egg, the answer is debatable, but most scholars agree that words help us form thoughts. For example, at times we may think we know what we want to say, but find that we don't know how to say it. However, the fact is that if we really knew what we wanted to say, we would probably have no trouble expressing it. There are other times when we speak and later wish that we hadn't. This usually occurs because we didn't think about what we were saying.

Erasing the effect of something you said is extremely difficult. You can correct or retract a statement, and you can even apologize for saying it, but you cannot eliminate the fact that you said it.

Politicians, for example, often try to assess how each word they speak might be interpreted by others. They do this because they know that what they say may not only place them in an awkward position, but it may also cost them an election or jeopardize national security. One such incident occurred during a primary campaign when George Romney, then the governor of Michigan, was seeking the Republican presidential nomination. At first, he supported United States involvement in Vietnam, but then he observed firsthand what was happening in that country. He immediately changed his position and advised that the United States leave Vietnam as soon as possible. When he was asked during the New Hampshire primary campaign why he had changed his view, he replied that originally he "had been brainwashed" about the situation. The word *brainwashed* carried such a powerful message that it literally cost Romney the primary and any hope of becoming president. His choice of language gave the impression that he was weak and easily persuaded—traits that could never be tolerated in the president of the United States. No matter how hard Romney tried to clarify what he meant, he could not overcome the stigma his statement created. *One word* caused Romney to lose his credibility and his bid for the presidency of the United States.

THINK ABOUT IT

"Language not only reveals a person's identity, who he is, but in some way it makes him the person he is."

Gerard Egan

When we communicate, we first get thoughts and then decide how we are going to express them. To do this effectively, we must know what language is and how to use it.

THE ELEMENTS OF LANGUAGE

Language, speech, and communication are three different, but related, phenomena. *Language* is a structured symbol system that allows us to express ideas and feelings to others; *speech* is one vehicle that we use to transmit language; and *communication* is the result we achieve if we succeed in our attempt to exchange meanings. Language is one means by which we communicate and speech is one way in which we use language. Of course, the fact that we possess language does not automatically mean that we can communicate, but we cannot communicate without language, and language would be useless if it did not convey meanings.

To clarify the relationship among language, speech, and communication, consider the fact that you can indicate an affirmative response to a question by nodding your head, thus using a sign to communicate without speech. You can also indicate the same response by writing *yes*, thus using written language to communicate without speech. If you were traveling in a foreign country and said *yes*, you might use language and speech without communicating.

The goal of this course is to help you get language and speech working together to produce effective communication. You can learn more about language by examining four of its key elements: sounds, words, grammar, and meaning.

Sounds

Language must be spoken before it can be written. Most of us are born with the physical mechanisms for making the speech sounds that are essential to create language. However, not all of us learn to produce the sounds in exactly the same way. Hence, languages and dialects sound strange or different to outsiders.

The **International Phonetic Alphabet (IPA)** was devised as a consistent and universal system for transcribing the speech sounds of all languages. We cannot simply rely on the letters of our alphabet or our spelling system because neither completely represents the sounds of our language. For example, the same letter may be pronounced in different ways—as is *g* in the words *go* and *gin* or *th* in the words *thin* and *then*. Furthermore, different letters may represent the same sound—as does the letter *c* in *cat* and the letter *k* in *kite*, or the letter *c* in *cite* and the letter *s* in *sight*.

The smallest functional unit of sound in a language is called a **phoneme.** In the English language there are 39 phonemes. Each phoneme is different enough from other phonemes to be useful in distinguishing meaning. If, for example, the vowel sound in *get* is distorted, the word could sound like *gate*. The two different vowel phonemes make it possible to distinguish one word from the other.

For language to exist, a series of sounds must be produced by successive movements of the speech organs. When we sound out a word—for example, kə myoo′ nə ka′ shən—we reduce the word into the sounds that compose it. When we successively put the sounds together, the parts form the word *communication*.

Words

Words are symbols that stand for the objects and concepts that they name. They represent agreed-upon sound combinations within our language community. For example, the sounds *h e l p* constitute a word because English speakers agree that they do. On the other hand, *z e l p*, while representing common sounds in our language, is not a word because this combination of sounds does not have an agreed-upon meaning.

When we speak, we put sounds together to represent ideas, concepts, feelings, and thousands of other things. A word can represent a thing itself—as *chair* represents the actual piece of furniture—or it can represent an abstract concept—as *freedom* represents the intangible qualities of self-determination and civil and political liberty.

Grammar

Just as language has rules that govern how sounds may be joined into words, it also has rules that govern how words may be joined into phrases and sentences. This second set of rules is its **grammar.** For example, in English, our grammar system requires that singular nouns take singular verbs while plural nouns take plural verbs: table *is*—tables *are*.

As we join sounds together to form words and join words together to form phrases, sentences, and paragraphs, we use our language's sound and grammar systems simultaneously. This ability to use the sounds and rules of language correctly is crucial to efficient and effective communication. It enables us to make up complete sentences and to understand the multiple-word sentences of others.

Despite the many rules that govern language, there is virtually no limit to the number of different messages that can be created. It has been estimated that in the English language there is the possibility of 100 quintillion twenty-word sentences.[1] This does not include sentences either shorter or longer than 20 words. Thus, the number is infinite. You only have to hear some of the excuses professors receive from students who miss an exam or a speech to know how creatively the English language can be used.

Meaning

The study of meaning, or the association of words with ideas, feelings, and contexts, is called **semantics.** If language did not have meaning, it would serve little or no purpose. Because words and word patterns can be repeated from person to person and from generation to generation, language becomes meaningful and useful as a tool for communication.

MINI-EXERCISE

In Lewis Carroll's *Through the Looking Glass,* Humpty Dumpty and Alice become involved in an argument about language and meaning:

"I don't know what you mean by 'glory,' " Alice said.

Humpty Dumpty smiled contemptuously. "Of course you don't—till I tell you. I meant there's a nice knock-down argument for you!"

"But 'glory' doesn't mean 'a nice knock-down argument,' " Alice objected.

"When I use a word," Humpty Dumpty said, in a rather scornful tone, "it means just what I choose it to mean—neither more nor less."

"The question is," said Alice, "whether you can make words mean so many different things."

"The question is," said Humpty Dumpty, "which is to be master—that's all."

Describe a situation in which you and another person had a misunderstanding based on the meanings of words. How did you resolve the misunderstanding? Explain what happened and what could have been done to prevent it.

We tend to associate language with specific meanings and to take that relationship for granted, but it is important to understand that, in fact, language is arbitrary and by itself has no meaning. This notion may seem to contradict our entire discussion so far. You may wonder how language can be a system with rules and meanings and still be arbitrary. However, in reality, language is arbitrary because it uses words, and words are symbols that merely represent people, things, concepts, and events. The relationships between words and things are not always logical or consistent. Why? Because the word is not actually the person, thing, concept, or event. For example, *chair, car, snake, communication, tall, black, money,* and *freedom* are merely words and not the entities they symbolize. Scream "Spider!" in front of someone who dislikes spiders and you will quickly see how words cause reactions—as if words were the actual thing! Words and meanings exist only in people's minds. Thus, those who study language say that *meanings are not in words but in people.*

THINK ABOUT IT

Whatever we call a thing, whatever we say it is, it is not. For whatever we say is words, and words are words and not things. The words are maps, and the map is not the territory.

S. I. Hayakawa

If someone were to say, "I hope you have a twif day," you would not know what he was talking about. However, if that person were to explain that when he says "twif" he means "nice," you would understand what he meant—even though you might think he was a little strange. If every time he sees you he uses the word "twif" instead of "nice," you would eventually associate "twif" with "nice" and automatically know exactly what he meant. The point is that "twif," the word (or symbol), is arbitrary because it does not mean a thing until people give it meaning. In the same way, words have no direct relationship to the person, thing, concept, or event they represent. The meanings of words can be classified in two ways: abstract versus concrete and denotative versus connotative.

Concreteness and Abstractness.   **Concrete words** are symbols for specific things that can be pointed to, physically experienced, touched, or felt. For example, words such as *car, book, keys,* and *dog* are concrete words. They represent specific tangible objects. Due to their specificity, the meanings of concrete words are usually quite clear. Consequently, communication based on concrete words leaves little room for misunderstanding, and any disagreement can be resolved by referring to the objects themselves.

Abstract words, on the other hand, are symbols for ideas, qualities, and relationships. Because they represent intangible things, their meanings depend on the experiences and intentions of the persons using them. For instance, words such as *right, freedom, truth,* and *trust* stand for ideas that mean different things to different people. Thus, the use of abstract words

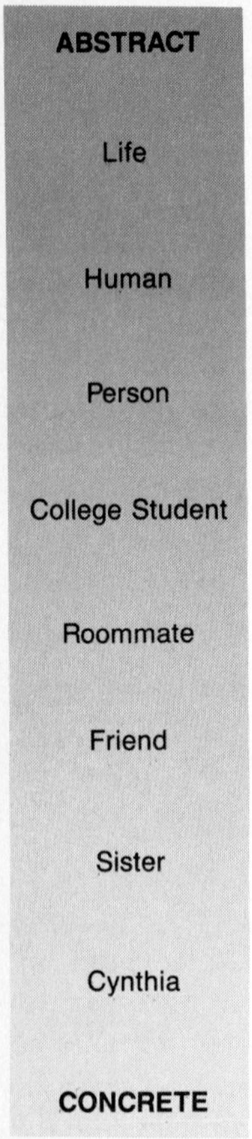

ABSTRACT

Life

Human

Person

College Student

Roommate

Friend

Sister

Cynthia

CONCRETE

Figure 3.1
*Concrete to
Abstract*

can easily lead to misunderstandings and result in ineffective communication, as illustrated by the following conversation:

STUDENT: Your tests are unfair.
INSTRUCTOR: Why do you say that?
STUDENT: They're unfair and it's impossible to get a high grade on them.
INSTRUCTOR: Do they include material that wasn't covered in class or in our readings?
STUDENT: No.
INSTRUCTOR: Do you mean the wording is too ambiguous for you to understand?
STUDENT: No.
INSTRUCTOR: What's unfair about them?

The problem here is that the student expects his instructor to understand what he means by the word *unfair,* but because *unfair* is an abstract word, its meaning can vary greatly from person to person and from situation to situation. To clarify his meaning, the student needs to use more concrete language—for instance, "Your tests are unfair because they contain too many items to complete in the time allotted." It is always a good idea to define or illustrate any abstract word that may be misunderstood.

Figure 3.1 illustrates how some words are concrete while others are abstract.

Denotation and Connotation.   The meanings of words can also be classified as either denotative or connotative. **Denotation** is the core meaning of a word—its standard dictionary definition. For example, the word *book* is defined as "a written or printed literary composition on consecutive sheets of paper bound together in a volume."

Connotation is the subjective meaning of a word. It is what a word suggests because of the feelings or associations it evokes. We attribute

MINI-EXERCISE

Arrange each group of words into a sequence ranging from the most abstract to the most concrete.

1. sport, basketball, National Basketball Association, Larry Byrd, physical activity, Boston Celtics
2. book, chapter, information, page, knowledge, paragraph, sentence, word, wisdom
3. assets, house, wealth, money, property, our house

connotational meanings to words based on our social and personal experiences. For example, the word *farm* has quite different connotations for a city person and a rural person. To a city person, a farm may simply be a place where crops are grown and animals are kept, but to a rural person, a farm represents a livelihood, a workplace, and a home.

The more communicators have in common in terms of their backgrounds, experiences, and attitudes, the more likely they are to see things in a similar way and to have similar meanings for the words they exchange.

MINI-EXERCISE

Consider the following situation:

Jill and her parents are discussing college. When the subject switches to Jill's boyfriend and the word *sex* is brought up, Jill immediately stops the discussion because she knows her parents' views on sex are much different from her own. The word simply has different meanings for Jill and her parents.

Jill cannot talk about sex with her parents because their differing connotations of the word result in misinterpretation and distrust. Discuss what can be done to prevent the occurrence of this kind of obstacle to communication. Who is at fault? Why?

LANGUAGE-BASED BARRIERS TO COMMUNICATION

As you can see, our use of language is an extremely complex process, yet many of us take language for granted. Although it takes little physical effort to say something to someone, it does take mental effort to ensure that what we say conveys our intentions. Even if we communicate what we may think is the perfect message, the possibility always exists that the receiver may misinterpret our message or find it ambiguous. Thus, the receiver must also make an effort to ensure that he or she receives the intended message.

Whether the problem lies with the sender or the receiver, as discussed in Chapter 1, we often blame communication for our difficulty—"the communication broke down," but this is a flimsy excuse. We must recognize that communication is nothing more than symbolic interaction and that because of communication's symbolic nature, there will always be the potential for misunderstanding. In fact, within the communication process there are numerous physical, mental, and cultural reasons for breakdowns to occur, and our use of language is one. Among the most common language-based barriers to effective communication are bypassing, inference confusion, indiscrimination, and polarization.[2]

Bypassing

What is *meant* by a speaker and what is *heard and understood* by the listener
are often different. Such misunderstanding between a sender and a receiver
is called **bypassing.** How many times have we said to ourselves or to
someone else, "But that's not what I meant"? The problem is that we forget
that language is symbolic. The words we speak or write are not the actual
objects, ideas, or feelings, but merely symbols that represent them. Here is
a classic illustration of bypassing:

> A motorist was driving down a highway when her engine suddenly stalled.
> She quickly determined that her battery was dead and managed to stop
> another driver, who consented to push her car to get it started.
>
> "My car has an automatic transmission," she explained to the other
> driver, "so you'll have to get up to 15 to 20 miles per hour to get me
> started."
>
> The man smiled and walked back to his car. The motorist climbed into
> her own car and waited for him to line up his car behind hers. She waited—
> and waited. Finally, she turned around to see what was wrong.
>
> There was the man—coming at her car at 15 to 20 miles per hour!
>
> The damage to her car amounted to over $1,000![3]

In this case, there is no question that communication took place, but the end result could not have been anticipated by either driver, given each one's understanding of the message sent or received. The driver of the stalled vehicle thought she knew exactly what she had communicated, and the other driver thought he knew exactly what had been asked of him, but the meanings of the message sent and the message received obviously were different—that is, bypassing took place.

Bypassing is usually the result of two false beliefs about language: (1) that each word has only one meaning and (2) that words have meaning in and of themselves.

An examination of our everyday language quickly illustrates that most words have multiple uses and meanings. For example, the *Random House Dictionary of the English Language* provides 60 different definitions for the word *call*, 30 for *fast*, 22 for *seat*, 29 for *see*, and 96 for *turn*. Thus, it is crucial that all of us as communicators, both senders and receivers, realize that words have multiple uses that can be interpreted differently by different people. Words often acquire a number of interpretations because meaning changes over time, varies from one culture or region to another, and depends on technical or common usage.

The belief that words have meaning in and of themselves is widespread, but the simple fact is that words themselves do not contain meanings. They only acquire meaning through the context in which they are used and by those using them. On the surface, this would appear to be a sensible enough phenomenon to accept—intellectually, but it is not always the case. During the past four or five years students in beginning speech communication classes were asked whether they believe words have meaning. The data, though not scientifically collected, suggest that better than 75 percent of them believe that to be true.

That some speakers and listeners bypass deliberately should not be overlooked. For example, politicians sometimes will say one thing in order to get people to believe or accept something else. When this occurs, there are ethical considerations that message senders and receivers should take into account. The issue of what is right or wrong and what is good or harmful must rest with the norms of society and one's own conscience.

The following techniques should help you to reduce the frequency of bypassing when speaking and listening. Bear in mind that the most these techniques can do is help, because there is little chance that bypassing will ever be eliminated.

Be Person-Minded, Not Word-Minded. To enhance understanding, we must think not only of the words and their meanings, but also of the persons using the words and of the meanings they give to those words. We must constantly remind ourselves: "This is what the word means to me, but what does it mean to the other person or persons?"

Query and Paraphrase.   Ask questions and paraphrase whenever there is a potential for misunderstanding that results from differences in background, age, sex, occupation, attitudes, knowledge, and perceptions. If you don't understand something or if you feel uncertain about what people mean, ask them to explain.

We can check our own understanding by paraphrasing the message in our own words to make sure that we received the message as it was intended. For example, all of us have probably been given directions that at first seemed very clear, but when we tried following them, we became confused. Paraphrasing is no guarantee that we will find our location, but it will provide a check on our comprehension and help the person giving the directions to gauge whether or not we understood. As the importance and complexity of a message increases, so does the necessity of paraphrasing.

Be Approachable.   We can encourage open and free communication by being easy to meet and deal with. The most frequent barrier to effective communication is an unwillingness to listen to others. To enhance communication, we must allow others to question and paraphrase what we say and show respect for what they say. Being receptive to others is not always easy, but we must make the effort in order to ensure a clear exchange of information.

Be Sensitive to Contexts.   We can reduce bypassing if we take into account both the verbal and the situational contexts in which communication occurs. The meaning of a word can be more precisely interpreted in terms of the words, sentences, and paragraphs that precede and follow it, and the setting in which communication takes place usually provides additional meaning.

REDUCING THE FREQUENCY OF BYPASSING

B̲e person-minded, not word-minded.
Query and paraphrase.
Be approachable.
Be sensitive to contexts.

Inference Confusion

Whenever we draw a conclusion from an observation, we are making an inference. **Inference confusion** occurs when people go beyond their actual observations to draw incorrect conclusions that they assume are correct.

Because we live in an environment where we must quickly sort and interpret the many stimuli that bombard our senses, we often make inferences. In many cases, inferences help us to understand our environment, but problems can arise when people communicate as if their inferences were actual observations.

Assume that you are walking down a city street and see a middle-aged man with torn clothes and a bloody nose stumble from an alley and yell for help. At the same time, you see a young teenager running down the street. The obvious conclusion would be that the teenage boy mugged the man. Is your conclusion based on fact (observation) or inference? At this point your conclusion is strictly inference. It might be accurate, but it is still an inference based only on what you think happened and not on what you actually saw.

Let's continue our example. Within a few moments a police officer comes on the scene and asks you what happened. You state with certainty, "The man must have been mugged; I saw the teenager who did it run away." Everything seems legitimate to this point, but is it? You didn't really see the teenager do anything but run, yet your communication implies that the teenager mugged the man. The choice of words and the perceptual linking of what did not occur were easy to make.

In an attempt to verify your statement, the police officer asks, "Did you see the teenager mug the man?" If you answer "No," then you are beginning to distinguish between observation and inference. If, on the other hand, you answer "Yes," you will have gone beyond what you observed to draw an inference.

You can probably think of many times when you or others have made incorrect inferences. It is easy to do. It is also relatively easy to learn to stay within our observations. The following characteristics differentiate statements of observation from statements of inference:

Statements of Observation	Statements of Inference
1. May be made only after or during an observation	1. May be made at any time
2. Are limited to what is actually observed	2. Go beyond what has been observed
3. May be made only by the observer	3. May be made by anyone
4. May be made only about the past or present	4. May be made about any time—past, present, or future
5. Approach certainty	5. Involve varying degrees of probability and chance

It may be difficult to avoid making inferences, but communication is clarified when we can distinguish between actual observation and inferences. For example, the witness might say, "I saw the man come from the alley and I saw the boy run, but I didn't see what else took place. I think the boy mugged the man, but I didn't see it."

REDUCING THE FREQUENCY OF INFERENCE CONFUSION

To distinguish between inference and observation, ask the following questions:

1. Did I personally observe what I am talking or writing about?
2. Do my statements closely correspond to, and not go beyond, my observations?
3. When I deal with important inferences, do I assess their probabilities?
4. When I communicate, do I label my inferences as such and encourage others to identify their inferences?

Indiscrimination

Indiscrimination is the neglect of individual differences and the overemphasis of similarities. Language plays a significant role in our tendency to see similarities even when none exist. Because of language, we are often more likely to generalize than to differentiate. For example, the abundance of categorizing nouns, such as *teenager, divorcé, student, professor, black, Southerner, liberal, friend, government, politician,* and *salesperson,* encourage us to focus on similarities. It is not unusual for us to say something like "All politicians are crooks," "The liberals are responsible for this problem," or "All students cheat in school." The problem is that we fail to distinguish between individuals, objects, and events. Such categorization results in stereotyping and frozen evaluations.

THINK ABOUT IT

Among the many problems of effective communication, none is more subtle or more widespread than the problem of prejudice.

Eldon L. Seamans

Sexist language is any language that expresses such stereotyped attitudes and expectations, or assumes the inherent superiority of one sex over the other.

Casey Miller and Kate Swift

Stereotypes. A **stereotype** is a relatively fixed mental picture of a class or group that is attributed to an individual member of that class without regard to his or her unique characteristics and qualities. Most stereotypes are considered to be negative, but they can also be positive—for example, "All liberals are hardworking," "All conservatives want peace," "All teachers are dedicated professionals," and "All environmentalists are concerned citizens." Whether the stereotype is negative or positive, the same problem exists: the differences in individuals are ignored.

Stereotyping is quick and easy to do because it does not require analysis, investigation, or thought. By precluding distinctions, stereotypes give us neat, well-defined, and oversimplified categories that facilitate our evaluation of people, situations, and events.

Frozen Evaluations. As discussed in Chapter 2, **frozen evaluation** is the tendency to look at people, things, and events as if they never change and to ignore any change that may have taken place. For example, when we think of ourselves, we seldom recognize the changes that we have gone through over time. Instead, most of us tend to see ourselves as the same person we were five, ten, or more years ago. Frozen evaluation is easy to do because it ignores the passage of time.

MINI-EXERCISE

Indicate the year in which each of the following news bulletins was probably made.

POPE CONDEMNS USE OF NEW "HORROR" WEAPONS

Vatican City—Prompted by widespread fears that new weapons of mass destruction might wipe out Western civilization, the Pope today issued a bulletin forbidding the use of these weapons by any Christian state against another, whatever the provocation.

MORAL ROT ENDANGERS LAND, WARNS GENERAL

Boston—The head of the country's armed forces declared here today that if he had known the depth of America's moral decay, he would never have accepted his command. "Such a dearth of public spirit," he asserted, "and want of virtue, and fertility in all the low arts to obtain advantages of one kind or another, I never saw before and hope I may never be witness to again."

The thoughts expressed in these two paragraphs could easily apply to what is happening today, but in fact, the first paragraph pertains to a statement made by Pope Innocent II in 1139 and the second quotes a comment made by George Washington in 1775.[4]

Did you think that these paragraphs referred to recent events? If so, you fell victim to indiscrimination. Discuss why such errors can occur in our language. How we can avoid or prevent them? Describe a personal experience which indiscrimination led to misunderstanding. What was the outcome? What could you have done to solve the problem?

Suggestions for Reducing the Frequency of Indiscrimination.   **Indexing** is a technique that can help you sort out differences among various members of a group and thus reduce indiscrimination. The goal of indexing is to identify how each person, object, or event is different and unique. When you hear someone say, "Politicians are corrupt," "College men are over-sexed," "Athletes are intellectually void," or any similar statement that classifies individuals, ideas, events, or things into a single category, you should immediately ask, "Which ones are you talking about?" For example, to increase specificity, you would ask, "Precisely which politicians are corrupt?" No matter what people may think, not all politicians are corrupt. Neither are all college men oversexed nor all athletes stupid. The point is that politician A is different from politician B, and politician B is different from politician C. The same is true of college men or athletes—they may belong to a class or group that has an identity and similar interests, but the group is composed of individuals, each different from the other.

Dating, another technique for reducing the occurrence of indiscrimina-tion, is a form of indexing that helps us to sort events, ideas, places, and people according to time. When we use dating, we acknowledge that things change over time and we add specificity to our statements by telling when something occurred. For example, the contexts of the statements in the mini-exercise could be greatly clarified merely by adding dates: Vatican City, 1139, and Boston, 1775. When we use dating to tell when something was true, we give our listeners valuable information that can increase their understanding of our intended message.

Polarization

Polarization is the tendency to view things around us in terms of extremes—either rich or poor, beautiful or ugly, large or small, high or low, good or bad, intelligent or stupid—even though most things exist in moderation. This phenomenon is referred to as the "either-or" or "black-or-white" syndrome and is usually aggravated by our choice of language.

MINI-EXERCISE

Supply the polar opposite for each of the following words:

>   all
>   high
>   fat
>   happy
>   correct

Now try to think of a word that would describe the middle ground between each pair of extremes. Which task was easier? Why?

Thinking in terms of polar opposites is simple and almost automatic. Coming up with a term that describes the middle ground between a pair of extreme opposites is more time consuming and often requires more than one word. In addition, people are less likely to agree on what actually constitutes the middle ground.

The most destructive consequence of polarization is the escalating conflict that results from the use of either-or terms to describe and defend our perceptions of reality. This is referred to as the *pendulum effect*. The pendulum represents a person's reality, which includes feelings, attitudes, opinions, and value judgments about the surrounding world. When the pendulum is hanging in the center, a person's perception is considered to be realistic, virtuous, intelligent, sane, honest, and honorable. Of course, most of us believe that, for the majority of the time, our pendulums are at or near the center.

When two individuals disagree in their perceptions of reality, their pendulums begin to move in opposite directions. The severity of the movement represents their differences and the convictions expressed by their language. As the conversation intensifies, each remark provokes a stronger and stronger reaction until both parties are driven to opposite extremes. For example, when two roommates argue over whose turn it is to clean, one may begin by saying, "It's your turn. I did it the last time." The other is likely to respond, "No, I did it the last time. Now it's your turn." If the disagreement continues and no solution is found, both will become firmer in their positions and their comments may turn into personal attacks: "You're always so messy and lazy." "And you're always so picky and critical." Eventually the situation may degenerate to the point where one or the other threatens to move out. Such an extreme outcome is typical of a discussion driven by the pendulum effect. Emotions may eventually run so high that the differences between the parties may seem insurmountable and a mutually agreeable settlement may seem unattainable.

Speakers can avoid the dangers of polarization by recognizing the potential for misunderstanding and by specifying degrees between extremes. For example, a statement such as "Nebraska is hot in the summer" is not as meaningful as it could be because the word *hot* is an overgeneralized extreme. To avoid confusion, further questions must be asked: "When it comes to hot, what is the basis of comparison (Florida or Minnesota)?" "Are Nebraska summers all the same or do they vary from year to year and from the northern part to the southern?" "What is the average summer temperature?" One way to resolve the problem of polarization is to state that "Nebraska summers can be hot. The average temperature is 85 degrees Fahrenheit, with lows around 74 degrees and highs around 105 degrees." It may take more words and time, but the risk of misunderstanding is substantially reduced.

THINK ABOUT IT

Note how language can be used to create deliberately ambiguous messages:

THE PENTAGON PRODUCTS PHILOSOPHY

That's why—right up front—we're willing to "tell it like it, to the best of our knowledge and belief, based upon available information and notwithstanding inaccuracies beyond our control, is." And our way of doing that is to give you, in plain English, five reasons why, dollar for dollar for dollar, it pays so much to shop with us—when you care enough to spend the very most.

Christopher Cerf and Henry Beard, *The Pentagon Catalog*

HOW TO USE LANGUAGE MORE EFFECTIVELY

On the surface, language may seem simple to use—people of all ages, cultures, and educational levels use language every day. Nevertheless, the ability to use language efficiently and effectively requires years of practice and study. While many variables affect our ability to use language effectively, three play key roles and merit special attention. They are accuracy, vividness, and appropriateness.

Accuracy

Using language accurately is as critical to a speaker as reading navigation instruments accurately is to an airplane pilot. The choice of a wrong word can not only distort your intended message, but it can also undermine your credibility. When you speak, your goal should be precision. Don't leave room for misinterpretation. You should constantly ask yourself, "What do I really want to say?" and "What do I really mean?" When necessary, consult a dictionary or thesaurus for the best choice of words to express yourself.

To gain a better selection of words, you must expand your vocabulary. Two of the best ways to do this are by listening to others and by reading. It also pays to become more conscious of words that you don't understand. Whenever you run into an unfamiliar word, first determine the context in which it is used. Then, either ask someone or consult a dictionary for its meaning. Once you have learned a new word, try to put it to use. Words that are not used are likely to be forgotten.

Learning new words and expanding your vocabulary takes effort, but with time and practice, it will become part of your daily routine. The more words you have to choose from, the greater your chances of communicating your exact meaning to others. One word of warning, however: Once you've developed a large vocabulary, avoid the temptation to use long or little-known words when short or common words would serve the purpose.

THINK ABOUT IT

I see one-third of a nation ill-housed, ill-clad, ill-nourished.

Franklin D. Roosevelt
Compare the above quote to one author's version of it:

It is evident that a substantial number of persons within the continental boundaries of the United States have inadequate financial resources with which to purchase the products of agricultural communities and indus-trial establishments. It would appear that for a considerable segment of the population, perhaps as much as 33.333 percent of the total, there are inadequate housing facilities, and an equally significant proportion is deprived of the proper types of clothing and nourishment.[5]

How do these speakers differ in their choice of words? How do their choices affect your emotions and your impression of them as speakers?

Remember that words may have different meanings for different people. Sometimes when our meaning is unclear, it is because we did not structure our statement effectively. Thus, our idea may be clear to us, but it may not be expressed accurately. For example, classified advertisers in newspapers frequently condense the content of their ads so much that their intended meaning becomes distorted or obscured. As a result, you'll see such ads as "1979 Cadillac hearse for sale. Body in good condition" and "Wanted to Rent—Four-room apartment by careful couple. No children." Obviously, these advertisers knew what they intended to communicate, but their failure to phrase their messages accurately interfered with their intended meaning.

When conversing, we can easily clear up any misunderstandings caused by scrambled sentence structure or poor word choice. But it is our responsibility to be aware of our listeners' reactions to what we are saying. If they appear confused or ask a question, we should rephrase our message more clearly.

Effective speakers do not assume that what is clear to them is necessarily going to be clear to their listeners. They are especially aware of this problem in situations such as public speeches, where the opportunity to ask questions may not be appropriate or possible. To avoid problems, they strive to make their meaning so clear that there is virtually no chance of misunderstanding. They try to ensure comprehension by using familiar words and concrete rather than abstract language.

MINI-EXERCISE

Change the following phrases and statements to make them more concrete and less likely to be misunderstood:

Sample: fresh fruit   an apple picked this morning
                a cold day
                a high evaluation
                a losing team
                She hit him several times.
                They made a lot of money.

Vividness

To communicate your message more effectively, make what you say seem alive, animated, and interesting. Language that is alive will bring a sense of excitement, urgency, and importance to what you say. To accomplish this, you must use language that is active and direct. Such language makes your thoughts sound forceful and dynamic. It tells your audience that they had better listen because what you have to say is important.

Using action verbs is a good way to create a sense of urgency and movement. For example, "They had realized their most cherished dream; they discovered the actual tomb of the Egyptian king they had sought for so long" is a sentence that shows action and excitement. Note how much more active and energetic it is than the dry and passive statement "The old tomb was found by the explorers."

To increase vividness, you should also avoid using clichés such as "happy as a lark," "blind as a bat," and "fit as a fiddle." Such phrases are overused; they sound unimaginative and they lack impact. You will be more likely to grab your audience's attention if you use fresh language to make old ideas sound new and exciting.

Appropriateness

Each time you speak, your listeners have specific expectations about the kind of language you will use. The kind of language that is appropriate varies from situation to situation. For example, the language you would use in addressing the president of your college or university would be much more formal than the language you would use when chatting with friends. You would be unlikely to call the president by a nickname and you would be equally unlikely to call a friend Dr. or Mr. or Ms. except in jest.

If the language you use is inappropriate for the situation, your credibility will suffer and your message may be misinterpreted or disregarded. It is therefore crucial to assess each speaking situation and adjust your language accordingly. In public situations, profanity, improper grammar, and slang are always inappropriate.

USING LANGUAGE EFFECTIVELY: KEY POINTS TO REMEMBER

Accuracy	Requires you to have a sufficiently large vocabulary
	Requires that you show concern for words and how they are used
	Requires that you know words have different meanings for different people
	Requires that you are aware of listeners' reactions to what you say
Vividness	Requires you to choose language that is alive, animated, and interesting
	Requires that you use language that is direct, forceful, and dynamic
	Requires that you use action verbs to create a sense of urgency
	Requires that your language be fresh and make old ideas sound new and exciting
Appropriateness	Requires that you be aware of your listeners' expectations and knowledge of language
	Requires you to realize that language appropriate for one situation may not be appropriate for another

SUMMARY   Learning how to use language is important for effective communication to
                 occur in any situation. Our ability to use language determines our success,
                 makes communication personal, and allows us to translate our thoughts,
                 feelings, and experiences into messages.

                 Language is a structured system of signs, sounds, gestures, or marks
                 used and understood to express ideas and feelings. It allows us to progress,
                 to cooperate, and to create and resolve conflict.

                 The misuse of language is more than just a matter of misusing words;
                 it also affects our ability to think. Thought and language, according to most
                 scholars, are inseparable. If our thoughts are not expressed clearly and
                 accurately, misunderstanding is inevitable. Once you have said something,
                 it is impossible to retract it. Thus, our choice of words used is important,
                 and mistakes can have serious repercussions.

                 Language is made up of your key elements: sounds, words, grammar,
                 and meaning. Language must be spoken before it can be written. Thus, it
                 is sound that allows us to have language. The *International Phonetic Alphabet*
                 is a system used for transcribing the speech sounds of all languages. The
                 phoneme is the smallest distinctive and functional unit of sound in a language.
                 For example, there are 39 phonemes in the English language.

                 When sounds are joined together in agreed-upon combinations, they
                 form *words*—symbols that stand for the objects and concepts they name.
                 Words, in turn, can be joined together to form phrases and sentences. The
                 rules that govern exactly how phrases and sentences must be constructed
                 form a language's *grammar.* A language's sound and grammar systems work
                 simultaneously to ensure effective and efficient communication.

                 The goal of communication is to exchange meanings. The study of
                 meaning, or the association of words with ideas, feelings, and contexts, is
                 called *semantics.* If language did not have meaning, it would serve little or
                 no purpose.

                 We tend to associate language with specific meanings and to take that
                 relationship for granted, but in reality, language is arbitrary because
                 language users arbitrarily pair words with meanings. Words are not actually
                 things or ideas, but symbols that represent things and ideas. Meanings,
                 therefore, are not in words but in people. Words can be *concrete*—very
                 specific—or they can be *abstract*—very general. Words also have a *denotative*
                 meaning, or dictionary definition, and a *connotative* meaning, which is a
                 social or personal definition.

                 Four common barriers to effective communication are bypassing, infer-
                 ence confusion, indiscrimination, and polarization. *Bypassing* is the misun-
                 derstanding that occurs between a sender and a receiver. It usually occurs
                 as a result of two false beliefs about language: (1) that a word has only one
                 meaning and (2) that words have meaning in and of themselves. To reduce
                 the frequency of bypassing, we should be person-minded, not word-minded;

be approachable; be sensitive to contexts; and we should query and paraphrase.

Inference confusion occurs when people go beyond their observations to draw incorrect conclusions that they assume to be correct. To reduce this problem, we must recognize that because inferences are easily made, we should question our assumptions and label our inferences, and expect others to do the same.

Indiscrimination is the neglect of individual differences and the overemphasis of similarities. It can lead to *stereotypes,* which are relatively fixed mental pictures of a class or group that are attributed to an individual member without regard to his or her unique characteristics and qualities. Indiscrimination can also lead to *frozen evaluations*—that is, the tendency to look at people, things, and events as if they never change and to ignore any changes that may take place. To help reduce misunderstandings due to indiscrimination, we can use *dating* and *indexing* to add distinguishing detail.

Polarization is the tendency to view things around us in terms of extremes. It can give rise to the *pendulum effect*—escalating conflict that stems from the use of either-or terms to describe and defend our perceptions of reality.

Effective use of language requires years of practice and study. Among the most important areas to address when attempting to improve language effectiveness are accuracy, vividness, and appropriateness. Accurate communication is precise and clear, thus leaving little room for misinterpretation. Vivid language makes messages come alive and grabs listeners' attention. Appropriate language ensures that a speaker's choice of words and manner of speaking suits the situation.

KEY TERMS

Abstract Words: symbols for ideas, qualities, and relationships.

Bypassing: the misunderstanding that occurs between a sender and a receiver.

Concrete Words: symbols for specific things that can be pointed to, physically experienced, touched, or felt.

Connotation: the subjective meaning of a word—what a word suggests because of the feelings or associations it evokes.

Dating: a form of indexing that helps to sort events, ideas, places, and people according to time.

Denotation: the core meaning of a word—its standard dictionary definition.

Frozen Evaluation: the tendency to look at events, things, or people as if they never change and to ignore any change that may have taken place.

Grammar: the rules that govern how words are put together to form phrases and sentences.

Indexing: a means of identifying how each person, object, and event is different and unique.

Indiscrimination: the neglect of individual differences and the overemphasis of similarities.

Inference Confusion: the tendency of people to go beyond their observations to draw incorrect conclusions that they assume are correct.

International Phonetic Alphabet (IPA): an alphabet of sounds devised to provide a consistent and universal system for transcribing speech sounds of all languages.

Language: a structured system of signs, sounds, gestures, and marks used and understood to express ideas and feelings among people within a community or nation, within the same geographical area, or within the same cultural tradition.

Pendulum Effect: the escalating conflict that results from the use of either-or terms to describe and defend our perceptions of reality.

Phoneme: the smallest distinctive and functional unit of sound in a language.

Polarization: the tendency to view things in terms of extremes—either good or bad, black or white, etc.

Semantics: the study of meaning, or the association of words with ideas, feelings, and contexts.

Stereotype: a relatively fixed mental picture of some class or group that is attributed to an individual member of that group without regard to his or her unique characteristics and qualities.

Words: symbols that stand for the objects and concepts that they name.

DISCUSSION STARTERS

1. Why is language so powerful?

2. How are thought and language related?

3. Why are language and communication not synonymous?

4. How is it possible that language can have rules and still be arbitrary?

5. The notion that meanings are in people is extremely important to the understanding of how we use language. Why is this so?

6. Which of the language barriers discussed in this chapter is the most likely to occur in everyday conversations? Why?

7. What advice would you give to someone about indexing and dating their communications?

8. How can language increase or reduce your credibility?

9. What does it mean to say that you use language effectively?

FURTHER READINGS

Elgin, S. H. *Gentle Act of Verbal Defense.* Englewood Cliffs, N.J.: Prentice-Hall—Spectrum Books, 1980.

Engel, S. Morris. *The Language Trap: Or How to Defend Yourself Against the Tyranny of Words.* Englewood Cliffs, N.J.: Prentice-Hall, 1984.

Hayakawa, S. I. *Language in Thought and Action.* 4th ed. New York: Harcourt Brace Jovanovich Inc., 1978.

Miller, Casey, and Kate Swift. *Words and Women.* Garden City, N.Y.: Anchor Books, 1977.

Mitchell, R. *Less Than Words Can Say.* Boston: Little, Brown, 1979.

Pei, M. *Weasel Words: The Act of Saying What You Don't Mean.* New York: Harper & Row, Publishers, 1978.

Rothwell, J. Dan. *Telling It Like It Isn't: Language Misuse & Malpractice/What We Can Do About It.* Englewood Cliffs, N.J.: Prentice-Hall, 1982.

NOTES

1. Miller, George A., *The Psychology of Communication* (Baltimore, Md.: Penguin, 1967).
2. Adapted from Haney, William V., *Communication and Organizational Behavior,* 3rd ed. (Homewood, Ill.: Richard D. Irwin, Inc., 1973), pp. 211–330; and *Communication and Interpersonal Relations,* 5th ed. (Homewood, Ill.: Richard D. Irwin, Inc., 1986), pp. 213–405.
3. Haney, 1973, p. 246.
4. Espy, Willard R., "Say When," *This Week,* 13 July 1952. First seen in Haney, 3rd ed., p. 396.
5. Chase, Stuart and Marian Chase, *The Power of Words* (New York: Harcourt Brace Jovanovich, 1954), p. 249.

CHAPTER 4

Nonverbal Communication

After studying this chapter, you should be able to:

1. Identify and explain eight forms of nonverbal communication.
2. Cite six common uses of nonverbal communication.
3. Tell why the four key characteristics of nonverbal communication are crucial to its use and interpretation.
4. Explain why nonverbal communication is difficult to interpret and understand.
5. Suggest ways to improve both the interpretation and use of nonverbal communication.

Nonverbal communication is any information that is expressed without using words. Thus, our tone of voice, body movements (for example, facial expressions, postures, and gestures), clothing, appearance, and use of space, touch, and time may communicate just as strong a message as our choice of words.

The inclusion of nonverbal behavior in the study of communication is relatively recent. We tend to take nonverbal communication for granted because it is so basic, but its importance is unmistakable when we realize how frequently nonverbal communication occurs.

Studies have revealed some fascinating facts about our use of nonverbal communication. For example, estimates show that the average person speaks for only ten to eleven minutes per day and that the average spoken sentence spans about 2.5 seconds. Other data suggest that in a normal two-person conversation, the verbal component conveys approximately 7 percent of the social meaning and the nonverbal component conveys approximately 93 percent of the social meaning.[1] These statistics indicate that in most situations, we spend more of our time communicating nonverbally than verbally.

Without realizing it, you often use nonverbal communication as the basis for many daily decisions. For example, whether or not you decide to approach your professor about turning in an overdue paper might depend on your perception of his or her nonverbal behavior. If he or she has an open office door, smiles, and appears friendly and approachable, you would probably conclude that this would be an appropriate time to discuss your late paper.

MINI-EXERCISE

The next time you are watching your favorite television program, turn the sound off for a few minutes and observe only the nonverbal signals. Then put the sound back on, but turn your back to the television and only listen. Which method provides you with more information about what is going on? Why?

Even though our culture is highly speech-oriented, more and more scholars, teachers, consultants, and others are recognizing the significant contribution of nonverbal behavior to the communication process. Thus, in this chapter we will examine all phases of nonverbal communication, including its forms, functions, characteristics, and interpretations. In addition, we will also discuss ways in which we can improve our own nonverbal communication.

FORMS OF NONVERBAL COMMUNICATION

Have you ever dressed up for a meeting, smiled at someone, sat in a specific seat in class, used your hands while talking, played with a pen or pencil, dimmed the lights to create a romantic atmosphere, played music loudly, looked someone directly in the eyes, kissed someone, pointed a finger, or burned incense to create a pleasant odor? If so, you have communicated nonverbally. Every day we perform a wide range of nonverbal behaviors without even thinking about them, yet such signals convey very definite messages about ourselves to others. It is because nonverbal communication is so diverse, common, and informative that we need to be more sensitive to its many different manifestations. Thus, in the following section we will examine some of the more significant forms of nonverbal communication, including body motions and facial expressions, physical characteristics, touch, space, time, paralanguage, artifacts, and environmental factors.

Body Motions and Facial Expressions

We can use body motions to create an infinite number of nonverbal messages. For our purposes, a **body motion** is any movement of the face, hands, feet, trunk, or other part of the body that communicates a message. One particularly significant category of body motions is **facial expressions,** which are movements of the face that directly translate, augment, or contradict verbal communication, or that are unrelated to verbal communication.

To make sense of thousands of different body movements and facial displays, a team of researchers devised a classification system based on the origins, functions, and coding of nonverbal behavior.[2] Their system divides body movements and facial displays into five categories: emblems, illustrators, regulators, affect displays, and adaptors.

Emblems.   Body movements that can be directly translated into words or phrases are called **emblems.** They include the hand signs for "OK," "I want a ride," peace, power, and the many other signs that we use as substitutes or replacements for specific words or phrases.

The meanings of emblems are like the meanings of words in that they are arbitrary, subject to change with time, and learned. Also, emblems do not necessarily mean the same thing from one culture to another.

Illustrators.   Body movements and facial expressions that accent, reinforce, or emphasize an accompanying verbal message are **illustrators.** Examples of ways people use illustrators might include an instructor underlining a word on the chalkboard to create emphasis, a child indicating how tall he is by holding his hand up, a softball player illustrating a batting swing by moving his or her arms in a particular motion, and children using their thumbs and fingers as if they were guns.

Regulators.   Nonverbal behaviors that control, monitor, or maintain the back-and-forth interaction between speakers and listeners are **regulators.** These cues tell us when to continue, repeat, hurry, elaborate, make things more interesting, or let someone else speak. Regulators include eye contact, shifts in posture, nodding of the head, and looking at a clock or wristwatch.

Affect Displays.   Nonverbal behaviors that express emotions and feelings are **affect displays.** Although your face is the primary means of expressing affect, your body may also be used. For example, you may slouch when you are sad, slam your fist on a table when you are angry, and jump up and down when you are excited. Affect displays communicate a variety of messages that repeat, contradict, supplement, supplant, or do not even relate to verbal messages.

Adaptors.   Nonverbal behaviors that help us to feel at ease in various communication situations are **adaptors.** They are the most difficult nonverbal signals to interpret because their meaning requires the most speculation. Scratching, playing with coins, sitting straight in a chair, grooming, and smoking are all forms of adaptors. We are especially likely to take such actions when we are trying to satisfy needs, manage emotions, develop social contacts, or deal with other stressful situations.

Adaptors fall into one of three categories:

1. **Self-adaptors** are generally not directed at others but, rather, serve some personal need. They include such common actions as scratching, smoothing your hair, and straightening your clothes.

2. **Object-adaptors** involve the use of an object or prop such as a pencil, a paper clip, keys, coins, a cigarette, a pipe, or jewelry. Although these objects have specific functions, they serve other purposes when used as adaptors. Most object-adaptor behaviors are unconscious. They help to release excess energy and tend to occur only when you are nervous or anxious.

3. **Alter-adaptors** are nonverbal behaviors learned from past experiences and from the manipulation of objects. They include: gestures used to protect yourself from others, such as putting your hands in front of your face; movements to attack others, such as assuming a fighting position; actions to establish intimacy with others, such as moving closer to someone; and attempts to withdraw from a conversation, such as moving toward a door. Several authors of contemporary books on body language contend that knowing how to interpret alter-adaptors can be a powerful tool for understanding others. They claim, for example, that the way a person crosses his or her legs may indicate sexual invitation, introversion, or aggressiveness. According to these writers, because alter-adaptors are performed unconsciously, they reveal our hidden desires or tendencies. To date, however, there is not sufficient proof to support these claims.

CATEGORIES OF BODY MOTIONS AND FACIAL DISPLAYS

Category	Key Characteristics	Examples
Emblems	Translate directly into words	The extended thumb of a hitchhiker
Illustrators	Accent, reinforce, or emphasize a verbal message	A child holding up his hands to indicate how tall he is while saying "I'm a big boy"
Regulators	Control, monitor, or maintain back-and-forth interaction	Eye contact, shift in posture, nod of head
Affect Displays	Express emotion and feelings	Sad face, slouching, jumping up and down
Adaptors	Help one feel at ease in communication situations	Scratching, grooming, playing with coins, fidgeting

Physical Characteristics

While body motions and facial expressions change quickly and can be controlled to some extent, physical characteristics—such as body type, attractiveness, height, weight, hair color, skin tone—are fairly constant and more difficult to control, especially in the course of a single interaction.

Physical Shape and Appearance. Physical shape and appearance play a significant role in our communication and relationships with others. In recent years, we have become obsessed with physical appearance and general health, spending billions of dollars each year on modifying, preserving, and decorating our bodies.

The reasons for our concern over appearance are varied, but there are indications that we have gradually acquired some stereotypes about body shapes that seem to influence how we react to and interact with each other. In one research study, people were asked to rate and compare silhouettes depicting three different body shapes—overweight, athletic, and thin—that were all the same height. The research subjects consistently rated the overweight people as older and shorter, and thought they were more old-fashioned, less strong, less attractive, more talkative, more warm-hearted and sympathetic, more good-natured and agreeable, more dependent, and more trusting of others. They rated athletic people as stronger, younger, and taller, and thought they were more masculine, better looking, more adventurous, more mature in behavior, and more self-reliant. They rated thin people as younger and taller, and thought they were more ambitious, more suspicious of others, more tense and nervous, less masculine, more stubborn and inclined to be difficult, more pessimistic, and quieter.[3]

Although this research suggests that people tend to make assumptions about personality and behavior characteristics based on body shape, there is little real proof that such judgments are accurate. As you learned in Chapter 3, operating on the basis of such stereotypes can lead to serious misunderstandings.

MINI-EXERCISE

Find photographs of either three males or three females who vary in attractiveness and are unlikely to be recognized by others. The first photograph should be of a very attractive person, the second should show an average-looking person, and the third should show an unattractive person. Show the photographs one at a time to some of your male and female friends and ask them to comment on each individual's attractiveness. Then ask them to imagine and describe each person's personality. Analyze the results of this research and report them to your class.

Attractiveness. In our society attractive people are generally treated more positively than those who are not. Numerous research studies have indicated that attractive people, when compared to unattractive people, are perceived to be more popular, successful, sociable, persuasive, sensual, and happy.

Physical attractiveness has an extremely powerful influence on everyday communication. For example, both men and women regard attractiveness as one of the critical factors in selecting a mate. It also affects credibility and thus plays a strong role in a person's ability to persuade others, and it helps in getting jobs and gaining higher salaries.

Attractiveness, however, can also be a liability. One research study found that being attractive can actually have negative consequences for women managers. Even when such women had reached top executive levels, their success was attributed to their looks rather than to their abilities, and they were consistently judged less capable than unattractive women managers. On the other hand, attractiveness was found to be an asset for men throughout their executive careers.[4]

Touch

"Reach out and touch someone" is a well-publicized slogan used by a national phone company. Although this company's ads suggest touching only in an abstract sense, the idea behind the ads is based on the fact that touch is a very personal and powerful means of communication. As one of our most primitive and yet sensitive ways of relating to others, touch is a critical aspect of our communication. It plays a significant role in giving encouragement, expressing tenderness, and showing emotional support, and it can be even more powerful than words. For example, when you've

just received some bad news, a pat on the shoulder from a friend can be far more reassuring than many attempted words of understanding.

The kind and amount of touching that is appropriate varies greatly from situation to situation, and depends on the individuals and their relationship with each other. For instance, at a business meeting, the participants may shake hands when they first meet, but other forms of touching are rare. In contrast, at a crowded party, touching is common—friends may hug and kiss when meeting, hold each other while dancing, sit near each other, or hold hands.

Space and Distance

Statements such as "Give me some room to operate," "That place was crowded," and "I need space"; signs such as "KEEP OUT," "Stay to your left," and "These seats are reserved"; and the bumper sticker that reads "Keep off my" followed by a picture of a donkey all illustrate our attempts to regulate the distance between ourselves and others. Such phenomena are of special interest to researchers in **proxemics,** the study of how we use space and the distance we place between ourselves and others when communicating.

Mini-Exercise

To see for yourself just how sensitive we are to space, try one or more of the following:

1. The next time you are in an elevator with just one other person, move as close to the other person as possible.
2. At the dinner table, inconspicuously move the salt, pepper, and other items on the table toward the person sitting across from you.
3. At the library, look for a person sitting alone at a large table and then, instead of sitting on the opposite side, sit right next to him or her.
4. Eat something generously seasoned with garlic or onion and talk to someone in a crowded room.

Describe what happened and why you think it happened.

The need for us to identify certain amounts of space as our own is an aspect of proxemics called **territoriality.** We often position markers such as books, coats, pencils, papers, and other objects to declare our space. The need for territory is so strong that in class we actually become upset when someone else sits in our seat, even though seating is not assigned. This uneasiness stems from our own desire to protect our territory. Similar reactions occur when someone enters a room without knocking or tailgates when driving—it's our territory and thus requires our permission to enter.

We usually pay little attention to the role of space in our communications, and more often than not we are only aware of its effect subconsciously. Yet the way those we communicate with use space gives us strong clues to what they are thinking and how they are reacting to us. Three variables—status, culture, and context—influence our use of space when communicating.

Status affects the distance that is maintained between communicators. Research shows that people of different status levels tend to stay farther apart than do individuals of equal status. Furthermore, people of higher status tend to close the distance between themselves and people of lower status, but seldom does the opposite occur.

Culture creates a wealth of differences in the way individuals use distance for communication. For example, Americans tend to stand farther apart during conversations than do people from many European and Middle Eastern cultures. Arabs, in contrast, consider it polite to stand close to the person with whom they are communicating. There are as many culture-based differences as there are cultures, and it is not unusual for one group to be perceived as cold and unfriendly and another as pushy and forward as a result of their use of space. The important thing to recognize is that not all cultures view distance in the same way.

Context also influences the space that is maintained between individuals. For example, people in line at an automated teller machine usually stand back far enough to give the person using the machine the feeling that his or her transaction is not being observed. But in supermarket checkout lines, shoppers ordinarily stand close together to avoid losing their places.

Time

People in our society are preoccupied with time. Everything seems to have a starting time and an ending time. There are people who are always on time and people who are never on time. There are people who use time wisely and people who waste time. We even go so far as to say that time is money.

Because we place such a high value on time, it plays a significant role in our nonverbal communication. We are particularly sensitive to people and events that waste or make exceptional demands on our time. Consider your reaction, for instance, when your date keeps you waiting, when an instructor continues to lecture after the bell has signaled the end of class, or when you are given only one day's notice about an upcoming test. Your feelings may range from confusion to impatience to indignation to outrage, but you will almost certainly not be neutral. To some extent, your reaction will depend on who the other person is. You will probably be more tolerant if the offending party is a close friend or relative, or someone who has great power over you. Thus, if a blind date keeps you waiting too long, you may decide to get up and leave, but if your professor is late for an office appointment, you will probably suffer in silence and continue to wait for his or her arrival.

We tend to have many expectations about how time should be used, and we often judge people by their use of time. For example, students are expected to be on time for class. Thus, students who are punctual are more likely to create a positive impression, while students who are consistently late may be perceived as irresponsible, lazy, or uninterested. Thus, we must be constantly aware of the messages we send through our use (and misuse) of time.

Paralanguage

Paralanguage is the way we vocalize, or say, the words we speak. Our use of words to convey a message is **verbal communication,** while the sounds that create the words can be considered nonverbal communication. For example, when you yell "Where are you going?" to get the attention of a friend walking across campus, the words themselves are verbal communication and the loudness of the words is nonverbal communication. We often rely more on paralanguage than on the words themselves when interpreting another person's message.

Note how the meaning of the sentence "Our friends are in the living room" varies according to the word that is emphasized:

1. **OUR** friends are in the living room. (not their friends)
2. Our **FRIENDS** are in the living room. (not our enemies)
3. Our friends **ARE** in the living room. (even though you do not think so)
4. Our friends are in **THE** living room. (the one you and I agree is a special place)
5. Our friends are in the **LIVING ROOM.** (and not in the bedroom, etc.)[5]

Even though the words are identical, each sentence creates an entirely different message, distinguished solely by the emphasis placed on specific words. Paralanguage includes *pitch* (how high or low the voice is), *vocal force* (intensity or loudness), *rate* (speed), *quality* (overall impression of the voice), and *pauses* or *silence.* The way we vary our voices conveys different meanings to our receivers. For example, a person who speaks quickly may communicate a message that is different from that of a person who speaks slowly. Even when the words are the same, if the rate, volume, pitch, and quality differ, the receiver's interpretations will also differ. Researchers estimate that 38 percent of the meaning of oral communication is affected by our use of voice—by *the way* something is said rather than *what* is said.[6]

On the basis of paralanguage, we make many judgments about what is being said, about the person saying it, about the speaking and listening roles, and about the credibility of the message. Of course, judgments about people based on paralanguage can be just as unreliable as judgments based on body type. We must, therefore, recognize the effect that paralanguage can have on our communication and adjust accordingly.

Mini-Exercise

I really love you.

Read the above statement aloud in four different ways: (1) with no expression at all, (2) as if you really do love the other person, (3) as if you actually despise the other person, and (4) as if you are desperate because the other person is leaving you.

Note that even though the words remain the same, the meaning changes. In what way does your voice change the meaning? What else do you notice about yourself each time you try to create a different meaning?

Artifacts

Artifacts are personal adornments that communicate information about a person. They include clothes, perfume, makeup, eyeglasses, hairstyles, beards and mustaches, automobiles, briefcases, and the many hundreds of other material cues that we use to communicate our age, sex, status, role, socioeconomic class, group membership, personality, and relation to others.

Effective communicators learn to adapt their use of artifacts to the specific situation. In that way they help to ensure that their intended message will prevail over any unintended message that may be conveyed by mere adornments.

Environment

Environment, as discussed in Chapter 1, is the physical and psychological surroundings in which communication occurs, including the furniture, architectural design, lighting conditions, temperature, smells, colors, and sounds of the location and the attitudes, feelings, perceptions, and relationship of the participants. The impact of the environment in which communication takes place has a lot to do with the individuals, their backgrounds, and their perceptions of what is important to them at the time of the interaction. The best environment allows a speaker's intended message to be delivered accurately. Thus, soft background music, dim lights, a log burning in a fireplace, a tray of hors d'oeuvres, and two glasses of wine would create the perfect environment for a romantic encounter, but would fail to create the proper atmosphere for a pregame pep rally.

The Functions of Nonverbal Communication

Without nonverbal communication our interaction with others would be boring. Nonverbal communication adds life to our exchanges by complementing, repeating, regulating, and accenting what we have to say. In addition, we often use nonverbal communication instead of words, and sometimes we even use it to deceive others.

Complementing Behavior

Nonverbal cues can be used to complete, describe, or accent verbal cues. This function is called **complementing.** For example, a golfer, after shooting a chip shot from about 75 yards, tells her partner that she missed the cup by inches and uses her thumb and index finger to show the distance. You can also use complementing behavior to express your emotions and attitudes. When saying hello to a friend, for instance, you show your genuine interest by displaying a warm smile and maintaining steady eye contact.

Repeating Behavior

We often use nonverbal behavior to repeat what we are expressing verbally. For example, a father attempting to keep his child quiet at an adult gathering may place his index finger to his lips while saying "shush!" The nonverbal action of the father is a **repeating** message because it conveys the same meaning as the verbal message.

Such repetition is especially common in sports. For instance, the referee on a basketball court shouts "traveling" while at the same time rolling his arms in a circular motion, and the baseball umpire cries "strike" while raising her right arm in the strike signal. In athletics, repeating nonverbal signals are deliberately used so that all players and spectators will know the official's call, even if they are out of earshot, but most repeating messages are sent without much thought. They are simply a natural part of our communicative behavior.

Regulating Behavior

Nonverbal cues can also be used for controlling the flow of communication, a behavior known as **regulating.** For example, we frequently use nonverbal signals to indicate that we want to talk, to stop another person from interrupting us when we are talking, or to show that we are finished talking and that the other person may take a turn. When we are listening, we may nod our head rapidly to suggest that the speaker hurry up and finish, or we may nod slowly to show that we want to hear more.

Senders may have a difficult time regulating their nonverbal cues because they may not even realize that they are sending them, but receivers are usually very aware of such signals. In class, for example, a professor receives a very clear message when students put on their coats or close their notebooks to indicate that class is over. While the students are merely recognizing that it is time for them to leave, the message the professor receives is quite different.

THINK ABOUT IT

Without nonverbal communication, a typical conversation might have to go something like this:

> "Hi, did you see the game last night? I'm done—it's your turn to speak."
>
> "No, but I did go to see the dance recital. Your turn—I'm done."
>
> "Thanks, the game was really great. Jeff Smith was really hot. He must have made . . . "
>
> "Do you mind? I'd like to say something."
>
> "Oh! You want talk about the recital some more—sure, go ahead."

What seems strange about this exchange? What changes would be created by the addition of nonverbal communication? What nonverbal cues would you add?

Accenting Behavior

Sometimes we use nonverbal cues for **accenting**—for emphasizing or punctuating our spoken words. For example, if a husband wants sympathy from his wife when he's not feeling well, he may tell her, in a weak voice, that he feels sick and give her a look that implies he is about to collapse. We often use our voices to highlight or accentuate what we are saying. A student trying to get his roommates to quiet down may quietly say, with little expression, "Will you guys please keep it down." If that doesn't work and the noise is really bothering him, he may raise his voice to indicate that he wants quiet immediately.

People who are excited or enthusiastic are more likely to use nonverbal cues for accenting than are people who are restrained, are having a difficult time expressing themselves, are not paying attention, or are not understanding what is being said. If used correctly in a public speech, accenting gestures and tones of voice can be especially effective ways of making a point clearer to an audience. In such cases, the gestures and changes in voice should appear natural and flow smoothly with the message.

Substituting Behavior

We often use nonverbal messages in place of verbal messages. Such **substituting** is common when speaking is impossible, undesirable, or inappropriate. For example, ramp controllers at airports use hand signals to guide planes to their unloading positions because the noise level is too high for spoken communication; friends will often exchange knowing looks when they want to say something behind another person's back; the hearing impaired use a sophisticated formal sign language in place of the spoken word; and people often use exaggerated gestures to communicate when they are separated by a considerable distance and shouting would be inappropriate.

Deceiving Behavior

We may purposely mislead others by using nonverbal cues to create a false impression or to convey incorrect information. Among the most common of such **deceiving** nonverbal behaviors is the "poker face" we assume when playing cards. We may also try to appear calm when we are really nervous or upset, and we often act surprised, alert, or happy when in fact we are feeling quite the opposite. In addition, we consciously try to manage our nonverbal behavior when we give a speech or attend a job interview in order to disguise our true purpose and emotions.

THE CHARACTERISTICS OF NONVERBAL COMMUNICATION

We can learn a great deal about other people by observing their nonverbal behavior, and they can learn much by observing ours. Of course, we can better interpret and use nonverbal communication if we understand some of its basic characteristics. Think, for example, of the far-reaching implications of the fact that through our nonverbal behavior we are always communicating something, whether we intend to or not. We must also consider that the interpretation of nonverbal cues depends on their context, that nonverbal communication is more believable than verbal communication, and that nonverbal communication is our primary way of expressing our feelings and attitudes toward others.

We Are Always Communicating

When another person is involved, you have to communicate. Whether you make eye contact, smile, frown, or try totally to ignore the other person, you are communicating something. Sometimes it is not what *is* said that is important, but what is *not* said. For example, not attending a meeting at which you were expected, coming late to an employment interview, wearing jeans when you were expected to dress more formally, wearing a suit when jeans were expected, talking about a sad situation with a smirk on your face, and speaking to someone, but never looking him or her in the eye, all convey strong messages. We all believe we can tell a great deal about people based on their facial expression, appearance (sex, race, height, physique), clothing, willingness to make eye contact, body movements, and posture.

To illustrate that we are always communicating, whether intentionally or unintentionally, consider the following example: Jack is always perfectly groomed and smells of expensive aftershave lotion. In contrast, George has shoulder-length hair and always wears sweatshirts and jeans. By just looking, we cannot really tell what the two men actually intend to communicate. Jack may simply be neat and use aftershave lotion because it feels good, or he may really want to communicate that designer clothes and expensive aftershave lotion are important to him. Similarly, George may simply like to dress comfortably, or he may be attempting to communicate that he disdains society's seeming obsession with outward appearances. Ultimately, it's not so much what Jack and George intend to communicate as what others perceive. Both students, whether they want to or not, are communicating something about themselves through their appearances.

Meaning Depends on Context

The context in which nonverbal communication occurs plays a crucial role in its interpretation. Pounding on a table to make a point during a speech means something entirely different from pounding on the table in response to someone calling you a liar. Direct eye contact with a stranger can mean something entirely different from direct eye contact with a close friend.

Richter; © 1982 The New Yorker Magazine, Inc.

When you communicate, your nonverbal and verbal cues usually supplement and support each other. Your appearance, tone of voice, eye contact, posture, and facial expression provide cues about the communication relationship. For example, when you talk to a friend, your relaxed tone of voice, eye contact, and posture reveal much about your friendship. Your nonverbal cues can tell your friend how much you value him or her, how comfortable you feel, and how intimate your relationship has become. Such nonverbal communication is interpreted within the context of your friendship and is complemented by casual and personal conversation.

Without an understanding of the context in which communication occurs, it is almost impossible to tell what specific nonverbal behavior may mean, and there are no guarantees that misunderstanding will not occur even when the context is fully understood. That is why we must think twice about our interpretation of others' nonverbal behavior and their possible interpretations of ours.

Nonverbal Communication Is More Believable

Most of us tend to believe nonverbal communication, even when it contradicts the accompanying verbal message. Consider, for example, the case of a student who tried to persuade his professor that he had a valid reason for not turning in a required paper. He explained that he had been working on the paper for several weeks and only had to finish typing it when his personal computer broke down. Throughout the conversation, the student appeared nervous, made little, if any, direct eye contact, and smiled at the wrong times. Based on this behavior the professor decided that the student was lying and thus refused to accept the story. She found that the student's nonverbal message was more convincing than his verbal one.

The Primary Way of Expressing Feelings and Attitudes

It is not unusual for us to detect other people's feelings of frustration, anger, sadness, resentment, or anxiety without their actually saying anything. This is because nonverbal communication is so powerful. If, as mentioned earlier, 93 percent of our messages are conveyed by nonverbal cues, then almost all of our feelings and attitudes are expressed through our nonverbal behavior.

We express many of our feelings with our body. For example, at a graduation party attended by many young children, one little girl entered with her parents and spotted a neighbor. She quickly turned up her nose and walked away. Her mother, running after her, asked why she had suddenly left, to which the girl replied, "I don't like that girl over there." The nonverbal communication really didn't need much explanation—it was obvious what the little girl was saying through her actions, whether intentional or unintentional.

INTERPRETING NONVERBAL COMMUNICATION

Nonverbal communication remains difficult to interpret and understand. If we are able to define, categorize, describe, and observe nonverbal communication, why do we still have difficulty interpreting it? There seems to be at least two good reasons.

Nonverbal Cues Have Multiple Meanings

Nonverbal communication is difficult to understand because a single behavior may have many different meanings. For example, a frown on a person's face may indicate unhappiness, sadness, anger, pain, thought, aggressiveness, disapproval, dejection, fear, fatigue, discouragement, disapproval, or a combination of these. Unlike words, most nonverbal cues lack acceptable dictionary definitions. Interpretations are also unreliable because they depend so heavily on our perceptions. Suppose, for example, that you have just walked out of a sad movie when you see a friend with tears in her eyes talking to her sister. It would be easy to assume that she was reacting to the movie. On the other hand, her crying could stem from many other causes, such as breaking up with her boyfriend, hurting herself, or hearing about a death in the family. Her tears could even stem from laughing too hard at something that occurred after the movie—assuming that she even attended the movie. Of course, some nonverbal behaviors, such as nodding the head for yes and shaking it for no, are consistent in both their meaning and their interpretation, but, unfortunately, they are the exception rather than the rule.

Nonverbal Cues Are Interdependent

The meaning of one nonverbal cue often depends on the correct interpretation of several other, simultaneous cues. For example, when someone enters a room, we not only see the person, but we also begin to select certain cues about him or her, such as gender, physical traits, facial expressions, voice characteristics, and clothing. Each depends on the others and tends to add to, or detract from, the total picture. This interdependency of nonverbal behaviors and our inability to perceive all aspects of any one nonverbal communication makes interpretation risky.

Many nonverbal behaviors are subtle and difficult to observe. A cue that one person notices immediately may be overlooked by another person, and thus multiple interpretations may be drawn from the same situation. In addition, while we may be highly aware of others' nonverbal behavior, we may be totally unaware of our own.

IMPROVING YOUR INTERPRETATION OF NONVERBAL COMMUNICATION

Because nonverbal communication is so complex, it is not always easy to interpret its meaning. Nonetheless, there are some things that you can do to reduce the problem. First, be observant of and sensitive to the nonverbal messages that you receive. Second, verify nonverbal messages that you are not sure of, or that may be inconsistent with other cues. Assume, for example, that a friend who used to visit regularly hasn't come over in several weeks. It might seem logical to conclude that she doesn't want to see you anymore, but then again, she may have gotten wrapped up in her studies, taken a part-time job, or fallen ill. To ensure an accurate interpretation of her behavior, it is crucial to consider all the possibilities and avoid jumping to conclusions. Because it is so tempting to make inferences based on nonverbal behavior, it is important to remember not to go beyond actual observations.

One method that can help you to determine the true meaning of a nonverbal message is descriptive feedback. When you use **descriptive feedback,** you check your understanding of another person's nonverbal behavior by describing your interpretation of it. Based on your description, the other person can then clarify his or her intended meaning.

TIPS FOR IMPROVING YOUR INTERPRETATION OF NONVERBAL BEHAVIOR

1. Remember that nonverbal messages don't always mean what you think they do. Thus, when you are unsure of someone's meaning, check it out before drawing your conclusions.
2. Be descriptive rather than judgmental when checking nonverbal messages that you do not understand. This allows the other person the opportunity to confirm or correct your perception.
3. Remember that the meaning of a nonverbal message depends on its context. Thus, the interpretation of the same cue may vary from person to person and from situation to situation.

Descriptive feedback is not always necessary, but when a message is inconsistent with the situation or other behaviors, or when you do not know whether you have accurately interpreted an important message, you should verify your perceptions with the other person. When using descriptive feedback, do not express agreement or disagreement—simply describe the message you believe was communicated. For example, if you interpret someone's behavior to indicate that he is uncomfortable around you, don't ask, "Why are you so nervous when I'm around?" Rather, describe the situation nonjudgmentally: "Jim, I get the impression that you may not be comfortable around me. Is that the case?" This allows the other person to explain without feeling defensive, and it enables you to avoid making inaccurate accusations that can limit your interpretations to your observations. When you provide descriptive feedback, you give the other person the opportunity either to confirm your perceptions or to explain what you did not understand.

IMPROVING YOUR NONVERBAL COMMUNICATION

We must be aware of the nonverbal messages we send to others. Fortunately, most of us do a good job of communicating nonverbally and thus don't need to make dramatic changes in the way we behave. Nonetheless, we cannot afford to ignore the effects of our nonverbal behavior or allow the nonverbal messages that we send to go unchecked, and if you find that others often misunderstand your intended meaning, you might want to examine how you communicate nonverbally.

There is no question that our nonverbal messages greatly influence how others perceive us and our communication. For example, an extremely bright and talented student was constantly being turned down for jobs that he should have been getting. When asked why he thought this was happening, he replied that he had no idea. To find out the problem, friends videotaped a mock interview in which he was interviewed by another student. When he reviewed the tape, he immediately noticed that he never looked at the interviewer. Instead, his gaze wandered about the room. This gave the impression that he lacked confidence and that he might not be totally candid in what he was saying. Once he knew why he was being rejected, he could try to change his behavior. To help him practice, his friends videotaped another interview session. This time, he was reminded to look at the interviewer each time his gaze wandered. After several such sessions, he grew more relaxed about looking at the interviewer and consequently appeared more confident and truthful in his communication.

TIPS FOR IMPROVING YOUR NONVERBAL COMMUNICATION

1. Recognize that the nonverbal messages you send strongly influence how others perceive you.
2. Be more aware of the nonverbal messages that you send.
3. Ask others for help in changing any distracting nonverbal behaviors that you may have.

Although changing your nonverbal behavior is not simple, it can be done with a little effort and desire. The key is to conscientiously examine how your nonverbal cues may be undermining your intended message. If you realize that you have distracting mannerisms, such as smirking, playing with coins, twisting your hair, shuffling your feet, or saying "you know" or "OK" too much, you can ask others to remind you when you start doing these things so that you can make a conscious effort to change.

SUMMARY

Nonverbal communication encompasses everything that we communicate to others without using words. It is not what we say, but how we say it with our tone of voice, body movements, appearance, and use of space, touch, and time.

There are eight categories of nonverbal communication behaviors: body motions and facial expressions, physical characteristics, touch, space, time, paralanguage, artifacts, and environment. All are intricately interdependent and, together with verbal communication, contribute to the total communication process. A *body motion* is any movement of the face, hands, feet, trunk, or other parts of the body that communicates a message. *Facial expressions* are movements of the face that can repeat, augment, contradict, or be unrelated to verbal communication. Body movements and facial displays may be classified as *emblems, illustrators, regulators, affect displays,* and *adaptors*. Adaptors that are not directed at others but serve personal needs are *self-adaptors*. *Object-adaptors* involve the use of an object or prop, and *alter-adaptors* are movements learned from our past experiences and from the manipulation of objects.

Physical shape and appearance play significant roles in the way we interact with one another. Physical attractiveness is an especially influential variable in everyday communication.

Touch is one of the most personal and powerful means of physically communicating with others. It can be even more powerful than words. The kind and amount of touching that is appropriate varies greatly from one situation to another and depends on the individuals and their relationship.

The way we use space and the amount of distance we place between ourselves and others gives strong clues about our thoughts and reactions. Researchers in *proxemics* are especially interested in *territoriality,* the need we all have to identify certain areas of space as our own. Status, culture, and context all influence our use of space when communicating.

Because we place such a high value on time, it too plays a significant role in our nonverbal communication. We tend to have many expectations about how time should be used and often judge people by their use of time.

Verbal communication is our use of words to convey a message, while *paralanguage* is the way we say those words. We often rely more on paralanguage than on the words themselves when interpreting another person's message.

Artifacts are material cues, such as clothes, hairstyles, and automobiles, that we use to communicate information about our age, sex, status, personality, and relation to others. To ensure clear understanding, effective communicators learn to adapt their use of artifacts to the specific situation.

The impact of the *environment* in which communication takes place has a lot to do with the individuals communicating, their backgrounds, and their perception of what is important to them at the time of the interaction. The best environment is one that allows an intended message to be communicated accurately.

Without nonverbal communication, our interactions with others would be boring and dull. Nonverbal communication adds life to our exchanges by *complementing, repeating, regulating,* and *accenting* what we have to say. In addition, we often use nonverbal communication as a *substitute* for words and sometimes we even use it to *deceive* others.

We can learn a great deal about other people by observing their nonverbal behavior, and they can learn much by observing ours. For example, it is important to realize that through our nonverbal behavior we are always communicating something, whether we intend to or not. We must also remember that the interpretation of nonverbal cues depends on their context, that nonverbal communication is more believable than verbal communication, and that nonverbal communication is our primary way of expressing our feelings and attitudes toward others.

Nonverbal behavior is consistently difficult to interpret and understand because (1) each cue has multiple meanings, and (2) the meaning of one nonverbal cue often depends on the correct interpretation of several other, simultaneous cues. To avoid misinterpretation, we must be observant of and sensitive to the nonverbal messages we receive, consider all their possible meanings, and avoid jumping to conclusions. The surest way to determine the true meaning of a nonverbal message is to use *descriptive feedback.* When we check our understanding of another person's nonverbal behavior by describing our interpretation of it, the other person can then confirm or clarify his or her intended meaning.

We must also be aware of the nonverbal messages we send to others. It is important to recognize that our nonverbal messages strongly influence how others perceive us. We should ask others for help in changing any distracting nonverbal behaviors we may have.

KEY TERMS

Accenting: the use of nonverbal cues to emphasize or punctuate spoken words.

Adaptors: nonverbal behaviors that help us to feel at ease in communication situations, such as twisting a ring, scratching, or playing with a pencil.

Affect Displays: nonverbal behaviors that express emotions and feelings.

Alter-adaptors: behaviors learned from our past experiences and from the manipulation of objects, such as putting our hands up to protect our face, moving closer to establish intimacy, and moving toward a door to end a conversation.

Artifacts: ornaments or adornments that communicate information about a person; they include clothes, perfume, makeup, hairstyle, jewelry, eyeglasses, and cars.

Body Motion: any movement of the face, hands, feet, trunk, or other part of the body that communicates a message.

Complementing: nonverbal cues that help to complete, describe, or accent verbal cues.

Deceiving: nonverbal cues used to purposely mislead others by presenting a false appearance or incorrect information.

Descriptive Feedback: a means of checking your understanding of another person's nonverbal behavior by describing your interpretation of it.

Emblems: body movements that have relatively direct translations into words or phrases.

Environment: both the psychological and the physical surroundings in which communication occurs; it encompasses the attitudes, feelings, perceptions, and relationships of the communicators as well as the characteristics of the location in which communication takes place.

Facial Expression: any movement of the face that can repeat, augment, contradict, or be unrelated to verbal communication.

Illustrators: body movements and facial expressions that accent, reinforce, or emphasize an accompanying verbal message.

Nonverbal Communication: information that is conveyed without words.

Object-adaptors: nonverbal behaviors that involve the use of an object or prop, such as a pencil, a paper clip, or keys for something other than its intended purpose.

Paralanguage: the way we vocalize, or say, the words we speak.

Proxemics: the study of how we use space and the distance we place between ourselves and others when communicating.

Regulating: the use of nonverbal cues to control the flow of conversation.

Regulators: nonverbal behaviors that control, monitor, or maintain the back-and-forth interaction between speakers and listeners.

Repeating: the use of nonverbal cues to repeat what was expressed verbally.

Self-adaptors: nonverbal behaviors that are generally not directed at others but, rather, serve some personal need, such as scratching oneself, smoothing one's hair, and straightening one's clothes.

Substituting: the use of nonverbal messages in place of verbal messages when speaking is impossible, undesirable, or inappropriate.

Territoriality: the need to identify certain areas of space as our own.

Verbal Communication: the use of words to convey a message.

DISCUSSION STARTERS

1. What is nonverbal communication?

2. Why do you think that nonverbal communication was not seriously studied until recently?

3. How does eye contact serve to develop relationships?

4. Do you agree or disagree with the notion that you cannot not communicate? Explain your response.

5. In your opinion, which nonverbal function contributes the most to your understanding of a message? Why?

6. What is paralanguage?

7. In what ways do vocal cues help us to make judgments about others?

8. Why do you think that nonverbal communication is more believable than verbal communication?

9. What does it mean to say that the interpretation of nonverbal communication depends on the context in which it occurs?

10. What can we do to help ourselves be more accurate in our interpretations of the nonverbal messages that we receive?

FURTHER
READINGS

Burgoon, J. K., and T. Saine. *The Unspoken Dialogue: An Introduction to Nonverbal Communication.* Boston: Houghton Mifflin, 1978.

Hall, Edward T. *Beyond Culture.* New York: Anchor Press/Doubleday, 1976.

Knapp, Mark L. *Essentials of Nonverbal Communication.* New York: Holt, Rinehart & Winston, 1980.

Leathers, D. G. *Successful Nonverbal Communication: Principles and Applications.* New York: Macmillan, 1986.

Mehrabian, Albert. *Silent Messages: Implicit Communication of Emotions and Attitudes.* 2nd ed. Belmont, Calif.: Wadsworth, Pub. 1981.

Malandro, L. A. and L. Barker. *Nonverbal Communication.* Reading, Mass.: Addison-Wesley, 1983.

Molloy, John. *Dress for Success.* New York: Warner Books, 1975.

Richmond, Virginia P., James C. McCroskey, and Steven K. Payne. *Nonverbal Behavior in Interpersonal Relations.* Englewood Cliffs, N.J.: Prentice-Hall, 1987.

NOTES

1. Birdwhistell, Ray L., *Kinesics and Context: Essays on Body Motion,* (Philadelphia: University of Pennsylvania Press, 1970), pp. 128–143.

2. Ekman, Paul, and W. V. Friesen, "The Repertoire of Nonverbal Behavior: Categories, Origins, Usage, and Coding," *Semiotica* 1 (1969):pp. 49–98.

3. Wells, W., and B. Siegel, "Stereotyped Somatypes," *Psychological Reports* 8 (1961):pp. 77–78.

4. "When beauty can be beastly," *Chicago Tribune,* 21 October 1966, p. 26a.

5. Ehninger, Douglas, Bruce E. Gronbeck, Ray E. McKerrow, and Alan H. Monroe, *Principles and Types of Speech Communication,* 10th ed., (Glenview, Ill.: Scott, Foresman and Company, 1986), p. 271.

6. Knapp, Mark L., *Essentials of Nonverbal Communication,* (New York: Holt, Rinehart & Winston, 1980), p. 7.

CHAPTER 5

Listening

After studying this chapter, you should be able to:

1. Explain why listening is an important skill to develop.

2. Distinguish between hearing and listening and outline the roles that the four elements of listening play in the listening process.

3. Define and illustrate the four functions of listening.

4. Identify six common barriers to effective listening and indicate how each may be overcome.

5. Discuss the two phases involved in listening with a critical ear.

6. Suggest specific guidelines for becoming a more effective listener.

Recently, a major manufacturing corporation spent more than $4 million on prime-time television and print advertising in a year-long campaign to build its image as a company that *listens* to its customers. Their slogan is: "Sperry . . . We Understand How Important It Is to Listen."

Sperry is not the first company to emphasize employee listening skills. In fact, senior executives of major corporations are often appalled by their workers' ineptness in this area, especially when it comes to young, new employees. This should come as no surprise considering that listening, analyzing, processing, and recording information are often neglected during formal education.

If you are a typical college student, you have probably been formally taught to read, write, and speak, but did any of your teachers ever present a systematic course in how to listen? Not much reliable data are available on the amount of listening training that is done in our schools. You probably never received any formal training and little, if any, informal training in this area. The purpose of this chapter, therefore, is to help you to become a more effective listener, and, as a result, a more effective respondent. To enhance your listening skills, you will need to understand the importance of effective listening, the elements of listening, the functions of listening, the most common barriers to listening, how to analyze and evaluate what you listen to, and the specific steps you can take to improve your listening.

JOE: Hi, Sue.

SUE: Hi.

JOE: How are you?

SUE: OK, but I'm in big trouble.

JOE: I'm OK too, but I've really been busy. It seems as if every professor has doubled the homework.

SUE: It looks as if I'm going to flunk calculus. My parents are going to kill me.

JOE: Oh! I know calc can be pretty rough. I've been so involved with my job that I've fallen way behind in my studies.

SUE: Well, I better go to class.

JOE: What kind of a problem are you having?

SUE: Never mind, I'll tell you later.

THE IMPORTANCE OF EFFECTIVE LISTENING

Most of the misunderstandings that arise in our daily lives are due to poor listening habits. According to many experts, many of us are poor listeners or do not listen at all, resulting in serious personal, professional, and financial problems. For students, poor listening can result in assignments

Figure 5.1

*Percentage of
Time Spent
Communicating*

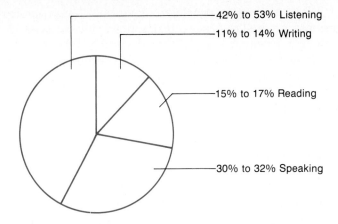

42% to 53% Listening

11% to 14% Writing

15% to 17% Reading

30% to 32% Speaking

done incorrectly, lower grades, missed appointments, misunderstood directions, and lost job opportunities.

It may surprise you to realize how much of your day you spend listening, but think about it—when you are not talking or reading, you are probably listening to something or someone. In fact, one study found that college students spend 42 to 53 percent of their communication time listening, but only 30 to 32 percent speaking, 15 to 17 percent reading, and 11 to 14 percent writing (see Figure 5.1).[1] As you will recall from Chapter 4, the average person spends about 10 minutes of each day speaking, a figure that reveals just how much time is left for listening to others, to television, to radio, to records, and to thousands of other sounds.

MINI-EXERCISE

Are you a good listener? Rate yourself by answering the following two questions:

1. What term best describes you as a listener?

      Superior   Excellent   Above Average   Average

            Below Average   Poor   Terrible

2. On a scale of 0 to 100 (100 = highest), how would you rate yourself as a listener?

Of all the people who have responded to these two questions, 85 percent rated themselves as average *listeners* or worse. Fewer than 5 percent rated themselves as superior or excellent listeners. On a scale of 0 to 100, the lowest self-rating was 10 and the highest was 90, with an *average rating* of 55. Based on these results, you would have to conclude that most people lack confidence in their listening ability. How do your self-ratings and those of your classmates compare to these general findings?

This questionnaire is distributed by the Sperry Corporation and was developed by Dr. Lyman K. Steil, President of Communication Associates of St. Paul, Minnesota.

When surveyed, people from virtually every profession as well as business graduates from a major university all wished they had more training in listening, since effective listening is the communication skill that contributes most to job success.[2-3] Such results leave little doubt about the significant role listening plays in society.

THE ELEMENTS OF EFFECTIVE LISTENING

Because most of us take listening for granted, we tend to think of it as a simple task. However, the listening process is actually quite complex. In fact, scholars still are not sure what listening is or what it involves. They do agree, however, that hearing and listening are not the same. While it is impossible to listen to sounds without first hearing them, it is possible to hear sounds without listening to them. So what is the difference between listening and hearing?

The greatest difference is that **listening** is an active process whereas **hearing** is a passive process. Listening takes energy, desire, and commitment—it doesn't just happen; we must make it happen. Hearing, on the other hand, occurs with little or no effort when we receive sound waves through our ears. Thus, a person can have excellent hearing (the physical ability to hear sounds) but be a terrible listener.

There are three levels of hearing and listening: (1) nonhearing, (2) hearing, and (3) thinking. Nonhearing is a passive process during which you neither hear nor listen. It occurs when you pretend to pay attention to a speaker while thinking about something else—as when you look at your professor in class and daydream about your upcoming vacation. You may even nod your head or say "OK," "yes," or "uh-huh" to give the appearance of concentration, but in reality you don't hear a word being spoken.

Hearing is the registering of sounds. You may remember hearing the sounds, but you do not allow them to penetrate beyond a superficial level. For example, when you play the radio while studying, you hear the music without really listening to it. The radio provides background sounds, but the music and lyrics are not recorded into your memory.

Thinking is not only hearing the sounds and remembering them, but also analyzing what is being said. This is the level at which actual listening occurs. Such listening involves a series of processes, including selecting, attending, understanding, and remembering.

Selecting

As mentioned in Chapter 2, we are constantly bombarded with more stimuli than we can decipher at one time. To make sense out of our environment, we must choose which stimuli we will listen to and which we will ignore. This process is called **selecting.** Thus, when we listen to something, we must pay attention and concentrate, especially since many other sounds

and potential distractions may vie for our attention at the same time. For example, at a party there may be loud music playing and other people talking. In order to listen to a friend speak, we must concentrate on his or her voice and exclude all other sounds and stimuli.

Stop reading for a moment and listen to the sounds around you. If, for example, a stereo is playing background music and you interrupt your reading to concentrate on a specific song, you are selecting the musical sounds over other stimuli. Selecting one source of sound does not automatically mean that you are listening, but at least you are in a position to begin the listening process.

Attending

Not only must you select what you are going to listen to, but you must also attend to it. That is, without attention, listening is impossible.

In Chapter 2, **attention** was defined as the mental process of focusing on specific stimuli while ignoring or downplaying other stimuli. Your attention span can be very brief (1 to 5 seconds), or it can be maintained for as long as you concentrate on a specific stimuli. The more things you notice around you, the less able you are to concentrate on any single thing, and the less able you are to listen effectively.

Understanding

The main difference between hearing and listening is **understanding.** Once you have selected and attended to sounds, you must attempt to understand them by assigning meaning to them. Although there is no commonly accepted explanation of how understanding occurs, it is known that your past experiences play an important role in the understanding process, and that you relate and compare new sounds to those you have heard in the past. To learn calculus, for example, you must first learn algebra. Thus, if you walk into a calculus class unprepared, you can select and attend to what the teacher is saying, but because you are unable to interpret the teacher's message, you will not understand the material being presented.

Remembering

When someone asks, "Are you listening to me?" and you answer "yes," you are, in a sense, saying that you are paying attention to what is being said. You are not indicating, however, that you understand the message or that you will remember it. **Remembering** is thinking of something again. The only way you can demonstrate that you have paid attention is by recalling what was said to you. Remembering, therefore, is a way of responding to what you have heard.

Unfortunately, many of us do not remember information for very long. Why we remember some things and not others is not completely clear. Certain evidence suggests that we remember approximately 50 percent of newly heard information—assuming that it is meaningful—but that after a month we forget more than half of it.[4]

MINI-EXERCISE

A simple experiment should illustrate how important memory is to listening. Read a two- or three-minute newspaper or magazine article to a friend and ask him or her to repeat the key information. Go through the same process with several other friends. Most people will be able to report only about 50 percent of what they've heard. Then, wait 24 hours and ask each person to repeat the information again. You will find that most will remember only about 25 percent of the original information, if that much.

As you can see, listening is not just a matter of paying attention. It is an extremely active and complex process that includes selecting, attending, understanding, and remembering. Although each aspect of the process is separate and distinct, all four are highly interdependent.

LEVELS OF HEARING

Nonhearing
Passive process
Excludes both
   hearing and
   listening

Hearing
Passive process
Sounds registered
   but not entered
   into memory
Excludes listening

Thinking
Active process
Sounds not only
   heard and
   remembered, but
   also thought about
   and analyzed
Includes listening,
   which involves
   selecting,
   attending,
   understanding,
   and remembering

THE FUNCTIONS OF LISTENING

You listen for many different reasons. You wake in the morning to the sound of an alarm clock or other noises, such as a roommate moving around, the sound of a radio coming from the next room, or the ring of a telephone. As you get dressed, you may listen to the voices of students talking outside your door, or to the sound of a police siren as it goes down the street. You may turn on your stereo and listen to music.

While having breakfast with your friends, you join in a heated discussion about the new 24-hour dormitory visitation rule. Then you rush off to an important lecture to get all the information you can for an upcoming exam.

That evening you decide to go to a rock concert. After the concert you go out for a snack, where you meet a good friend who is really upset over receiving a low grade on a test. You listen to your friend and try to comfort him by showing that you understand how he feels.

Throughout this day you have listened to many different people and things for a variety of purposes. For example, you listened to the alarm clock in order to know that it was time to get up; you listened to your friends' opinions at breakfast in order to evaluate the new dorm policy; you listened to your troubled friend in order to understand his feelings; and you listened to the rock concert for pure enjoyment. In each case, listening served a different function and required different listening skills.

Let's look at each of these functions in greater detail. Then, later in the chapter, you will examine the skills you need to improve in each area.

Listening for Information

Earlier it was pointed out that you spend approximately 42 to 53 percent of your time listening. As a college student, you probably spend most of that time **listening for information**—that is, listening to gain comprehension. You listen to your speech communication teacher discuss process, perception, nonverbal and verbal communication, famous speakers, and similar topics in order to learn about speech skills. Each day you listen for such information as news, weather forecasts, sports scores, directions, orders, assignments, names, and locations.

Evaluative Listening

Whenever we listen to judge or to analyze information, we are using **evaluative listening.** Because we are trying to discriminate, we listen with a critical ear. For example, after purchasing a car, a new owner heard a squeak coming from the front end. He rolled down the window and did some evaluative listening—that is, he tried to pinpoint the exact location of the bothersome noise. Speech communication teachers often listen to students' speeches both to discriminate between good and poor presentations, and to evaluate them—that is, to assign grades. Ideally, we should always listen critically by constantly judging evidence, arguments, facts, and values. We are constantly bombarded by messages asking us to believe, accept, or buy things; for our own protection, we must evaluate everything we listen to. Later in this chapter, we will present specific guidelines for evaluating what we hear.

Empathic Listening

Empathic listening, which serves to comfort or help ourselves or others, includes understanding and information seeking, but usually excludes judgment (discrimination and evaluation). A friend who calls, for example, to bemoan how everything has gone wrong that day is more than likely asking not to be judged, but to be understood, empathized with, and consoled.

Most of us find it difficult to avoid making judgments when we listen to someone else's problems, but that is exactly what we must do if we hope to listen with empathy. Having someone listen empathically is a healing and soothing process that can often help us gain perspective on our problems.

When listening to others with empathy, we need not feel their emotions, but we should strive to understand them. Empathic listening indicates that we are aware, appreciative, and understanding of another person's feelings. Caring about someone requires a great deal of sensitivity as well as the ability to communicate that sensitivity. It is not easy to listen; it is even more difficult to listen with empathy. If, however, we fail to empathize with others, we also fail to understand them.

No two people can experience the same event in exactly the same way. Yet, for some reason, most of us believe that other people should perceive things just as we do. Only when we accept the great differences in people's perceptions can we understand them.

Listening for Enjoyment

When we listen purely for pleasure, personal satisfaction, and appreciation, we **listen for enjoyment.** We usually listen to music, for example, simply because we enjoy it. The same is true when we turn on the stereo, attend a concert, watch a "sitcom," or go to a movie.

Despite its somewhat lighter function, listening for enjoyment involves more than merely sitting back and letting sounds enter our ears. To enjoy listening to something, we must also understand it and be able to evaluate it. Thus, even when we listen for enjoyment, we are busy selecting, attending, understanding, and remembering.

BARRIERS TO EFFECTIVE LISTENING

Why are most people poor listeners? The answer to this question is surprisingly complex. Because listening is a part of the communication process, which is constantly changing, and because we are human, the quality of our listening changes from time to time and from situation to situation. Thus, we are more effective listeners in some circumstances than we are in others. The reasons for our ineffectiveness vary dramatically, and some of the factors that affect listening effectiveness are under our control while others are not. The following six barriers to effective listening are particularly common and significant.[5]

Indifference to the Topic or Speaker

Your level of interest and the amount of importance you place on a subject or speaker usually govern how much effort you put into listening. Of course, the decision that a subject or person is uninteresting or boring automatically implies that the information is not important. What appears to be dull or insignificant, however, may very well be vital enough to make the difference between passing or failing an exam, doing an assignment correctly or incorrectly, and learning or not learning.

Perhaps we are indifferent because we have heard the person speak before or have had some experience with the topic and thus believe that we will not learn anything new. Usually, this kind of defeatist attitude stems from not understanding the topic or from thinking that we already know what is going to be said. Often, however, we leave the situation complaining that we were bored stiff, only to learn later that we missed something worthwhile.

By deciding not to listen we may not only miss something of value, but also waste our own time and energy as well as the speaker's. Furthermore, poor listening can be costly in terms of lost friendships, opportunities, and more. We may think that the time spent ignoring or blocking out a speaker can be used for better things and occasionally we may be right, but a more creative approach is to consider how we can use the information to our advantage. Many good ideas have been generated from information that seemed boring at the time. The key point to remember is that subjects are not interesting or uninteresting by themselves; our own active investigation and consideration of every idea presented to us finally determines a subject's suitability, application, and acceptability.

Criticizing the Speaker Instead of the Message

Think of how many times you have sat in a classroom and judged a speech by the number of "ahs," "ums," and "OKs" the speaker used. How many times has your opinion been influenced by a speaker's volume, mispronunciations, or accent? Have you ever missed a message because you were focusing on a speaker's mismatched shirt and tie, bizarre earrings, facial expressions, physical appearance, skin color, or ethnic background?

Of course, speakers should do everything in their power to eliminate personal quirks that may distract others' attention from their message, but listeners must also share the responsibility. An effective listener must be able to overlook the superficial elements of a person's delivery style or appearance in order to concentrate on the substance of the presentation.

Concentrating on Details, Not Main Ideas

Most of us listen for specific facts, such as dates, names, definitions, figures, and locations, assuming that they are the important things to know. But are they? In some situations, specific facts are needed, but most of the time we are given too many details to process into our memories. As a result, we walk away with a smattering of disjointed details and no idea how they relate to each other and to the total picture. In addition, when we listen only for facts, we often forget to analyze and evaluate the message, and lose sight of the possibility that the general ideas may be more significant than the details that surround them.

Most experts in listening generally agree that it is better to analyze the situation first to determine the nature of the message. Then, if you decide that specific facts are important, you should listen for them. If, however, it is more important to assess the speaker's general message, focus on the ideas rather than the individual facts. As a result, you will not only find it easier to remember details and understand how they relate to each other, but you will also have a better understanding of the speaker's message.

Avoiding Difficult Listening Situations

Most of us find it difficult to keep up with the vast amount of information available and to understand the increasing complexity of technical data that confront us each day. At these times we tend to cope in one of two ways. Either we try too hard to concentrate on what is being presented, or we give up and ignore what the speaker has to say. In either case, we usually fail to understand what is being said.

A great deal of concentration and energy is needed to overcome the tendency to ignore or avoid what may appear to be a difficult and confusing subject. The best approach is usually to ask questions, even though it may seem inconvenient, inappropriate, or embarrassing. For example, some people find that physicians tend to overestimate their patients' ability to understand complex medical terminology and procedures. Thus, even when these doctors are trying to be helpful, they often talk over their patients' heads. It then becomes the listener's responsibility to gain understanding. The patient should stop the physician and ask questions, or at least point out that he or she does not yet understand. The same principles apply to the classroom. You should never hesitate to ask when you don't understand something, because without understanding, you cannot learn.

Sometimes you may not listen to a classroom instructor presenting new and difficult information because you lack motivation, but once again, the responsibility falls on you, the listener. You must take the energy and time to listen. If you regularly tune out difficult presentations, make a conscious, continuous effort to listen to such communication. Your confidence and competence should improve, along with your ability to cope with such situations.

Tolerating or Failing to Adjust to Distractions

Distractions constantly arise to disrupt our concentration. There are many distractions that we can control. As listeners, we have the responsibility to adjust to or compensate for distractions and to focus on speakers and their messages. If, for example, noise from another room competes with the speaker, the listener should not think, "I can't hear, so the heck with it." Rather, the listener has the responsibility to close the door, ask the person who is creating the noise to be quiet, move closer to the speaker, or, as a last resort, ask the speaker to talk louder.

Some distractions must be overcome through mental rather than physical effort. A baby crying in the background can easily become a major distraction, or it can be merely a minor nuisance that we overcome by forcing ourselves to listen more intently to the speaker. We know that the human ear is capable of hearing a coin hit the pavement on a crowded, noisy city street, but that doesn't mean that everyone in the vicinity must stop and react to it. By tuning in to certain sounds, those of us with normal hearing can selectively filter out extraneous noise and distractions, and focus on the sounds that make up the messages that are meaningful to us.

If we cannot modify external noise, we must alter our own internal listening behavior to understand the speaker's message.

Faking Attention

At one time or another everyone has pretended to pay attention to something or someone. This is a lot like playacting: You appear to listen intently, but your mind is definitely somewhere else. You might even smile in agreement, when all you are really doing is maintaining eye contact. In class you may pretend to be taking notes, although your mind is not following what is being said. In fact, you may not be thinking of anything in particular. What you are actually doing is deceiving yourself into believing that you are accomplishing something.

Pretending to pay attention may become a habit. Without even realizing what you are doing, you may automatically tune out a speaker and let your mind wander. If, after a speech, you cannot recall the main purpose or the essential points presented by the speaker, you were probably faking attention. While it may seem harmless, such deceptive behavior can lead to misunderstandings and cause people to question your credibility and sincerity.

Although these six barriers to effective listening are the most common and problematical, they are not the only ones, nor do they operate independently. In fact, several barriers often work together to disrupt our listening, but fortunately, because listening is a learned behavior, we can learn to overcome the obstacles that interfere with our listening effectiveness.

INEFFECTIVE VERSUS EFFECTIVE LISTENING HABITS

Bad Listener	*Good Listener*
Tunes out topic—thinks it's boring	Finds areas of interest
Criticizes the speaker	Judges content rather than delivery
Listens only for details	Listens for ideas
Avoids difficult material	Exercises mind
Is easily distracted	Resists distractions
Fakes attention	Challenges, weighs the evidence, listens attentively

ANALYZING AND EVALUATING MESSAGES

As listeners, our goals may be more than just to understand a message. We may also need to judge the accuracy of the information presented, determine the reasonableness of its conclusions, and evaluate its presenter. At these times, we face a listening situation in which we must be critical: Is the message true? Is it based on solid evidence? Is it complete? Is it logical? Is the speaker's motivation for presenting the message ethical?

In today's society we are constantly confronted with many choices and decisions. For example, we are exposed to about 65 to 90 commercial messages each day in addition to all the interpersonal messages we receive at school, home, work, and recreation. Since we are limited in the amount of experience we can acquire on our own, we must depend on others for information and advice. Thus, we must evaluate and assess that information in order to make judgments about its value and utility. Listening with a critical ear involves two phases: (1) assessing the values and intent of those to whom we listen, and (2) judging the accuracy of the conclusions that we draw from the messages we receive.

Assessing the Motivation Behind a Message

Assessing a speaker's motivation generally involves several stages of information processing: (1) making a judgment about the values of the person we are listening to, (2) making a comparison between our standards and those of the speaker, and (3) determining the appropriate response to the message based on our judgment of its worth as presented.

Values are central to the communication process and to each individual's perceptual system. Even though we often take values for granted, they strongly influence our behavior. In communication, values affect our perception and interpretation of both the messages we send and the messages we receive. The first consideration in listening, therefore, is to examine the message in order to determine the speaker's values.

Of course, we should not automatically dismiss a message merely because the speaker's values conflict with our own. However, anytime we are confronted with a message that differs from our own views—one that asks us to do something, buy something, or behave in a certain way—we should be aware of the purpose behind it. We all face tremendous pressures to conform, and sometimes conformity means going against our principles. In these cases, we should be careful to recognize the motivation behind the message.

Judging Conclusions from a Message

In order to make accurate judgments about important messages, ask yourself the following questions:

1. Is the speaker qualified to draw the conclusion?
2. Has the speaker actually observed what he or she is talking about?
3. Does the speaker have a vested interest in his or her message?
4. Is there adequate evidence presented to support the conclusion?
5. Is the evidence relevant to the conclusion?
6. Is there contrary evidence to what has been presented?
7. Does the message contain invalid or inadequate reasoning?

MINI-EXERCISE

How do you think the following people would rate you as a listener? Use a scale of 0 to 100, with 100 being the highest rating.

1. Your best friend
2. Your boss or teacher
3. Your roommate or a co-worker
4. Your parents

After you have rated yourself, go to each person and ask him or her to rate you too (without disclosing your self-ratings, of course). Then compare the ratings. Were they the same? If not, why not?

SUGGESTIONS FOR IMPROVED LISTENING

With appropriate knowledge and practice, all of us can become better listeners. First, we must take listening seriously and acknowledge that no one can do it for us. Then we must recognize that a willingness and desire to improve are essential to increased listening effectiveness. Finally, we must begin to think of listening as an *active* process that requires our conscious participation. Passive listening is fine in some situations. For example, listening to the stereo while carrying on a casual conversation with a friend isn't likely to create problems. However we must also be able to identify cases in which active listening is crucial, and we should react accordingly. To listen more effectively, we must put energy and concentration into the process and constantly remind ourselves that listening is vital to communication.

Here are some specific suggestions for improving your listening behavior:

Be Prepared to Listen

Although this suggestion may seem quite obvious, few people prepare themselves to listen. Many assume that listening is going to happen by itself and that no preparation is necessary. This assumption is wrong— *hearing* will happen by itself, but listening will not.

Conditioning yourself for listening is important. Your attention span, which is directly related to your ability to listen, depends on your physical and mental condition at a given moment. If you are tired, your capacity to listen actively is severely reduced. Therefore, whenever possible, it's a good idea to determine your goals in advance and prepare to listen accordingly. If you are able to plan ahead and know what you want to gain from a situation, you can motivate yourself to maintain the high energy level needed to listen effectively.

Behave Like a Good Listener

To be an effective listener you must act like an effective listener. Here are some guidelines for effective listening:

1. **Stop Talking.** You cannot listen while you are talking.

2. **Do Not Interrupt.** Interrupting is not only rude, but also distracting to both the speaker and the listener. If you are speaking, or thinking about speaking, you can't give your full attention to what the other person is saying.

3. **Empathize with the Other Person.** Try to put yourself in the other person's position in order to understand what the communication means from his or her point of view.

4. **Concentrate on What Is Being Said.** Actively focus your attention on the message, the ideas, and the speaker's feelings toward the message.

5. **React to the Ideas Expressed, Not to the Person Talking.** It is difficult at times to separate the message from the speaker, but when listening, it is always the message that must take priority. If, for example, someone shouts that your dorm is on fire, you are not going to ignore the message just because you dislike the person giving it. Effective listening requires open-mindedness and the ability to evaluate the content of a message without regard for personal reactions to the source.

6. **Look at the Speaker.** Looking at the speaker enables you not only to listen, but also to compare his or her verbal and nonverbal messages. Observing the speaker's facial expressions, eye contact, and gestures can aid your interpretation. Be careful, however, not to be unduly influenced by the speaker's nonverbal messages or choice of words.

Looking at the speaker also helps you to concentrate and conveys your interest in the message. When speakers sense their audience's interest, they tend to communicate with more enthusiasm, making the task of listening a little easier.

7. **Ask Questions.** At appropriate times, if you do not understand something, need clarification, or want to show that you are listening, ask questions. This will help the speaker gauge the clarity of his or her message and ensure more accurate communication.

8. **Be Flexible in Your Views.** Even if you disagree, you must be receptive to others' opinions in order to gain new information. There is nothing wrong with questioning another's point of view, but you should at least listen. Then, if you disagree, you can either reject the information or rebut the speaker's standpoint.

9. **Listen for Main Ideas.** The key to good listening is to grasp the total picture. Facts are often important, but they are only one aspect of a message. Facts, as suggested earlier in this chapter, are easy to forget. In many cases, therefore, it is better to concentrate on principles, concepts, and general thoughts than on details. Most speakers are trying to make one or two

significant points. They use details, such as examples, statistics, and definitions to support these points. Of course, you should not ignore the supporting details, but knowing them will do you little good if you do not understand the main ideas.

10. **Take Notes.** Closely related to effective listening is note taking, an activity usually associated with the classroom but not limited to it. In fact, it is wise to take notes in any lengthy and difficult listening situation. Here are several ways to improve your note-taking skills:

- *Determine Whether Notes Are Appropriate.* This is a subjective decision, but common sense will usually tell you whether to take notes or not. If you plan to use the information immediately and have a strong memory, notes may not be necessary. On the other hand, if you must retain the information for a long period of time or have a weak memory, notes may well be the appropriate solution.
- *Determine What Kind of Notes to Take.* Notes can be taken in several different ways. You may prefer to jot down key words, a partial outline, or a complete outline.

The *key word format* is best used to remember only the specific points in a message. For example, to remember the definition of the word *process* as it is used in communication, list such key words as *ongoing, changing,* and *no beginning or end.* Your choice of key words must be highly descriptive and thorough, however, if you hope to make sense of your notes in the future.

When using the *partial outline format,* write key ideas in full with only enough detail to help you remember the main concept. This form of note taking is most appropriate when there is no need to recall all the information, or when you are only interested in certain aspects of the message. A partial outline need not be formal. For example, if you were taking notes on a speech about improving your diet, your partial outline might look like this:

DATE: January 15, 1988
TOPIC: Improving one's diet and health
SPEAKER: Dr. Jane Smith, health expert from University of Nebraska
PURPOSE: To provide suggestions on improving students' eating habits and general health

I. Balanced diet is important to a healthy life
   A. Foods from all three groups:
      proteins, fats, and carbohydrates
   B. Meats, vegetables, and cereal
II. Exercise with balanced diet is important
   A. Walk, swim, or do some other physical activity
   B. Exercise at least three times a week for approximately 15 minutes or more each time

Prepare a *complete outline,* which means outlining virtually the entire presentation, if you want to retain all the information that is presented. This form of note taking would require you to list all the main ideas and subordinate ideas as they are presented. For example:

Class Notes: Life Sciences 101

I. Circulatory System
   A. Heart
      1. Structure
         a. Atria—2 chambers that receive blood
         b. Ventricles—2 chambers that expel blood
         c. Valves
            (1) Aortic
            (2) Pulmonary
            (3) Auriculo-ventricular, called A-V valves
      2. Cardiac cycle—flow of blood through heart
         a. Into atria
         b. Into ventricles
         c. Ventricles contract—blood expelled into blood vessels
   B. Blood vessels
      1. Structure
         a. Innermost layer—flat endothelial cells
         b. Second layer, tunica media—elastic and contractile fibers
         c. Outermost layer, adventitia—connective tissue and some contractile fibers
      2. Types
         a. Arteries—carry blood from heart
         b. Veins—carry blood back to heart
         c. Capillaries—carry blood from arteries to cells and from cells to veins
II. Respiratory system
    Etc.

The problem with outlining is that some speakers' presentations will not be well organized, thus making it difficult to create a complete and systematic outline.

- *Keep Notes Clear and Brief.* Don't try to write everything down. Write clearly and thoughtfully so that you can read your notes later, and keep your comments brief to give yourself time to study the speaker and think about what is being said.
- *Review Your Notes Later.* Reviewing as soon after the speaking event as possible will help you to recall and learn the information. Some people find it helpful to annotate, reorganize, or even rewrite their notes before filing them away for future reference.

Of course, care must always be taken to avoid getting so involved in note taking that effective listening is forgotten. Note taking should be used only as an aid to listening—never as a substitute for it.

SUMMARY   People place high priority on good listening skills. Until quite recently, the listening process was taken for granted primarily because it seemed so obvious, but people are now recognizing that listening is a complex process that must be carefully cultivated because it is so crucial to effective communication.

Hearing is a passive process, whereas listening is an active process. *Hearing* is the physiological process in which sound is received by the ear. *Listening*, which requires energy, desire, and commitment, involves selecting, attending, understanding, and remembering the sounds we hear. *Selecting* is the process of choosing what we are going to listen to. *Attention* is the mental process of focusing on specific stimuli while ignoring or downplaying other stimuli. *Understanding* is the assigning of meaning to the stimuli that we have selected and attended to. *Remembering* is recalling something by an act of memory—thinking of something again. While each of these functions is separate and distinct, all are also interdependent.

Listening serves four principal functions: (1) *listening for information* enables us to gain comprehension; (2) *evaluative listening* occurs when we intend to judge or analyze information; (3) *empathic listening* seeks to provide comfort through increased knowledge and understanding; and (4) *listening for enjoyment* creates pleasure, personal satisfaction, and appreciation.

Many obstacles prevent us from listening effectively. For example, we often decide in advance that the topic or speaker is boring, uninteresting, or unimportant. We may criticize the speaker instead of the message, concentrate on details rather than on main ideas, avoid difficult listening situations, permit distractions to interfere, or fake attention. These obstacles to effective listening do not operate independently—several of them can occur at one time. Because listening is a learned behavior, we can learn to overcome some of these bad listening habits.

We listen not only to understand, but also to judge the accuracy and reasonableness of the information presented by a speaker. Each day we are confronted by hundreds of messages, and to make wise decisions about them, we must listen with a critical ear. This involves two steps: assessing the values and intent of the speaker, and judging the accuracy of the conclusions we draw from the messages we receive.

We can improve our listening ability in two ways: by being mentally and physically prepared to listen and by behaving like a good listener. To be a good listener, we need to stop talking and avoid interrupting, empathize with the other person, concentrate on what is being said, react to the ideas and not to the person talking, ask questions when we do not understand something, be flexible in our views, listen for main ideas, and take notes.

KEY TERMS

Attention: the mental process of focusing on specific stimuli while ignoring or downplaying other stimuli.

Empathic Listening: listening that includes understanding and information seeking, but usually excludes making judgments.

Evaluative Listening: listening to judge or to analyze information.

Hearing: the passive, physiological process in which sound is received by the ear.

Listening: the active process of receiving aural stimuli by selecting, attending, understanding, and remembering.

Listening for Enjoyment: listening purely for pleasure, personal satisfaction, or appreciation.

Listening for Information: listening to gain comprehension.

Remembering: recalling something by an act of memory—thinking of something again.

Selecting: the process of choosing what we are going to listen to.

Understanding: the assigning of meaning to the stimuli that we have selected and attended to.

DISCUSSION
STARTERS

1. Why do we take the listening process for granted?

2. What could you say to persuade someone of the importance of listening? Support your arguments with evidence.

3. How would you go about teaching a person to be a more effective listener?

4. What are the differences between listening and hearing?

5. What makes listening so much more complicated than hearing?

6. What role does memory play in the listening process?

7. Why is it important to understand the different functions of listening?

8. What does it mean to listen with empathy?

9. Why don't we listen effectively?

10. What are the three most important things to remember about note taking?

FURTHER
READINGS

Banville, Thomas G. *How to Listen—How to Be Heard.* Chicago: Nelson-Hall, Inc., 1978.

Burly-Allen, M. *Listening: The Forgotten Skill.* New York: John Wiley & Sons, 1982.

Floyd, J. J. *Listening: A Practical Approach.* Glenview, Ill.: Scott, Foresman and Co., 1985.

Steil, L. K., L. L. Barker, and K. W. Watson. *Effective Listening: Key to Your Success.* New York: Random House, Inc., 1983.

Wolf, F., N. C. Marsnik, W. S. Tacey, and R. G. Nichols. *Perceptive Listening.* New York: Holt, Rinehart & Winston, 1983.

Wolvin, A., and C. G. Coakley. *Listening,* 2nd ed. Dubuque, Iowa: Wm. C. Brown, Pubs., 1985.

NOTES

1. Rankin, Paul, "Listening Ability," *Proceedings of the Ohio State Educational Conference's Ninth Annual Session,* 1929; Barker, Larry, R. Edwards, C. Gaines, et al., "An Investigation of Proportional Time Spent in Various Communication Activities by College Students," *Journal of Applied Communication Research* 8(1980):pp. 101–109.

2. Di Salvo, Vincent, "A Summary of Current Research Identifying Communication Skills in Various Organizational Contexts," *Communication Education* 29 (July) 1980:pp. 283–290.

3. Di Salvo, Vincent, David C. Larsen, and William J. Seiler, "Communication Skills Needed by People in Business," *Communication Education* 25(1976):p. 274.

4. Dietze, A. G. and G. E. Jones, "Factual Memory of Secondary School Pupils for a Short Article Which They Read a Single Time," *Journal of Educational Psychology* 22(1931):pp. 586–598, 667–676.

5. Nichols, Ralph, "Factors Accounting for Differences in Comprehension of Materials Presented Orally in the Classroom," Unpublished Doctoral Dissertation, University of Iowa, Iowa City, 1948; Hirsch, Robert O., *Listening: A Way to Process Information Aurally,* (Dubuque, Iowa: Gorsuch Scarisbrick, Pubs., 1979), pp. 36–41.

PART II

PUBLIC COMMUNICATION

CHAPTER 6

Getting Started: Topic Selection and Audience Analysis

After studying this chapter, you should be able to:

1.   Describe how to choose a topic for a speech.

2.   Assess whether the topic you've selected is appropriate for you, your audience, and your speech situation.

3.   Formulate both the general and specific purposes of your speech.

4.   Analyze your audience's point of view.

5.   Explain what information a speaker should gather about an audience when preparing a speech.

6.   Interpret data from an audience analysis and apply this data to your specific speech situation.

- Shawn is preparing a ten-minute oral report for his history class based on the research he has done on the Vietnam War.
- Kelley has recently been elected student council president. Tonight is the council's first meeting and Kelley must persuade the other council members of the importance of the goals and objectives she has set for the coming school year.
- As a member of the Future Farmers of America, Mark will speak to a group of high school students about the importance of the organization and try to convince them to join.
- Megan, a seventh-grade student teacher, is about to present her first lecture on how to use BASIC computer language.

Each of these students is preparing for a public speaking event. **Public speaking** is the presentation of a speech, usually prepared in advance, during which the speaker is the central focus of an audience's attention. In Chapter 1 we stated that the ability to communicate is one of the most important skills a person can possess in our society. Because speechmaking is such a vital and significant form of communication, it is the focus of this chapter and Chapters 7 to 11.

The two most frequent concerns of beginning speechmakers are "I don't have anything worthwhile to say" and "I'm too nervous to speak in front of others." Both of these worries are addressed in detail in this chapter and in the others that follow. You may have your own reasons for doubting the need to learn how to develop and present a speech, but whatever they are, you must be willing to set them aside. Learning about speechmaking will not only help you become a more effective speaker, but it will also help you to develop better writing, listening, organizing, researching, and reasoning skills.

THE IMPORTANCE OF EFFECTIVE SPEECHMAKING

People who believe that they will never have to give speeches consequently feel that learning about speechmaking is a waste of time. A survey of 202 randomly selected blue-collar workers in a medium-sized city, however, found that almost half of these workers had given speeches to ten or more people at least once during a previous two-year period. They spoke to community organizations, to church groups, to students in courses they were taking, and to members of their unions. The more education they had, and the higher their economic status, the more likely they were to make speeches. The report also observed that college graduates were even more likely to give speeches than nongraduates.[1]

In another survey, 67 out of 71 top corporate executives in the United States stated that training or competence in public speaking was essential for a person in middle management.[2] While public speaking isn't the only skill required for a successful business career, it is considered necessary by those who have reached the top.

THINK ABOUT IT

When Jim Wickless was in high school, he enrolled in a speech class largely against his will. "I would never have taken it if it hadn't been required," Wickless said. "But it turned out to be one of the most important courses I've ever had."

Wickless' public speaking ability has come in handy in his seven years on the Lincoln Board of Education. He speaks frequently to community groups, testifies before the state legislature, and in his spare time lectures on speech writing in a public speaking class at Southeast Community College. Next year he's scheduled to become president of the Nebraska Association of School Boards, a position which will afford more opportunities for speechmaking.

Earlier this year Wickless tried to make speech a requirement for high school graduation, but couldn't persuade the rest of the board to go along with him. In his reelection campaign he argues that Lincoln students need better training in three key areas: oral and written communication, critical thinking skills, and foreign languages. All three subjects, he says, are vital to students' future in a competitive society of changing careers and international markets.

1. In your opinion, should a course in speech communication be required for high school graduation? Why or why not?
2. Should a course in speech communication be required for college graduation? Why or why not?
3. In what ways is oral communication vital to students' future in a competitive society of changing careers and international markets?

Excerpt from Bob Reeves, "Wickless finds speech class was valuable lifetime lesson," *Lincoln Star,* April 21, 1987, p. 8.

SELECTING A SPEECH TOPIC

Selecting a topic is the first step in preparing a speech. As illustrated by the speech topics presented at the beginning of this chapter, the choice of topics is often prompted by the situation, the needs of others, and the position and qualifications of the speaker.

The following example shows how a speaker (requested by a phone caller to speak at an annual luncheon) would narrow his or her speech topic.

CALLER: My name is Jane Smith and I'm with the state retailers' association. We're having our annual conference in your city

this year on Wednesday, April 20. You have a reputation as a fascinating speaker on the topic of communication, so we were wondering if you would be willing to speak at our conference.

SPEAKER: Let me look at my calendar. Yes, I am available on that day.

CALLER: Good! We would like you to talk about the importance of communication to retailers. You would be speaking at approximately noon, during our luncheon. We would like you to speak about 30 to 45 minutes and then allow about 15 minutes for questions. Is that OK?

SPEAKER: Yes, but I do have a few questions. How many people will be attending?

CALLER: About 65 to 75.

SPEAKER: Who will these people be?

CALLER: They are mainly retailers—people who either own their own small businesses or manage large department stores.

SPEAKER: Could you be more specific?

CALLER: Yes, the business owners tend to have small clothing stores or sporting goods stores—something like that. The managers may be from supermarkets or companies like Sears or Wards.

SPEAKER: Can you be more specific about the topic you would like me to cover?

CALLER: I'll have Sue Jones, our president, call you—she can provide you with more details.

Similar circumstances accompany most invitations to speak. People, whether well-known speakers or not, are usually asked to discuss a topic within their area of expertise. For example, a teacher may be asked to speak on computers in the classroom, a business person may speak on the economy, and a farmer may speak on the high price of farm equipment.

Classroom speaking situations are similar to these examples except that the instructor is the person requesting the speech. Here is a typical classroom speech assignment:

> Your first speech will be a five- to seven-minute informative presentation. You may choose your own topic, but it must be related to a sociopolitical issue and cannot focus on how to do something. For example, an acceptable topic would be "Solar Energy: The Fuel of the Future," while an unacceptable topic would be "How to Water Ski in Five Easy Steps."

The Subject Area

Selecting a topic can often be frustrating, but it need not be if you are willing to consider a wide range of possible topics. There are two simple rules for beginning your search for a speech topic.

Rule 1: Select a topic that interests you and that you know something about.

Choosing a topic that is familiar and interesting to you should make the development and delivery of your speech a little easier. The more you know about a subject, the easier it is for you to speak about it. If you think that you don't know any subject well enough to present it to others, remember the following example. A student insisted he didn't know of any topic that would be of interest to others. He was majoring in construction technology, so his teacher suggested that he think about an aspect of this field that interested him the most. The student later presented a fascinating speech on the history and technique of skyscraper construction. The speech gained the student new respect among his peers, who were impressed by his knowledge.

On the other hand, there may be a topic that you have a strong interest in, but know little about—violence in our society, for example. The necessity of giving a speech presents an ideal opportunity for you to learn about a topic and at the same time fulfill a class assignment.

Rule 2: Select a topic that will be of interest to your audience.

If an audience perceives a speaker's topic to be relevant and stimulating, they are more likely to pay attention and respond favorably. If you are unable to think of an interesting subject to speak on, two methods may help you out.

First, compile a self-inventory of topics that you know about and find interesting. For example, list books and newspaper articles that you've read, television shows that you watch, hobbies that you enjoy, sports that you participate in, and community, regional, state, or national issues that concern you.

MINI-EXERCISE

Complete the following self-inventory by supplying as many answers as you can for each category; then examine each of your answers to determine if it can be a viable speech topic.

	Books Recently Read	*TV Shows*	*Newspaper Articles*
SAMPLE:	*In Search of Excellence*	Cosby Show	U.S. Ships Arms to Iran

	Hobbies	*Sports*	*Community Issues*
SAMPLE:	Coin Collecting	Volleyball	New Recreation Facility

	State Issues	*Regional Issues*	*National Issues*
SAMPLE:	Improving Education	Farm Crisis	Drugs

If your self-inventory doesn't help you come up with a topic, try brainstorming. **Brainstorming** is a technique used to generate as many ideas as possible in a limited amount of time. Simply set aside a short period of time (two to five minutes) for intensive concentration and write down all the ideas you can think of that might be used as topics. To keep things simple, just write key words or phrases. The goal of brainstorming is to generate a great many ideas, so no word or phrase is inappropriate. For example, you might produce the following list:

politics	dance	drunk	rock
video	sex	crime	sports
health	technology	human services	radio
war	justice	agriculture	business
space	energy	housing	education

These words could provide the bases for many speeches. Therefore, after listing as many thoughts as you can, you need to select those that appeal to you and develop them further. The term *technology,* for example, could serve as the springboard for an entirely new list:

computers	air travel	auto industry	health
lasers	microwaves	weapons	space

With a little effort, brainstorming can help you generate a number of potential speech topics.

MINI-EXERCISE

Use brainstorming to generate several topics that you might use for your next speech. What criteria would you use to determine the best topic for your presentation? Using the criteria you have established, determine which topic you will use.

Assessing the Appropriateness of a Topic

Once you have identified a possible speech topic, the next step is to determine whether it is appropriate for your situation, your assignment, and your audience. Begin by asking yourself if your topic is *worthwhile.* That is, does it merit the audience's attention? Will the audience see a relationship between you and the topic and between the topic and themselves? Will the topic meet the objectives of the assignment?

Other important questions to ask include the following:

1. Does the audience have sufficient knowledge and background to understand the topic?
2. Can you make the topic understandable to everyone in the audience?
3. Is the topic of sufficient interest to you that you will be motivated to present it effectively?
4. Do you have adequate knowledge of the topic?
5. If you are not already familiar with the topic, will you be able to learn enough about it to give an informed speech?
6. Is the topic appropriate for the situation in which you will present it?

Narrowing and Focusing Your Topic

Once you have determined that your topic is appropriate, the next step is to decide whether it is focused and specific enough to meet the time limit and the goal of the assignment. This step can save you much time and trouble in the long run because a topic that is well focused is much easier to research than one that is too general. For example, if you selected the

topic "The Problems with American Education," you could work for years and still not cover all the information that is available. If you restricted your scope, however, to problems with American education during the past five years, you would begin to reduce the time frame of your literature search. You could narrow the topic even further by concentrating on a single problem with American education during the past five years, and so on. Each time you define, narrow, and focus your topic, you increase its potential depth.

The more abstract a topic, the more important it is to narrow and focus it to meet the constraints of a speech situation. For example, a member of a university's debate team started the process of selecting a topic for her ten-minute informative speech by expressing an interest in pop culture. To narrow the topic, she decided to examine only pop culture fads. As soon as she recognized the abundance of such fads, she began to focus more specifically on video games. While thinking about video games as a fad and as an element of pop culture, she decided to be even more specific and limited her attention to the effects of video games on children. This continuous narrowing and focusing of the topic enabled the student to focus her research and content development on a single, well-defined area of interest.

DETERMINING THE GENERAL AND SPECIFIC PURPOSES OF YOUR SPEECH

The **general purpose,** or overall goal of a speech, is usually to perform one of three overlapping functions—to inform, to persuade, or to entertain. Rarely does a speech serve only one function. Even though most classroom speech assignments are intended to emphasize a single function, the speeches themselves may contain aspects of all three functions. For example, the speech about the effects of video games on children is meant to inform, but this does not mean that the speech cannot contain some persuasive and entertaining elements as well.

Speeches that Inform

When the general purpose of your speech is to inform, you are expected to convey your knowledge of a particular subject. Thus, an **informative speech** should enhance an audience's knowledge and understanding by explaining what something means, how something works, or how something is done. A key assumption is that the majority of your audience does not already know the information you are planning to present. Thus, you are presenting information to your audience in much the same way that teachers do when they present information to their classes.

When a topic is controversial, for example, "Using Condoms as a Means of Preventing AIDS"—speakers whose general purpose is to inform should not take sides. They should allow audience members to draw their own conclusions. The goal of an informative speech is to present information clearly and accurately while at the same time making the learning experience as enjoyable as possible for the audience.

Speeches that Persuade

Providing information is part of all presentations, but the speech that persuades goes several steps further in order to influence or change the attitudes or behavior of listeners. Thus, while the focus of an informative speech is on conveying information by explaining, reporting, or demonstrating, the goal of a **persuasive speech** is to advocate or gain acceptance for the speaker's point of view. For example, a student preparing a persuasive speech may decide to advocate that a new recreational building be financed with student fees. In order to win the audience over, he will have to present evidence to justify his position. It is impossible to persuade without giving information.

MINI-EXERCISE

Listed below are some topics for informative speeches. How would you convert each one into a topic that would be appropriate for a persuasive speech?

INFORMATIVE: Nine Steps to a Healthy Body
PERSUASIVE: Daily Exercise Will Save Your Life

1. INFORMATIVE: Understanding the Use of the Microcomputer
   PERSUASIVE:

2. INFORMATIVE: Solar Energy: A New Power Source
   PERSUASIVE:

3. INFORMATIVE: Star Wars: The Defense System of the Future
   PERSUASIVE:

4. INFORMATIVE: The Farm Crisis
   PERSUASIVE:

Speeches that Entertain

The function of an **entertainment speech** is to provide enjoyment and amusement, as does an after-dinner speech. This does not mean, however, that an entertaining speech cannot be both informative *and* persuasive, or that informative and persuasive speeches cannot be entertaining. The principal difference among these three kinds of speeches depends on which function (informing, persuading, entertaining) the speaker puts the most emphasis on.

General Versus Specific Purposes

The reason for stating a general purpose is to provide direction for a speech's content. In the classroom, a speech's general purpose is usually specified as part of the assignment. Outside the classroom, it may or may not be specified. When the general purpose is not identified, you must determine it for yourself. To be a successful speaker, you must know exactly what you plan to accomplish by speaking.

Once you have determined your general purpose, you are ready to state your specific purpose. A **specific purpose** can be stated in a single phrase that defines precisely what you intend to accomplish in your speech. Recall that the student who chose pop culture as her original topic ended up with an entirely new topic—video games—as a result of the narrowing process.

She was then ready to develop a statement of her specific purpose. The statement she devised was: "To inform my listeners about the three major effects of video games on children." Note that this statement is clear and concise. It tells the listeners exactly what the speaker intends to do and what she wants them to know.

Formulating a Specific Purpose Statement

An effective specific purpose statement identifies the general purpose of the speech, the target audience, and the exact topic to be covered. These three pieces of information significantly help the speaker to develop and deliver the speech. Note that in the video games example, the speaker's specific purpose statement cites the general purpose of the speech, which is to inform. It also identifies the audience, which is important because different audiences may require different information. For example, if a speech is to be presented to children only, to adults only, or to both children and adults, the content will have to be adjusted to fit the group. Thus, while the general and specific purposes are the same, the content of the speech will vary depending on the listeners' backgrounds, knowledge, and attitudes toward the topic.

The careful writing of a specific purpose statement is important to all aspects of *planning, researching,* and *developing* a successful speech. The following guidelines should help you write effective specific purpose statements:

1. The specific purpose statement should include a verb that describes the general purpose of the speech.

INCORRECT: Video games and children.
  CORRECT: To inform the audience of three effects of video games on children.
           Note that in the correct statement, the inclusion of the verb clarifies what the speaker hopes to accomplish.

2. The specific purpose statement should be limited to one distinct thought or idea.

INCORRECT: To inform the audience of the three effects of drugs and the four best ways to avoid alcohol abuse by teenagers.
  CORRECT: To inform the audience of the three most dangerous effects of drugs on teenagers.
           The incorrect statement is too long and contains more than one subject. In fact, an entire speech could be developed around either idea. It is best to select only one idea and refine it as the purpose for the speech.

3. The specific purpose statement should not be a question.

INCORRECT: How does capital punishment affect society?
  CORRECT: To persuade the audience that capital punishment can be extremely harmful to society.
           While the question indicates the topic, it is not a clear or complete specific purpose statement because it fails to specify the general purpose of the speech.

4. The specific purpose statement should be concise and carefully worded.

INCORRECT: The effects of a permissive society can be extremely harmful to children and can also create a society that eventually becomes desensitized to reality.

CORRECT: To persuade the audience that a permissive society can only lead to the breakdown of law and order.

The incorrect statement tries to cover too much, is too general, and doesn't clearly state what is to be achieved in the speech.

Stating your general and specific purposes makes it easier to develop your speech. Both statements can guide your thinking and planning and thus focus the thrust and aims of your speech. You should be ready to revise your specific purpose, however, throughout the development stages of the speech. As you research a topic, for example, you may find additional information that will lead you to revise your thinking. Or, you may learn something about your audience that will make you want to revise your approach.

MINI-EXERCISE

What is wrong with each of the following specific purpose statements? How would you correct them?

1. What is euthanasia?
2. To inform the audience about sailing.
3. To persuade the audience that a need exists for quality education in our society.
4. Skydiving can be fun.

ANALYZING YOUR AUDIENCE

Audience analysis is the collection and interpretation of data about the basic characteristics, attitudes, values, and beliefs of an audience. Analyzing your audience is an essential step in developing and delivering a speech. An audience becomes actively involved in a speech and reacts not only to the speaker, buy also to the subject, to what is said, to how it is said, to other audience members, and to the situation. Thus, the more you know about your audience, the better you can adapt your speech to them.

Selecting a topic, narrowing it, and determining its specific purpose all require some understanding and knowledge of the target audience, as does the remainder of the development process—selecting and organizing the content, developing the introduction and conclusion, and delivering the speech. Because knowledge of the audience is so important to a speaker's success, in this section we examine the audience's point of view, kinds of audience members, key information to find out about an audience, methods for researching audiences, and how to adapt a speech to an audience.

THINK ABOUT IT

Effective speakers are audience-minded. They know to whom they are speaking and why they are speaking to them. They are also aware of the response they wish to gain from presenting their speech. Developing a presentation with the audience in mind is the best way to achieve the goal of your speech.

Understanding the Audience's Point of View

An **audience** is a collection of individuals who have come together for a specific reason—to listen to a speech. Each individual, however, may have a variety of personal reasons for being present. Students, for example, come to class not just to listen to lectures, but because they are required to attend as part of their speech assignment.

The reason individuals come together to form an audience is an important point that every speaker should consider when planning a speech. If people join an audience because they wish to listen to a speech, then it is reasonable to assume that they also want to hear something that is meaningful to them. People are egocentric. Most individuals ask the same basic questions about their involvement in an audience: What is in it for me? Why is this important? How will this specifically affect me?

These questions suggest that as you develop a speech topic, you should recognize that your audience will be judging what they hear based on their past experiences and on the relevance of the information presented. The more you know about your audience's past experiences, familiarity with and attitude toward your subject, and the reason they are present, the easier it is for you to develop a speech that is meaningful to them.

THINK ABOUT IT

Imagine that you are an expert on reading and have been asked to speak on the topic "How to Teach Children to Be More Effective Readers." You have spent many hours getting ready for the speech and are now prepared to present it. But are you really prepared? Have you thought about the members of your audience? Who are they? What do they know about reading? What is their attitude toward reading?

Would you present the same information to an audience of professionals who teach reading as you would to parents who want their children to become better readers, to children who are indifferent about reading, or to a combination of all three groups—teachers, parents, and children? What results would you expect if you used the same approach for all three audiences? What results would you expect if you varied your approaches?

Captive Versus Voluntary Participants

Many kinds of people make up an audience and many reasons determine why people attend speeches, but there are basically only two kinds of audience participants—captive and voluntary.

Captive Participants.   Audiences required to listen to a particular speaker are **captive participants.** They are present, but usually *not by choice.* Varying degrees of captivity exist from member to member within each audience— that is, some people may resist participation more than others.

Even though few circumstances (at least in this country) force a person to be in an audience, some situations demand attendance to avoid a penalty. For example, a teacher often requires attendance during speech presentations, an employer requires employees to attend new product demonstrations, or a military leader orders troops to attend lectures on their military maneuvers. In such situations, audience members either must be present or cannot leave without being noticed or penalized for doing so. To be effective, a speaker must recognize when he or she is dealing with captive participants.

Voluntary Participants.   In contrast to captive participants, **voluntary participants** choose to hear a particular speaker or speech because of some interest or need. True volunteers attend only because of what they expect to hear. There is no other motivation for their presence.

In practice, the difference between captive and voluntary participants is not always easy to distinguish because many situations that appear to be voluntary on the surface may actually be captive. The reverse may also be true. The deciding factor is whether the participants are required to listen or not. For example, students may be required to attend a lecture and may also be tested on what the speaker says. They are definitely captive participants. On the other hand, children may be required to attend church with their parents, but may not be expected to listen to what's going on. In such a case, they are voluntary participants.

Captive audience participants, therefore, have little or no choice—they must be present and they are supposed to listen. Volunteer audience participants have more choice—whether or not they listen is up to them. This difference is important for you to know because your objective as a speaker should be not only to gain your audience's attention, but also to get them to listen.

Speakers addressing voluntary audiences have a definite advantage over those addressing captive audiences: they do not have to spend as much effort persuading their audiences to listen. Voluntary participants already have at least one thing in common—they all want to listen to the speaker. For example, at a fund-raiser for a political candidate, the audience members are there because they support the candidate and want to hear what he or she has to say.

Key Audience Information

Two kinds of information—demographic and psychological—should be gathered about an audience. Demographic data are the vital statistics that help us group people into categories. Psychological characteristics are more intangible and strongly influence an individual's reaction to a speaker, a topic, and the surroundings in which a speech takes place.

Demographic Information. In a **demographic analysis,** a speaker researches an audience in terms of such basic information as age, gender, cultural or ethnic background, education, occupation, religion, geographic location, and group membership. The more similar the demographic characteristics of audience members, the easier it is for a speaker to adapt to their needs and interests. For example, if an audience consists of only 17- and 18-year-olds, the speaker has only a one-year age difference to deal with. On the other hand, if the audience members' ages span from 5 to 85 years, the speaker will have a more difficult time trying to adapt to the broad differences in this age range.

Age.   Age may not seem important, and for some topics and situations it isn't, but knowing that members of the audience differ in age can help the speaker select a range of appropriate examples and evidence. An age difference between the speaker and the audience can also alter what and how messages are expressed. For example, if the speaker is young and the audience is elderly, or vice versa, both the speaker's and the audience's experiences may play a critical role in how a subject is approached or perceived.

Sex.   Gender is an important demographic characteristic, but it can present problems. Considering it as a difference among audience members can be tricky because social, political, and economic distinctions between women and men change rapidly in our society. Not only have the attitudes of each sex toward the other changed, but so have the attitudes of each sex toward itself. Women have taken a greater role in activities that were once exclusively male dominated and vice versa. Thus, speakers must always be sensitive to potential gender-based biases. Although some topics may still be more appropriate for one sex than the other, clear-cut distinctions are becoming increasingly rare.

Cultural or ethnic background.   Cultural or ethnic background is often not considered as thoroughly as it should be, even though a tremendous diversity of backgrounds exists in our society. Whenever possible, you should be sensitive to the different groups that may be present to hear your speech.

The following communication variables are culturally determined and influence interactions between and among members of different ethnic backgrounds:

- Attitudes
- Social status within the group
- Thought patterns
- Expected behaviors
- Use of language
- Use of spatial relationships
- Meanings of words
- Time
- Nonverbal expressions

Each of these variables determines and regulates how an individual creates and interprets messages. Thus, a speaker who does not take these factors into account may embarrass and insult an audience.

Education.   Although it may be impossible to find out exactly what an audience knows and understands about a specific topic, it is important to ascertain their general educational level. Knowing whether most listeners have completed high school, college, or graduate school can help you to gauge their intellectual level and experience and to adapt your speech accordingly.

Occupation.   Knowledge about audience members' occupations can also tell you something about their probable interest in and familiarity with a subject. For example, you might not consider being a student an occupation, but it is. Because you are a student, your education, your major, and your career choice are all probably of high interest to you. Similarly, lawyers would be interested in topics related to the law, teachers in education, and parents in raising children.

Religion.   Speakers must be as sensitive to religion as they are to ethnicity. That is, they must recognize issues that touch on religious beliefs and treat them with respect. Most audiences will include people holding varying beliefs, so a broad awareness is required. If you plan to speak on an issue that may have religious ramifications, you should evaluate how your message will affect audience members. Otherwise, you run a high risk of offending and/or losing the attention of some or all of your audience.

Geographic origins.   Knowing the geographic origins of your audience can help you to adapt your speech to them. For example, most people from rural communities probably know and care more about agricultural topics than do most people from large urban areas. People from the South may not be interested in fuel oil to heat their homes, but if they live in an oil-producing state, they may be interested in the price of a barrel of oil.

Group membership.   Finally, the audience's group membership should be considered when you are developing and delivering a speech. A group is a collection of individuals who have joined together for some common cause or purpose that may be social, professional, recreational, or charitable.

Recognizing that individuals in your audience come from groups with special interests can help you to relate your speech directly to their needs and concerns. Of course, it isn't always possible to reach out to every group in your audience, but by appealing to the largest group possible you can create strong attention and interest. For example, a student who belonged to a sorority decided to inform her audience about the many important ways in which sorority and fraternity functions extend beyond mere social activities. Her audience consisted of 24 students, 18 of whom were not affiliated with any Greek group. Knowing this, she began her speech by talking about her thoughts of Greek organizations before she became a member. By first pointing out her reservations about such groups, she created a common understanding between herself and her listeners. Had her audience, on the other hand, included 18 sorority and fraternity members, they would have thought her topic and its introduction was boring.

Psychological Information.   In a **psychological analysis,** a speaker collects data about audience members' values, attitudes, and beliefs. It is an extension of the demographic analysis. A psychological analysis seeks to determine how the audience will react to the speaker, the speaker's topic, and the surroundings in which the speech is presented. The size of the audience, the physical setting for the presentation, the knowledge level of the audience, and the attitude of the audience toward the speaker, the topic, and the situation all play vital roles in the planning, development, and delivery of a speech.

Size.   The number of audience members has a considerable psychological effect on a speaking situation and strongly influences how a speech should be delivered. For instance, the larger the audience, the more difficult it is to use an informal, conversational speaking style. Size also influences how visual aids are used and affects the speaker's use of language and gestures. There is a difference between speaking to 10 or 35 people, as in a typical classroom speech assignment, and speaking to 100 or 350 people in an auditorium. Effective speakers know this and plan their presentations to meet the requirements of each situation.

Physical setting.   In evaluating the physical setting, consider such factors as the room size, ventilation, seating arrangement, lighting, speaker's platform, and potential for using visual aids. Some professional speakers require specific physical settings and will refuse to give their presentations if their conditions can't be met. Unfortunately, you do not have that choice in a classroom assignment. You can, however, assess the physical setting and make sure to take full advantage of what is available to you.

The seating arrangement of your audience is often predetermined, as it is in classroom settings, but sometimes a slight modification may make your presentation more effective. For example, a speech professor was asked to address a group of 30 police officers. He purposely arrived early so he could see the room and assess the speaking conditions. The seats were arranged classroom-style—that is, the chairs were in uniform rows directly in front of a raised speaker's podium, on which stood a large wooden lectern with a microphone. The professor felt that the setting was organized too formally and would inhibit his presentation, so he quickly rearranged the room by placing the chairs in a semicircle and moving the speaker's podium off to one side. These simple changes gave his presentation a more casual feeling and encouraged audience involvement.

Knowledge level.   The extent of an audience's knowledge about a topic has a tremendous effect on the outcome of a speech. For example, if an audience has little or no background in a topic and the speaker does not realize this, both the audience and the speaker may become frustrated. The audience's frustration is similar to the frustration of students with no math background who are trying to learn calculus from a teacher who assumes they have been well prepared. The speaker may feel like the calculus teacher. When an audience isn't ready to receive information, or when the information is too technical for them to understand, the speaker must present the material in terms everyone can understand.

On the other hand, a speaker must also adjust his or her presentation to a knowledgeable audience. A physician addressing a medical conference would not spend a lot of time explaining familiar medical terms. To do so would insult the intelligence of the other physicians in attendance. Even though people are apt to be more interested in subjects they know something about, an audience does not want to hear familiar information unless the speaker can present a new twist or add to their existing knowledge. For example, a student decided to present a four- to six-minute informative speech about the lead pencil—a subject that would seem to be too familiar and of limited interest to other students. After interviewing his classmates, the speaker noted that they all had the same limited response: "What can you say about a lead pencil other than it is made of lead and wood and is used for writing?" Based on his analysis, the student developed a creative and fascinating speech; he turned a supposedly dull topic with little substance into a unique and interesting experience for his audience. Although his delivery style was casual and entertaining, he provided detailed information about the history of the lead pencil and its effect on society. The speech was a great success.

Attitude toward the speaker.   The audience members' attitudes toward the speaker, the subject, and the situation strongly influence how a speech should be developed and delivered. If you know your audience's attitudes in advance, you can adjust to accommodate them, as the following example proves.

Two speech professors arrived late to a workshop they were offering on effective communication. Anxious to start, the professors said little about themselves and quickly launched into their main topic. Fifteen minutes into the presentation, they noticed that most of the participants were not paying attention and appeared confused. Finally, a student asked, "Who are you?" When the speakers replied that they were speech communication professors and listed their credentials and qualifications, the audience settled down and became attentive.

As this example illustrates, an audience's attitude toward a speaker can make the difference between success and failure. Audience members always formulate some attitude toward a speaker. Effective speakers recognize this fact and adjust their presentations accordingly.

Attitude toward the topic.   The audience's attitude toward the topic is just as significant as their attitude toward the speaker. If audience members do not relate to a topic, the speaker will have a difficult time getting them to listen. For instance, a student chose to speak on individual retirement accounts for his persuasive speech. He researched the subject thoroughly and practiced its delivery. His presentation was enthusiastic, but his audience remained cool and uninvolved. The problem was that the speaker failed to consider the age of his audience members (mostly eighteen- to twenty-year-old students). Saving for retirement was not high on their priority lists. The speaker could have made his speech more relevant by discussing young people's indifference toward retirement saving and convincing them that they should be concerned now.

Attitude toward the situation.   Finally, the speaker must examine the audience's attitude toward the situation in which the speech is presented. A key question to ask is: Why is the audience gathered? The audience's expectations influence their attitude toward the situation, which in turn affects the speaker and the topic.

Knowing in advance the prevailing attitudes of your audience toward you, your topic, and the situation should help you to plan, deliver, and ultimately achieve the specific purpose of your speech.

Methods of Audience Research.   Once you recognize what is important to know about your audience, the next step is to determine the best method of obtaining the necessary information. The three most common ways of gathering information about an audience are through observation, survey interviews, and questionnaires.

Observations.   Probably the easiest method of audience research is **observation,** in which the speaker watches audience members and notes their behaviors and characteristics. Although this approach relies strictly on the speaker's subjective impressions, it can be useful. For example, when asked to give a presentation to the Home and School Association, a professor relied on her observations of previous meetings to determine the kinds of information her audience would like to know. Based on past audience behavior she had observed, she made inferences about the people likely to attend her presentation. She felt safe in assuming, for example, that men and women who attend Home and School Association meetings are interested in improving the quality of their children's education and in learning how to become better parents. Her observations were basically sound because she had made them over a two-year period.

Mini-Exercise

Create a list of things that you have learned about your classmates by observing their behavior. Which pieces of information would be especially helpful to you in choosing a topic and developing a speech to deliver to them?

No doubt you have already learned a great deal about your classmates through observation. You already know the number of students in your class, the number of males and females, and their approximate ages. Through introductions, general conversation, and other interactions, you might know what subjects these students are majoring in, what campus groups they belong to, whether they hold jobs, what their interests are, and so on. You also have the unique opportunity to hear each of them give speech presentations. By listening carefully to each speech and observing others' reactions, you can learn a great deal about your classmates' attitudes, interests, values, and knowledge.

By now you also know the size of the classroom, the location of the speaker's podium (if there is one), the seating arrangement, the availability of audiovisual equipment, and other physical features of the environment. All of this information can help you when planning your speech presentation. In addition, you have had the opportunity to observe your instructor and to learn his or her views and expectations for your classroom performance. Thus, you can gather much information merely by being sensitive to what is going on around you.

Survey interviews.   A **survey interview** is a carefully planned and executed person-to-person question-and-answer session during which the speaker tries to discover specific information that will help in the preparation of a speech. Its purpose is to establish a solid base of fact from which to draw conclusions, make interpretations, and determine future courses of action. This method of audience research can be highly productive. To be most useful, however, surveys require a great deal of planning and organization. Consequently, this approach can consume much time and energy. Specific interviewing skills are discussed in more detail in the next chapter.

It is often impossible or impractical to survey every audience member. In such cases, you may prefer to use random sampling. In **random sampling,** a small group of interviewees is chosen from a larger group using a selection method which ensures that each individual has an equal chance of being selected. You can create your own random sample by writing each class-mate's name on a small piece of paper, placing all the names in a box, and then drawing out slips of paper equal to the number of students you wish to interview. If you have a truly random sample, the information you obtain should closely resemble the information you would have obtained if you had interviewed the entire audience.

Survey interviews can also be done over the telephone. After completing the survey, the interviewer usually codes the data, calculates totals, and tabulates percentages. The final stage is to analyze what the percentages mean and how they can be used in developing the speech's message.

To be successful, a survey interview requires preplanning and testing to make sure that the questions will be understood and will yield the desired information. Here are some guidelines that should help you get started:

1. Will the interviewees understand what is wanted and why?
2. Are the questions clear without further explanation?
3. Will the questions elicit the kind and amount of information desired?
4. How much probing will be necessary?
5. Will interviewees react negatively to any questions?
6. Are the answer categories adequate?
7. Do any of the questions reflect the interviewer's own biases?
8. Can the responses be tabulated easily and meaningfully?

Questionnaires. A **questionnaire** is a set of written questions that is distributed to respondents to gather desired information. The same questioning techniques used in survey interviews are also used in questionnaires. In some cases, questionnaires are more practical and take less time than interviews. They can be administered to large groups of people at the same time and respondents can remain anonymous, which often leads to greater honesty and openness.

To be successful, questionnaires must be skillfully planned. Although learning to develop good questionnaires takes much time and practice, here are some simple guidelines that should help you get started:

1. Decide exactly what information you want to gather.
2. Decide on the best method for making multiple copies of your questionnaire.

TABLE 6.1 *Sample Questionnaire*

Directions: Please check the response that indicates how strongly you agree or disagree with each statement. Do not write your name on this questionnaire.

1. War destroys the finest of a nation's young.

    _____ Strongly agree
    _____ Slightly agree
    _____ Undecided
    _____ Slightly disagree
    _____ Strongly disagree

2. War is sometimes necessary because defending what is right is more important than maintaining peace.

    _____ Strongly agree
    _____ Slightly agree
    _____ Undecided
    _____ Slightly disagree
    _____ Strongly disagree

3. Immoral acts committed by the armed forces of a country do not reflect the moral decay of its people.

    _____ Strongly agree
    _____ Slightly agree
    _____ Undecided
    _____ Slightly disagree
    _____ Strongly disagree

4. Generally, Americans believe in self-determination and self-government.

    _____ Strongly agree
    _____ Slightly agree
    _____ Undecided
    _____ Slightly disagree
    _____ Strongly disagree

3. Decide when, where, and how to distribute the questionnaire.
4. Plan the introduction to the questionnaire. Will the respondent need specific instructions?
5. Make sure your questions are clear and understandable.
6. Limit the number of possible responses to each question.
7. Keep the questionnaire as brief as possible.

Table 6.1 shows a typical questionnaire. Note that it provides simple instructions, it is brief, the questions are clear, and the number of possible responses is limited.

Knowing your audience is important to the planning of your speech. The easiest way to find out about your audience is through observation. Your success with this method will depend on the amount of experience you have with your audience and your ability to make accurate inferences. For most classroom situations, observation will yield adequate information, but if you seek more specific data, you may want to use a survey interview. A survey interview takes a lot of planning and time and is not very efficient. However, it does provide an opportunity to get information in person and to probe when necessary. Finally, if you are dealing with a large group, you may decide to gather information by using a questionnaire. Although good questionnaires take time to write, they can be administered more quickly than interviews and often yield more candid responses.

Analyzing Your Results and Adapting Them to Your Audience

The goals of observing, survey interviewing, and administering questionnaires are to learn about your audience and to discover any patterns in the information you have gathered. What conclusions can you draw? How certain can you be of them? How can you use what you've learned to improve your speech?

If your analysis is thorough and correct, you should have a fairly good picture of your audience—their relevant demographics, interests, knowledge levels, and attitudes toward the topic, the speaker, and the general situation.

Although your findings will rarely be uniform, you should be able to reach some general conclusions. You may find, for example, that 70 percent of your respondents strongly disagree that capital punishment should be used in our society, 15 percent have no opinion, and 15 percent strongly agree. These data suggest how your listeners will react to you and your speech. If your purpose is to persuade them that capital punishment should be used in our society, you will need to adjust your speech to meet a potentially strong opposition. To do so, you must answer two key questions: "How will you get those who oppose you to listen to what you have to say?" and "What can you say to include those who have no opinion or who strongly agree with you?"

Although it is never easy to win over people who oppose your views, you can try by discussing their views first and then by leading the audience into a discussion of your views. You should also use credible and unbiased sources that people are more likely to accept. In addition, you should acknowledge that your listeners' views have as much merit as yours, but assert that your views foretell a better solution to the crime problem.

If your research indicates that your audience has little or no opinion about the information you are presenting, you need to provoke their interest. Begin by telling why they should listen to what you have to say and by showing how the topic relates to them personally. Focus on helping them recognize the benefits and importance of your topic, and remember that clearly communicating your own enthusiasm can also help to generate their interest.

Finally, when you are dealing with an audience that agrees with you and what you have to say, you need to acknowledge that you all share the same point of view. For example, if you and your audience agree that a new auditorium should be built, note your shared agreement and then go on to talk about what can be done to get the new facility built. In the process, you might try to strengthen their beliefs.

The crucial point is that no matter what your audience's position on your topic may be, your research enables you to identify it in advance. You can use this information to pursue your specific purpose. Of course, the more information you have available to you, the better equipped you will be to adapt your speech to your audience.

MINI-EXERCISE

Your specific purpose is to persuade your classmates that a higher student fee is needed to support more student activities on campus. Your survey of your class indicates that 30 percent favor the increase, 50 percent are moderately opposed, 10 percent are strongly opposed, and 10 percent don't care one way or the other. Explain how you might plan your speech to meet your audience's views.

SUMMARY

Public speaking is the presentation of a speech, usually prepared in advance, during which the speaker is the central focus of an audience's attention. The ability to speak in front of others will not only aid you in your career, but will also help you to develop writing, listening, organizing, researching, and reasoning skills. A great deal of time and effort are required to become a capable speaker, but the rewards are well worth it.

When selecting a topic, choose an area that you already know something about and that is of interest to you and your audience. Two methods of finding topics are *self-inventory*—an analysis of your own interests—and *brainstorming*—an attempt to generate as many ideas as possible in a limited amount of time. Once you have selected a subject, you must determine its appropriateness for you and your audience. Then you need to narrow and focus your scope to meet the situation and time requirements.

A speech should serve one of three *general purposes: to inform,* enhance the audience's knowledge and understanding; *to persuade,* attempt to advocate or gain acceptance for the speaker's point of view; or *to entertain,* provide enjoyment and amusement. Rarely, however, does a speech serve a single general purpose exclusively. More often, the three purposes overlap.

Part of the narrowing and focusing of a speech is the formulation of a specific purpose—a single phrase that specifies precisely what the speech is intended to accomplish. The clearer the specific purpose is, the easier it is to plan, research, and develop a successful speech.

Effective speakers know that they must tailor their speeches to their *audience.* The more speakers know about their audience's past experiences, knowledge and attitudes toward a subject, and reasons for attendance, the easier it is to develop speeches that are meaningful and relevant. An *audience analysis* can provide the kind of basic information a speaker needs to ensure success.

Although audience members vary greatly in their personal traits and reasons for attendance, they can be divided into two basic categories based on the nature of their participation. *Captive participants* are audience members who are required to hear a particular speaker or speech, while *voluntary participants* are audience members who choose to hear a particular speaker or speech because of some personal interest or need.

To be fully prepared, a speaker needs to gather two kinds of information about an audience—demographic and psychological. In a *demographic analysis*, a speaker researches an audience to discover such basic information as age, gender, cultural and ethnic background, education, occupation, religion, geographic location, and group membership. In a *psychological analysis*, a speaker collects data about audience members' values, attitudes, and beliefs. It is an extension of the demographic analysis and usually builds on it. A psychological analysis seeks to determine how the audience will react to the speaker, the speaker's topic, and the surroundings in which the speech is presented. The size of the audience, the physical setting for the presentation, the knowledge level of the audience, and the audience's attitude toward the speaker, toward the topic, and toward the situation all play vital roles in the planning, development, and delivery of a speech.

The three most common ways of gathering information about an audience are through observation, survey interviews, and questionnaires. The *observation* method relies on the speaker's perceptions of the audience's behaviors and characteristics. It is the easiest way to gather information about an audience, but its accuracy relies on the amount of experience a speaker has had with the audience and his or her ability to draw reliable conclusions. The *survey interview* is a carefully planned and executed person-to-person question-and-answer session. Its purpose is to gather facts about the audience that will help the speaker to plan a course of action. Because survey interviews can be very time-consuming, many speakers will use a *random sampling* to avoid having to talk to every audience member. Finally, some speakers use a *questionnaire*, or set of written questions, to gather information. This is a very efficient way to reach large numbers of people all at one time.

No matter what information-gathering technique you use, you must analyze the results with the goal of understanding the audience and discovering any patterns that will help in the development of your speech. A thorough and correct analysis should give you a fairly good picture of your listeners—their relevant demographics, interest and knowledge levels, and attitudes toward your topic, you as the speaker, and the general situation. Once you have completed your analysis, you can use your findings to adapt your speech to the needs and interests of your audience. As a result, your audience should have little difficulty answering the question "What's in it for me?"

KEY TERMS

Audience: a collection of individuals who have come together for a specific reason—to hear a speech.

Audience Analysis: the collection and interpretation of data about the basic characteristics, attitudes, values, and beliefs of an audience.

Brainstorming: a technique used to generate as many ideas as possible in a limited amount of time.

Captive Participant: a person who is required to hear a particular speaker or speech.

Demographic Analysis: the collection and interpretation of characteristics (age, sex, religion, and so on) about individuals that excludes values, attitudes, and beliefs.

Entertainment Speech: a speech whose main function is to provide enjoyment and amusement.

General Purpose: the overall goal of a speech, which is usually to perform one of three overlapping functions—to inform, to persuade, or to entertain.

Informative Speech: a speech that enhances an audience's knowledge and understanding by explaining what something means, how something works, or how something is done.

Observation: an audience research method in which the speaker watches audience members and notes their behaviors and characteristics.

Persuasive Speech: a speech that attempts to change listeners' attitudes or behavior by advocating or trying to gain acceptance for the speaker's point of view.

Psychological Analysis: the collection and interpretation of data about audience members' values, attitudes, and beliefs.

Public Speaking: the presentation of a speech, usually prepared in advance, during which the speaker is the central focus of an audience's attention.

Questionnaire: a set of written questions that is distributed to respondents to gather desired information.

Random Sampling: a method of selecting a small number of interviewees from a larger group so that every individual has an equal chance of being selected.

Self-Inventory: an analysis of one's own interests used in choosing a speech topic.

Specific Purpose: a single phrase that defines precisely what is to be accomplished in a speech.

Survey Interview: a carefully planned and executed person-to-person question-and-answer session during which the speaker tries to discover specific information that will help in the preparation of a speech.

Voluntary Participant: a person who chooses to hear a particular speaker or speech.

DISCUSSION STARTERS

1. Why is it important to be an effective speaker?

2. How can being an effective speaker help you to be more successful?

3. Name three speakers whom you find to be especially effective. What contributes to their effectiveness?

4. Your best friend has been asked to give a speech, but the topic has been left open. What advice would you give him or her about choosing an appropriate topic?

5. Describe the criteria you would use to determine whether a speech topic is appropriate for you and your audience.

6. Why are a general purpose and a specific purpose statement necessary to the development of a speech?

7. In what ways can an audience analysis help you in the development and delivery of a speech?

8. Why do you think most people are egocentric? What can a speaker do to take this into account?

9. Which audience, in your opinion, would be easiest to address: an audience of captive participants, an audience of voluntary participants, or an audience of both captive and voluntary participants? Why?

10. You are preparing to speak on the need for stricter laws governing illegal drugs and are uncertain of your audience's views. What should you know about your audience? How would you go about getting the information you need?

11. Why is it important to know your audience's attitudes toward you before you give a speech?

12. What information can a psychological analysis of your audience provide?

13. What can you do to adapt your speech to your audience?

FURTHER READINGS

Dance, Frank E. X., and Carol Zak-Dance. *Public Speaking*. New York: Harper & Row, Publishers, Inc., 1986.

Ehninger, Douglas, Bruce E. Gronbeck, and Alan H. Monroe. *Principles of Speech Communication*. 9th Brief Edition. Glenview, Ill.: Scott, Foresman and Company, 1984.

Hunt, Gary T. *Public Speaking*. 2nd Ed. Englewood Cliffs, New Jersey: Prentice-Hall, 1987.

Linkugel, Wil A., R. R. Allen, and Richard L. Johannesen. *Contemporary American Speeches: A Sourcebook of Speech Forms and Principles*. 5th Ed. Dubuque, Iowa: Kendall/Hunt, 1982.

Lucas, Stephen E. *The Art of Public Speaking*. 2nd Ed. New York: Random House, Inc., 1986.

Ryan, Halford Ross. *American Rhetoric from Roosevelt to Reagan: A Collection of Speeches and Critical Essays*. Prospect Heights, Ill.: Waveland Press, Inc., 1983.

Sprague, Jo, and Douglas Stuart. *The Speaker's Handbook*. Harcourt Brace Jovanovich, San Diego, 1984.

Verderber, Rudolph F. *The Challenge of Effective Speaking*. 6th Ed. Belmont, Calif.: Wadsworth, 1986.

NOTES

1. Kendall Edgerton, Kathleen, "Do Real People Give Speeches?", *Central States Speech Journal* 25, No. 3 (Fall 1974): pp. 233–235.

2. Trent, Jimmie D., and W. Charles Redding, "A Survey of Communication Opinions of Executives in Large Corporations," Unpublished Special Report, No. 8, Purdue University, (September, 1964).

CHAPTER 7

Gathering and Using Information

After studying this chapter, you should be able to:

1. Identify three principal sources of information about a speech topic and indicate how each contributes to the research process.

2. Use the library to gather information for a speech.

3. Cite four guidelines that can make the research process more efficient and effective.

4. Explain how testimony, examples, definitions, and statistics can be used to support and clarify a speaker's message.

5. Employ supporting and clarifying materials to enhance the impact of a speech.

Dana has been working part-time in the radiology lab at a local hospital. She knows from her work that lasers are fast becoming the technology of the future in the health care industry. Therefore, when she needed to present an informative speech in her communications class, she decided to speak on the medical uses of the laser in the United States.

To prepare for her speech, Dana interviewed several radiologists and surgeons about their use of lasers. She read an article about the latest developments in laser technology, but when she sat down to outline her presentation, Dana realized that she didn't have enough information to speak for the five to seven minutes required by her instructor. Because she wasn't going to work for a few days, she decided to research her subject more thoroughly in the school library. There she found more than enough additional information to fulfill her assignment.

By the time Dana had finished gathering information, she had drawn on her own personal experiences, spoken with other people, and read the most recent printed sources she could find. By being so thorough in gathering information, she had taken a crucial step toward developing a first-rate speech.

Gathering information takes time and effort, but it is one of the most rewarding aspects of developing a speech. It is rewarding because you learn from the information that you gather and because without such information, you couldn't make a speech. The information that you gather eventually becomes the backbone of your speech. Consequently, your speech can only be as good as the information you use. For this reason, this chapter focuses on how to research a topic and how to use the information you find to support and clarify what you have to say.

GATHERING INFORMATION

Some professional speakers believe that every ten minutes of speaking time requires at least ten hours of research and preparation time. Though such a rule of thumb is arbitrary, it is not unusual for speakers to devote at least that much time to research. Therefore, it is wise to start gathering materials for your speech as soon as possible. How much information is enough? There is no magic amount, but the more information you have, the better equipped you are to design and develop your presentation and adapt it to your audience. Of course, quality is more important than quantity—especially when your time is limited. That is why it is important to develop your research skills. The more skilled you become at doing research, the better use you will make of your time.

Using Yourself as a Source of Information

If you want to make the best use of your time and gather the best information, where should you begin? The most often suggested answer is with yourself. You are one of the most valuable sources of information available. Your personal experiences can contribute to the contents of your speech. Recall that in Chapter 6, when we discussed how to choose a speech topic, we suggested that you begin by examining your own interests. Chances are, if you're excited about a topic, you can inspire excitement in your listeners as well. Probing your own knowledge of a subject can also help you organize your thoughts, develop a research plan, and, eventually, save you a great deal of time.

The Interview as a Source of Information

Of course, you may not always have firsthand experience with a topic, or your own knowledge may not be sufficient. In such cases, you may want to interview other people for information. A good interviewer can often discover information that could never be obtained from other sources.

As we discussed in Chapter 6, an **interview** is a carefully planned and executed person-to-person question-and-answer session during which a speaker tries to discover specific information that will help in the preparation of a speech. An important characteristic of an interview is that it involves the constant exchange of messages between two individuals—that is, both persons interchange the roles of sender and receiver as they respond to one another. In addition, an interview includes messages that may be nonverbal as well as verbal, and unintentional as well as intentional. Like all communication, no two interviews can ever be identical. They will vary from person to person, from topic to topic, and from situation to situation.

Due to its personal nature, an interview calls for the same skills and insight as social conversation. It also requires careful preparation, including the establishment of a clear, well-thought-out plan for obtaining the needed information.

Above all, an effective interviewer should be able to adapt his or her interview to the other person. For this to occur, at least one and preferably both of the participants should have an understanding of listening and feedback (Chapter 5), nonverbal communication (Chapter 4), and interpersonal communication (Chapter 12).

Planning an Interview. You need to consider many things before you actually interview someone. First, you must determine the kind of information you seek and formulate a clear and concise general objective. Then, you must decide whom to interview and how to budget your time during the interview so that it will be as productive as possible.

Interviewees. Selecting the right persons to interview is essential in determining the quality of the information you will receive. You should ask yourself the following questions:

- Which individuals have the information I need?
- How credible are they?
- Are they willing to share this information openly and honestly with me?
- Who is accessible?

Interviewees are usually selected because of their particular positions or expertise. Because they usually hold high positions, they may have unusually busy schedules, so you should always set up an appointment for an interview.

Before the interview, try to get as much background information as possible on both your topic and your interviewee. The more background information you have, the better equipped you will be to conduct the interview. Obtaining information about the topic or the person may require some library work or may even involve interviewing others in preparation for the main interview.

MINI-EXERCISE

Whom would you consider interviewing if you were planning to speak on the following topics?

Subject Area   *Interviewees*
The High Cost of Auto Insurance   An insurance agent
                                                         The state director of insurance
                                                         Several insurance policyholders

Air Traffic Safety
Prison Reform
The High Cost of Education
Test-Tube Babies
Corruption in Athletics

Which individuals would be more likely to give you unbiased information? Why?

Organizing the interview. An interview usually has three identifiable segments—an opening, a body, and a closing. Each can vary in content and length. What is included in each segment depends on you, your purpose, the inteviewee, and the situation.

1. *The Opening:* The **opening** can vary from a brief introduction to a lengthy explanation. During the opening, you should try to put your interviewee at ease, state your purpose, and provide appropriate background information, if needed. A typical introduction might be:

> Good morning, Dr. Kay. My name is Julie Smith and I'm a student at the university. I'm delighted that you're willing to visit with me. I know how busy you must be, so I'll only take about 15 minutes of your time. As you know from our phone conversation, I'm interested in learning more about you and the new computer facilities. I'm taking a speech communication course and will be giving a speech on this topic. I'd like to tape-record the information because I'm not good at note-taking and I want to make sure I get everything you say as accurately as possible. Do you mind? Good. Let's begin.

Openings, of course, may be much shorter, but when you and the interviewee do not know each other, it is important to be as informative as possible. Many times, the success or failure of the interview is determined by the way the opening is handled.

2. *The Body:* The **body,** which is the main part of an interview, consists of the questions and answers. The body may be flexible, with no specific plan or sequence, or it may follow a specific outline, with little or no flexibility. Within the general limitations of the purpose, the situation, and

the persons involved, interviewing methods may vary widely. Some situations, such as an audience analysis, require a highly structured interview format to ensure that all interviewees are asked the same questions. In contrast, a news conference may require more flexibility to make sure that the questions are adapted to the interviewee's responses. In more informal settings, two interview formats are likely to be used: nonscheduled and moderately scheduled.

In a **nonscheduled interview,** the interviewer follows a central objective or a list of possible topics and subtopics. The discussions on the "Phil Donahue Show" and the "Tonight Show" with Johnny Carson, for example, are nonscheduled interviews. The principal advantages of this format are its openness, which permits greater probing, and its flexibility, which allows changes in the direction of the discussion. The primary disadvantage is that the interviewer must be highly skilled.

In a **moderately scheduled interview,** the interviewer works from a prepared list of basic questions or topics accompanied by related possible probes. This kind of interview might be sequenced as follows:

1. What do you like most about the team-policing concept in your community?
   a. What about police service?
   b. What about the crime rate?
   c. What about home security?
2. What do you think of our city's beautification program?
   a. What about the trees on Main Street?
   b. What about the new streetlights?
   c. What about wider streets?

The greatest advantage of the moderately scheduled interview, especially for inexperienced interviewers, is that it is easy to use because it is planned in advance. Preplanning relieves the interviewer from concentrating too much on the questions that need to be asked, but at the same time, it allows for probing and flexibility. In addition, this method shows the interviewee that the interviewer is well prepared for the interview.

3. *The Closing:* The final portion of the interview process is the **closing.** As the interviewer, you must, at some point, decide that you have obtained all possible information, or that you have used up your time. You must then be ready to conclude the interview, a step that can be one of the most difficult aspects of interviewing. Closing should be done with sensitivity and timing, so that the meeting is not stopped too abruptly or carried past the point of relevancy.

The ability to end an interview effectively comes from experience and knowing how to control the direction of a conversation. In most instances you can end an interview easily by expressing appreciation to the interviewee for his or her cooperation and time. Then, you should summarize the information you have learned. Do not close, however, until you have either reached your interview objective or accomplished as much of your objective as time will allow. If you have not achieved your purpose, indicate that a future meeting may be necessary. Never overstay your welcome!

Other Considerations.   Factors such as dressing appropriately, being punctual, and listening attentively can also contribute to the success of an interview. Because attire can make a difference in how you are received, you must use your judgment when determining what to wear in a given situation. Presenting a businesslike appearance shows that you respect the person you are interviewing. Being on time for an interview is essential. One of the most disrespectful things an interviewer can do is to be late, so plan to be at least ten minutes early. If, for some reason, you will be late, call the interviewee as soon as possible to notify him or her. Finally, give the interviewee your undivided attention throughout the discussion.

The best way to ensure an effective interview is to use common sense and to prepare yourself as much as possible beforehand. For a more detailed discussion about interviewing and interviewing strategies see Chapter 15.

The Library as a Source of Information[1]

After class one day, a student came to her teacher and said, "I can't find enough information on my topic." "Oh?" the professor inquired in a tone of surprise, knowing that the topic was space technology. "What did you find in the library?" The student quickly responded, "I didn't go to the library." The professor didn't know whether to laugh, cry, or just feel sorry for the student. How sad that this student had not considered the library as a resource for her speech.

Making use of library resources does require some effort, but once you understand how the system works—and most libraries use essentially the same system—you will find that it is the most useful and beneficial resource for speech preparation. If you do not know how to locate reference materials, now is the time to learn. Start by taking a tour or attending one of the orientation sessions that many libraries offer. Some also provide educational packages with instructions on how to use the library. If you do not utilize your library, you will be at a disadvantage not only in your speech class, but in all your other classes as well.

After your tour or orientation session, you need to practice using the library. There are four principal sources of information in the library: yourself, the librarian, the card catalog, and the reference department.

Start with Yourself.   To create an effective speech, you must be willing to go to the library and work hard on your research. But you can save much time and effort if you determine in advance what information you are seeking. For example, if your specific purpose is to inform your audience of the effects of pornography on society, begin your library search armed with the key words *pornography, pornography effects,* and *pornography and society.* As you search the subject catalog and the reference indexes, you will

FIGURE 7.1

Card Catalog
Listings of the
Same Book by
Author, Title,
and Subject

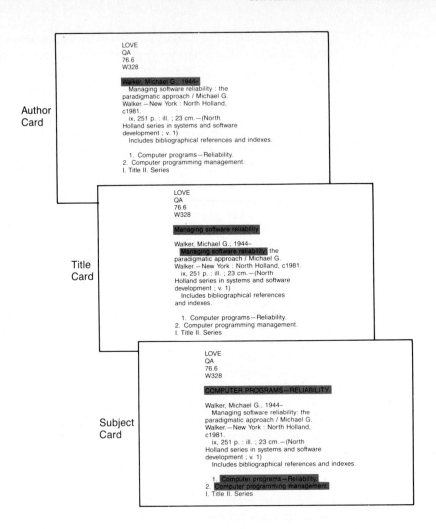

probably find a number of words related to your key words and you may discover that some of your key words are not listed. You can then adjust your search accordingly. Knowing what you want, however, is still the best starting place for a library search.

Ask the Librarian. Librarians are exceptionally well trained to serve you and anyone else who needs information. Helping library users is part of their job. When you don't know how to find something—ask! Some students are afraid to request assistance, but even experienced library users frequently seek help from the librarian, an expert who is your most valuable resource when searching for information.

Use the Card Catalog. The card catalog, an index to all the books in the library, is designed to be a quick and easy means of locating materials. Most card catalogs list books in three ways: by author's last name, by title, and by subject. Figure 7.1 illustrates the three kinds of listings. Entries in the card catalog are listed alphabetically.

Periodicals, which include magazines, professional journals, newspapers, and serials, are listed by title or by the name of the issuing body, such as Modern Language Association or American Council on the Teaching of Foreign Languages. To find a specific piece of information or a magazine article, you must go to the reference department.

Use the Reference Department. Most library research begins in the research department, which contains all the books needed for easy access to specific subject areas. Available here are dictionaries, almanacs, biographical aids, encyclopedias, yearbooks, newspapers, atlases, bibliographies, indexes, and guides to periodical literature.

There are many different specialized indexes—for example, Agriculture & Natural Resources Indexes, Business, Economics & Statistics Indexes, Biology & Life Sciences Indexes, Computer Indexes, Education Indexes, and History Indexes—that provide information about virtually every subject. (See the Appendix at the end of this chapter for a more complete list.) But the index that is probably the most widely used by beginning speech students is the *Readers' Guide to Periodical Literature.* This useful index to popular periodicals lists articles from over 190 different magazines. Issues of the guide, published semimonthly or monthly, are bound separately for the latest publications and are bound in volumes for publications that are a year or more old.

Entries in the *Readers' Guide* are listed alphabetically by author and subject. For example, if you are interested in the most recent information on computers, look in the latest issue of the *Readers' Guide* under the subject heading "computers." If "computers" is not listed, keep searching earlier issues until you find it. Each article that has been written about computers is also listed alphabetically. The *Readers' Guide* also lists subheadings for special areas related to computers. A typical listing would look like this:

SUBJECT HEADING: COMPUTERS

SUBHEADING: Educational Use

ARTICLE: The impact on today's children. C. Spencer. il Pers Comput 10:153–7 O '86.

The citation includes the article's title, the author's name, the title of the periodical, the volume, the pages, and the date.

The *Readers' Guide,* if used correctly, can be an extremely valuable resource. However, many other indexes can be used to locate information on various subjects. If you are uncertain or don't know what is available, ask the librarian.

Finding materials is generally quite simple, especially after you have familiarized yourself with the library and its organization. Since most libraries have so many kinds of materials shelved in so many locations, they assign retrieval numbers and codes in order to provide complete addresses for all of them. The retrieval numbers and codes tell you exactly where materials are located and in what form they can be found. If you have trouble locating any material, see the librarian. He or she will guide you.

Commonly Used Resources.   Because magazines, journals, and newspapers have the most recently available information on a subject, they are the most often used resources for speech writing. If you want to know the latest opinions and trends for almost any social, political, or economic issue, weekly magazines and newspapers will probably be your best resources. Or, if you are looking for specific scientific research, journals may be your best alternative.

Because magazine and newspaper articles are usually brief and written for a general audience, they are very rich sources of basic information for speeches. Given their briefness, you can read several articles in order to gather differing points of view. In addition, libraries not only have local and state newspapers, but they also usually have major newspapers from all over the world, which can provide you with an even broader perspective.

Encyclopedias are another good starting place for ideas and introductory information, particularly in fields with which you are unfamiliar. Libraries usually have a variety of encyclopedia sets that contain short articles written by experts.

If you do not know what your library has to offer, take time to learn about it. The search for knowledge is never easy, but thought and preparation will enable you to find ample information about almost any speech topic.

Suggestions for Doing Research

There are few shortcuts to doing good research, but ways do exist that make research more enjoyable and less tedious. Here are several suggestions:

1. *State a Clear Purpose Before Starting Your Research.* Knowing what information you want to find makes researching a topic much easier. If, for example, the purpose of your speech is to inform your audience about the importance of maintaining a good diet, the key word in your purpose statement would be *diet.* Therefore, your search for information should begin with *diet,* followed by *maintaining* and the *importance* of a good diet. Thinking of other key words will help lead you to topics related to diet, such as *nutrition* and *health.* Considering all the possible areas of research in advance will help to eliminate the potential frustration of not knowing what to look for.

2. *Begin Your Research Early.* Because finding appropriate materials takes time, you should start your research as soon as possible. If you wait until the last minute, you may discover that the materials you need are unavailable or that it takes longer to find them than you anticipated.

MINI-EXERCISE

Before you reach for that first catalog drawer, take a few minutes. Relax. Analyze your topic and plan your approach. Warm up your brain.

One good way to begin is to see if you can break your topic down into component parts. Let's say you are interested in finding out about Japanese management techniques, particularly those related to dealing with employees. One way to break this subject down is to list the key words *management, employees, Japan.* Or, if you are looking for material about course content in Christian schools, you might break your subject down into the key words *course content, schools, Christian religion.*

The next step is to expand your list of key words to include phrases that help to further define your topic. In the first example, you might choose *personnel management* and *employment policies.* In the second, *curriculum* would be an alternative to *course content. Schools* and *Christian religion* could be expressed as *denominational schools, church-supported education, sectarian schools,* and *parochial schools.*

This process allows you to clarify what you want before you begin the search process and helps you overcome one of the most common obstacles to good subject researching—a too-narrow view of the terminology needed to define a subject. Try this procedure with your own subject.[2]

3. *Maintain a Bibliography of Sources.* As you find sources in the card catalog and periodical guide, copy them in the same form onto a sheet of paper or index cards (3" × 5" or 4" × 6"). List each item separately and make notes about its importance to your speech presentation. Although this can be a rather tedious job, it is essential that you keep track of the material you find.

4. *Take Notes.* Efficient and accurate note-taking is a must. Once you have located information, you must either record it by hand or photocopy it for later use in writing your speech. Whether you wish to quote a statement verbatim or only summarize or paraphrase it, you must record the original information accurately and completely. Take plenty of notes and always make sure that the source is fully and accurately indicated, as shown by the sample note cards in Figure 7.2. Nothing is more frustrating than having information and not knowing where it came from. Recording the source will also be helpful if you need to return to it for additional information. The more information you obtain, the better. You should always plan on having more than you will actually need to write your speech.

FIGURE 7.2

Sample Note
Cards

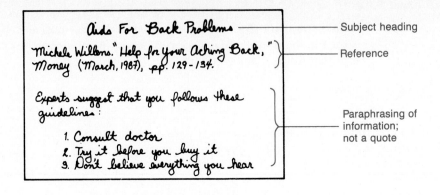

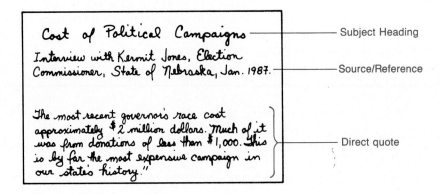

USING YOUR RESEARCH

Over 2000 years ago, Aristotle, a famous Greek scholar, wrote that there are essentially two parts to every speech—a statement and its proof. Aristotle's description is still valid today. How you clarify and support ideas in your speech is a consideration that should not be taken lightly.

THINK ABOUT IT

Consider the following statement:

> Students of today are far more advanced than the students of a decade ago. Today's students, for example, have access to computer technology, which has allowed them to advance at a much faster rate.

On the surface, this statement seems to have validity, but is it accurate and will an audience accept it at face value?

Audiences generally accept information based on one of two factors: the speaker's perceived believability or the perceived believability of the information itself. Thus the statement in the "Think About It" box would be more acceptable to most audiences if it were made by a well-known educator and researcher than if it were made by a student. Regardless of its source, a statement should be clearly explained and adequately supported. Most listeners require some proof or specific data before they completely accept a statement. Consequently, effective speakers *clarify* and *justify* each main idea in their speeches with a variety of supporting and clarifying materials.

Supporting and clarifying materials bring life to a speech. They can make the content of a speech appealing, vivid, exciting, meaningful, acceptable, and more useful to listeners.

MINI-EXERCISE

Compare these two paragraphs:

1. To what extent do males and females differ in the way they learn and communicate? The sexes are psychologically similar in many respects. Although some of the differences may have a biological basis, the existing evidence is conflicting.
2. To what extent do males and females differ in the way they learn and communicate? Eleanor Maccoby and Carol Jacklin, two widely respected psychologists and authors, report in their book, *The Psychology of Sex Differences*, that "the sexes are psychologically much alike in many respects." Although some of the differences in behavior—such as the superior verbal ability of girls and accelerated math skills of boys—may have a biological basis, a great deal of conflicting evidence surrounds such differences.

Which paragraph do you find to be more meaningful? More acceptable? More interesting? More useful? Why?

The quantity and quality of a speaker's supporting and clarifying materials plus the speaker's ability to use them correctly usually make the difference between a mediocre speech and a very good one. Thus, in this section we will focus on the basic kinds of supporting and clarifying materials used in speeches: testimony, examples, definitions, and statistics.

Citing Testimony to Support and Clarify

When speakers use opinions or conclusions of recognized witnesses or authorities, they are using **testimony**. Testimony usually supports or reinforces points that speakers want their audiences to accept. The value of testimony is related both to the listeners' opinion of its acceptability and to the speaker who presents it.

Consider this paraphrased opening of a student's speech:

> You try to stop yourself, but for some reason you can't. The child keeps on screaming, "Mommie, Mommie, please don't hit me anymore!" You've lost control and until your rage subsides, you can't stop, even though you know you should. Not until you are caught or you do something severely harmful is anything done about it. When it's all over, you have inflicted the worst kind of human atrocity on your own child. How do I know this? Because I used to beat my own child until I got help.[3]

The young woman who gave this speech had her audience's attention not only because of the story she was recounting, but also because she had the courage to relate what she had done and how she had overcome it. Her abuse of her own child did not enhance her believability and create acceptance for what she was saying, but her willingness to admit that she was personally involved in her topic did.

The use of testimony usually adds trustworthiness to what a speaker says—a necessity for all speakers who are not yet established as experts on their chosen speech topic. The speaker's own experience can be an excellent form of testimony, as in the previous example. But when the speaker's experience is insufficient, then the use of a recognized and trusted authority can be invaluable in gaining listeners' acceptance.

Testimony can be used as either supporting or clarifying material, or both. Here is an example of testimony that supports and clarifies:

> The following statement by the American Automobile Association sums up experiments too numerous to mention and represents the best current professional opinion on automotive safety: "We know that seat belts, if used properly and at all times, can save hundreds of lives each year. By 'used properly' we mean that both the shoulder and seat belts must be fastened."[4]

Here the speaker adds support by citing the American Automobile Association as a source of information and at the same time clarifies what seat belts can do—if "used properly" they can save lives.

Testimony can be either quoted directly, as the speaker did in the seat belt example, or paraphrased, as in the example about child abuse. Paraphrasing is an effective method of condensing a long text or clarifying a passage that is too technical for audience members to understand. Sometimes audience members tune out speakers who use long and complex quotations. Thus, restating long quotations in your own words adds interest and makes the source's words fit in with the tone of your speech.

Short Quotations.   The quotations you use in a speech should make your ideas clear and memorable. Certain statements are so well phrased that they could not be stated any better. An example is this forceful and unforgettable statement by John F. Kennedy in his 1960 presidential inaugural address: "Ask not what your country can do for you—ask what you can do for your country." Always quote such statements word for word.

The Importance of Accuracy.   Misquoting someone can be embarrassing but, even worse, it can destroy your believability. Always double-check each quotation for its accuracy and source, and never use a quotation out of context. Finally, if you paraphrase, make sure you do not violate the meaning of the original statement.

Qualified Sources.   The person you quote should be a qualified authority on the subject to which the testimony relates. To hear athletes endorse tennis shoes or movie stars endorse cosmetics is common and fairly believable since they use such products in their work. But when celebrities advertise products completely unrelated to their expertise, their testimony becomes less believable.

The qualifications of the person or organization that you are citing should be consistent with the point you are making. Listeners will find you and your speech more believable when you use qualified sources.

Unbiased Sources.   Testimony should meet two essential tests: the person who is cited must be qualified by virtue of his or her skills, training, expertise, recognition and reputation; and the testimony must be acceptable and believable to your listeners.

For maximum believability, the testimony you use should also come from objective sources. Using objective and neutral authorities is particularly valuable when your subject is controversial. In trying to persuade an audience, for example, that today's automobiles are safer than those of a decade ago, it is more convincing to quote the American Automobile Association or the National Safety Council than the president of an automotive manufacturing company. Listeners tend to be suspicious of opinions from a biased or self-interested source. When citing testimony, avoid using celebrities' names solely because they are well known. The best testimony comes from a person whose expertise is related to the topic and who is recognized by your listeners.

USING TESTIMONY: SOME TIPS

- Use testimony when you need expert opinion to support what you say.
- Use recognized, qualified, unbiased, and trusted authorities whenever possible.
- Cite sources completely and accurately.
- Keep quotations short and relevant to what you are saying.
- Paraphrase long and difficult quotations in your own words.
- When you use a quotation, make sure that it is absolutely accurate.

Presenting Examples to Clarify

An **example** is a simple, representative incident or model that clarifies a point. Examples are useful when you are presenting complex information to listeners who are unfamiliar with a topic and when you are informing or instructing. Brief examples, illustrations, analogies, and restatements are four kinds of examples that help to make things clearer for an audience.

Brief Examples. A **brief example** is a specific instance that is used to introduce a topic, drive home a point, or create a desired impression. The following brief example was used to introduce a subtopic related to the main topic of genius:

> One of the most striking findings that runs through the research on creativity is how hard creative geniuses work. For example, Edison once said, "Genius is 1 percent inspiration and 99 percent perspiration."

A series of brief examples can also be used to create a desired impression:

> Edison himself held 1093 patents. Albert Einstein wrote 248 publications. Pablo Picasso averaged 200 works of art a year. Wolfgang Amadeus Mozart had more than 600 compositions to his credit before he died at age 35.

Brief examples can be used in limitless ways to help support or clarify a point you wish to make.

Illustrations. An **illustration,** or extended example, is a narrative, case history, or anecdote that is striking and memorable. Illustrations often exemplify concepts, conditions, or circumstances, or demonstrate the findings that have been obtained through the acceptance of a plan or proposal.

If an example is not fully explained or detailed, but refers to a single aspect or event, it is an illustration. Because illustrations go into more detail than brief examples, they are useful in establishing proof. When the earlier examples regarding genius are put together, they form the following illustration:

> One of the most striking findings that runs through the research is how hard these creative giants work.
>
> "Genius is 1 percent inspiration and 99 percent perspiration," according to Thomas Alva Edison. It seems he was right.
>
> Edison himself held 1093 patents. Albert Einstein wrote 248 publications. Pablo Picasso averaged over 200 works of art a year. Wolfgang Amadeus Mozart had more than 600 compositions to his credit before he died at age 35.
>
> "For the most part, they tend to start earlier and end later," Simonton says. "The idea of early burnout—that if you start early, you end early—is not true."
>
> "Something appears to drive these creators to venture into the world of truth or beauty at an early age, to contribute masterworks at a hectic pace and to continue their creative endeavors until late in life."[5]

An illustration provides depth and explanation to the point a speaker is trying to make. It also gives the information more meaning. An illustration may be either factual or hypothetical. A **factual illustration** tells what has actually happened, while a **hypothetical illustration** tells what could or probably would happen given a specific set of circumstances.

A hypothetical illustration, because it is conjecture, asks listeners to use their imaginations. Such examples are often short stories that relate to a general principle or concept. One instructor used the following hypothetical example to help her students envision how to use their voices when delivering an emotional speech:

> Imagine that an angry mob has accused your friend of a crime—a serious crime—and that they are going to hang him because they believe he is guilty, even though you know he isn't. Your only chance to save your friend is to persuade the unruly mob that he is innocent.

This episode, even though it is hypothetical, demonstrates that people who are involved in serious situations must use their voices to make their point. The speech to the mob would have to be vivid, forceful, convincing, and delivered at a highly emotional level.

The use of a hypothetical illustration can be particularly effective when it involves the listeners. The more realistic the situation, the more likely it is that the listeners will become involved. Despite the desirability of realism, however, a speaker should always specify whether an illustration is factual or hypothetical.

Analogies.   An **analogy** is a comparison of two things that are similar in certain essential characteristics. Analogies explain or prove the unknown by comparing it to the known.

There are two kinds of analogies: figurative and literal. A **figurative analogy** draws comparisons between things in different categories. For example, the thermostat, whose workings are understood by most people, could be used to explain communication feedback. The thermostat reacts to the temperature in a room and sends messages back to the furnace. In like manner, communication feedback provides reactions to a communicator. A **literal analogy** compares members of the same category—for example, two universities, two football teams, or two cities.

Most speech topics offer many opportunities to use analogies. Generally, figurative analogies make ideas clear and vivid, while literal analogies supply evidence to prove points. Not only are analogies an effective and creative means of proving a point and clarifying information, but they are also efficient because they use fewer words to communicate information.

Restatements.   A **restatement** is the expression of the same idea using different words. It includes the use of summaries, synonyms, rephrasing, and repetition. In contrast to restatement, repetition is the expression of the same item using the *same* words.

Restatement does not provide evidence, but it often has a persuasive effect. If well planned, restatement adds clarity and meaning to a message. Martin Luther King, Jr., in his famous "I Have a Dream" speech, used both repetition and restatement to make his point:

> I say to you today, my friends, so even though we face the difficulties of today and tomorrow, I still have a dream. It is a dream deeply rooted in the American dream.
>
>   I have a dream that one day this nation will rise up and live out the true meaning of its creed, "We hold these truths to be self-evident, that all men are created equal."
>
>   I have a dream that one day on the red hills of Georgia the sons of former slaves and sons of former slave owners will be able to sit down together at the table of brotherhood.[6]

King repeated the phrase "I have a dream that one day . . . " six times in the course of his speech, and each time he made the same point by using a different example to support the conclusion that one day all people will be treated equally.

Another example of restatement can be seen in the following:

During the last part of the season, our football team was inconsistent and often scored fewer points than our opponents. Putting it another way, our defense did not hold up through the last half of the season as well as our offense. In still a different sense, this means that if we are going to win the national championship, we must work together as a team and strengthen our weak areas.

Thus, you can see that restatement can be a valuable method of presenting an idea from several different perspectives.

USING EXAMPLES: SOME TIPS

- Whenever possible use factual examples to add authenticity to your presentation. A factual example builds on the basic information presented and adds believability to both you and your speech.
- Use examples that are realistic and relate directly to your discussion. If you try to generalize from unusual or rare situations, you risk undermining your believability.
- Make sure that your examples are authentic, accurate, and verifiable. Always give credit to the source of an example so that your listeners can verify it. °

Using Definitions to Explain

You must define all unfamiliar words and concepts for your audience. Nothing is more bothersome to an audience than a speaker who uses terminology that they do not understand. You can use several different kinds of definitions to keep your audience's attention.

Logical Definitions. A **logical definition,** the most common form used by speakers, usually contains two parts: a term's dictionary definition and the characteristics that distinguish the term from other members of the same category. For example:

> *Sociology* is defined as an academic field of study—the science of society, social institutions, and social relationships. Its focus of study is the origin, development, organization, and function of human society.

This definition states exactly what sociology is and how it differs from other academic fields, such as communication, anthropology, biology, and chemistry. As a result, the listener should fully understand what the speaker is talking about.

Operational Definitions. An **operational definition** is used to explain how an object or concept works. Some operational definitions merely illustrate the steps that make up a process. For example:

> *Selective perception* is the choosing of stimuli we want to perceive and the ignoring of stimuli we do not want to perceive.
>
> The *mean* is the result of adding all the scores in a set of scores and dividing by the number of scores in the set.

Operational definitions can also explain how conceptual terms are measured:

> A *communicative apprehensive person* is defined as a person who scores 90 or above on the Personal Report of Communication Apprehension Test.

Definitions by Example. A common and effective method of explaining a term or concept is to use a **definition by example.** The example may be either spoken or literal. Look at the following:

> When I speak about large universities, I mean institutions such as the Universities of Wisconsin, Southern California, or Minnesota, each of which has an enrollment of over 30,000 students.
>
> A slalom water ski has a large fin on the bottom. Here is what it looks like. (The speaker shows an actual ski, diagram, or picture.)

Defining unfamiliar terms or concepts, especially those that are technical or complex, is a must if you expect your audience to understand and accept your speech. In most cases, it is better to offer too much explanation than too little. On the other hand, you do not want to patronize your audience by explaining the obvious.

USING DEFINITIONS: SOME TIPS

- Keep definitions short and to the point. Do not make your explanation more complex than necessary.
- Use clear and concise language that your audience can easily understand.
- Define a term or concept whenever you suspect that your audience may not understand what you mean or if multiple interpretations are possible.
- Make your definitions come alive for your audience by providing examples.

Supplying Statistics to Summarize

Numerical data that show relationships between and among phenomena (variables, observations, collections), or that summarize and interpret many examples are known as **statistics.** Every day we are confronted with numerical analyses. We read, for example, that the earth's population is over 5 billion, that the gross national product has increased by one-tenth of 1 percent, that in the past two years the enrollment at the university has declined from 23,500 to 22,100, that 17 percent of all married couples prefer to have 1.7 children, and so on. Although statistics can point out some interesting information, they can be difficult to interpret.

Statistics enable speakers to summarize a large amount of data rapidly, to analyze specific occurrences or instances, to isolate trends, and to predict future events. Like examples, statistics are used to clarify and support a speaker's position. For example, consider these two statements:

> Many Americans were killed and wounded in the Vietnam conflict.
> Recent Department of Defense figures document that over 40,000 American men and women were killed and over 300,000 were wounded in the Vietnam conflict from 1961 to 1970.

The first statement, though accurate, does not tell us specifically what is meant by "many." Its vagueness makes it weak. The second statement, because it cites specific numbers, gives listeners a clearer picture of the situation and is thus more convincing.

Statistics can be used to emphasize the seriousness or magnitude of a particular issue, as seen in the following example:

> The October 23, 1983, issue of the *New York Times* reported some startling facts. It released the findings of the Gallup Poll Organization, who stated that there are about 500,000 incidents each year in which children of divorced couples are kidnapped by one of their parents.[7]

Statistics can also be informative:

> A glance at the statistics concerning survival rates best demonstrates the organ transplant's workability today. The *New York Times* June 19, 1983,

magazine edition reported that the one-year survival rate for heart transplant patients is 65 percent. Liver transplant patients have a 70-percent survival rate according to the October 1, 1983, issue of *Science News,* with the longest surviving patient living 13 years after the transplant. Even more interesting is the amount of success with kidney transplants, which now command a 90 to 97 percent survival rating.[8]

Statistics can be used in many ways to support or clarify your position on a given subject, but it is important to use them correctly.

Statistical Measures.   To accurately use and understand statistical data in speeches, you should know some basic statistical terminology. The four most commonly cited statistics are the mean, the median, the mode, and the range.

The **mean,** often referred to as the average, is the result of adding all the scores in a set of scores and dividing by the number of scores in the set. Note, for example, the sample data provided in Table 7.1. The scores of all nine students in Group A total 744 points. To find the mean, divide 744— the total of all the scores—by 9, the number of students in the group. In this way you find that the mean is 82.67. The mean for Group B would be similarly calculated: 739 ÷ 9 = 82.11.

The **median** is the middle score in a series of numbers. Because it is the middle score, half the scores are above the median and half are below it. In Table 7.1, since there are nine scores, the middle score is the fifth one. Thus, in Group A the median is 83 and in Group B it is 80.

TABLE 7.1   *Computing Statistics*

Here are two sets of scores from two different groups of students who took the same test:

	Group A	Group B
	90	95
	88	87
	86	87
	85	85
	83	80
	79	79
	79	77
	79	75
	75	74
	744	739
Mean (÷ 9)	82.67	82.11
Median (middle score)	83	80
Mode (most frequent score)	79	87
Range (highest and lowest numbers)	75 to 90	74 to 95

The **mode** is the most frequent score in a series of numbers. In Table 7.1, the mode in Group A is 79 because three students received that score. In Group B, two students scored 87, so that is the mode.

The **range** is the highest and lowest numbers in a series of numbers. The range for Group A is 75 to 90, and for Group B it is 74 to 95.

Knowing a set of data's mean, median, mode, and range is not enough. You must also ask yourself which data best represent each group's scores. When comparing the two sets of scores, which data provide a better analysis? The answers to these two questions depend on the point you are trying to make and what you wish to compare. Selecting the most appropriate statistics is a matter of interpretation and emphasis, and it is here that statistics can be misleading.

Choosing the Best Statistics.   Darrell Huff, in his book *How to Lie with Statistics,* clearly and concisely illustrates how numbers an be manipulated and distorted.[9] The classic notion that "numbers don't lie" has to be taken in the context of how they are used. Suppose, for example, you are told that the mean (average) salary of professional football players is $160,000.[10] Assuming that this figure is correct, does it reflect the actual salaries that football players make? Yes, to a degree it does, but let's look at the data from another perspective.

Suppose that the median salary of a professional football player is $105,000—that is, half the players make more and half make less than $105,000 a year. In addition, the most frequent salary—the mode—is around $90,000, and the range of all football players' salaries runs from a low of $45,000 to a high of $1.5 million per year. Looking at all these data—the mean, or average salary of $160,000; the median, or mid-range salary of $90,000; and the range of salaries from $45,000 to $1.5 million—we can see that quite a discrepancy exists. In fact, there is a $70,000 difference between the average and the most frequently paid salary, and almost $1.5 million separates the lowest paid player from the highest paid.

How would you use these statistics in your speech? That depends on your purpose. If you wanted to report that professional football players earn high salaries, you would probably use the mean. Or, looking at only a few superstars, you could present calculations to show that some players earn as much as several thousand dollars an hour. However, it is likely that no single statistic represents the true picture of what professional football players are paid. Thus, it is important for speakers to cite several statistics and listeners should ask questions about statistical data, especially when they are not given all the figures they need to form a clear and accurate interpretation of the actual situation.

Making the Most of Statistics.   Following five simple guidelines will help you to make the most of the statistics you've gathered.

1. *Make sure that the statistics you use are from reliable and neutral sources.* The motives of the source of any statistics must be carefully assessed. For

example, if you heard two sets of data representing fuel economy per gallon of gasoline—one prepared by the Chrysler Corporation and the other by the Environmental Protection Agency—which would you expect to be more reliable? Although the Chrysler Corporation's data may be perfectly accurate, there would be a tendency for listeners to believe that their data are biased. It would be to a speaker's advantage, therefore, to use the more neutral source—in this case, the Environmental Protection Agency.

There are times, however, when it may be difficult to identify the most neutral source. For example, whose statistics would you use if you wished to inform your audience about the United States' strength in nuclear weapons—the Department of Defense or the Americans for Peace? Here the choice is debatable unless you intend to take a position on the issue. Remember, statistics can be used in many different ways and can thus influence interpretations and outcomes.

2. *Take time to explain the statistics you are using.* Interpret and relate your statistics to your listeners. Consider the following use of statistics:

> The diameter of the sun is about 865,000 miles, about 109 times the diameter of the earth. Because the sun is about 93 million miles from the earth, it does not appear larger than the moon. But the sun's diameter is 400 times as large as that of the moon. The sun is also almost 400 times farther from the earth than is the moon.
>
> If the sun were the size of a skyscraper, the earth would be the size of a person. The moon would be the size of a cocker spaniel standing next to the person.[11]

This explanation makes statistics meaningful by clearly comparing and contrasting the size and distance of the sun and the moon. When using data that listeners may have difficulty understanding or visualizing, try to provide the appropriate comparisons and contrasts in order to make the data more meaningful.

3. *Use statistics sparingly.* Statistics are difficult to comprehend, so if you use too many, you run a high risk of boring or confusing your audience. Use statistics only when necessary, and make sure they are easy to understand. The following example would be difficult for even the most attentive listener to comprehend:

> If my new proposal is accepted, we will have at least a 20-percent increase in production efficiency and at least a 50-cent per unit cost reduction according to our 1990 projections. This, I might add, means a 10-percent or minimum 35-cent per unit cost reduction over the next five to six years. What this all adds up to is a 15-percent increase over this time period and an eventual profit of $110,000 per year. That will also give us a 6-percent depreciation allowance.

4. *Round off large numbers when possible.* Listeners understand and remember figures better when they are not complicated. For example, it is easier to remember 10,000 than 9997. While it's true that the Statue of

TABLE 7.2   *A Simplified Way of Presenting Statistics*

		Dividends	
	Net Sales	*Net Earnings*	*Dividends Per Share*
1st Quarter	$ 44,000	$ 2900	$.10
2nd Quarter	50,000	3500	.15
3rd Quarter	55,100	4500	.20
4th Quarter	56,700	5000	.22
Total	$205,800	$15,900	$.67

Liberty's torch rises 305 feet and 1 inch, or 92.99 meters, above the base of the pedestal, it is less complicated to say that the torch rises 305 feet, or 93 meters. Unless an exact figure is needed, round off most statistics to the nearest whole number.

5. *Sometimes the best method of presenting statistical information is to display it visually.* Using visual aids saves explanation time and also makes statistics easier to understand. Compare the clarity of the following with the simplicity of the visual aid in Table 7.2:

> The first quarter net sales were $44,000, which created a net earning of $2900, thus producing a 10-cent dividend per share. The second quarter net sales were $50,100, leading to a net earning of $3500 for a 15-cent dividend per share. The third quarter net sales of $55,100 created a net earning of $4500 for a 20-cent dividend per share. And the fourth quarter net sales of $56,700 produced a net earning of $5000, or a 22-cent dividend per share. The total net sales were $205,800, with a total net earning of $15,900 paying a total dividend per share of 67 cents.

Note that all the words in the verbal example can be summed up in a simple four-column table.

USING STATISTICS: SOME TIPS

- Make sure that the statistics you use come from reliable and neutral sources.
- Plan to take time to explain the statistics you are using.
- Use statistics sparingly—too many can make your presentation too complex and boring.
- Round off large numbers and fractions when possible.
- Display statistics visually whenever possible in order to save explanation time.

FIGURE 7.3

Visualizing
Statistical Data

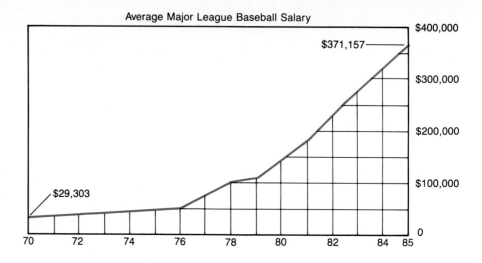

Figure 7.3 presents another example of how complex data can be summarized and presented in a visually interesting way. Note how the artwork makes it much easier for the reader to understand the comparisons of salaries. Chapter 9 discusses in detail the use of visual aids in a speech presentation.

SUMMARY

Many beginning speechmakers do not appreciate the important role that gathering information plays in the speech development process, yet most professional speakers consider it essential. Although it takes time and effort to gather good information, the result will be a more effective speech.

A wide variety of resources is available to help you locate information for your speech. Often, the best starting place is yourself. Even if you are not an expert on your topic, you probably have some knowledge of it. If your personal experiences do not suffice, you will need to obtain information from others or from the library.

Through interviews you can collect opinions from others who have firsthand knowledge of your topic. An *interview* is a planned person-to-person question-and-answer session aimed at gathering information. First, you should determine the specific purpose of your interview. Then you should select the interviewees who will be most able to help you meet your purpose. The number of individuals who can be interviewed and who have special knowledge on various topics is infinite.

Interviews can be an especially productive way of gathering information because they can provide more in-depth and up-to-date information than newspapers or magazine articles, they furnish information that is not covered in published materials, and they serve as an excellent way to question experts who have specialized backgrounds.

An interview has three identifiable segments: the *opening,* the *body,* and the *closing.* An informal information-gathering session is usually organized as a *nonscheduled interview,* in which the interviewer follows a central objective or list of possible topics and subtopics, or as a *moderately scheduled interview,* in which the interviewer uses a prepared list of basic questions or topics along with related investigative questions.

The library is one of the most valuable sources of information for your speech. There are four principal sources of information in the library: yourself, the librarian, the card catalog, and the reference department. You should have a working knowledge of the library and know what you want to find before you begin your search. Trained librarians are available to help you when you are having difficulty. The card catalog, an alphabetical index to all the books in the library, is designed to be a quick and simple means of locating materials. Most card catalogs list books in three ways: by author's last name, by title, and by subject. Periodicals are also listed by title or by name of issuing organization. Most library research begins in the reference department, which contains all the sources needed for easy access to specific subject areas. The reference department contains dictionaries, biographical aids, encyclopedias, yearbooks, atlases, indexes, and guides to periodical literature.

To simplify your research process, know what you want to find, begin early, record citations accurately and completely, and take clear notes of the information that will benefit you in writing your speech.

The information you gather then becomes the lifeblood of your speech. Although a speaker's believability and delivery are critically important to the success of a speech, how effectively he or she uses research to support and clarify main points usually makes the difference between a good speech and a poor one. The four basic kinds of supporting and clarifying materials used in speeches are testimony, examples, definitions, and statistics.

When speakers cite opinions or conclusions of recognized witnesses or authorities, they are using *testimony.* This technique benefits student speakers who have not yet established themselves as experts on the topics they present. Several guidelines should be observed when presenting testimony: (1) use short quotations, (2) quote and paraphrase accurately, (3) use qualified and unbiased sources.

Examples are the most useful form of supporting and clarifying material. There are four different kinds: (1) the *brief example*—a specific instance used to introduce a new topic, drive home a point, or create a desired impression, (2) the *illustration*—an extended *factual* or *hypothetical* example that is striking and memorable, (3) the *analogy*—a *figurative* or *literal* comparison of two things that are similar in certain essential characteristics, and (4) the *restatement*—an expression of the same idea using different sets of words. When presenting examples, use factual cases whenever possible, relate them to the topic you are discussing, make them realistic and believable, provide verifiable sources, and give proper credit to the originator.

Speakers who are sensitive to their audiences realize the importance of defining unfamiliar terms. There are three basic forms of definitions: (1) the *logical definition*, which is the most common, consists of a term's dictionary definition and a description of how the term differs from other members of the same category, (2) the *operational definition* explains how an object or concept works, and (3) the *definition by example* explains terms and concepts through the use of spoken or literal examples. When using definitions, keep them short, use clear and concise language, explain every term that you suspect your audience may not understand or could misinterpret, and provide examples when appropriate to clarify meanings.

Statistics are beneficial because they enable speakers to summarize a large amount of data rapidly, they aid in analyzing specific occurrences or instances, and they help to isolate trends and predict future events. The four most commonly cited statistics are the *mean*, the *median*, the *mode*, and the *range*. Statistics should be accurate, meaningful to your audience, used sparingly, representative of your claims, and taken from a reliable source.

KEY TERMS

Analogy: a comparison of two things that are similar in certain essential characteristics.

Body: the main part of an interview that consists of the questions and answers.

Brief Example: a specific instance that is used to introduce a topic, drive home a point, or create a desired response.

Closing: the final portion of the interview process in which the interviewer thanks the interviewee and sums up his or her findings.

Definition by Example: the use of either a spoken or a written example to explain a term or concept.

Example: a simple, representative incident or model that clarifies a point.

Factual Illustration: tells what has actually happened.

Figurative Analogy: a comparison of things in different categories—for example, a heart and a pump.

Hypothetical Illustration: tells what could or probably would happen given a specific set of circumstances.

Illustration: an extended example, narrative, case history, or anecdote that is striking and memorable.

Interview: a carefully planned and executed person-to-person question-and-answer session during which a speaker tries to discover specific information that will help in the preparation of a speech.

Literal Analogy: a comparison of members of the same category—for example, two churches, two businesses, or two states.

Logical Definition: the most common form of definition used by speakers, it usually contains two parts: a term's dictionary definition and the characteristics that distinguish the term from other members of the same category.

Mean: a statistic often referred to as the average, it is obtained by adding all the scores in a set of scores and dividing by the number of scores in the set.

Median: the middle score in a series of numbers; half the scores are above the median and half are below it.

Mode: the most frequent score in a series of numbers.

Moderately Scheduled Interview: an interview format in which the interviewer has listed the basic questions or topics to be discussed with possible probes included under each question or topic.

Nonscheduled Interview: an interview format in which the interviewer follows a central objective or a list of possible topics and subtopics; there is no formalized order of questions and there are no anticipated responses.

Opening: the introduction to an interview in which the interviewer explains the purpose of the interview, establishes rapport, and provides background information, if needed.

Operational Definition: a definition that explains how an object or concept works; some operational definitions merely illustrate the steps that make up a process.

Range: the highest and lowest numbers in a series of numbers.

Restatement: expression of the same idea using different words; it includes the use of summaries, synonyms, rephrasing, and repetition.

Statistics: numerical data that show relationships between and among phenomena (variables, observations, collections) or that summarize and interpret many instances.

Testimony: the opinions or conclusions of recognized witnesses or authorities.

DISCUSSION STARTERS

1. What advice would you give to a beginning speech student about gathering information for a speech?

2. Why is it important to examine what you know about a topic before you consult with others or use the library?

3. Why is an interview a particularly productive way of gathering information?

4. What advice would you give a person who has never conducted an interview? What would he or she need to know to be an effective interviewer?

5. You have just entered the library to research your speech topic, which is gun control. You want to learn as much as possible about this subject. Where would you begin?

6. How would you describe the reference department in a library?

7. What is the purpose of using supporting and clarifying materials in a speech?

8. If you are not an expert on a given subject, what kind of supporting material should you use? Why?

9. You are helping a friend write a speech. The purpose is to persuade the audience that capital punishment in our society is unnecessary. Your friend wants to cite the Law and Order Association as the main source. Is this a good source? Why or why not?

10. What is the difference between an illustration and a brief example?

11. You are instructing a group of college students in the use of examples. What tips would you give them for using examples in their speeches?

12. What do a hypothetical illustration and a figurative analogy have in common? Cite examples and explain.

13. It is usually best to define unfamiliar terms for your audience. Can you think of times when you should not? Explain.

14. What tips would you give a speaker who uses many technical terms that the audience is unlikely to understand?

15. What is the difference among a median, a mode, and a mean?

16. If you were comparing the salaries of teachers, doctors, and lawyers, which would provide the best comparisons—medians, modes, or means? Explain.

17. As a receiver of information, what cautions should you take when you hear someone using statistics?

FURTHER
READINGS

Ayres, Joe, and Janice M. Miller. *Effective Public Speaking*, 2nd Ed. Dubuque, Iowa: Wm. C. Brown, Publishers, 1986.

Ehninger, Douglas, Bruce E. Gronbeck, and Alan H. Monroe. *Principles of Speech Communication*, 9th Brief Ed. Glenview, Illinois: Scott, Foresman and Company, 1984.

Fletcher, Leon. *How to Develop & Deliver a Speech*, 3rd Ed. New York: Harper & Row, Publishers, 1985.

Hunt, Gary T. *Public Speaking*, 2nd Ed. Englewood Cliffs, N.J.: Prentice-Hall, 1987.

Lucas, Stephen E. *The Art of Public Speaking*, 2nd Ed. New York: Random House, 1986.

Samovar, Larry A., and Jack Mills. *Oral Communication Message and Response*, 6th Ed. Dubuque, Iowa: Wm. C. Brown, Publishers, 1986.

Sprague, Jo, and Douglas Stuart. *The Speaker's Handbook.* San Diego, Calif.: Harcourt Brace Jovanovich, 1984.

NOTES

1. Information contained in this section was reviewed by Eva Sartori and Scott Stebelman of the University of Nebraska Library staff.

2. Thornton-Jaringe, Judith E., *Do you ever feel confused about where to start once you get to the library?* (Lincoln, Nebr.: The University of Nebraska Libraries, 1983).

3. Student's name withheld to protect her right to privacy.

4. "Buckle Up," American Automobile Association Brochure, 1985.

5. "Motivation: A Key to Creative Works," *Sunday Journal-Star* (Lincoln, Nebr., February 3, 1985), p. 3D.

6. From "I Have A Dream" by Martin Luther King, Jr., Copyright © 1963. Reprinted by permission of Joan Davis.

7. Ferrari, L. David, "Parental Kidnapping" in *Winning Orations* (Mankato, Minn.: Interstate Oratorical Association, 1984), p. 10.

8. Levy, Irma, "Transplantation: The Miracle of Life" in *Winning Orations* (Mankato, Minn.: Interstate Oratorical Association, 1984), p. 80.

9. Huff, Darrell, *How to Lie with Statistics.* New York: W. W. Norton, 1954.

10. The data do not reflect actual salaries of professional football league players. The account is an example only.

11. *The World Book Encyclopedia*, World Book, Inc., 1984, vol. 18, p. 780.

APPENDIX: PERIODICAL INDEXES ARRANGED BY SUBJECT DISCIPLINE

I. GENERAL SUBJECT INDEXES

1. General Information Indexes

   Alternative Press Index
   Magazine Index—reel-to-reel
   microfilm reader
   Readers' Guide to Periodical Literature

2. a. General Humanities, Literature and History Indexes

   Arts & Humanities Citation Index
   British Humanities Index
   Humanities Index

2. b. General Social Sciences Indexes

   Social Sciences Citation Index
   Social Sciences Index
   P.A.I.S.

2. c. General Science Indexes

   General Science Index
   Science Citation Index

II. SPECIFIC SUBJECT INDEXES

1. Agriculture and Natural Resources Indexes

   Bibliography of Agriculture
   Biological & Agricultural Index
   Selected Water Resources Abstracts
   World Agriculture Economics & Rural Sociology Abstracts

2. Anthropology Indexes

   Abstracts in Anthropology
   Anthropological Index to Current Periodicals
   Anthropological Literature

3. Architecture Indexes

   Architectural Periodicals Index
   Art Index
   Avery Index to Periodicals

4. Art Index

   Art Index

5. Astronomy Indexes

   General Science Index
   Science Citation Index

6. Biology and Life Sciences Indexes

   Biological Abstracts
   Biological and Agricultural Index
   Ecology Abstracts
   Wildlife Review

7. Book Review Indexes

   Book Review Digest
   Book Review Index
   Combined Retrospective Index to Book Reviews in:
      Humanities Journals, 1802–1974
      Scholarly Journals, 1886–1974
   An Index to Book Reviews in the Humanities

8. Business, Economics and Statistics Indexes

   American Statistics Index
   Business Periodicals Index
   Business Index
   Index of Economic Articles
   Index to International Statistics
   Predicasts F & S Index: Europe
   Predicasts F & S Index: International
   Predicasts F & S Index: United States
   Statistical Theory & Method Abstracts
   Statistical Reference Index
   The Wall Street Journal Index
   Work Related Abstracts

9. Chemistry Index

   Chemical Abstracts

10. Computer Indexes

    ACM Guide to Computing Literature
    Computer and Control Abstracts
    Computer & Information Systems Abstracts Journal
    General Science Index

11. Criminal Justice Indexes

   Criminal Justice Periodical Index
   Criminology & Penology Abstracts
   Social Sciences Index

12. Dissertation Indexes

   Comprehensive Dissertation Index
   Dissertation Abstracts International

13. Education Indexes

   Business Education Index
   *Current Index to Journals in Education
   (CIJE)*
   Education Index
   Educational Administration Abstracts
   ERIC Indexes: See *Current Index to
   Journals in Education (CIJE)* and
   Resources in Education
   Exceptional Child Education Resources
   Multicultural Education Abstracts
   Resources in Education
   *School Organization & Management
   Abstracts*

14. Engineering Indexes

   Applied Science and Technology Abstracts
   Engineering Index
   Ergonomics Abstracts

15. Film Studies and Media Broadcasting
   Indexes

   Film Literature Index
   Magazine Index—reel-to-reel
   microfilm reader
   Readers' Guide to Periodical Literature
   Topicator

16. Geography Indexes

   *Geographical Abstracts/Geo Abstracts:
   Annual Index*
      V.1 Index to Parts A,B,E,& G—
      Physical Geography
      V.2 Index to Parts C,D,& F—
   Social/Economic Geography
   Social Sciences Citation Index
   Social Sciences Index

17. Geology Indexes

   General Science Index
   Science Citation Index

18. Government Documents Indexes

   American Statistics Index
   C.I.S. Annual: Index & Abstracts
   *Cumulative Subject Index to the Monthly
   Catalog of U.S. Government
   Publications:*
      1895–1899
      1900–1971
   *Cumulative Title Index to United States
   Public Documents, 1789–1976*
   Government Documents Rollfiche
   Reader—reel-to-reel microfilm reader
   Index to U.S. Government Periodicals
   *Monthly Catalog of U.S. Government
   Publications*
   P.A.I.S.

19. Health, Physical Education,
   Recreation and Dance Indexes

   Behavior Medicine Abstracts
   Index Medicus
   Physical Education Index
   Physical Fitness/Sports Medicine
   Sports Bibliography

20. History Indexes

   America: History and Life
   Arts & Humanities Citation Index
   Historical Abstracts
   Humanities Index

21. Journalism Indexes

   Communication Abstracts
   P.A.I.S

22. Linguistics, Language and Literature
   Indexes

   Arts & Humanities Citation Index
   British Humanities Index
   Essay and General Literature Index
   Humanities Index

*Linguistics and Language Behavior
Abstracts (LLBA)
M.L.A. Bibliography*

23. Mathematics Indexes

*General Science Index
Mathematical Review
Science Citation Index*

24. Medicine, Nursing and Hospital
    Literature Indexes

*Behavior Medicine Abstracts
Cumulative Index to Nursing & Allied
Health Literature
Hospital Literature Index
Index Medicus
International Nursing Index
Nutrition Abstracts & Reviews, Series A:
Human & Experimental*

25. Music Indexes

*Music Article Guide
Music Index
RILM Abstracts of Music Literature*

26. Newspaper Indexes

*Chicago Tribune
Christian Science Monitor
Los Angeles Times
New York Times
Newsbank
The Times Index of London:*
    *1790–1939
    1940–present*

27. Philosophy Indexes

*Arts & Humanities Citation Index
British Humanities Index
*Humanities Index
Philosopher's Index*

28. Physics Index

Physics Abstracts

29. Political Science Indexes

*C.I.S. Annual: Index & Abstract
Combined Retrospective Index to Journals*

*in Political Science, 1886–1974
International Bibliography of Political
Science
International Political Science Abstracts
P.A.I.S.
Sage Public Administration Abstracts
U.S. Political Science Documents
Social Sciences Citation Index
Social Sciences Index*

30. Psychology Indexes

*Child Development Abstracts &
Bibliography
Index to Periodical Literature on Aging
Psychological Abstracts
Psychological Documents
Social Sciences Citation Index
Social Sciences Index
Women Studies Abstracts*

31. Religion and Theology Indexes

*Religion Index One: Periodicals
Religious and Theological Abstracts*

32. Sociology and Social Work Indexes

*Gerontological Abstracts
Inventory of Marriage & Family
Literature
Sage Family Studies Abstracts
Sage Race Relations Abstracts
Social Sciences Citation Index
Social Sciences Index
Social Work Research & Abstracts
Sociological Abstracts
Urban Affairs Abstracts
Women Studies Abstracts*

33. United Nations Indexes

*United Nations Documents Index—
v.1(1950)–v.24(1973)
Undex: U.N. Documents Index. Series
A,B,C—(1970–1978)
Undoc: Current Index: U.N. Documents
Index—v.1(1979) to the present
U.N. Index to Proceedings of the General
Assembly—(1950 to the present)*

CHAPTER 8

Organizing and Outlining

LEARNING OBJECTIVES

After studying this chapter, you should be able to:

1. Identify the purposes and contents of the three main parts of a speech.

2. Select and appropriately state the main points of your speech.

3. Assess the five patterns of organization and choose the one that best suits your speech's topic and purpose.

4. Use transitions, signposts, and internal summaries to connect the thoughts in your speech.

5. Compose an effective introduction and an effective conclusion for your speech.

6. Prepare a complete sequence of preliminary, full-content, and presentational outlines for your speech.

John has decided that he is going to bake a cake for Tracy's birthday. Never having baked a cake before, he asks the help of Tracy's friend, Jennifer, who used to work in a bakery.

JENNIFER: What kind of cake do you want to make?

JOHN: I don't know. I think Tracy likes chocolate cake.

JENNIFER: How about a German chocolate?

JOHN: Sounds great! I think I've got the mix.

JENNIFER: What do the directions say?

JOHN: HEAT oven to 350 degrees. Grease and flour pan. BLEND in large mixer bowl on low speed for 30 seconds: Cake mix, 1 1/2 cups water, 1/3 cup vegetable oil, and 3 eggs.
BEAT medium speed 2 minutes, or 300 strokes by hand.
BAKE 35 to 40 minutes.
COOL 10 minutes, remove from pan and frost.

JENNIFER: OK, we need milk, eggs, and vegetable oil.

JOHN: Got it!

JENNIFER: First we'll pour the cake mix into the mixing bowl and then add our milk, eggs, and vegetable oil in that order. John, you can mix it. Turn the blender on medium speed.

JOHN: OK! It's ready. Now what?

JENNIFER: Pour the mix into the baking pan and spread it evenly.

JOHN: Done!

JENNIFER: Now put it in the oven for 30 to 40 minutes.

JOHN: The timer is going off—the cake appears to be done.

JENNIFER: Yes, it's done. Now take it out and let it cool before we frost it.

A simple activity like baking a cake requires organization—if you want the cake to taste good, that is. For example, the first step in baking a cake is to choose a recipe. This is similar to selecting a topic for a speech. The second step is to set out all the needed ingredients. This corresponds to a speaker's research process. The third step is to add the ingredients to the batter in the order prescribed by the recipe. A speaker organizes the elements of his or her speech in much the same way.

If you have ever baked a cake, you know how important organization is in getting the job done effectively and efficiently. Naturally, differences exist between cake baking and creating a speech, but there are some important similarities. If you randomly put ingredients in a cake pan and bake them in the oven, your chances of creating a delicious cake will diminish dramatically. In parallel, if you randomly join all the information you have gathered for a speech, your chances of creating a meaningful and effective speech will diminish dramatically.

THINK ABOUT IT

"If I was organized I'd be dangerous."
Anonymous

So far, in this section of the book, we've discussed topic selection, determining a speech's general and specific purposes, analyzing the audience, gathering information, and distinguishing kinds of supporting and clarifying materials. These are all crucial steps in the speechmaking process, but for a speech to make sense, it must be organized. Therefore, in this chapter, we will examine how to bring all the elements of your speech together through organizing and outlining.

ORGANIZING YOUR SPEECH

Organizing is the arranging of ideas or elements into a systematic and meaningful whole. If you have already thoroughly researched your topic, you can ease your writing task through careful organization. All speeches are organized into three main parts: the introduction, the body, and the conclusion. Since the body is the main part of any speech, we will examine it first.

The Body

The **body** of a speech presents the main content that develops the speaker's general and specific purposes. To ensure that the body of your speech is well organized, your content must be divided into main points that are thoughtfully selected and stated, limited in number, and carefully ordered, connected, and supported.

Select and State Your Main Points.   **Main points,** which are the principal subdivisions of your speech, are critical to the achievement of your specific purpose. Assume that the specific purpose of your speech is to inform your audience about the most significant causes of automobile accidents in the United States. To determine the main points, ask yourself two questions: "What are the causes of auto accidents?" and "Which causes are the most significant ones?" By asking these questions, assuming that you have already thoroughly researched your subject, you can begin to determine the main points of your speech. The following is a list of possibilities.

SPECIFIC PURPOSE: To inform my audience of the three most significant causes of auto accidents in the United States.

MAIN POINTS:
    I. Manufacturing defects in automobiles are a significant cause.
    II. Driving too fast for conditions is a significant cause.
    III. Driving under the influence of alcohol is a significant cause.

These three main points, or causes, form the basic structure of the body of the speech. Each additional significant cause (depending on how *significant* is defined) means an additional main point and a change in the number of causes stated in the specific purpose.

Relate the Main Points to Your Specific Purpose. The main points of a speech usually evolve from the specific purpose. As discussed in Chapter 6, the specific purpose should be carefully developed and written. Suppose your specific purpose is to inform the audience of the origin and mission of the Special Forces in our armed services. This specific purpose establishes two main points: the origin of the Special Forces and the mission of the Special Forces. The speech would be organized as in the following example.

SPECIFIC PURPOSE: To inform the audience about the origin and mission of the Special Forces branch of the armed services.

MAIN POINTS:
    I. The origin of the Special Forces branch of the armed services occurred because of a variety of needs.
    II. The mission of the Special Forces branch of the armed services is to provide expertise in emergency situations.

Let's start from another perspective. Assume you have been assigned to give a speech that will persuade your audience to adopt a particular point of view. From your research on computers and your belief that they are making our society very impersonal, you decide to discuss the harmful effect computers have on interpersonal relationships. The main points for this speech do not evolve as readily as they did in the previous examples, but as you begin to think about your topic, you will also begin to refine your specific purpose. First, state your general purpose as in the following example.

GENERAL PURPOSE: To persuade my audience that computers can be harmful to interpersonal relationships.

At this point you should ask the question, "Why are computers harmful to interpersonal relationships?" As you generate answers, you begin to determine the main points of your speech. You conclude that two key reasons support your view: computers are mere machines without the ability to react on their own, and computers limit the amount of personal contact people have with each other. At this point you should refine your specific purpose to match your main points. In this case you might state it as in the following example.

SPECIFIC PURPOSE: To persuade my audience that there are two reasons that computers can be harmful to interpersonal relationships.

MAIN POINTS: I. Computers are harmful because they are machines that cannot react on their own.
                    II. Computers are harmful because they limit personal contact with others.

State Your Main Points Carefully.   Main points, like the specific purpose, should be carefully developed and written, and they should also be specific, vivid, relevant, and parallel in structure.

Be specific.   The more specific the main points, the less confusion they will create and the more meaningful they will be to an audience. Each main point in a speech should be independent of the others and simple to understand. Compare the following:

Ineffective	*Effective*
I. Nuclear power is the most efficient fuel in our society, but it has been historically misunderstood by most people.	I. Nuclear power is the most efficient fuel in our society. II. Nuclear power has been historically misunderstood by most people.

Be vivid.   The more vivid the main points, the more likely they are to create interest and help organize the speech. The main points should be thought provokers and attention grabbers that stand out from the supporting materials. It is more vivid to say, "The proposed federal regulation regarding birth control for anyone under 18 would have a devastating effect on teenagers' lives!" than to say, "The proposed federal regulation requiring family planning clinics that receive federal funds to notify parents of anyone under the age of 18 who wishes to use birth control devices would have a devastating effect on teenagers." Vivid phrasing should be realistic, not overstated, and appropriate to the ethical standards of the occasion.

Show relevance of main points.   Main points that are relevant to the audience's immediate interests encourage greater involvement and empathy. For instance, instead of saying "Air pollution has reached high levels," say "Air pollution *in our city* has reached high levels." Using direct references to the audience whenever possible increases the link between you, what you are saying, and your audience. Audience members like to know how the speaker's subject affects them and why they should listen.

Create parallel structure.   Finally, main points should be parallel in structure—that is, the same pattern of wording should be used when possible. For example:

Not Parallel
  I. Child pornography has been a serious problem in our community.
  II. Our community is experiencing increased amounts of child pornography.
  III. Child abuse has increased because of the pornography in our community.

Parallel
  I. Child pornography has been a serious problem in our community.
  II. Child pornography has increased in our community.
  III. Child pornography has caused an increase in child abuse in our community.

The second example follows a consistent pattern and therefore should be easier to work from and remember. Audiences usually have only one opportunity to hear a speech. Therefore, anything you can do to make the main points stand out from the rest of the content is to your benefit.

Limiting the Number of Your Main Points.   The number of main points in your speech will depend on at least three considerations:

  1. The content to be covered in the speech, especially the amount and complexity of the supporting materials for each point
  2. The time available to deliver the speech
  3. The amount of information that your audience can reasonably be expected to comprehend and remember from one speech

The time available for most classroom speech assignments is limited by practical considerations. As a result, most speeches have no more than five main points and the majority have between two and three.

Try to balance the amount of time that you devote to each main point. For example, if you are assigned a five- to seven-minute speech, plan for the introduction and conclusion to take about two minutes. The remaining time should be equally distributed among the main points. Of course, this is just a guideline. It isn't always possible to balance the main points exactly, nor should you. The nature of some speech topics requires that some main points be emphasized more than others.

An audience should be able to sort out and recall each main point. This is impossible if there are too many. Common sense tells us that three points are easier to remember than five or more. Thus, as a speaker, you must set reasonable expectations for both your listeners and yourself. If you have too many points and a limited amount of time, you will be unable to develop each point thoroughly enough to make it clear, convincing, and memorable.

Order Your Main Points. Once you've identified your main points, you must decide their order of presentation. This takes serious analysis, for the order determines your speech's structure and strategy. Which will be the most effective order of presentation depends on your speech's topic and purpose. Another determining factor is your audience. One of the five basic patterns of presentation is used in most speeches: time-sequence, spatial, problem-solution, cause-effect, or topical.

The time-sequence pattern. The **time-sequence** or **chronological pattern** is an order of presentation that begins at a particular point in time and continues either forward or backward. The key is to follow a natural time sequence and avoid jumping haphazardly from one time to another. This pattern is especially useful for tracing the steps in a process, the relationships among a series of events, or the development of ideas. The history of photographic technology, the steps in setting up an advertising display, and the development of the computer in today's society are all topics that lend themselves to the time sequence. Here is an example of a time sequence that moves forward from a specific date:

SPECIFIC PURPOSE: To inform my audience about the historical development of softball.

MAIN POINTS:
    I. In 1887, softball was developed as an indoor game.
    II. In 1895, softball was adapted as an outdoor game.
    III. In 1933, softball was sanctioned by the Amateur Softball Association of America.

In contrast, a reverse-order time sequence begins at a specific date and works backward chronologically. For example, a speech discussing advertising trends in the auto industry, organized in reverse-order time sequence, could start as follows:

SPECIFIC PURPOSE: To inform my audience of the trends in auto advertising beginning with today's advertising and retracing to the 1950s.

MAIN POINTS:
    I. In the 1980s, advertisements emphasized fuel economy.
    II. In the 1970s, advertisements emphasized how well a car rode.
    III. In the 1960s, advertisements emphasized the size of the car.
    IV. In the 1950s, advertisements emphasized the power of the car.

The time-sequence pattern can also be used to explain a process or describe how to do something. Such topics as the development of our space industry, the evolution of the computer, and how to make wine, bake bread, use CPR in an emergency, or water ski all have specific steps that must be presented in sequence if the result is to be successful.

The spatial pattern. In a **spatial pattern** of presentation, the content of a speech is organized according to relationships in space. This method is especially appropriate for presentations that describe distances, directions, or physical surroundings. For example, a spatial pattern might be used to describe each area in a factory's floor plan, the floor-by-floor plans for a building, or how to get from one location to another by moving from east to west, north to south, center to outside, clockwise, and so on. A spatial pattern describes the relationships among all the main points. Here is an example of a speech's main points organized by spatial pattern:

SPECIFIC PURPOSE: To inform my audience of the floor plan of the new police department.

MAIN POINTS: I. The official records are kept in the east wing.
                                  II. The training division is in the west wing.
                                 III. The jail is in the north wing.
                                 IV. The reception area and offices are in the south wing.

Both the time-sequence and the spatial patterns are well-suited for informative speeches.

The problem-solution pattern.   A speech that follows the **problem-solution pattern** is usually divided into two parts: the problem and the suggested solution. The problem is usually defined as a need, doubt, uncertainty, or difficulty, while the suggested solution remedies or eliminates the need, doubt, uncertainty, or difficulty without creating other problems. For example, a problem-solution approach could be used to address such topics as the lack of a sufficient exercise facility for students, the discovery that the new water treatment plant does not seem to be working correctly, the fact that there is no way to be sure that the new crime-stopper program will work, or the belief that the university has had a difficult time retaining quality faculty members.

The problem-solution pattern, if used correctly, should do more than just present a problem and a solution; it should help the audience to understand both the problem and the solution as well as why the solution will work. For example, a speech that advocates a change in production techniques might follow this problem-solution pattern:

SPECIFIC PURPOSE: To persuade my audience to accept the needed production changes in order to meet the demand for the product.

PROBLEM: I. The assembly line is not producing enough finished products to meet the demand.

SOLUTION: II. There must be cooperation among all of the workers.

The problem-solution pattern usually includes three to five of the following elements:

1. *A definition and description of the problem*, including its symptoms and size
2. *A critical analysis of the problem*, including causes, current actions, and requirements for a solution
3. *Suggestions of possible solutions*, including descriptions of each plan's strengths and weaknesses

    4. *A recommendation of the best solution,* including a thorough justification of its superiority over other proposed solutions

    5. *A discussion of the best solution put into operation,* including a description of how the plan can be implemented

Although the problem-solution pattern can be used for informative speeches, it is best suited for persuasive presentations.

The cause-effect pattern. The **cause-effect pattern** is an order of presentation in which the speaker first explains the causes of an event, problem, or issue, and then discusses its consequences. Causes and effects may be presented in two different sequences. A speaker may either (1) point out certain forces or factors and then show the results that follow from them, or (2) describe conditions or events and then point out the forces or factors that caused them.

In using the cause-effect pattern to discuss the effects of computers on students' job placement, a speaker might begin by recounting recent developments in computer procedures that have led to a more accurate analysis of students' skills and then show that, as a result, the number of students who have obtained first jobs in their chosen fields has increased dramatically. The speaker might also reverse the process and first point out that the number of jobs that students are landing in their chosen fields is the result of more accurate computer analysis of their skills.

Regardless of the exact sequence, a speech organized by cause and effect has two main points—a description of the factors that are the *cause* and a prediction or identification of the subsequent *effect.* Such topics as eating disorders in young adults, television violence, heart disease, and new approaches to improving memory all lend themselves to the use of the cause-effect pattern.

Using the cause-effect pattern, a speech on the need to raise taxes to support education might be arranged in either of the following ways:

SPECIFIC PURPOSE: To persuade my audience that the cost of education is the result of poor management.

CAUSE: I. School officials have planned poorly, overspent, and mismanaged tax dollars since 1984.

EFFECT: II. Because of the mishandling of tax dollars, taxes were raised to compensate for the shortfall in funds necessary to run our public high school.

Or:

EFFECT: I. Taxes should be raised to make up for the shortfall in funds necessary to run our public high school.

CAUSE: II. Poor planning, overspending, and mismanagement of funds by school officials have been the primary contributors to the need for a tax increase.

Because the cause-effect pattern can be used in a variety of ways, it is a useful format for either informative or persuasive speeches. As long as the cause can be directly related to the effect that you are trying to prove, this pattern can be an excellent choice for many different topics.

The topical pattern.   The **topical pattern** is an order of presentation in which the main topic is divided into a series of related subtopics. Each subtopic becomes a main point in the speech and all main points are joined to form a coherent whole. In this way, the topical pattern is a unifying structure.

The topical pattern is most likely to be used when none of the other patterns of organization can be applied to the topic or purpose of a speech. Speech topics such as the advantages of running, study habits that can improve your grades, uses of the video camera, and barriers to effective listening can easily be organized using the topical pattern.

Here is how the topical pattern could be used to organize a speech about the barriers to effective listening:

SPECIFIC PURPOSE: To inform my audience about the four greatest barriers to effective listening.

MAIN POINTS:
    I. Language distractions are barriers to effective listening.
   II. Factual distractions are barriers to effective listening.
  III. Mental distractions are barriers to effective listening.
  IV. Physical distractions are barriers to effective listening.

When the topical pattern is used correctly, each main point should be consistent and related to the others. Because the topical pattern is versatile, it can be adapted to most speech purposes.

Choosing the Best Pattern of Organization.   We have already emphasized the importance of matching your speech's pattern of organization to your topic and your purpose. You must also consider another key factor—your audience. The wise speaker anticipates responses from the audience. Thus, if your prespeech audience analysis indicates that important questions or objections are likely to be raised, you should arrange your main points to meet those objections. For example, if you are advocating that a lottery be legalized in your community and are certain that your audience is likely to ask whether a lottery will bring crime into the community, you may structure your presentation as follows:

SPECIFIC PURPOSE: To persuade my audience that a lottery will benefit the community.

MAIN POINTS:
    I. Lotteries are one of the most economical ways to raise revenues.
   II. Lotteries are cost-efficient.
  III. Lotteries are safe to operate and are crime-free.

No matter what pattern you select, you should be careful to use only that pattern when sequencing your main points. For example do not organize some of your main points by time sequence and others by cause and effect.

Connecting the Main Points.   A conversation can move from one unrelated topic to another without losing meaning or impact, but for a speaker to communicate effectively with an audience, the thoughts in his or her speech must be systematically connected. The three most common connecting devices that speakers use are transitions, signposts, and internal summaries.

Transitions.   **Transitions** are phrases and words used to link ideas. They form a bridge between what has already been presented and what will be presented next. Transitions are typically used between the introduction and the body of a speech, between main ideas, between supporting materials and visual aids, and between the body and the conclusion. A transition can review information that has already been presented, preview information to come, or summarize key thoughts. Here are some typical transition statements that might be made in a speech:

> Let me move on to my next point. . . .
> Now that I have discussed the history of the frisbee, I would like
>   to move on to its uses. . . .
> Turning now . . .
> The final point I would like to make is . . .
> Another example might be . . .
> Keeping in mind the four items I have discussed, we arrive at the
>   following conclusions. . . .

Signposts.   **Signposts** are words, phrases, and short statements that let the audience know what is ahead. Some typical signposts are:

> Let me first illustrate . . .
> My second point is . . .
> In conclusion . . .
> As you look at my chart . . .
> Next you should consider . . .
> Finally . . .

Questions can also be used as signposts:

> Why does our tuition continue to increase?
> What does all this mean for us?
> How can we solve this problem?
> Who, then, is responsible?

Such questions draw the audience's attention to a forthcoming answer. A signpost, then, prepares an audience for what to expect next—just as a traffic sign warns of a coming curve in the road. It also alerts the audience that the upcoming information is important. For example:

> The most essential aspect of this is . . .
> Let's look at possible solutions to . . .
> The only thing you need to know is . . .

Internal summaries.   An **internal summary** is a short review statement that should be given at the end of each main point. Here is an example:

INTERNAL
SUMMARY

Let me briefly summarize what I have said so far. Inflation is the number-one factor contributing to our rising costs. For every percent that inflation increases, we must raise tuition by four percent. The problem of inflation must be solved. . . .

Internal summaries are extremely useful in helping the audience to follow along when a presentation is lengthy or complex.

CONNECTING THOUGHTS

TRANSITIONS	Phrases and words used to link ideas
SIGNPOSTS	Words, phrases, and short statements that let the audience know what is ahead
INTERNAL SUMMARIES	A short review of key information made after each main point

Supporting the Main Points.   Main points by themselves are nothing more than assertions, but as we explained in Chapter 7, an audience needs supporting and clarifying materials in order to accept what a speaker says. Therefore, it is imperative that each main point in a speech be supported and that the support be relevant and logically organized. When supporting materials are included, the body of a speech expands to look like this:

SPECIFIC PURPOSE:

To persuade my audience to take action against the malpractice nightmare in the health care industry.

MAIN POINT:

I. The symptoms of the malpractice crisis affect all of us.

SUPPORT AND
CLARIFYING
MATERIAL:

A. Medical malpractice is in what the American Medical Association calls "a crisis situation."
   1. *Fortune Magazine,* on February 15, 1985, explained that since 1975, the number of malpractice suits has gone up 500 percent.
   2. *Forbes Magazine,* in June 1985, revealed that the average settlement in a malpractice suit in 1984 was $950,000, nearly three times the average of 1983.[1]

Your supporting materials should be clearly related to the specific purpose and the main points of your speech.

The Introduction

Experienced speakers usually develop their introduction after, not before, the body of their speech. An **introduction** is an opening statement that serves two important functions: it orients the audience to the subject and it motivates them to listen. Thus, your introduction should prepare your audience for the body of your speech by clearly stating your specific purpose and by arousing interest and attention. While orienting listeners to the subject is usually considered more important, every effective speaker recognizes that without the attention and interest of the audience, no message can be conveyed successfully.

Your introduction, or preview, should be based on the information you gathered in your audience analysis. If your analysis was accurate and thorough, you should understand your audience's frame of reference and how it might differ from your own. Your introduction should include:

1. Background information
2. A clear statement of purpose
3. A forecast statement (a signpost statement)
4. Information to establish or improve your believability

Base your background information on what your audience knows or does not know about your subject. This is the appropriate time to set the stage, define terms, and establish the significance of your topic for your audience, as the speaker did in the following example:[2]

SETTING
THE STAGE

Twenty-five-year-old Scott Wilson, a gardener at a Florida condominium, accidentally sprayed the herbicide he was using on his face and hands. He had used the chemical many times in the past and that's why he simply washed his face and hands and returned to work—even though his shirt was still dripping wet. Five days later, Scott Wilson was rushed to the hospital barely breathing.

DEFINITION OF
TERM

Paraquat, the herbicide that Wilson was using, kills plants within hours by disrupting the photosynthetic process, causing individual cells to collapse. . . .

SIGNIFICANCE OF
TOPIC

Paraquat, in diluted form, is also a herbicide of choice for thousands of home gardeners. Its brand name is Ortho Spot Weed and Grass Control.

Design your introductory comments to gain the attention and interest of your audience. You must hold their interest and attention throughout your entire presentation, but that task will be easier if you can capture them during your introduction.

A standard way of gaining initial attention is simply to point out the reasons for presenting your speech. This is easily done in story form. For example:[3]

ORIENTING
MATERIAL

"When I was a kid," recalls author and columnist Pete Hamill, "the library gave us the world. My brother and I would get up early on Saturday mornings and wait on the library steps to be the first ones in the building."

Today our nation boasts of 100,000 public, university, and community libraries which circulate over one billion books each year. It is safe to say that each one of us has shared and enjoyed the adventure, excitement, and knowledge that our libraries offer through their collections of books, periodicals, and materials.

REASON TO LISTEN   But, in spite of their contributions to each one of us, the library systems of the United States are in the midst of a quiet, but serious crisis. With obstacles to funding, inflation, rising book costs, thefts and mounting expenses, our libraries are in serious trouble. . . . Because of its importance to all of us, it is necessary for us to examine this problem.

You may also arouse attention by:

1. *Referring to the subject or occasion.* You may be asked to speak on a special occasion, such as a holiday, founders' day, graduation, or anniversary. Here is a sample introduction related to an occasion:

> I am very honored to have been asked to give a speech in celebration of Public Education Week. This is truly a special occasion because our public educational system has made this community what it is today.

2. *Using personal references.* Whenever you can relate your own experience to a speech, do so. Personal experiences make your speech more meaningful to your audience and show them that you know what you are talking about. Here is how a speaker used a personal experience to introduce his speech on the joys of running:

> I used to be overweight and out of shape, and my grades were quite low. Now I've lost weight, I'm in much better physical shape, and my grade point average has increased. The reason for all of this is that I started to run each day.

3. *Asking rhetorical questions.* A rhetorical question is a question for which no answer is expected. Asking rhetorical questions in an introduction usually encourages an audience to become intellectually involved. Such questions can also be used to create suspense. Here is how one student used rhetorical questions to involve her audience in a speech about buying a new stereo:

> What is the best stereo on the market today? Which brand of stereo will give you the most for your money? These questions are often asked by those of us who are about to purchase a new stereo. My purpose today is to answer these questions for you.

4. *Presenting a startling statement.* This technique can be used when you want to shock or surprise your audience. It is an extremely effective attention getter, as shown by the following example:

> Big Dan's Tavern certainly didn't appear to be anything special to the young mother of two who crossed its threshold for the first time to make a simple purchase. Try as she may, though, she will never forget the barroom, because when the youthful mother entered it—her nightmare began. She endured more shame and terror that night than most of us probably will ever have to face. She was stripped, assaulted, and raped by four men for over an hour. She pleaded for mercy or aid and yet more than 15 other bar patrons simply stood and watched the spectacle. One man brushed aside

her pleading hands as he moved out of the way. Another helped hold her on the pool table for the convenience of the attackers. Many cheered and applauded, but no one called the police.[4]

5. *Using humor.* A funny story or relevant joke can not only gain the attention of your audience, but also get them to relax. One speaker began his talk as follows:

> The last time I gave a speech to this large a group an audience member raised his hand in the back row and shouted, "I can't hear you." Immediately, a hand went up in the front row and the person asked, "Can I move back there?" Now I know all of you want to hear me, so I'll try to speak loud enough, and if I don't, I'll know why some of you are moving to the back row.

6. *Using quotations.* Sometimes a quotation can grab your audience's attention, and if cited accurately, it can also add to your believability. A student talking about the future started her speech as follows:

> Lew Lehr, a former president of the 3M Company, one of the companies cited in the popular best seller, *In Search of Excellence,* wrote "The future belongs to those who see opportunity where others see only problems." The future is ours, but we must see it as an opportunity to excel. Our college education equips us for this opportunity. Today, I want to talk to you about what the twenty-first century will bring to each of us.

Suggestions for Developing Your Introduction

1. Keep your introduction relatively brief—between 5 and 20 percent of your total content.
2. Allow plenty of time to prepare your introduction carefully. Because it is critical to the success of your speech, it should not be rushed or written at the last minute.
3. Make your introduction creative and interesting. To accomplish this, think of several different introductions and choose the most effective one. Remember that the key to a successful introduction is making it relevant to your speech topic.
4. As you research your speech, watch for material to use in your introduction. Keep a notebook or file of interesting quotations, stories, humorous statements, and other items that might liven up your opening.
5. Develop your introduction after you have completed the main part of your speech. It's easier to create a relevant introduction after you have determined the content and direction of the body.
6. Write out your introduction word for word. This section is too important to improvise or leave to chance. In addition, writing it out will give you confidence and help you get off to a strong start.

A Sample Introduction.   The following introduction was part of a college student's award winning speech:[5]

BACKGROUND AND
ATTENTION GETTER

One year ago, two of my professors, Steve and Mary, were involved in a head-on collision with a drunk driver. Steve was killed instantly. Mary was critically injured and was not expected to live. The case was especially tragic because Steve and Mary had two young daughters and no will. Without a will, the state was required to take possession of the children, despite the fact that friends and family were more than willing to raise them.

REASON TO LISTEN

SIGNIFICANCE OF
TOPIC

PURPOSE
STATEMENT

FORECAST
STATEMENT

Over 60 percent of all Americans die without a will, and most of us don't even consider writing a will until relatively late in life. To those of us in the prime of our lives, the thought of writing a will of our own seems morbid and unnecessary. That simply isn't true. The fact is that each of us needs some kind of will, and most of us don't have the least idea of how to go about writing one. My purpose today is to convince each of you that having a will is important. We will discuss why people avoid writing a will, what a will is and why we need one, and finally, how we can obtain a will.

The Conclusion

Your **conclusion** should focus your audience's thoughts on the specific purpose of your speech and bring your most important points together in a condensed and uniform way. You may also use your conclusion to spell out the action or policies you recommend to solve a problem. In every case, your conclusion should reinforce what you want your audience to remember. Effective speakers often conclude a speech by doing the following things.

1. *Summarizing the main points.* In closing, the speaker repeats the main points of the speech. This is particularly helpful in informative speeches or any time you want your audience to remember your main points. For example, the speaker who informed her audience of the four greatest barriers to effective listening concluded her speech as follows:

> In summary, let me review the barriers that have the most impact on our listening. They are language, factual, mental, and physical distractions. If you remember these and how they affect listening, you will be a more effective listener.

2. *Issuing a challenge or appeal.* This kind of conclusion is especially effective when your purpose is to persuade your audience to take some form of action. The following conclusion was used in a persuasive speech on how to eliminate illiteracy in our society:

> Finally, our involvement must begin from the very simplest of tasks. We must observe our own friends, students, and classmates. It isn't easy for an adult to admit he or she can't read. If you suspect someone is having difficulties, tactfully encourage him or her to take advantage of the literacy programs that exist. A little compassion and understanding can make the difference between the number of those that do participate and those that don't.[6]

3. *Citing a quotation*. Citing a memorable quotation can be a good way to leave a lasting impression on your audience. When it is relevant and reinforces your specific purpose, a quotation can give your speech additional authority and help to increase your believability. A student speaking on the right to die with dignity concluded her speech as follows:

> If we can adopt these two requirements, we can forever banish death as a grim reaper. As former New York Senator Jacob Javits said shortly before his death, "The right to die with dignity is profound, moral, and essential."[7]

Because your conclusion is as important as any other part of your presentation, you should give it the same amount of attention. Be especially careful to avoid using it to add new information. Instead, use your conclusion to:

1. Reinforce your specific purpose
2. Review your main points
3. End with a final thought

Signal your audience that your speech is nearing its end by using such phrases as "in conclusion," "finally, let me end by," "in closing," or "my purpose has been." Each of these prepares your audience for your concluding remarks.

SUGGESTIONS FOR DEVELOPING YOUR CONCLUSION

The following hints should help you to develop a strong conclusion for any speech:

1. Your conclusion should be brief and should end with a definite summarizing statement. It should account for between 5 and 15 percent of the content of your speech.
2. Your conclusion should not contain information that was not already mentioned in either the introduction or the body of your speech.
3. Your conclusion, like the other parts of your speech, should not be rushed. It should be carefully thought out and relevant to the specific purpose of your speech.
4. Consider several possible endings and then settle on the one that best serves the purpose of your speech. Leave your audience with an impact that will make your speech memorable.
5. Write out your conclusion word for word. Then learn it well so that you can end your speech smoothly and confidently.

A Sample Conclusion. The following conclusion was part of a college student's award-winning speech:[8]

<table>
<tr>
<td>SIGNAL OF
SPEECH'S END
SUMMARY OF MAIN
POINTS

APPEAL FOR ACTION</td>
<td>To sum up, I have attempted to give you some of the reasons why art should be such a vital part of the curriculum of our schools. We, as concerned citizens, need to appeal to the large number of well-intentioned citizens who are not aware of the consequences of their actions against the arts. In some areas parents are forming boosters for the arts, which are similar to athletic boosters. This is something perhaps you could start in your own community. Also, plans are now afoot for the launching of a National Association for Education in the Arts, which could form the spearhead of a movement to exert pressure on policymakers.</td>
</tr>
<tr>
<td>MEMORABLE FINAL
THOUGHT</td>
<td>We all understand that a germinating seed needs the right surroundings to grow. If the environment becomes sterile, the plant will cease to grow or if it does survive, it will not be healthy. We, as gardeners for our lawns, provide the proper environment for those lawns. Are we willing to accept less for children? True, the damage to a crop or lawn without proper care is obvious, but the damage to the independence and creative thinking of our children, while less obvious, is a loss to us all.</td>
</tr>
</table>

OUTLINING YOUR SPEECH

Outlining is one of the most difficult (and therefore mistakenly avoided) steps in preparing a speech. *Outlining* and *organizing* are somewhat similar terms. **Outlining** is a standardized approach to arranging written materials into a logical sequence, often referred to as the blueprint or skeleton of a speech. **Organizing,** on the other hand, is simply the arranging of something in a systematic and meaningful way. Both involve the arranging of information to form a meaningful sequence, but outlining is a more rigorous, written process.

Because outlining requires more detail than organizing, your outline should help unify and clarify your thinking, make relationships clear, and provide the proper balance and emphasis to each point as it relates to your specific purpose. Outlining also helps to ensure that your information is both accurate and relevant.

As you prepare your outline, you will gain an overview of your entire presentation. This should help you to gauge the amount of support you have for each of your main points and identify any points that need further development.

The Three Stages of Outlining

The actual process of outlining usually requires three steps:

1. Create a preliminary outline that identifies the topic and the main points to be covered in the speech.

2. Expand the preliminary outline into a full-content outline that clearly and fully develops the speech's content.
3. Condense the full-content outline into a presentational outline for easy delivery.

The Preliminary Outline.   A **preliminary outline** is a list of all the main points that you may decide to use in your speech. For example, suppose that you are preparing a four- to six-minute persuasive speech on safety regulations for compact/light trucks and passenger vehicles.[9] Because of the limited amount of time you have to give your speech, you know that you cannot possibly cover everything related to your topic. And because your general purpose is to persuade, you will need to focus your speech's content in that direction. So, recalling what you have already read about topic selection, analyzing your audience, gathering information, and using supporting and clarifying materials, you determine your specific purpose: To persuade your audience that safety standards should be established for compact/light trucks and passenger vehicles. Based on this specific purpose, you can prepare a preliminary outline of possible main points, as shown in Table 8.1. Once your possible main points are arranged in this way, you will find it easier to analyze your thoughts. You can then decide exactly which main thoughts to include in your speech and choose the best order for presenting them.

TABLE 8.1   *Sample Preliminary Outline*

TOPIC:	Safety regulations for compact/light trucks and passenger vehicles
GENERAL PURPOSE:	To persuade
SPECIFIC PURPOSE:	To persuade my audience that safety regulations should be adopted for light/compact trucks and passenger vehicles.
POSSIBLE MAIN POINTS:	1. The existing safety regulations for light/compact trucks and passenger vehicles
	2. Production standards of light/compact trucks and passenger vehicles
	3. The need for additional safety regulations for light/compact trucks and passenger vehicles
	4. The growing popularity of light/compact trucks and passenger vehicles
	5. Recent improvements in safety standards for automobiles
	6. Why safety standards haven't been adopted for light/compact trucks and passenger vehicles
	7. The effects that the lack of safety regulations for light/compact trucks can have on society

The Full-Content Outline.   A **full-content outline** is an expansion of the main points selected from the preliminary outline. When done correctly, it is a detailed skeleton of a speech with all main and secondary points written in complete sentences (see Table 8.2). A full-content outline helps a speaker to clarify and polish his or her thoughts because:

1. a main point that cannot be written in a complete sentence is probably weak or invalid and does not belong in the speech;
2. writing a complete sentence for each point requires thought;
3. such an outline shows the flow of the speech and whether the sequence is logical and effective;
4. the outline illustrates the relationship of each point to the specific purpose and enables the speaker to analyze how each point contributes to the total presentation;
5. the outline is a form of communication in itself that serves as an excellent summary of the text and can be used by others to see the main points of the presentation;
6. the outline helps to make each topic sentence clear and shows transitions from point to point.

The full-content outline should close with a bibliography that lists all the sources used in preparing the speech. This includes books, magazines, and interviews—any source that either the speaker or the listener might want to refer to in order to learn more about the subject. A sample bibliography is illustrated in Table 8.2.

Because it serves so many purposes, a full-content outline is an essential part of planning any speech. Writing a full-content outline is not necessarily an easy task, but once the job is completed, it makes the rest of the preparation and delivery of a speech much easier.

GUIDELINES FOR WRITING A FULL-CONTENT OUTLINE

1. Cover the three main parts of your speech in your outline: introduction, body, and conclusion—with appropriate transitions.
2. Identify each main point in your speech with a Roman numeral (I, II, etc.).
3. Follow standard outline style to ensure consistency in symbols and indentation.
4. Use only one idea per symbol.
5. State each main heading (such as I, A, 1) as a single sentence.
6. Give subpoints to every Roman numeral statement in the body of your speech. All main points and subpoints must have at least two parts— that is, there can be no I without a II, no A without a B, no 1 without a 2, and so on.
7. The body will usually contain two, three, or four Roman numerals.
8. Be sure that the outline makes sense from one symbol to the next.

TABLE 8.2   *Full-Content Outline*

TITLE:	A Cruel Hoax
TOPIC:	Safety regulations for compact/light trucks and passenger vehicles
GENERAL PURPOSE:	To persuade
SPECIFIC PURPOSE:	To persuade my audience that safety regulations should be adopted for light/compact trucks and passenger vehicles.

Introduction

ATTENTION-GETTING AND ORIENTING MATERIALS	It isn't surprising that a consumer culture which eats light food, drinks light beer, and performs light aerobics also drives—in ever-increasing numbers—light/compact vehicles. Light/compact vehicles
DEFINITION	include pickups, minivans, jeeps, sport utility vehicles, and station wagons built on truck chassis.
	The truth is that light cuisine frequently isn't, light beer frequently isn't, and light aerobics are still a sweaty proposition. As for light/compact vehicles, . . . Well, Diana Richards saw the light by accident.
STORY	Diana Richards, a 36-year-old credit manager, was driving her pickup home after a hard day at work when she was sideswiped by a car.
STARTLING STATEMENT	Knocked unconscious, she awoke to the horrifying discovery that her foot was missing. Later, most of her lower leg was amputated. Ms. Richards
QUOTATION	described the sense of betrayal she felt: "I always thought that a truck had more protection. I couldn't believe how it crumbled. It was just like
ANALOGY	someone took aluminum foil and just wadded it up. And it crumbled so bad—and then when I saw the other people's car and how it was hardly even hurt, I kept asking, why did ours fall apart?"
SIGNIFICANCE OF TOPIC	Diana Richards' case, as presented on the June 10 television program, "Newsmagazine 1986," is not unique. Each year, thousands of Americans are tragically maimed or killed as a result of light/compact vehicle accidents. Many lives could be spared if it weren't for a lethal combination
SPECIFIC PURPOSE	of legislative perversity and manufacturers' callousness. Today, I would like to tell you why safety regulations should be adopted for light/compact
FORECAST	trucks and passenger vehicles. I will examine the lack of safety standards on light/compact vehicles, the costs to each of us, the reasons for the absence of adequate safety standards, and the solutions that must be
SIGNPOST	adopted. I will begin by talking about the lack of safety standards.

Body

MAIN POINT WRITTEN AS FULL SENTENCE— IDENTIFICATION OF PROBLEM	I. Light/compact vehicles are dangerous due to the lack of safety regulations.
	   A. Light/compact vehicles are exceedingly popular.
	      1. Ford Motor Company expects to sell 4.4 million vehicles this year alone.

SUPPORTING MATERIAL	2. People are buying them because of their near car-like comfort, according to the *Wall Street Journal*.
	   B. Light/compact vehicles are exceedingly dangerous.
	      1. Max Bramble is just one example of the danger of driving a compact vehicle.

             a. His pickup was hit from behind with such force that it was crushed.

             b. Max suffered brain damage and died.

      2. Each year thousands of people die or sustain serious injuries as a result of driving compact vehicles.

             a. Between 1982 and 1984 the number of deaths related to driving compact vehicles nearly doubled.

             b. There are 35 deaths for every 100,000 compact pickups registered, compared to 21 per 100,000 for all cars registered.

INTERNAL SUMMARY

TRANSITION

So far I have shown you how dangerous light/compact vehicles are by providing specific examples and statistics. They are not only dangerous, but they also cost society money.

MAIN POINT

II. Light/compact vehicles, because they are not regulated, cost each one of us money.

SUPPORTING MATERIALS

    A. Unregulated light/compact vehicles cost us in terms of higher health care, lost wages, and increased insurance premiums.

    B. It cost society as a whole, according to the National Safety Council, $1 billion last year.

INTERNAL SUMMARY

TRANSITION

There is a tremendous cost to each of us because there are no regulations—it costs both in dollars and in lives. Why isn't something being done?

MAIN POINT

III. Two reasons are often cited for the lack of safety standards for light/compact vehicles.

SUPPORTING MATERIAL

    A. Manufacturers assert that light/compact vehicles are safer than other vehicles because they are manufactured to meet other car standards and thus should be safe.

    B. Manufacturers claim that most accidents are the driver's fault and that no number of standards will change that.

INTERNAL SUMMARY
TRANSITION

It is clear that the manufacturers do not see safety standards as the solution to the problem—they blame the driver. What is the solution?

MAIN POINT— SUGGESTED SOLUTIONS

IV. There are two solutions to the problem of light/compact vehicle safety regulations.

    A. We must take action to protect ourselves when we buy light/compact vehicles.

        1. Purchase light/compact vehicles that have safety features such as steel-reinforced beams.

        2. Wear a seat belt at all times while driving or riding in a light/compact vehicle.

    B. Congress must do something to pass legislation to improve the standards of light/compact vehicles.

INTERNAL SUMMARY

We therefore must help ourselves and get Congress to pass legislation if we are going to improve the safety standards of these vehicles.

Conclusion

TRANSITION

SUMMARY OF MAIN
POINTS

APPEAL

After examining the absence of light/compact vehicle standards, the cost
to each of us, the reasons for their absence, and the appropriate corrective
measures, the choice is clear. Either we can adopt and enforce simple
safety standards that ensure adequate protection to those involved in
accidents with light/compact vehicles, or we can ignore the carnage that is
visiting our nation's highways, and, like Diana Richards and Max
Bramble, risk "seeing the light . . . by accident."

Bibliography

General Accounting Office Report to the Congress, July 6, 1978.
Landis, David. "Big Deals Abound for Small Trucks," *USA Today*,
     February 2, 1987, p. 10E.
Levin, Doron P. "As Small Trucks Gain in Popularity, Questions
     Arise About Their Safety," *Wall Street Journal.* March 20, 1986, p.
     33.
National Safety Council Report.
Transcript from television show, "Newsmagazine 1986," June 10,
     1986, Vol. 1, No. 1.

TABLE 8.3   *Sample Presentational Outline*

TITLE:	A Cruel Hoax
TOPIC:	Safety regulations for compact/light trucks and passenger vehicles
GENERAL PURPOSE:	To persuade
SPECIFIC PURPOSE:	To persuade my audience that safety regulations should be adopted for light/compact trucks and passenger vehicles.

Outline

SELF-REMINDERS
ABOUT DELIVERY

DON'T READ NOTES

SLOW DOWN — LOOK AT AUDIENCE — PAUSE

Introduction
   I. Consumer culture—light foods, light beer, light aerobics, also
      light/compact vehicles.
      A. List types of vehicles
      B. Diana Richards Story
         1. 36-year-old credit manager
         2. Lost foot
         3. 1,000 Americans—"Newsmagazine 1986" television
            show

BRIEF PAUSE

STATEMENT OF
PURPOSE

II. Safety regulations should be adopted
    A. Lack of safety standards
    B. Reason for lack of standards
    C. Solution to problem

SIGNAL THAT BODY
AND MAIN POINTS
ARE COMING

Body

I. Light/compact vehicles are dangerous
    A. Exceedingly popular
        1. Ford/4.4 million vehicles

CITING SOURCE
HELPS SPEAKER TO
REMEMBER AND
QUOTE REPORT
DATA ACCURATELY

        2. Buying because of comfort—*Wall Street Journal*
    B. Exceedingly dangerous
        1. Max Bramble story
        2. Thousands die or sustain serious injuries
            a. 1982–84 deaths doubled
            b. 35/100,000 pickups
               21/100,000 cars

REMINDER OF
INTERNAL SUMMARY
AND TRANSITION

(So far I have shown danger by providing examples and statistics. . . .)

REMINDERS OF KEY
TERMS AND
SOURCES

II. Not regulated—cost everyone money
    A. Higher health care, lost wages, increased insurance
    B. National Safety Council—$1 billion last year

(Tremendous cost to each. Why isn't something done?)

INTERNAL SUMMARY
AND TRANSITION

III. Two reasons
    A. Manufacturers—safe enough
    B. Manufacturers—drivers at fault

(Manufacturers don't see problem. What is the solution?)

PAUSE

PAUSE DESIGNED
TO HIGHLIGHT KEY
POINT

IV. Two solutions
    A. Protect ourselves
    B. Congress must act

INTERNAL SUMMARY
AND TRANSITION

(Must help ourselves and get Congress to pass legislation)

REMINDER TO
SPEAK SLOWLY

SLOW DOWN

SIGNAL THAT
CONCLUSION IS
COMING

Conclusion

I. Absence of light/compact standards
II. We can adopt and enforce safety standards . . . or we can ignore the carnage
    A. Diana Richards and Max Bramble
    B. "Seeing the light . . . by accident"

Mini-Exercise

Reorganize the scrambled order of the following outline to include main points and all supporting points. Place the number that corresponds to each sentence in the blanks provided. Each sentence can be used only once.

    I.

        A.

            1.

            2.

        B.

            1.

            2.

   II.

        A.

        B.

        C.

Topic: The Financial Crunch in State Universities

1. Costs of operation are rising.
2. There are several possible solutions for this financial crisis.
3. Colleges must improve lobbying in the legislatures.
4. Revenues and sources of income are declining.
5. Colleges must hold the line on new hiring.
6. Salaries of faculty and staff are increasing.
7. State legislatures are cutting back on support.
8. State universities face a financial crisis.
9. Current programs now cost more.
10. Tuition revenue is not keeping pace.
11. Students must pay a greater percentage of their educational costs.

The Presentational Outline.   A **presentational outline** is a condensation of the full-content outline that eases delivery by minimizing detail and listing key words and phrases in place of full sentences (see Table 8.3). This is the outline that you will actually work from when you deliver your speech. The advantages of the presentational outline are that it is more concise, requires less space, is more comprehensible at a glance, and is easier to use when speaking.

Your presentational outline should include your main points and sufficient clarifying and supporting material to aid you in your presentation. It may also include your complete introduction and conclusion, although the choice is up to you. Its most important contents are the key words and phrases that will remind you of the points you want to make. But remember to be brief. If your presentational outline is too complex and detailed, you can easily get too involved in your notes and thus lose contact with your audience.

SUMMARY

Organizing is the arranging of ideas or elements into a systematic and meaningful whole. It requires planning, time, and know-how. Most speeches are organized into three main parts: the introduction, the body, and the conclusion.

The *body,* which is the main content of a speech, develops the speaker's general and specific purposes. It consists of the main points of a speech plus the supporting and clarifying materials. The *main points,* which are the principal subdivisions of a speech, are critical to the accomplishment of a speaker's specific purpose. Main points should relate to the specific purpose, be stated carefully, and be limited in number.

One of five basic patterns is used in most speeches. (1) The *time-sequence pattern* begins at a particular point in time and continues either forward or backward. (2) The *spatial pattern* organizes the main points according to their relationship in space. (3) The *problem-solution pattern* first discusses a problem and then suggests solutions. (4) The *cause-effect pattern* illustrates logical relationships between the cause of something and its subsequent effect. (5) The *topical pattern* divides a speech topic into a series of related subtopics. The pattern of presentation should match the topic and the speaker's specific purpose.

The main points of a speech are connected to one another by transitions, signposts, and internal summaries. *Transitions* are words and phrases used to link ideas. *Signposts* are words, phrases, and short statements that let an audience know what is coming. *Internal summaries* are short reviews of what was said under each main point. Main points cannot stand alone; they must be supported and clarified.

The *introduction* and *conclusion* are usually developed after the body of the presentation has been completed. The introduction serves two principal functions: to orient the audience to the topic and to motivate them to listen. The main functions of the conclusion are to focus the audience's thoughts on the specific purpose and to bring together the most important points in a condensed and uniform way.

Outlining provides a written account of the main features and ideas of a speech that can then serve as a blueprint or skeleton. During the outlining process, a speaker produces a preliminary outline, a full-content outline, and a presentational outline. The *preliminary outline* lists all possible main points and forms the basis for early decisions about a speech's content and direction. A *full-content outline* expands on the preliminary outline by detailing all the main and secondary points in full-sentence form, and a *presentational outline* condenses the full-content outline into the key words and phrases that will aid the speaker in delivering the speech. When you have completed the outlining process, you should have an extremely clear picture of exactly what you will say and how you will say it.

KEY TERMS

Body: the main content of a speech that develops the speaker's general and specific purposes.

Cause-Effect Pattern: an order of presentation in which the speaker first explains the causes of an event, problem, or issue, and then discusses its consequences.

Conclusion: a closing statement that focuses the audience's thoughts on the specific purpose of a speech and brings the most important points together in a condensed and uniform way.

Full-Content Outline: an expansion of the main points selected from the preliminary outline, it is a detailed skeleton of a speech with all main and secondary points written in complete sentences.

Internal Summary: a short review statement that should be given at the end of each main point.

Introduction: an opening statement that orients the audience to the subject and motivates them to listen.

Main Points: the principal subdivisions of a speech.

Organizing: the arranging of ideas or elements into a systematic and meaningful whole.

Outlining: a standardized approach to arranging written materials into a logical sequence, often referred to as the blueprint or skeleton of a speech.

Preliminary Outline: a list of all the main points that may be used in a speech.

Presentational Outline: a condensation of the full-content outline that eases delivery by minimizing detail and listing key words and phrases in place of full sentences.

Problem-Solution Pattern: an order of presentation that first discusses a problem and then suggests solutions.

Signposts: words, phrases, or short statements that indicate to an audience the direction a speaker will take next.

Spatial Pattern: an order of presentation in which the content of a speech is organized according to relationships in space.

Time-Sequence (Chronological) Pattern: an order of presentation that begins at a particular point in time and continues either forward or backward.

Topical Pattern: an order of presentation in which the main topic is divided into a series of related subtopics.

Transitions: phrases and words used to link ideas.

DISCUSSION STARTERS

1. How can a speech's organization affect an audience?

2. Why should the main points of a speech be carefully developed and written?

3. What usually determines the number of main points in a speech?

4. What should be done to make a speech's main points more meaningful to an audience?

5. Why is it important for a speaker to understand the different patterns for ordering the main points in a speech?

6. Why is the introduction so important to a speech's overall effectiveness?

7. What should the introduction of a speech accomplish?

8. What suggestions would you give beginning speakers about how to develop the introduction of a speech?

9. What should the conclusion of a speech accomplish?

10. What suggestions would you give beginning speakers about how to develop the conclusion of a speech?

11. How do the three kinds of outlines differ?

FURTHER READINGS

Boyd, Stephen D., and Mary Ann Renz. *Organization and Outlining: A Workbook for Students in a Basic Speech Course.* Indianapolis: Bobbs-Merrill, 1985.

Haynes, Judy L. *Organizing a Speech: A Programmed Guide.* 2nd ed. Englewood Cliffs, N.J.: Prentice-Hall, 1981.

Sprague, Jo, and Douglas Stuart. *The Speaker's Handbook.* San Diego: Harcourt Brace Jovanovich, Publishers, 1984.

Wall, K. Wayne. *Fundamentals of Outlining: A Self-Teaching Program.* Dubuque, Iowa: Kendall/Hunt, 1983.

NOTES

1. Stolts, Michael, "The Malpractice Malaise," *Winning Orations, 1986* (Mankato, Minn.: Interstate Oratorical Association, 1986), pp. 117–118.

2. Blashfield, Mickey, "The Paradox of Paraquat," *Winning Orations, 1984* (Mankato, Minn.: Interstate Oratorical Association, 1984), p. 37.

3. Edwards, David J., "Dewey or Don't We? Saving Our Libraries," *Winning Orations, 1984* (Mankato, Minn.: Interstate Oratorical Association, 1984), p. 70.

4. Randles, Billy, "My Brother's Keeper," *Winning Orations, 1984* (Mankato, Minn.: Interstate Oratorical Association, 1984), p. 49.

5. Johnson, Laurel, "Where There's A Will There's A Way," *Winning Orations, 1986* (Mankato, Minn.: Interstate Oratorical Association, 1986), p. 59.

6. Braaten, Joan, "It's English," *Winning Orations, 1984* (Mankato, Minn.: Interstate Oratorical Association, 1984), p. 66.

7. Gerlach, Brenda, "America—The Land of the Free?" *Winning Orations, 1986* (Mankato, Minn.: Interstate Oratorical Association, 1986), p. 104.

8. Stalnaker, Tamara, "Elevation to the Beautiful Life," *Winning Orations, 1984* (Mankato, Minn.: Interstate Oratorical Association, 1984), pp. 92–95.

9. This example is based on "A Cruel Hoax," a speech written by Mary B. Trauba for the 1987 oratory contest competition. Permission to use "A Cruel Hoax," which has won several national oratory contests, was acquired from Mary B. Trauba, a student at the University of Nebraska, and Jack Kay, the director of Forensics and Chair of the Department of Speech Communication, University of Nebraska—Lincoln.

CHAPTER 9

Delivering Your Speech

LEARNING OBJECTIVES

After studying this chapter, you should be able to:

1. Describe the roles that ethics, knowledge, preparation, and self-confidence play in effective speechmaking.

2. Discuss the symptoms and causes of speech anxiety and suggest five methods of controlling this problem.

3. Analyze the pros and cons of the four basic methods of speech delivery.

4. Identify the vocal and physical factors that contribute to an effective delivery.

5. Tell how each of the most commonly used visual aids can enhance a speech presentation.

6. Specify how speakers can polish their delivery.

DIONNE: *(seeing Bill standing in an empty room, talking)*
What are you doing?

BILL: I'm practicing my speech.

DIONNE: Do you always practice by talking in an empty room?

BILL: No, not all the time, but it helps me feel more at ease.

DIONNE: Don't you get nervous when you have to give a speech?

BILL: A little, I guess. But, if I'm prepared and I've practiced enough—it's a piece of cake. I really like speaking in front of others.

DIONNE: You've got to be kidding.

You may find it hard to believe, but the most enjoyable part of the speechmaking process is the actual presentation of the speech to the audience. The hard part is behind you. You've done your researching and organizing, so now you can focus on the last step—delivery.

The effectiveness of your speech presentation depends not only on what you say, but also on how you say it. Therefore, to help you improve your presentation skills, we will discuss the qualities of effective speakers, how to manage anxiety, the features of an effective delivery, the different methods of delivery, the vocal and physical aspects of delivery, how to use visual aids, and how to polish your delivery.

THE QUALITIES OF EFFECTIVE SPEAKERS

By cultivating certain personal qualities, you as a speaker can enhance the likelihood that your listeners will accept your message. The most effective speakers are ethical, knowledgeable, prepared, and self-confident.

Ethics

Ethics—an individual's system of moral principles—plays a key role in communication. Because we are responsible for what we tell others, we should always hold the highest ethical standards. As speakers, we must communicate to our audience that we are honest, sincere, and of high integrity.

As listeners, we are also responsible for what we accept from others. Therefore, we should verify the integrity of the information we receive. See Chapter 5 for a complete discussion of listening and the responsibilities of the listener.

THINK ABOUT IT

An ethical speaker:

- Does not distort or falsify evidence.
- Does not use false reasoning.
- Does not make unsupported attacks on an opponent.
- Does not deceive an audience about his or her intent.
- Does not use irrelevant emotional appeals to divert attention from the basic argument.
- Does not pose as an authority when he or she is not.[1]

Knowledge

Knowledge is a speaker's greatest asset. Knowing your subject is essential if you plan to reach your listeners. Those who have become noted speakers are almost always avid readers. To be knowledgeable and to enhance your understanding of events, people, and values, you must read and be observant of things around you. From experience you know that it is easier to talk about things and events that you are familiar with than those you are not. As an educated person, you should keep abreast not only of past international, national, regional, and local events, but of current events as well. You should read all kinds of books, at least one trade magazine, and one daily newspaper in addition to listening to news broadcasts and documentaries.

Preparation

People rarely make speeches without some preparation, and the most successful speakers are those who are well prepared. A successful speech is somewhat like a successful date, business meeting, or athletic event: all require planning, preparation, and work. In an article entitled "Motivate Your Team—The Vince Lombardi Way," Jerry Kramer, a former football player for the Green Bay Packers, relates the following story as told by Max McGee, who used to play left end for the same team:

> Lombardi [a famous head coach], according to McGee, was very angry at the team. Lombardi told the team that they were going to go back to the beginning—back to the fundamentals.
> He then picked up a football and said, "This is a football."
> McGee responded quickly, "Wait a minute, Coach, you're going too fast."

McGee's humorous story contains an important message: Even if you are a pro, it is wise to prepare ahead of time and to know the fundamentals. Whether playing football or delivering a speech—for the beginner as well as for the experienced speaker—preparation and knowledge of the fundamentals are important.

THINK ABOUT IT

Wil Linkugel, a professor of speech communication at the University of Kansas, told this story:

A student athlete was delivering a speech to the class. The student, speaking in a monotone voice, kept reading from a prepared script. Finally, Professor Linkugel interrupted the student.

PROFESSOR: Why don't you put down your notes and just tell us what your notes say?

STUDENT: I can't do that. I'll never get it right.

PROFESSOR: Let's see what you can do.
The student tried speaking without his notes, but the result, although greatly improved, left much to be desired.

STUDENT: I'll never do this right!

PROFESSOR: In practice, if you were running a pass pattern and you didn't do it right, what would your coach make you do?

STUDENT: We'd run it over again.

PROFESSOR: How many times would you run it over?

STUDENT: As many times as it would take to get it right.

Self-Confidence

Self-confidence is so essential to becoming an effective speaker that most of this book's content is aimed at helping you to improve and strengthen this quality. Anxiety can be especially damaging to a speaker's self-confidence. Because self-confidence is influenced so strongly by anxiety, we will discuss this problem in detail.

MANAGING THE ANXIETY OF SPEECHMAKING

If you suffer from the fear of speaking before an audience—a condition known as **speech anxiety,** it may help to know that you are not alone. In fact, even the most experienced speakers confess to having some anxiety about speaking before a group, but they are able to control it.

Understanding a particular fear is difficult unless you have personally experienced it. The following story illustrates this point. Mary's brother-in-law's back bothers him when he lifts heavy objects. She used to think that he was making excuses for being lazy until she pinched a nerve in her back and experienced the pain her brother-in-law has long suffered. The message was very clear to her: it isn't easy to understand someone else's problem unless you have experienced it yourself. The next time her brother-in-law complained about his back, Mary was more sympathetic.

If you have had the opportunity to speak before a group, you probably know a little about speech anxiety, the number-one fear of Americans, according to a national survey.[2] The important thing to remember is that having some anxiety about giving a speech before a group is normal. It only becomes a serious problem when you cannot control your anxiety or choose not to communicate.

Not everything that is faced can be changed, but nothing can be changed until it is faced.

James Baldwin

Communication Apprehension

Communication apprehension, the severest form of speech anxiety, is the chronic fear or avoidance of all interactions with others. It can be seen in individuals who either consciously or subconsciously have decided to remain silent. They perceive that their silence offers them greater advantages than speaking out, or that the disadvantages of communicating outweigh any potential gains they might receive.

Among the fears of those with communication apprehension is the fear of speaking before a group. However, everyone who fears speaking before a group does not necessarily suffer from communication apprehension. That term refers to the much deeper problem of virtually cutting oneself off from most communication with others.

The Symptoms of Speech Anxiety

Speech anxiety is a more specific term used to describe the discomfort of people who fear speaking before a group. It occurs when our bodies secrete hormones and adrenaline that eventually overload our physical and emotional responses. These chemical reactions are similar to those you might experience if you suddenly meet a growling dog or a person holding a gun. Your heart begins to beat faster and your blood pressure begins to rise. Consequently, more sugar is pumped into your system. In addition, your stomach may begin to churn. When you experience these reactions, you may feel as if your body is operating in high gear and that little or nothing can be done about it.

Speakers who experience speech anxiety often display these visible signs:

VOICE	Quavering Too soft Monotonous; nonemphatic Too fast
FLUENCY	Stammering; halting Awkward pauses Hunting for words; speech blocks
MOUTH AND THROAT	Swallowing repeatedly Clearing throat repeatedly Breathing heavily
FACIAL EXPRESSIONS	No eye contact; rolling eyes Tense face muscles; grimaces; twitches Deadpan expression
ARMS AND HANDS	Rigid and tense Fidgeting; waving hands about Motionless; stiff
BODY MOVEMENT	Swaying; pacing; shuffling feet.[3]

These behaviors can occur separately or in any combination, depending on the degree of anxiety the speaker is experiencing.

Speakers suffering from speech anxiety may also make telling statements. For example, they may offer self-critical excuses or apologies such as "I'm not any good at this anyway," "I didn't really prepare for this because I didn't have enough time," or "I never was able to say this correctly." Instead of improving the situation, these comments tend to draw more attention to speakers' nervousness and thus magnify the problem. Among the other indicators of anxiety are such physical symptoms as profuse sweating, dry lips, and blushing, and such observable behaviors as lack of eye contact, an unenthusiastic tone of voice, poor posture, a crackling voice, and a resigned facial expression.

Speakers who suffer from speech anxiety often overestimate how much the audience notices about their behavior. The audience, on the other hand, tends to underestimate or overlook a speaker's anxiety. Audiences cannot detect, for example, a speaker who is experiencing butterflies unless the butterflies cause an observable reaction or the speaker's voice sounds nervous.

Causes of Speech Anxiety

Just as physicians can better treat an illness if they know its cause, so can people better reduce and control speech anxiety if they can determine the underlying problem. Many people with speech anxiety treat only the symptoms and tend to ignore the causes, but trying to remove the symptoms without understanding the causes is usually a losing battle.

Most speech anxiety begins at a very early age as a result of negative feedback in the home. For example, children who are not encouraged to communicate or are punished for doing so are likely to learn that communicating is undesirable and that silence is beneficial. They will then avoid communication because it is not rewarded. As these children continue to avoid communicating, others may unknowingly contribute further to their fear by asking questions such as "Cat got your tongue?" or "You're afraid to talk, aren't you?", thus making them feel inadequate and perpetuating the fear and anxiety associated with communicating.

People may also develop speech anxiety if they constantly hear that speaking in front of others can be a terrible experience or if they are told immediately before giving a speech, "Don't worry about it—you'll do fine," which reinforces the notion that something can go wrong. If speakers believe that something can go wrong and that they might make fools of themselves, they are apt to lose confidence and develop speech anxiety.

In our society, success, winning, and "being number 1" are too often considered all-important. When we can't be the most successful we sometimes consider ourselves failures. No one likes a failure. Thus, we are apt to feel that success brings rewards and failure brings punishment. If you are a winner, you are praised and if you are a loser, you are ridiculed. As a result, we place tremendous pressure on ourselves and others to be successful.

When we haven't been successful at something, we are often told to try again, but if the consequences of the failure are dramatic and if the payoff for success doesn't seem worth the effort, we may prefer to avoid the situation. Avoidance may result in punishment, but we may perceive that as better than trying to do something and failing. Sometimes society is more lenient. For example, in an athletic contest we assume that there will be a winner and a loser. No one likes to lose, but playing your best and losing is often acceptable. When someone makes a mistake in a speech, however, we may be more critical. Rather than acknowledge that the person is making an honest effort, we may perceive him or her as inadequate or unskilled. Consequently, the stress created by fear of making mistakes in front of others may be so great that it produces anxiety and sometimes complete avoidance of a speech situation.

Among the other most common causes of speech anxiety are:

- Fear of physical unattractiveness
- Fear of social inadequacy
- Fear of criticism
- Fear of the unknown
- Fear of speech anxiety
- Conflicting emotions
- Excitement from anticipation[4]

Note that each of these reactions to a speechmaking situation is learned, and because speech anxiety is a learned behavior, the only solution for its sufferers is to examine the potential reasons for their anxiety and learn how to use this knowledge to manage their discomfort.

Treating Speech Anxiety

While speaking before a group may produce stress and anxiety, few people allow their nervousness to prevent them from trying and succeeding. In fact, as mentioned earlier, even well-known speakers feel some nervousness before giving a speech, but they have learned to control it. The key to successful control of your anxiety is the desire to control it. To cope with speech anxiety we must realize that the potential for failure always exists, but that we can't let it stop us from trying. If we allowed the possibility of failure to overwhelm us, we probably would never do or learn anything. A child beginning to walk is a prime example of how most of our learning occurs. At first, the child wobbles, takes a small step, and falls. But when the child falls, someone is usually there to offer help, support, and encouragement to continue. In addition, the child usually is determined to walk regardless of the difficulties. Speechmaking, like learning to walk, involves many of the same processes: help, support, and encouragement are important, but the essential ingredient is *determination* to succeed.

There are no simple cures for speech anxiety—only ways to reduce, manage, or control it so that it does not interfere with your presentation. Experts, for example, suggest that selecting a topic you *enjoy* and *know* something about helps to reduce anxiety since the more you know about a subject, the easier it is for you to talk about it.

Being prepared can also reduce anxiety. Many kinds of preparation can help. For example, know your audience, know the physical surroundings where you are going to speak (such as the room size, lighting, placement of microphone and audiovisual equipment), and convince yourself that you will be successful. *Confidence* plays a key role in controlling anxiety.

Practice is another good way to gain a feeling of preparedness. The better you know the content of your speech and your delivery plan, the more comfortable you will feel about your presentation. Few things are done without some practice. For example, the quarterback who executes a perfect touchdown pass, the gymnast who scores a 10 in the floor exercise, the actress who presents a flawless performance, the student who draws beautiful pictures, the person who passes the road test for a driver's license, and the person who gives a polished and interesting speech have spent hours—and sometimes years—in practice.

Giving a speech and completing a pass play in a football game are not exactly the same thing, but both require similar preparation. The successful pass play requires research, organization, learning, observation, practice, willingness to work hard, ability to perform, confidence, knowing your opponent's defenses (or knowing your audience), and timing. A successful speech presentation requires all of the aforementioned factors in addition to knowing your audience and selecting an appropriate topic.

CONTROLLING SPEECH ANXIETY

1. Realize that almost everyone has some anxiety about presenting a speech—you are not alone.
2. Select a topic that you are familiar with and that you enjoy.
3. Know your audience and the surroundings where your presentation will take place.
4. Prepare yourself mentally for success. Believe that you are going to be successful and you probably will be.
5. Practice!

METHODS OF DELIVERY

An effective delivery conveys the speaker's purpose and ideas clearly and interestingly so that the audience attends to and retains what was said as it was intended by the speaker. The effectiveness of a speech, therefore, depends both on what is said and how it is conveyed. No two speakers are alike. For example, it is unlikely that anyone could deliver Martin Luther King, Jr.'s, "I Have a Dream" speech as effectively as he did. This speech, widely regarded as a masterpiece, was delivered on August 28, 1963, to over 200,000 people who had gathered in Washington, D.C., to participate in a peaceful demonstration to further the cause of equal rights for black Americans. If you've ever heard a recording of this speech, you know how his delivery affected his audience. King had a rich baritone voice modulated by the cadence of a Southern Baptist preacher and the fervor of a crusader. Although the words of the speech can be repeated and the style of Martin Luther King, Jr., can be imitated, the setting, timing, and circumstances cannot be reconstructed. Thus, the effect that King had on that day in August 1963 can never be repeated.

A poorly written speech can be improved by effective delivery, and a well-written speech can be ruined by ineffective delivery. Yet there is no single set of hard and fast rules that will guarantee an effective delivery in every situation. The only consistent rule is that you must be yourself! Of course, as a beginning speaker, you probably have many questions about how to deliver a speech: "How many notes should I use?" "Will I need a microphone?" "Where and how should I stand?" "Where or at whom should I look?" "How many and what kinds of gestures should I use?" "How and when should I use my visual aids?" "How loud should I speak?" "How quickly or slowly should I speak?"

Such questions are valid, but their answers will vary from person to person and from situation to situation. In the end, effective delivery comes from practice under the direction of a competent instructor. It also grows from an awareness of self and a knowledge of what effective delivery is.

Although a speech may be delivered in many different ways, the four most common methods of delivery are impromptu, memorized, manuscript, and extemporaneous.

Impromptu Delivery

When using the **impromptu method,** a speaker delivers a speech without any preplanning or preparation whatsoever. You have used this method many times, perhaps without even realizing it. Whenever you speak without prior preparation, whether in response to a question in class, to a sudden request at a business meeting, or to a comment made by a friend, you are using the impromptu method of delivery. The more formal or demanding the situation, the more most speakers prefer to avoid this approach. At times, however, you have no choice. In such cases, muster your self-control, relax, and concentrate on what you wish to say. The lack of preparation time distinguishes the impromptu method from other methods of delivery and forces speakers to depend solely on their ability to think on their feet.

Memorized Delivery

The **memorized method** of presentation requires that you memorize your speech in its entirety, usually from a word-for-word script. This kind of delivery is used for short presentations, such as toasts, acceptance speeches, and introductions, and is also commonly used by speakers in contests and on lecture circuits. Speakers frequently memorize certain parts of their speeches, including examples, short stories, statistics, quotations, and other materials that they can call up at the appropriate time. Politicians, salespeople, tour guides, and others often have a memorized "pitch" or speech to fit their needs.

Memorizing has one advantage: You can concentrate less on what you have to say and focus more on your delivery. Of course, this is only true if you are extremely self-confident and have memorized your speech so completely that you don't need to think abut each word. The disadvantage of the memorized delivery is its lack of flexibility—it doesn't allow for much, if any, adaptation to your audience. Beginning speakers face another disadvantage: they may forget what they want to say and become embarrassed. In addition, it is very difficult to deliver a memorized speech without sounding mechanical. To present a memorized address effectively, therefore, requires a great deal of practice and confidence.

Manuscript Delivery

A speaker who uses the **manuscript method** of delivery writes the entire speech out in advance and presents it word for word. As a result, such a speaker is never at a loss for words. A speaker should use a manuscript when every word, phrase, and sentence must be stated precisely. On the other hand, speakers who work from manuscripts are less able to adapt to the reactions of the audience and thus may sound mechanical.

If you plan to speak from a manuscript, keep the following in mind:

1. *Write your manuscript for the ear.* There is a difference between material written for silent reading and material written to be read aloud. The silent reader can examine a previous sentence for reference and can reread a thought several times if it is unclear the first time, but a person listening to a speech cannot.

2. *Prepare your manuscript in an easy-to-read format.* Typing it triple-spaced should help. Use special marks to note the points that you plan to emphasize.

3. *Think about what you are saying.* The presence of a manuscript often tempts a speaker to read words instead of thoughts. To avoid this problem, try to sound spontaneous and give meaning to the manuscript.

4. *Practice reading out loud, preferably with the help of a tape recorder.* The key to success is to sound as if the thoughts you are reading are fresh. The manuscript should be presented with enthusiasm, vigor, and interest.

Extemporaneous Delivery

The **extemporaneous method** uses a carefully prepared and researched speech, but the delivery appears to be spontaneous. The extemporaneous delivery style is the most commonly used in speech classrooms. It falls somewhere between the memorized or manuscript deliveries and the impromptu delivery. The extemporaneous method requires careful preparation and research, but in return creates an impression of spontaneity and projects a definite conversational quality. Speakers who use this method depend on only a brief presentational outline or a few notes, key words, or main points to keep on track. They choose the actual wording of their speech at the time of delivery.

An extemporaneous speech may at first seem as difficult as an impromptu speech, but in fact it is much easier. Because it eliminates memorization and manuscript writing, it leaves more time for preparation and practice. Thus, once you have prepared your outline, you can begin to practice your delivery. The goals of the extemporaneous method are to be conversational and to create the illusion of spontaneity. Each time you practice your speech, the wording should be somewhat different, although your purpose should remain the same.

The extemporaneous method of delivery is advantageous because it gives you better control of your presentation than does the impromptu method, it allows for more spontaneity and directness than either the memorized or the manuscript methods of delivery, and it is more adaptable to a variety of speaking situations. Most teachers as well as professional speakers prefer to use the extemporaneous method.

METHODS OF DELIVERY

	Advantages	*Disadvantages*
Impromptu	Spontaneous Flexible Conversational	No time for preparation Can be inaccurate Difficult to organize Can be stressful

Memorized	Good for short speeches
	Speaker can concentrate
	  on delivery
	Easier to maintain high
	  eye contact
	Prepared in advance
		Inflexible
		Requires lots of practice
		  and repetition
		Speaker can forget or lose
		  place
		Difficult to adapt to
		  audience response
		May sound mechanical

Manuscript	Good for technical,
	  detailed, and sensitive
	  reports
	High accuracy
	Can be timed to the
	  second
	Prepared in advance
		No flexibility
		May sound mechanical
		Difficult to adapt to
		  audience response

Extemporaneous	Flexible Conversational Prepared Organized	May be intimidating to inexperienced speakers

VOCAL AND PHYSICAL ASPECTS OF DELIVERY

As mentioned earlier, the effectiveness of a speech depends both on what is said and how it is conveyed. Basically, without solid content and valid sources, nothing is worth communicating, but without effective delivery, information cannot be clearly and vividly presented.

Because your audience is the ultimate judge of your effectiveness, you must use your delivery to involve them in your speech. Each audience member likes to feel as if he or she is being addressed personally. Therefore, try to think of your presentation as a conversation and your audience as your partners in dialog. Then use your voice and body to reinforce this impression.

Vocal Aspects

Many beginning speakers overlook the important role that voice plays in delivery. As you speak, your voice should be pleasant to listen to, clearly express your thoughts, and express a range of emotions. These three essential aspects of voice are often referred to as quality, intelligibility, and variety.

Vocal Quality.   **Vocal quality** is the overall impression a speaker's voice makes on his or her listeners. Voices may be harsh, nasal, thin, mellow, resonant, or full-bodied. Attitude can affect the quality of the voice and tell listeners whether the speaker is happy, confident, angry, fearful, or sad. Vocal quality is also a highly accurate indicator of the presenter's sincerity.

Intelligibility.   A speaker's **intelligibility** is determined by vocal volume, distinctiveness of sound, clarity of pronunciation, and the stress placed on syllables, words, and phrases. To determine the proper volume, you must be aware of the size of the room and listeners' reactions. (Do listeners look as if they're straining to hear you, for example?) The keys to high intelligibility are self-awareness and consideration for your listeners.

Vocal Variety.   **Vocal variety** is the combination of rate, force, and pitch variations that adds to a speaker's overall vocal quality. Such variety gives feeling to your delivery and adds emphasis to what you say.

Rate is the speed at which a speaker speaks—usually between 125 and 150 words per minute. Speaking at the appropriate rate requires self-awareness. A rate that is too fast or too slow or that never changes can damage the impact of your message. It is also important to recognize the value of pauses. By changing your rate of speech, a pause can be an effective means of gaining attention and adding emphasis to an important point. Essentially, pauses punctuate thoughts.

Vocal **force** is the intensity and volume level of the voice. As mentioned earlier, you must choose a volume level that is comfortable for your audience. In addition, however, you can use force to communicate your ideas with confidence and vigor. You can also increase force to emphasize an important point or to regain lagging interest. By learning how to use force, you can greatly increase your effectiveness as a speaker.

Pitch refers to how low or high the voice is on a tonal scale. Variety in pitch can serve a number of functions. For example, changes in pitch can eliminate monotony and add emphasis to key words.

Obviously, any change in rate, force, or pitch makes a word, phrase, or sentence stand out. The greater the amount of change or the more sudden the change is, the more emphatic the word or statement will be. So remember, the keys to vocal variety and effective delivery are the contrasts a speaker uses to make selected ideas seem more important than they would seem otherwise.

Physical Aspects

Among the physical factors that can affect delivery are personal appearance, body movement, gestures, facial expressions, and eye contact. Each of these must be well coordinated and relevant to the purpose of your speech.

Personal Appearance.   Personal appearance—the way a speaker dresses, grooms, and presents him- or herself to others—is an extremely important consideration. Typical student attire is not always acceptable. The general rule is to use common sense in dressing for the occasion. Often, first impressions are based on appearance. As a result, your audience may draw quick and hard-to-change opinions about your attitudes toward them and yourself. In this way, appearance can affect your believability.

Although we do not know much about the exact role of personal appearance and its effect on communication, we do know that appearance does influence interpersonal responses and, in some situations, is the primary determinant of listeners' responses. In addition, personal appearance—which includes attractiveness, body build, hair, and clothes—can have a profound impact on a speaker's self-image and therefore affect how he or she communicates with others. As simple—and even superficial—as it may seem, looking your best does help you to convey your message.

Body Movement.   Body movement is closely related to personal appearance. This includes posture, which should be relaxed and natural. Avoid slouching. Because an audience's attention instinctively follows moving objects, your motions should be easy and purposeful. The use of movement—stepping to the side, forward, or backward—can aid in holding attention and communicating ideas more clearly. Purposeful movement, along with posture, can indicate confidence and convey a positive self-image.

Gestures.   **Gestures** are movements of the head, arms, and hands that help to illustrate, emphasize, or clarify an idea. To avoid looking forced, gestures should be spontaneous. For example, when you are involved in a conversation that you have strong feelings about, your gestures come naturally. If you are sad, angry, or happy, you find yourself automatically making gestures that express your emotions. To obtain equally natural gestures when giving a speech, you need to be equally involved in what you are saying. If you concentrate on getting your message across, rather than on your gestures, you will find yourself moving more freely and naturally.

When you are first learning how to give a speech, using gestures may seem a bit uncomfortable. To overcome this problem, practice using gestures in front of others who are willing to make positive suggestions to help you improve. Be assured that as you give more and more speeches, you will find that gesturing becomes more natural and easier to do. Soon, without even thinking, you'll be using strong and smooth-flowing gestures that help to hold your audience's attention and add meaning to your message.

BEHAVIORS THAT CAN DETRACT FROM YOUR DELIVERY

General Delivery:
Speaking too quickly
Speaking too slowly
Sighing
Nervous smiling or laughing
Choppy pacing

Face
Deadpan or serious look
Facial contortions (such as scowling)
Listless or apathetic look

Hands
Fidgeting
Waving or other meaningless motions
Toying with objects
Clenching fists

Eyes
Shifty glances
Rolling movements
Looking at the floor
Looking at one side of the room
Looking at the ceiling

Staring
Lack of sustained eye contact

Voice
Sing-song speech patterns
Monotone voice
Nasal twang
Mumbling
Speaking too softly
Speaking too loudly
High pitch
Shrillness, stridency
Lack of variety in pace, volume

Body
Tense, stiff posture
Sloppy posture
Hunched shoulders
Wiggling

Feet
Shuffling
Shifting weight
Crossing legs

Facial Expressions. **Facial expressions** are configurations of the face that can reflect, augment, contradict, or be unrelated to a speaker's vocal delivery. They account for much of the emotional impact of a speaker's message. Your face is a very expressive part of your body. It quickly and accurately tells your audience a lot about you—for example, whether you are serious, happy, worried, or angry. Because your audience will read a great deal into your facial expression, it is important to look warm and friendly. Such an expression will inform your listeners that you are interested in them as well as in what you are saying. Of course, your topic, your purpose, the situation, and your audience will all determine exactly what facial expressions will be appropriate as you progress through your speech.

Eye Contact.   **Eye contact**—the extent to which a speaker looks directly at audience members—is associated with facial expression. Although facial expressions indicate a speaker's feelings about the message, eye contact seems more related to a speaker's feelings about the listeners. According to some authorities, eye contact is the most important physical aspect of delivery because it indicates interest and concern for others and implies self-confidence. Most speech communication teachers recommend that you look at your audience most of the time you are speaking.

Looking at the members of your audience establishes a communicative bond between them and you. Failure to make eye contact is the quickest way to lose listeners. Speakers who ignore their audiences are often perceived as tentative, ill at ease, insincere, or dishonest.

Your eye contact with your audience should be pleasant and personal. Give your listeners the feeling that you are talking to them as individuals during a casual conversation. When speaking to a small audience (5 to 30 people), try to look at each individual for a few seconds at a time. To avoid looking shifty, move your eyes gradually and smoothly from one person to another. For larger groups, it is best to scan the audience and occasionally talk to a specific member or members. Do not look over people's heads, and avoid staring, which can give the impression that you are angry or hostile. Your eyes should convey that you are confident, sincere, and speaking with conviction. The message your audience should get from your eye contact is that you care about them and about what you are saying.

At first, establishing eye contact with an audience may make you feel uncomfortable, but as you gain experience, you will begin to feel more at ease. You will soon find that making eye contact puts you in control of the situation and helps you to answer such questions as: "Can they hear?" "Do they understand?" "Are they listening?"

USING VISUAL AIDS

Visual aids are materials and equipment, such as key words, diagrams, models, real objects, photographs, tables, charts, and graphs that speakers may use to enhance their speeches. Students often think that the only time they will be required to use visual aids is in classroom speech assignments. In reality, however, speeches using visual materials are presented quite frequently, and many speeches depend on them. For example, imagine an architect explaining the floor plans for a new high-rise office building without a drawing, model, or photograph; a company executive explaining this year's annual profits and losses compared to last year's without a chart, graph, or diagram; a coach explaining a football play without a chalkboard or overhead projector; a teacher telling her class where Athens, Greece, is located without a map or globe; or a salesperson selling a product without showing it.

The Advantages of Visual Aids

If "one picture is worth a thousand words," then visual aids are an excellent way to strengthen and reinforce the development and proof of a point. Such aids are a special form of supporting and clarifying materials because they combine both verbal and visual modes of presentation. When carefully designed and used, visual aids can help a speaker to:

1. Save time
2. Gain attention and hold interest
3. Clarify and support main points
4. Reinforce or emphasize main points
5. Improve retention

Research has shown that audiences remember information longer when it is accompanied by visual aids.[5]

Kinds of Visual Aids

There are many different kinds of visual aids and methods of presenting them. The most frequently used kinds of visual aids are key words, real objects, models, diagrams, pictures, tables, and graphs, while the most frequently used methods of presentation are chalkboards, posters, projections, and handouts.

Key Words.   Displaying key words in writing is a simple way to highlight main points and important ideas. This approach helps the audience to focus on the most significant words and concepts being presented and, therefore, to understand and recall them more easily. Key word visuals can be easily prepared in advance. When designing them, use contrasting colors so that the lettering stands out from the background as vividly as possible. The lettering should be neat and large enough to be easily and understood. The following is an example of a key word visual:

> Treatments for
> Communication
> Apprehension
>
> **Systematic
> Desensitization**
>
> **Behavior Modification**
>
> Cognitive Modification
>
> **Rhetrotherapy**

Real Objects.   A real object is any article related to the speech topic that a speaker displays or demonstrates, such as a musical instrument, piece of sporting equipment, or kind of food. Using a real object can make your topic more immediate and interesting, but it can also create problems if the object is too large, too small, or too impractical. Pets, for example, are often unpredictable and can be distracting before, during, and after a speech. When displaying the actual article is not practical because of size or cost, a model should be considered.

Models.   A model—a representation of a real object—allows a speaker to conveniently enlarge or shrink an object to an appropriate size for display. For example, it would be impractical to show the actual circuitry of a microchip, which is no larger than a pinhead, or the inside of an actual space shuttle, which is not only enormous but also inaccessible to most people.

Models can also be lifesize. Currently, cardiopulmonary resuscitation (CPR) is a very popular and important subject. To demonstrate this procedure, speakers often use life-size dummies of humans. In this case, too, models are practical alternatives to the "real thing." When models are neither available nor practical, a photograph or diagram may be used.

Photographs and Prints.   A photograph is an excellent device for explaining details and surroundings. One student, speaking on artistic style, brought prints of several paintings to illustrate the differences between them. Another student, who spoke on the construction of the Egyptian pyramids, showed photos that she had taken on a vacation trip. She realized that the originals were too small, so she had them enlarged for effective use in the classroom. The typical photograph is usually too small to be seen clearly unless the speaker moves through the audience or passes it around. In both instances, the advantage of using photos is somewhat diminished because the audience tends to pay more attention to the pictures than to what is being said.

Drawings, Sketches, and Diagrams.   When photographs or prints are unavailable or lack adequate detail, a drawing, sketch, or diagram may be used. Don't worry if you're not artistic, because most drawings used in classroom speeches are relatively simple.

For example, Figure 9.1 is a simple line drawing used to describe how a classroom can be divided in a beginning speech communication course. The diagram simply shows the division of the room for various functions and makes a professor's explanation of a seating arrangement much easier for students to comprehend.

Similarly, a speaker might use an architect's blueprint, a chart illustrating a company's organizational structure, a sketch of the basic positions for waterskiing, or a map of various segments of land. Virtually anything can be diagrammed or sketched.

FIGURE 9.1   THE PSI CLASSROOM

Simple Line
Drawing

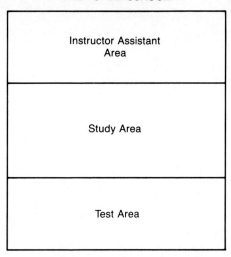

In technical presentations or briefings, a diagram may be used to illustrate three-dimensional relationships. The two most common three-dimensional diagrams are the cutaway view and the exploded view, as illustrated in Figures 9.2 and 9.3. The cutaway allows an observer to see the inner workings of an object, while the exploded view shows the systematic relationship of separate parts to the whole object. The most effective diagrams are drawn to scale and represent the real object or process as accurately as possible.

Tables and Graphs.   Tables and graphs are used mainly to display statistics. A table is merely an orderly arrangement of data into columns to highlight similarities and differences, as shown in Table 9.1.

Tables conveniently display large amounts of data in a relatively small space, but remember that a complex or lengthy (and perhaps boring) table will require an equally complex and lengthy explanation. As with any visual aid you decide to use, a table must be concise, simple, and clear so that the

FIGURE 9.2

Cutaway Diagram

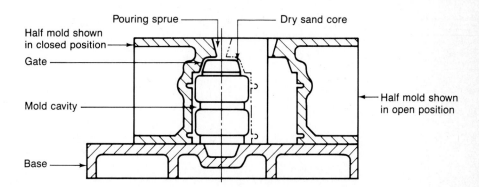

FIGURE 9.3

Exploded
Diagram

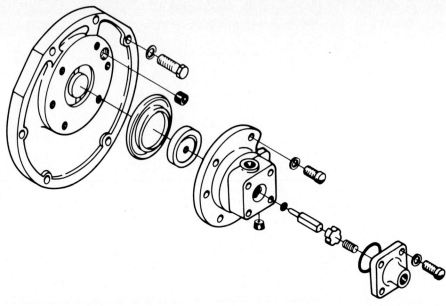

TABLE 9.1   *Illustration of a Table*

Highest-paid teams
A comparison of 1984 and 1985 average salaries for major league baseball teams,
and where they rank:

1985 rank	1984 rank	Team	1985 avg.	1984 avg.	Players
1	1	N.Y. Yankees	$546,364	$458,544	26
2	5	Atlanta	$540,988	$402,689	27
3	12	Baltimore	$438,256	$360,204	27
4	3	California	$433,818	$431,431	32
5	7	Milwaukee	$430,843	$385,215	27
6	14	Los Angeles	$424,273	$316,530	28
7	4	Chicago Cubs	$413,765	$422,194	32
8	10	Detroit	$406,755	$371,332	26
9	15	San Diego	$400,497	$311,199	26
10	6	Philadelphia	$399,728	$401,476	28
11	13	Pittsburgh	$392,271	$330,661	26
12	20	N.Y. Mets	$389,365	$282,952	29
13	16	Boston	$386,597	$297,878	28
14	19	St. Louis	$386,505	$290,886	26
15	17	Toronto	$385,995	$295,632	28
16	18	Kansas City	$368,469	$291,160	28
17	9	Houston	$366,250	$382,991	28
18	8	Oakland	$352,004	$384,027	28
19	2	Chi. White Sox	$348,488	$447,281	27
20	22	Cincinnati	$336,786	$269,019	27

Source: Major League Baseball Players Association

important information is easy to spot. Lengthy and complex data are often better illustrated by a graph.

Graphs help to make statistical data vivid and illustrate relationships among data in ways that are easy for your audience to grasp. The line graphs, as illustrated in Figure 9.4, are particularly helpful for clarifying comparative data over time. Such graphs can help you to trace trends and show increases and decreases over a span of days, months, or years. Note in Figure 9.4, for example, that the sharp downward slope of the line strongly emphasizes how sharply farm population dropped between 1920 and 1985.

Bar graphs are another simple way to show comparisons. For example, note how much easier it is to compare the data depicted in the bar graph in Figures 9.5 and 9.6 than the data presented in the table in Table 9.1. Whenever possible, visual aids should present only one or two basic relationships so that your audience can quickly grasp your point.

Pie graphs derive their name from their shape and are used to illustrate proportional divisions of a whole set of data. Each wedge of the pie represents a percentage of the whole. Pie graphs are often used to show distribution patterns and to illustrate national, state, or local budgets. Note in Figure 9.7 that the pie graph starts with a radius drawn vertically from the center to the twelve o'clock position. Each segment is then drawn in clockwise, beginning with the largest and continuing down to the smallest. A pie graph should be divided into no less than two and no more than eight segments.

FIGURE 9.4

Line Graph

How Farm Portion of Population has dropped

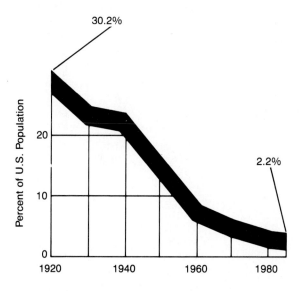

SOURCE: CENSUS BUREAU

FIGURE 9.5

Bar Chart

Mountain Aviation, Inc.
Composition of Employees by
Race and Sex, 7/1/85

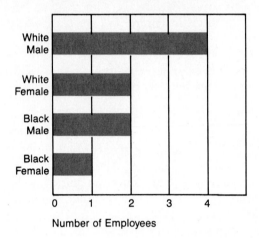

FIGURE 9.6

Bar Chart

Mountain Aviation, Inc. vs. Aviation Industry:
Composition of Employees by Race and Sex, 7/1/85

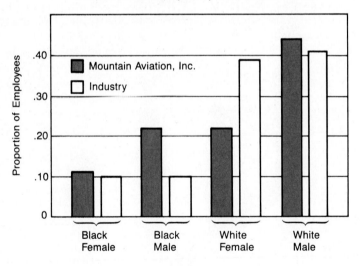

FIGURE 9.7

Pie Graph

Imports of Selected Countries as Percentages of GNP

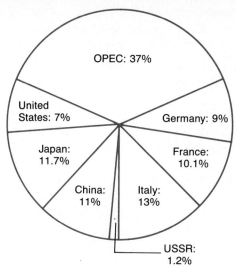

Chalkboards. The chalkboard is the most readily available method of presenting visual aids, at least in most classrooms. Here are several things to consider when you are planning to use a chalkboard:

1. When will you put your information on the board? Preferences vary from speaker to speaker and from instructor to instructor. Some instructors may prefer that you write on the board before you speak, but others will ask that you write while you speak. If putting the information on the board before you speak will not interfere with other presentations and if you can cover what you have written, preparing the board in advance can simplify your delivery. To be safe, ask your instructor which approach he or she prefers.

2. How should you write on the board? This, of course, depends on the size of the room and your writing skills. Your writing should always be large and neat enough for everyone in the room to read. The appearance of your writing on the board communicates a message about you and your speech. Thus, you want what you write to create a positive impression.

3. How should you use the board when delivering your speech? Even when reading from the board, you should always try to face your audience. Use a pointer, a ruler, or your outstretched arm to help guide your listeners to the information you want them to focus on.

The chalkboard is a convenient visual device, but if it is not used properly it can be more of a distraction than a help. Practice writing on the board before your speech. This will give you an idea of how it feels to write on the board, and you will be able to determine the size necessary for your letters to be seen by those sitting in the back row.

Posters.   Posters are another commonly used method of presenting infor-mation visually. The greatest advantage of posters is that they can be prepared in advance, which makes the speaker seem more efficient and professional. Many of the same guidelines for writing on the board also apply to using posters. Here are some suggestions:

1. Posters should be neat and orderly in appearance.
2. Writing and illustrations should be large enough for everyone in the audience to read.
3. The content of posters should be kept simple. Include only the information that is essential to make your point. Too much information will make the poster look cluttered and will inter-fere with the audience's understanding.
4. Look at your audience rather than at the poster. Using a pointer will aid you in maintaining eye contact with your listeners.
5. You should practice using your poster until you feel comfortable with it. Plan where you will place it to ensure that your audience can see it. If an easel is not available, check to see if there are clips on the board for hanging posters or if you will need to use masking tape. If you must use masking tape, make large loops of tape and place them on the back of the poster in advance. Then, when you are ready to display the poster, merely place it on the board, pressing firmly on the tape loops to secure it. If you have more than one poster, you can place several of them on the board at once, or you can display each individually as you need it. When choosing a poster, make sure that it is made of firm cardboard so that it will support itself if you have to stand it in a chalk tray or on a table.

Projected Visuals.   The most common projected materials are slides, movies, overhead transparencies, and videotapes. The projection of such visuals requires planning and familiarity with the mechanical equipment to be used. Each format has advantages and disadvantages, so knowing what each can and cannot do is vital. For example, showing slides and movies requires a totally darkened room and the projectors may be noisy, but both enable you to show places and things that may otherwise be impossible to visualize. Films and videos can add motion, color, and sound, but they can be costly and often tend to dominate a presentation by literally replacing the speaker for a period of time.

The most popular projected visual is the overhead transparency. These materials can be prepared in advance or created during a presentation, and whether prepared by the speaker or a professional, they are relatively inexpensive. In addition, overhead projectors are easy to use and do not require a darkened room.

When using an overhead projector, consider the following:

1. Make sure the projector is focused correctly so that everyone in the room can read what is on the transparency.
2. Make writing and drawings large enough to be seen clearly by everyone.
3. Conceal information on the transparency until it is needed.
4. Use a pointer (pencil or pen) to direct the audience's attention to what is being discussed.
5. Practice using the overhead. Check it out beforehand to make sure that everything is working correctly.

Mechanical devices, because of their potential for breakdown, require a back-up method. It is a good idea to always carry a spare bulb to install in case the first one burns out. Also, bring along copies of visual aids in handout form, just to be safe.

Handouts. Handouts can be a useful means of presenting information to your audience. They are particularly helpful if you are unable to use any other method. Among their advantages are that they can be prepared in advance and that each audience member receives a personal copy as a review of your speech. On the other hand, handouts can also become a distraction. Merely passing them out can interrupt the flow of your presentation, and audience members may pay more attention to your handouts than they do to your speech itself. As a result, you should only use handouts when you have no other alternative or when you have a creative reason for doing so.

TIPS ON USING VISUAL AIDS

1. Display visual materials only while you are using them. Do not distract your audience by showing your visuals too early or by leaving them on display after you've finished talking about them.
2. Ensure that everyone can see your visual aids by making them large and bright.
3. Do not talk to your displayed objects. Discuss them while maintaining eye contact with your audience.
4. Keep your visual aids on display long enough to ensure that everyone has ample opportunity to absorb their information.
5. Do not stand in front of your visual aids. Using a pointer can help you to avoid blocking your audience's view.

Choosing and Using Visual Aids

When planning to use visual aids, keep the following hints in mind:

1. Visual aids should serve a need—that is, they should never be used just for the sake of using them. In fact, visual aids are not appropriate for some speeches. In other cases, visual aids can get a point across better than words alone. For example, it is easier to show an audience how to tie shoes than it is to tell them. Furthermore, it is easier *both* to tell *and* to show them how to tie shoes than it is *either* to tell *or* to show them only.

2. Visual aids should be planned and adapted to the audience and the situation. For example, the size of the visual aid and the distance between you and your audience should be considered. The visual material should be kept simple and free from too much detail.

3. Visual aids should not dominate or take over a speaker's job. They should supplement but never replace the speaker. When planning a speech, do not rely too heavily on visual aids, but instead, use them to help elaborate or explain a point or idea.

4. Visual aids should look as professionally prepared as possible. Neat and accurate materials will create a positive impression on the audience and reflect favorably on the competency of the speaker. Visuals should be bright, attractive, and legible, as well as free from factual and spelling errors.

5. Visual aids should be practical—easy to prepare, use, and transport.

6. Visual aids that are not original or that contain information that is not yours require documentation. Cite your source either directly on the piece where your audience can see it or in the context of your speech.

POLISHING YOUR DELIVERY

The best way to polish your delivery is to practice, practice, practice. Exactly *how much* practice you will need depends on a number of considerations, including how much experience you have speaking before audiences, how familiar you are with your subject, and how long your speech is. There is no magic amount of time that will make your delivery perfect.

If your speech is not to be memorized, make sure to use slightly different wording in each run-through. When you *memorize* a speech, it's possible to master the words without mastering the content. Your goal should be to *learn* your speech, which will mean that you have mastered its ideas.

In practicing your delivery, it is important to start with small segments. For example, practice the introduction, then one main point at a time, and then the conclusion. After you have rehearsed each small segment several times in isolation, practice the entire speech until you feel that you have mastered the content and that the ideas flow smoothly.

If possible, practice in the same room where you will speak or under similar conditions. This helps you to see how things look from the front of the class and to plan where you should place your visual aids and notes.

Your last practice session should leave you with a sense of confidence and a desire to present your speech.

Practice using your notes in the same way that you plan to use them in your speech presentation. Speakers' notes may vary from a few key words to an entire manuscript. Most speech instructors limit their students' notes to a few 3" × 5" cards, but some may not permit the use of any notes. These instructors contend that if students first get used to speaking without notes, they will use them more judiciously when notes are eventually allowed. Above all, a speaker's notes should not create a distraction.

TIPS ON USING NOTE CARDS

1. Write large enough to let you read your notes at a glance.
2. Write on only one side of the card. Otherwise it becomes too easy to lose your place.
3. Number your cards in order.
4. Write only necessary information. Use key words or phrases whenever possible.
5. Practice using your notes. Know them so well that you can maintain eye contact with your audience.

If you have prepared your speech well, you should not need a lot of notes. A few key words or phrases should be enough to help you recall what you wish to say. Your notes should be brief and written large enough so that you can read them instantly from a distance. For example, you should be able to fit the notes for a 6- to 10-minute speech on a single 3" × 5" note card if you use only key words or ideas as reminders. If your speech contains quotations or statistics that must be accurately presented, a separate 3" × 5" card may be necessary. If you use visual aids, they can also serve as notes because they remind you of what to say.

If you intend to use visual aids, practice using them too. Decide when and how you will display them. If you can, take them to the room where you will speak to test their visibility and effectiveness. Feeling comfortable using your visual aids will make you feel more confident about your whole speech.

Finally, concentrate on what you are saying and to whom you are saying it. Above all, be yourself.

SUMMARY An effective speaker is ethical, knowledgeable, prepared, and self-confident. Unfortunately, *speech anxiety*—the fear of speaking before an audience—can severely undermine a speaker's self-confidence. In reality, speech anxiety is quite common, and almost everyone who speaks before a group experiences it to some extent. The important thing is to be able to control it. Speech anxiety can be reduced by selecting a topic that you know and enjoy, preparation, practice, and knowing the surroundings in which your presentation will take place.

Communication apprehension—the chronic fear of interacting with others—is the severest form of speech anxiety. An individual who suffers from communication apprehension will actually remain silent rather than risk communicating. Everyone who fears speaking before a group does not necessarily suffer from communication apprehension.

The effectiveness of your speech presentation depends not only on what you say, but also on how you say it. Appearance, body movements, gestures, facial expressions, eye contact, and vocal characteristics all contribute to an effective speech delivery. Speakers who successfully combine all these factors convey their purpose and ideas clearly and interestingly so that their audience attends to and retains the intended message.

A poorly written speech can be improved by effective delivery and a well-written speech can be ruined by an ineffective delivery. Yet there are no hard and fast rules that will guarantee every speaker an effective delivery in every situation. The only consistent rule is that you must be yourself!

Although a speech may be delivered in many different ways, the four most common methods of delivery are impromptu, memorized, manuscript, and extemporaneous. An *impromptu* speech is delivered without planning or preparation. A *memorized* speech is presented from memory, usually based on a word-for-word script. The *manuscript* method of delivery relies on a written speech and is read word for word. And an *extemporaneous* speech is a carefully prepared and researched presentation for which the speaker uses few notes and tries to be spontaneous.

Many beginning speakers overlook the important role that voice plays in delivery. The three essential aspects of voice are *vocal quality*—the overall impression of the voice, *intelligibility*—the clarity of the sounds and the pronunciation of the words, and *vocal variety*—the *rate, force,* and *pitch* variations that add life to a speaker's voice. In addition, many physical factors contribute to the success of a presentation. These include *gestures*—the movements of head, arms, and hands to help illustrate, emphasize, or make a point; *facial expressions*—the configurations of the face that can reflect, augment, contradict, or be unrelated to what is being said; and *eye contact*—the extent to which a speaker looks directly at audience members. Effective eye contact establishes a bond between the speaker and the audience and makes each listener feel as if he or she is being addressed personally.

Many different kinds of *visual aids* can be used to enhance a speaker's words. When visual aids are used as supporting and clarifying materials, they save time, gain attention, reinforce or emphasize main points, and improve retention. The most frequently used visual aids are key words, real objects, models, diagrams, pictures, tables, and graphs.

The projection of visual aids requires some preplanning and familiarity with the mechanical device to be used. The most common projected visuals are slides, overhead transparencies, movies, and videotapes. Other methods of presenting visual aids include chalkboards, posters, and handouts.

The best way to polish your delivery is to practice. The amount of time spent rehearsing a speech will determine how effective your delivery will be.

KEY TERMS

Communication Apprehension: the severest form of speech anxiety—a chronic fear or avoidance of all interactions with others, it can be seen in individuals who either consciously or subconsciously have decided to remain silent.

Extemporaneous Method: a delivery style in which the speaker carefully prepares the speech in advance, but delivers it with only a few notes and with a high degree of spontaneity.

Eye Contact: the extent to which a speaker looks directly at audience members; associated with facial expression.

Facial Expressions: configurations of the face that can reflect, augment, contradict, or be unrelated to a speaker's vocal delivery.

Force: the intensity and volume level of the voice; an aspect of vocal variety.

Gestures: movements of the head, arms, and hands that help to illustrate, emphasize, or clarify an idea.

Impromptu Method: a delivery style in which a speaker delivers a speech without any preplanning or preparation whatsoever.

Intelligibility: a speaker's vocal volume, distinctiveness of sound, clarity of pronunciation, and stress placed on syllables, words, and phrases.

Manuscript Method: a delivery style in which a speaker writes the speech in its entirety and then reads it word for word.

Memorized Method: a delivery style in which a speaker memorizes a speech in its entirety, usually from a word-for-word script.

Pitch: how low or high the voice is on a tonal scale; an aspect of vocal variety.

Rate: the speed at which a speaker speaks, normally between 125 words and 150 words per minute; an aspect of vocal variety.

Speech Anxiety: the fear of speaking before an audience.

Visual Aids: all materials and equipment, such as key words, diagrams, models, real objects, photographs, tables, charts, and graphs, that speakers may use to supplement their words.

Vocal Quality: the overall impression a speaker's voice makes on his or her listeners.

Vocal Variety: the combination of rate, force, and pitch variations that adds to a speaker's overall vocal quality.

DISCUSSION STARTERS

1. Which quality of an effective speaker—ethics, knowledge, preparation, or self-confidence—would you say is the most important? Why?

2. Why do you think most people are so fearful of speaking before an audience?

3. Your best friend must give a speech and is frightened about it. What advice would you give to help him or her manage this fear?

4. How would you distinguish between an effective and an ineffective speech delivery?

5. Can a poorly written speech be made to sound good? Why or why not?

6. On what bases should a speaker select one method of delivery over another?

7. If you were to develop an evaluation form to assess a speaker's vocal delivery, what factors would you include and how would you evaluate them?

8. In your opinion, what distinguishes the voice of an outstanding speaker from that of an average speaker?

9. What nonverbal behaviors distinguish effective speakers from ineffective speakers?

10. Why should a speaker use visual aids in a speech?

11. If you were advising beginning speakers, what would you tell them about using notes in their first speech?

12. Based on the information you learned in this chapter, what advice would you give to a beginning speaker about delivery?

FURTHER READINGS

Cooper, Morton. *Change Your Voice, Change Your Life*. New York: Macmillan, 1984.

Hahner, Jeffrey C., Martin A. Sokolof, Sandra Salisch, et al. *Speaking Clearly: Improving Voice and Diction*, Second ed. New York: Random House, 1986.

MaKay, John. *Speaking with an Audience: Communicating Ideas & Attitudes*. New York: Thomas Y. Crowell Co., 1977.

Richmond, Virginia P., and James C. McCroskey. *Communication Apprehension, Avoidance, and Effectiveness*. Scottsdale, Ariz.: Gorsuch Scarisbrick, Pubs., 1985.

Samovar, Larry A., and Jack Mills. *Oral Communication: Message and Response*, Sixth ed. Dubuque, Iowa: Wm. C. Brown Pubs., 1986.

NOTES

1. Wenburg, John, and William W. Wilmot, *The Personal Communication Process*, (New York: John Wiley & Sons, Inc., 1973), p. 69.

2. Bruskin Associates, "What Are Americans Afraid of?" *The Bruskin Report*, No. 53, 1973.

3. Mulac, Anthony, and A. Robert Sherman, "Behavioral Assessment of Speech Anxiety," *Quarterly Journal of Speech*, 60, No. 2 (April 1974): p. 138.

4. Buehler, E. C., and Wil Linkugel, *Speech: A First Course*, (New York: Harper & Row Pubs., 1962).

5. Zayas-Baya, Elena P., "Instructional Media in the Total Language Picture," *International Journal of Instructional Media* 5 (1977–78): pp. 145–150.

CHAPTER 10

Informative Speaking

After studying this chapter, you should be able to:

1. Tell why information is powerful.
2. Select an informative speech topic that focuses on an object, process, event, or concept.
3. Gain an audience's attention by generating a need for your information and showing its relevance to their needs and interests.
4. Demonstrate how to use organization, language, and definitions to increase your audience's understanding of your topic.
5. Explain how avoiding assumptions and personalizing information can contribute to the success of an informative speech.
6. Deliver an effective informative speech.

PATTY:	John, do you know where the 501 Building is?
JOHN:	I don't know. Ask Sue, I think she had class there last semester.
PATTY:	Sue, do you know where the 501 Building is?
SUE:	I think it's located next to Ferguson Hall. No, I don't know.
PATTY:	John thought you had class in that building last semester.
SUE:	No, but Ethan did.
PATTY:	Ethan, do you know where the 501 Building is?
ETHAN:	Sure. Do you know where the Big Red Shop is located?
PATTY:	Yes.
ETHAN:	It's one block south of the Big Red Shop on the same side of the street. It's the only building on that block. You can't miss it.
PATTY:	Thanks.

HEATHER:	Can you help me with my chemistry?
RICK:	Sure. What do you need help with?
HEATHER:	The problems on pages 55 and 60 in the workbook. I just don't understand them.
RICK:	Okay. Let's start with the problem on page 55.

DAVE:	Professor Jones, would you please explain the differences between *homophily* and *heterophily?*
PROFESSOR JONES:	Of course. Homophily refers to the degree to which interacting individuals are similar in certain attitudes. Heterophily is the opposite of homophily—it is the degree to which someone is different from us in various attributes. Let me give you some examples . . .

Each of the preceding examples illustrates someone wanting information and someone giving it. *The American Heritage Dictionary of the English Language* defines **information** as "the act of informing or the condition of being informed; communication of knowledge—knowledge derived from study, experience, or instruction." This definition makes the act of informing seem fairly simple, doesn't it? Yet, when you think about the amount and kinds of knowledge that you send and receive in a single day, providing information really isn't simple at all. Have you ever tried to teach someone how to perform CPR (cardiovascular pulmonary resuscitation), use a word processor, or play a card game? If you have, you know it takes time and care to present information in proper sequence and in amounts small enough to ensure that the listener understands correctly.

Teaching, or informing others, can be a rewarding and satisfying experience, but if you lack the required skills, it can also be frustrating. To help you in this area, we will discuss how to present knowledge by means of the informative speech. This type of speech is one of the most often assigned in the speech communication classroom because of its far-reaching practicality. You will find that knowing how to present information clearly and systematically will be a great benefit to you both personally and professionally throughout your life.

Mini-Exercise

Watch "Sesame Street" and analyze the instructional strategies that are used to teach children. What does the show do to get children to remember information? What does it do to keep their attention? Why is this show so successful at getting young people to learn? How could you adapt some of the show's delivery techniques to an informative speech?

Information and Power

Being informed helps to reduce our uncertainty of things we know little about. Thus, it is logical that the person who possesses and controls information has power. When people need information about something they know little about, they tend to turn to those who can provide the necessary information. For example, in the dialog at the beginning of this chapter, the person who has the desired information has the power to share it or not to share it. The more important a piece of information is to you and the greater your desire to have it, the more valuable that information is to you. Thus, the person who has the information you want gains control over you because of his or her power to give or withhold the knowledge you seek.

The ability to communicate information is essential in our society. One trend that futurists appear to agree on is the increasingly important role that information will play in our progress. In fact, over the years, we have moved from an economy based on agriculture and heavy industries, such as steel, machinery, and automobile manufacturing, to an economy based on knowledge industries, such as research, health services, banking, training, and communications. During the 1950s, only about 17 percent of our labor force held information-related jobs. This figure has now increased to almost 60 percent. This demand puts even more emphasis on workers' needs for greater skills in producing, storing, and delivering information. Much of the information we send and receive is written, but most is spoken. For example, teachers, trainers, consultants, media specialists, salespersons, technicians, doctors, nurses, lawyers, elected officials, and managers all depend on oral communication.

THINK ABOUT IT

Imagine a clock face to visualize our place in history:

> Let the clock stand for the amount of time humans have had access to
> writing systems. Our clock would thus represent something like 3000
> years, and each minute would stand for 50 years. On this scale, there
> were no significant media changes until about nine minutes ago. At that
> time, the Western culture developed the printing press. About three
> minutes ago, the telegraph, the photograph, and the locomotive arrived.
> Two minutes ago we invented the telephone, the rotary press, motion
> pictures, the automobile, the airplane, and the radio. And one minute
> ago, we developed the talking picture.[1]
>
> Television has appeared in the last 30 seconds, the computer in the last
> 15, and communication satellites even more recently. Crammed into the
> last 10 seconds are not only several hundred thousand new books, but
> low-cost electronic and laser technologies that promise almost unlimited
> opportunity to produce, store, retrieve, and deliver messages.[2]

THE GOAL OF INFORMATIVE SPEAKING

The general goal of informative speakers is to increase the knowledge of
their listeners. There is a very fine distinction between informing and
persuading. The informative speech is meant to increase knowledge,
whereas the persuasive speech is meant to alter or change attitudes and
behavior. Information can be presented without any attempt at persuasion,
but persuasion cannot be accomplished without attempting to inform.

The difference between the two is best explained through the following
examples. A car salesperson must rely on persuasion to sell cars. However,
to persuade someone to buy a car, the salesperson will probably spend a lot
of time informing him or her about the advantages of buying a specific
model. The salesperson might be highly successful in increasing the
customer's knowledge and understanding of the car (informing) yet he or
she may fail at inducing the customer to buy the car (persuading). Persuasion
takes place when a person stops presenting information to increase understanding and begins to present information to encourage or alter behavior.

A math professor, in explaining a complex problem, is attempting to
help students understand how the problem can be solved. Here the professor
is not hoping to persuade the students of how it should be done, but is
trying to help them gain the knowledge and understanding they need to
find the solution on their own. Of course, the professor could add an
element of persuasion if he or she tried to show that one way of solving the
problem was better than another, but that would probably be less important
than teaching the basic problem-solving skills. Above all, the professor's
specific goal is to teach (inform), while the car salesperson's specific goal is
to sell (persuade).

The key to understanding the difference between information and persuasion lies in recognizing that although *information may contain some elements of persuasion, all persuasion must provide information.* Therefore, what separates an informative speech from a persuasive one is the goal of the speaker. Persuasion will be discussed in more detail in the next chapter.

TOPICS FOR INFORMATIVE SPEECHES

It is surprising when students believe they have little to inform others about. Most students have a wealth of information and a vast list of potential topics based on what they have learned from their classes, reading, and other experiences. For example, geography, agriculture, computer science, social science, sex education, driver education, first-aid training, art, music, physical education, political science, sociology, chemistry, health, and on-the-job experiences can all offer potential topics for an informative speech.

In Chapter 6 two rules for selecting a speech topic were presented:

RULE # 1: Choose a topic that interests you and that you know something about.

RULE # 2: Choose a topic that will be of interest to your audience.

If something interests you, chances are it will also be of interest to others. Roland, for example, has been involved with computers ever since he can remember, first with video games and then with his own personal computer. In high school, he took a few programming classes, and now, as a college major in computer science, he has learned much about the most recent technological advances in the field of graphic arts and design programming. This specialized knowledge made a natural topic for his informative speech. Yet, at the time of the assignment, Roland never even thought of it. Only after his speech professor spent some time asking him about his interests did he decide to speak on graphic design. The assignment required the use of visual aids. Roland already had many available aids to choose from, including flow charts of his computer programs and the graphics that he and others had designed. He was also able to expand his experiences and knowledge by interviewing professors and doing more research on a subject that he really cared about.

For the past semester, Cindy has been an intern volunteer for a local family crisis line. Her responsibilities include answering phone calls from troubled people and referring them to experts and organizations that can help them with their problems. Given this experience and her major in clinical psychology, Cindy wisely chose to give her informative speech on the growing role of crisis lines in serving the mental health needs of local communities.

Roland and Cindy are probably no different from most of you. At first, they doubted that they had anything worthwhile to speak about. Like them, if you stop to think about your past experiences and interests, you will probably discover that you too have a great deal to share with others.

Remember, informative speeches may focus on objects, processes, events, or concepts.

Objects

Speeches about objects examine concrete subjects, such as people, animals, structures, and places. Here are some specific purpose statements for informative speeches on objects:

- To inform the audience about the main architectural features of a gothic cathedral.
- To inform the audience about the anatomy of the heart.
- To inform the audience of what to look for when buying a word processor.
- To inform the audience about the life of Martin Luther King, Jr.

Processes

When discussing a process, a speaker explains how something works or how something is done. Here are a few samples:

- To inform the audience how to make a flower arrangement.
- To inform the audience how to write a resumé.
- To inform the audience how to make beer.
- To inform the audience how drugs affect our bodies.

Speeches about processes generally serve two purposes: to increase understanding and to teach someone how to do something. Process speeches are usually organized in chronological (time) order—that is, they proceed step-by-step from the beginning of the process to its end.

Events

Informative speeches about events discuss happenings or occasions. Among the many possibilities are:

nuclear accidents	earthquakes
the Vietnam conflict	Rose Bowl parades
landing on the moon	marathons
cancer	the sinking of the Titanic
the Challenger explosion	the assassination of John F. Kennedy

Each of these topics is fairly general and thus needs to be narrowed for short time limits. Some appropriate specific purpose statements are:

- To inform the audience about why the U.S. got out of Vietnam.
- To inform the audience about the latest developments to cure cancer.
- To inform the audience about why the space shuttle Challenger exploded.
- To inform the audience about the 1987 Boston Marathon.

INFORMATIVE SPEECH TOPICS: A SAMPLE LIST

Here are some possible topics for informative speeches. Of course, this list is by no means exhaustive, and the topics are not necessarily titles of speeches, but may reflect specific purposes or broad areas that need to be narrowed to fit assigned time limits or other requirements set by your instructor.

New Approaches to Instruction: The Technology of Education
Investment: The Stock Market Game
College Drug Use
Architecture: A Form of Communication
Lasers in the Operating Room
Sensitivity Training
Sexual Practices in the 1980s
Pornography
Solar Energy
Jealousy
Quarreling Can Be Constructive
The New Drug Society
Immigration: A U.S. Tragedy
Marriage and Communication
Street Gangs Are Organizations
Agriculture's Newest Technologies
Agribusiness: Boom or Bust?
Strip-Search Abuse
Animal Rights and Scientific Research
The Computer: The Ultimate Invasion of Privacy
Missing Children
The New Tax Laws
AIDS: What Is It?
Effortless Exercise
Drugs in Athletics
Fast Food: A Nation at Risk
What Is the Future's Market for Computers?
Your Body Is an Image of You
Competition: A Fact of Life in Our Society
Single Parents
Genetic Cloning
The Criminal: No Room in Our Jails
Individualized Instruction

Concepts

Speeches about concepts deal with more abstract topics, such as beliefs, theories, ideas, and principles. Here the challenge is to make the subject matter more concrete so that the audience can more easily understand it. Concept-based topics might include:

communication	learning theory
sexism	liberalism
Buddhism	taxes
love	open society

Taken alone, these topics are too vague to be meaningful. If you were to ask a dozen people what each term means, you would probably receive a dozen different answers. Thus, it is the speaker's responsibility to narrow and focus the subject so that the audience understands his or her intended meaning. Here are some specific purpose statements based on more general abstract topics:

- To inform the audience of some common misconceptions about communication.
- To inform the audience about the two most important principles in learning theory.
- To inform the audience about the necessity of taxes.
- To inform the audience about the nature of an open society.

Speeches about concepts take extra time and effort to develop because of their abstract nature. These speeches require the use of concrete examples, definitions, and clear language.

Whether a speech is about an object, a process, an event, or a concept is not always clear, because a subject may cross from one category to another. Often the difference rests with the specific purpose that the speaker chooses to emphasize. Therefore, it is important to decide how you want to treat your subject and then develop your speech accordingly. If you are unsure of your approach, you may want to review Chapter 6 for more specific information about topic selection and how to determine which topics may be best suited for you and your audience.

PREPARING AND DEVELOPING AN INFORMATIVE SPEECH

The previous chapters on public communication relate directly to the principles and skills of informative speaking. All aspects of topic selection, audience analysis, information gathering, preparation of supporting and clarifying materials, and organizing, outlining, and delivering a speech are crucial to the effectiveness and eventual success of your informative presentation. In addition, you should know the goals and strategies involved in a presentation, including how to compete with such distractions and noises as students coming in late, the noise of an airplane, the humming of a lawn mower, and listeners' whispering in the audience. Such interferences should not be ignored if you plan to be successful in transmitting information to others. To achieve your main goal of increasing knowledge, you must strive to attain two subgoals: gain your audience's attention and increase their understanding.

Gaining Audience Attention

Motivating the audience to pay attention is critical to the success of any speech. To accomplish this you should generate a *need* for the information and show its *relevance* to your listeners. A student once asked his professor why the audience had not paid attention to his informative speech on the harmful effects of smoking. He had failed to consider two things when selecting and preparing his speech: no one in the class smoked and everyone already knew, or at least thought they knew, the harmful effects of smoking. As a result, the audience thought it was unnecessary to pay attention. If the speaker had analyzed his audience, he could have made the appropriate adjustments. Then he might have started his speech by saying:

> I realize that none of you smoke and that's good. I also realize that you probably know a lot about the harmful effects of smoking. But did you know that smoke from other people's cigarettes can be just as harmful to you—or even more harmful—than smoking yourself? Let me explain.

In this way, he would attempt to pique the audience's curiosity and their need to know by asking a **rhetorical question**—that is, a question asked to stimulate thinking, but to which no answer is expected. Here are some other examples of rhetorical questions used to open speeches:

- Scientists have been working for years on the cure for the common cold and I believe that I have found it. Do you know what I discovered?
- Do you want to know a sure way to raise your grades?
- Do you know why the number of drug-related deaths among college students is on the rise?
- What is the best way to keep your weight down?
- What do you think is the most important skill you can learn in college?

People are also more likely to pay attention when they feel that a speech relates directly to them. A speaker who gives an audience a reason to listen by relating his or her topic to their needs and interests creates **information relevance.** Thus, to ensure your listeners' attention, you should ask yourself if the information you intend to present is relevant to them, and, if it is not, how you are going to make it so. One student presented an extremely well-researched speech on air pollution and its effects on people. He used a variety of excellent examples about pollution on the east and west coasts, but never related them to his listeners, who were from the Midwest. To make his speech more relevant, he needed to relate pollution on each coast to that in the Midwest and provide more information on why Midwesterners should be concerned about the effects of pollution.

Another speaker talking about space technology and its contribution to our daily lives used several examples to make her topic relevant and useful to her audience. In discussing products that were specifically developed for use in space but now have become part of our everyday lives, she mentioned Velcro as a replacement for zippers. She pointed out that because of its success, Velcro is now commonly used in clothing, shoes, handbags, and many other items. She then held up a jacket to illustrate how Velcro works. The audience immediately recognized the relevance of the student's topic.

Information that is perceived as new also attracts the attention of an audience. Whenever this fact is mentioned, some students immediately respond, "But there isn't anything new to present." Actually, "new" does not necessarily mean that you have to present a new topic or something that the audience has never heard of before. It does mean, however, that you need to devise a new view or angle to a topic. There are many subjects that we have heard about many times, such as abortion, capital punishment, gun control, drugs, and the use of seat belts. But a speaker who provides a fresh perspective on a familiar topic makes it more interesting and thus increases the chances of holding the audience's attention by contending that not all illegal drugs should be banned because some can be medically helpful for certain diseases. She began in the following manner:

> You have read and heard so much about cocaine, crack, heroin, and other illegal drugs that you are probably sick of the subject, but these drugs are not all bad. You may, at first, think that I am too liberal, but my mother is on drugs and I am glad of it. You see, my mother is suffering from cancer and the only relief she can get is from the small doses of heroin she receives each day to ease the pain. Today, I am going to inform you about the need for certain illegal drugs that aid our sick and dying.

This approach is not necessarily new but it is different. Rather than taking a stand either for or against the banning of illegal drugs, she focused on certain instances in which the use of illegal drugs can be beneficial. This also helped her to stay within the guidelines of the informative speech.

Increasing Understanding

Once you have gained your listeners' attention, you have created the opportunity to increase their understanding. Understanding is the ability to interpret, grasp, or assign meaning to an idea. You can increase your audience's understanding by systematically organizing your presentation, choosing appropriate language, and providing clear definitions.

Organizing. In a well-organized speech, ideas are arranged in a clear and orderly sequence that makes the material easier to follow and understand. Effective organization helps to increase the speaker's believability and improves the audience's comprehension and retention of information. Two organizational techniques that aid listeners' understanding are planned repetition and advance organizers.

Planned repetition is the deliberate repeating of a thought in order to increase the likelihood that the audience will understand and remember it. The repetition of information generally helps us to remember things more completely. For example, we often repeat a new acquaintance's name several times to make sure that we will remember it later.

The power of repetition is so great that it is the guiding principle behind most TV commercials. Although we may find it bothersome, the constant repetition of the same commercial reminds us of the product and thus increases the chances of our purchasing it. You can use this same principle in an informative speech to get your audience to remember key ideas. For example, you might say, "The relationship among thought, language, and reality is called linguistic relativity—the relationship is called linguistic relativity. Once again, the relationship between thought, language, and reality is called linguistic relativity." Or "The combination is 37–45–72–6. That's 37–45–72–6."

Advance organizers—statements which warn that significant information is coming—signal the listener to pay attention. Some common advance organizers are "This is very important," "Listen to this," "Now get this," and "You will need to know the following." These warnings get the attention of your audience and emphasize that the forthcoming information is both necessary and important. Teachers use advance organizers to make sure that students know what is essential. They will say, for example, "This will probably be included on your next test," "The following is extremely vital if you are going to understand the overall concept," or "The next three points are crucial to your understanding of the problem." Advance organizers also serve as previews of main points. For example, a speaker might say, "There are three parts to a speech: the introduction, the body, and the conclusion." Then he would go on to discuss each part in detail.

Choosing Language. It is extremely important to match your level of language to the knowledge your audience already possesses about your topic. Always appropriate is the familiar expression KISS: "**K**eep **I**t **S**imple, **S**tupid!" If you are speaking with experts or with people who are familiar with your topic, you will be free to use technical terms, but if your audience is unfamiliar with your subject, you will need to choose your words carefully and define any special terms. In some cases, you will even want to avoid technical terms altogether. This may be necessary when such terms would only confuse your audience or when your audience lacks the ability or background to understand them. Sometimes a speaker's use of too many technical terms will turn an audience off or even create hostility. A speaker should choose his or her language carefully to avoid creating unnecessary problems. When possible, choose words that are concrete over words that are abstract and use descriptions to make your points clearer.

Abstract versus concrete words. To increase your audience's understanding, try to use as many concrete words as possible. As discussed in Chapter 3, **concrete words** are symbols for specific things that can be pointed to, physically experienced, touched, or felt. Thus, concrete words stand for specific places, objects, or acts: Howard Smith; Lincoln, Nebraska; your personal computer; writing a letter to a friend. When you use concrete language to define and explain, your listeners will form mental pictures that are similar to your own. For example, if you say that something is the size of a dime, all of your listeners should form a fairly accurate and similar picture of the size you have in mind. Because of their specificity, concrete words leave less room for misinterpretation and misunderstanding.

In contrast, **abstract words** refer to ideas, qualities, or relationships. For example, democracy (an idea), evil (a quality), and love (a relationship) are all abstract words. Their meanings depend on the experiences and intentions of the persons using them. A speaker who says that "the local food program is good for the people" may mean either that the food in the program is nutritious or that the program as a whole is beneficial. Because of its lack of precision, abstract language may leave listeners confused about the speaker's true intent.

For example, in her speech, Cynthia stated: "There are many things I don't like about our defense spending." Because this statement is too general and vague, it had little impact on her audience. A more precise statement would have been, "There are two things I don't like about our defense spending: it costs taxpayers $200 billion each year, and it takes money from desperately needed education and health programs." The second statement is concrete and specific, and thus more forceful and clear.

Abstract words allow listeners to choose from a wide range of personal images, while concrete words help listeners to focus on the specific image that the speaker has in mind. Thus, as you prepare an informative speech, you should try to choose the most concrete words possible.

Description. To make something more concrete, a speaker will often describe its size, quantity, shape, weight, composition, texture, color, age, strength, or fit. Words used to describe something are called **descriptors.** The more descriptors a speaker uses that relate to the listeners' experiences, the greater the likelihood that the message will be understood. Here is how Jim used descriptors in talking about the construction of a building:

> The first requirement when constructing a building is a sturdy foundation. The underlying groundworks for the foundation are called footings. Footings are usually made of concrete and range from about 1 foot in depth for a house to 10 feet in depth for a building with 20 floors. The width of footings ranges from 1 foot to the width of an entire building, depending on the soil's composition and its ability to support construction. Concrete, the result of mixing lime, concrete, stone, sand, and water, is prepared for use. This mixture is gray, has the consistency of cake batter, and pours like lava

coming down the side of a volcano. When concrete dries, it becomes as hard as steel. At first it is white, but it turns gray after it is cured, or finished for use.

Through his explanation, Jim gave meaning to the word *footing* by using size, quantity, color, composition, texture, and strength descriptors. His vivid, colorful language appeals to the senses, thus making a meaningful and lively presentation for his audience.

MINI-EXERCISE

How would you make the following more meaningful and vivid by using the descriptors to characterize size, quantity, shape, weight, composition, texture, color, age, strength, or fit?

1. A cruise ship you were on
2. A mountain you climbed
3. An airplane you flew on
4. A house you lived in
5. A resort hotel you stayed at
6. A city you visited

Defining.   One way to ensure your audience's understanding is to define all potentially unfamiliar and complex words. Consider the importance of definitions in the following cases: Jane had been involved in computer programming and in her speech discussed "flow sheets" and "GIGO"; Mike spoke on "euthanasia"; Sally presented her informative speech on the "squeal rule"; and Jim, in his speech on language and culture, spoke about the problem of "ethnocentrism." In each situation, many in the audience may not have understood the speaker's subject unless the basic terms were explained. For example, flow sheets are written instructions that programmers use to set up the step-by-step operations to be performed by the computer, and GIGO is computer jargon meaning "garbage in garbage out"—or rather, you get out of the computer what you put into it. Euthanasia is the act of painlessly putting to death a person suffering from an incurable and painful disease. A doctor uses the squeal rule when he or she tells the parents of a teenage girl that she is using birth control pills. And, finally, ethnocentrism is the belief in the inherent superiority of one's own group and culture.

As you probably recall from Chapter 7, the most common form of definition used by speakers—the logical definition—usually contains two parts: (1) the dictionary definition, and (2) the characteristics that distinguish the term from other members of the same category. You most likely remember that an operational definition explains how an object or concept works and that a definition by example explains a term or a concept by using examples, either verbal or literal, to illustrate a point. In addition, there are four other methods of clearly defining a term for your listeners: contrasts, synonyms, antonyms, and etymologies.

Contrasts. A **contrast definition** is used to show or to emphasize differences. This type of definition is helpful when you want to distinguish between similar terms. For example, an informative speaker discussing communication apprehension and speech anxiety differentiated one term from the other by stating that communication apprehension is a trait or global anxiety, while speech anxiety is a state or situational anxiety. A person suffering from communication apprehension may also have speech anxiety, but a person with speech anxiety may not have communication apprehension. A contrast definition may also point out differences in causes and effects. Thus, the speaker might point out that people with communication comprehension actively avoid all interactions with others, while people with speech anxiety merely feel a bit of controllable discomfort when addressing an audience.

Synonyms. The use of synonyms can also help clarify the meaning of a word. A **synonym** is a word, phrase, or concept that has exactly the same or very nearly the same meaning as another word, term, or concept. In describing a communicative extrovert, a speaker referred to "willingness to talk openly," "uninhibited speech," and "ability to speak in any situation without reservation." Each phrase describes the behavior that might be exhibited by a person who is a communicative extrovert.

Antonyms. In contrast, an **antonym** is a word, phrase, or concept that has the opposite meaning of another word, phrase, or concept. For example, a communicative extrovert is the opposite of someone with communication apprehension. Such a person is not shy, reserved, unwilling to talk, or afraid to speak. On the contrary, he or she greatly enjoys talking with others.

Etymologies. An **etymology** is a form of definition that traces the origin and development of a word. One student used etymology to explain how the Olympic Games got their name. In the Greek system of telling time, an Olympiad was the period of four years that elapsed between two successive celebrations of the Olympian, or Olympic, Games. This method of figuring time became common about 300 B.C., and all events were dated from 776 B.C., the beginning of the first known Olympic Games. Such a definition provides the audience with a novel way to remember key information. The *Oxford English Dictionary* and the *Etymological Dictionary of Modern English* are excellent sources of word etymologies.

Whenever there is any possibility that your audience may not understand a term or concept, select the kind of definition that will provide the clearest explanation. In some instances more than one kind of definition may be necessary. To err by overdefining is better than to provide an inadequate definition that leaves your audience wondering what you are talking about.

Mini-Exercise

A speaker's presentation of information is judged on five criteria:

1. Accuracy
2. Clarity
3. Interest
4. Relevance
5. Comprehension

How would you apply these criteria to an informative speech presented in class?

Hints for Effective Informative Speaking

Almost everything covered in the text to this point is relevant to informative speaking and audience participation. However, adhering to the following two key steps should be particularly helpful in ensuring your success: avoid assumptions and personalize the information.

Avoid Assumptions

A student began speaking on CPR by emphasizing how important it is and why it saves lives. However, she failed to explain that the acronym CPR stands for cardiovascular pulmonary resuscitation; she assumed that everyone already knew that. Most of the audience did understand, but a number of people did not. In addition, some knew what the acronym meant, but did not know how the technique worked. Because at least half of the class was unfamiliar with the technique, they found the speaker's presentation confusing and frustrating. One simple, mistaken assumption undercut all the work she'd put into her speech.

To avoid making assumptions:

1. Ask yourself if your listeners will already know what you are talking about. Here is where an audience analysis may be appropriate. Randomly select some of your classmates and ask them what they know about your topic and its related terminology.
2. If you believe that even one audience member may not understand, take the time to define and explain your topic.
3. If you believe that a majority of your audience already knows what you mean, simply say something like, "Many of you probably know what euthanasia is, but for those who don't, it is . . . " In this way, you acknowledge those who already know and help those who do not.

4. It is always best not to assume too much. You are better off assuming that your audience needs introductory information, especially if there is any doubt in your mind. You can always move through your basic definitions and explanations quickly if your audience already seems to understand, but it is difficult to regain their interest and attention if you start out by talking over their heads.

Personalize the Information

When you relate your topic directly to your listeners so that they can see its relevancy to themselves, you are personalizing your information. Judy presented a speech about nutrition and the eating habits of people in the United States. It was an interesting speech, but the audience didn't understand what it had to do with them. In revising her speech, Judy surveyed students in her dorm and class about their eating habits. Then she personalized the information for her audience as follows:

> Bad eating habits can cause problems that you may not be aware of. In a survey I took, I found that many college students like yourselves fail to eat a variety of foods from the four basic food groups every day. In fact, my data indicate that 61 percent of you—that is more than half of you—do not eat balanced meals. Furthermore, I found that 50 percent of you skip breakfast at least five times a week.
>
> What does this mean to you? According to nutrition experts, people who eat balanced meals are more motivated and less tired than people who don't eat balanced meals. In fact, those of you who drink a can of pop and eat a candy bar for breakfast—and you know who you are—are more likely to have high blood pressure, lack ambition, feel highly stressed, and fall prone to chronic diseases later in life.

While information that is relevant helps to maintain attention, information that is personalized not only holds attention, but also gains interest. People like to be entertained while being enlightened. For example, think of your most effective instructors. Chances are that they take ordinary material and personalize it into meaningful, interesting knowledge. Listening to a string of facts can be boring and frustrating, but a speech comes to life when it contains personal illustrations.

People are also interested in others. If they were not, there would be no *National Enquirer, Star,* and *People* magazines, or programs like "Life Styles of the Rich and Famous" and Johnny Carson's "Tonight Show." Stories about human events are much more likely to touch listeners than are cold, hard statistics. Thus, whenever possible, try to personalize your information and dramatize it in human terms. Relate it to specific people or situations that your audience members know and care about.

One student began an informative speech about the Heimlich maneuver, a technique used to clear the throat of someone who is choking, by relating the story of a four-year-old boy who saved his three-year-old friend. The boy, who had watched a television show in which the maneuver was used to save the life of one of the main characters, simply reenacted what he had seen. By using this dramatic, real-life episode, the student was able to grab her audience's attention and prepare them for her discussion of who developed the technique, how it works, and how many lives it has saved.

To personalize information:

1. Use examples and information that specifically relate to your audience.
2. Draw conclusions that your audience can identify with and explain what the conclusions may mean to them.
3. Refer to people who are similar to your audience members—for example, student athletes, nontraditional students, minority students, foreign students, or engineering students.
4. Refer to topics and events that affect your listeners, such as campus activities, local laws, athletic and social events, cultural programs, or career decisions.

CHECKLIST FOR PREPARING AN INFORMATIVE SPEECH

1. Have you selected a topic that is appropriate for an informative speech?
2. Is the topic one in which you are interested?
3. Have you chosen a topic that will allow you to inform your audience about something they do not already know?
4. Will you be able to cover your topic adequately in the given time limit?
5. Have you worded your specific purpose to ensure that it meets the objective of the informative speech?
6. Have you selected and worded your main points so that they are clear and meet your specific purpose?
7. Are you providing adequate clarifying and supporting material to ensure that your audience will understand everything you are talking about?
8. Have you organized your speech according to the guidelines of effective organization specified in Chapter 8?
9. Have you avoided assumptions and personalized the information as much as possible?
10. Have you sufficiently practiced your delivery?

A SAMPLE INFORMATIVE SPEECH WITH COMMENTARY

The following adaptation of a speech written by James Kimble, University of Nebraska student, illustrates many of the strategies discussed in this chapter. Permission to reprint this speech was given by Dr. Jack Kay, Department of Speech Communication Chair and Director of Forensics, University of Nebraska-Lincoln, Nebraska.

I Forgot

SPECIFIC PURPOSE: To inform the audience about how memory affects what we do.

JIM BEGINS WITH A LITTLE HUMOR
THAT TIES IN WELL WITH HIS SPEECH
TOPIC. HE ALSO BEGINS TO
ESTABLISH THE RELEVANCY OF HIS
TOPIC TO HIS AUDIENCE AND USES A
RHETORICAL QUESTION TO GAIN THE
AUDIENCE'S ATTENTION.

As the old saying goes, "Education is what you have left over after you have forgotten everything you have learned." Unfortunately, I can't seem to remember who first told me that. And that's not a rare occurrence. In fact, we all lose the ability to retain over 95 percent of what we experience in our day-to-day lives. For instance, how many of you can remember the names of all your teachers, from kindergarten all the way through high school? Though you probably knew them quite well at one time, they've begun to fade away, just like many other things that have happened to you in your past.

JIM INCLUDES A PLANNED
REPETITION OF HIS STATISTICS
ABOUT THE LOSS OF MEMORY,
EMPHASIZING THE POSITIVE SIDE OF
IT. HE ALSO COMPARES THE HUMAN
MIND TO THE COMPUTER IN AN
ATTEMPT TO MAKE AN ABSTRACT
NOTION MORE CONCRETE.

Although 95 percent of what we experience is filed away in our subconscious, defying all efforts at retrieving it, the 5 percent that we do retain helps our mind to exceed the best and most modern computers in capacity, flexibility, and speed. Our conscious memory span reaches back almost as far as our life span—for some of us, this will someday exceed 80 or 90 years. Memory is something that we use every second that we are alive and, therefore, is important to each one of us.

JIM STATES HIS SPECIFIC PURPOSE
VERY CLEARLY. THEN HE PROVIDES
AN ADVANCE ORGANIZER STATEMENT
OF THE MAIN POINTS. FINALLY, HE
MAKES A STRONG CASE FOR WHY HIS
AUDIENCE SHOULD LISTEN TO WHAT
HE HAS TO SAY.

Today we'll examine memory and exactly how it affects everything we do. To begin with, I'll pose the question "What is memory?" Then I'll examine three types of memory: first, sensory; then motor skill; and finally semantic or verbal memory. My purpose is to help us understand more about ourselves, because when we understand how we think, we can understand how other people think.

JIM BEGINS HIS FIRST MAIN POINT
AND TIES IT DIRECTLY TO HIS
AUDIENCE. HE THEN ASKS A SERIES
OF RHETORICAL QUESTIONS. NEXT,
HE POINTS OUT THAT DEFINING
MEMORY IS NOT EASY AND THAT THE
AUDIENCE SHOULD NOT EXPECT A
SIMPLE ANSWER.

By the time you die, your brain will have processed and absorbed billions of items—words, faces, objects, scenes, facts, images, concepts, verbal expressions—all contained within the gray matter inside your head. How is this possible? Just what is memory? Well, what is love? What is time? Do we exist? The answer to all of these questions is the same. That is, we don't know! All we can do at this time is theorize. And theorize we have.

HE BEGINS HIS EXPLANATION OF
WHAT IS KNOWN ABOUT MEMORY.
WHEN HE USES A TECHNICAL TERM,
HE DEFINES IT TO MAKE SURE THAT
HIS AUDIENCE WILL UNDERSTAND.
HIS LAST SENTENCE IS A TRANSITION
TO HIS SECOND MAIN POINT.

Scientists inform us that anything and everything we experience causes a physical change within the structure of our brains called an *engram*. Engram means "written on"— in this case, written on the brain. How we can selectively take these engrams from our subconscious thought into our conscious, or why we sometimes can't, still isn't clear. But what has become clear is that there are three distinct types of memory. Let's examine the first of them.

IN THIS PARAGRAPH JIM CITES HIS FIRST SOURCE. HE THEN INVOLVES THE AUDIENCE BY USING TWO EXAMPLES THAT ARE FAMILIAR TO THEM. HE CHOOSES VIVID EXAMPLES THAT HIS LISTENERS CAN IDENTIFY EASILY.

Sensory memory, as Lee Edson describes in his book, *How We Learn*, is memory that we associate with the senses. Most of you can visualize President Reagan's face and voice, even though he's not here. Or perhaps you can imagine my fingernails scratching along a chalkboard—some of you can even hear it. These are both examples of our sensory memory—experiences that our minds "chalk up" to one of our senses.

JIM POINTS OUT THAT EACH OF US HAS SOME SPECIAL SENSE AND PROVIDES EXAMPLES OF WELL-KNOWN PEOPLE WHO HAD SPECIAL MEMORY SKILLS. JIM THEN CITES HIS SECOND SOURCE. HE CONTINUOUSLY RELATES TO HIS AUDIENCE THROUGH EXAMPLES.

Each of us has one particular sense that plays a larger role in helping us with our memories. Some notable examples are Beethoven, Mozart, and Wagner, who had incredible auditory memories. Napoleon and da Vinci were both blessed with incredible visual memories—in laymen's terms, photographic memory. Most of us do have strong visual recall, but, as Allan Baddely tells us in his book, *Your Memory: A User's Guide*, our auditory recall, in most cases, is even stronger. For instance, shortly after loved ones die, we often have trouble visualizing their faces, yet for many years afterwords, we can often hear their voices in our heads. Unfortunately, for some people, hearing a dead person's voice every time they look at his or her picture can become a little unsettling. So sensory memory isn't necessarily always a good thing. Although it may be incredibly helpful for retention, it is not always pleasant.

JIM NOW MOVES INTO THE SECOND TYPE OF MEMORY. HE EXPLAINS THIS SKILL THROUGH AN EXAMPLE. HE COMPARES IT TO THE FIRST TYPE OF MEMORY AND EXPLAINS IT THROUGH ANOTHER EXAMPLE. HE AGAIN RELATES THE NOTION DIRECTLY TO HIS AUDIENCE.

More vital than sensory memory is motor skill memory. This is the retention and recall, even after long periods of nonuse, of our physical movements. Imagine if you couldn't remember how to walk or how to move your jaw up or down to eat. These are both very important motor skills. If you didn't have motor skill memory, which enables you to recall how to make various physical movements when you want to, life would be pretty miserable.

JIM USES MORE EXAMPLES TO CLARIFY HIS POINT. NOTE THAT ALL OF JIM'S EXAMPLES ARE COMMON AND EASY FOR HIS AUDIENCE TO PICTURE. HE THEN CITES HIS THIRD SOURCE.

All humans have the unique ability to bring back motor skills learned decades earlier. Once you've learned to ride a bike or swim, you'll be able to do these activities for the rest of your life. In the same way, we never forget how to grasp objects, or how to control our eyelid movement. Forgetting how to move the muscles that perform such operations is generally unheard of—except in cases of some mental or physical illness. Our motor skill memory is nearly all-pervasive. In fact, Donald and Eleanor Lair, in their book *Techniques for Efficient Remembering*, claim that motor skill functions do not involve memory. They are reactions, like sneezing, or physiological processes such as digestion. Obviously, our motor skill memory is important to each one of us.

JIM'S DESCRIPTION OF THE THIRD
TYPE OF MEMORY AGAIN IS RELATED
TO HIS AUDIENCE MEMBERS.

The third type of memory is semantic, or verbal, memory. What we remember in this area are things that we've heard, read, or thought. If you know the capital of France or if you can recite the chemical formula for salt, then you know how to use your semantic memory.

JIM RELATES ANOTHER EXAMPLE
DIRECTLY TO HIS AUDIENCE. BY
CONSTANTLY REMINDING HIS
LISTENERS THAT HIS TOPIC IS
RELEVANT TO THEM PERSONALLY,
JIM HOPES TO MAINTAIN THEIR
ATTENTION.

For most of us, skill or deficiency in semantic memory determines whether or not we do well in school. For those of you with strong semantic memory, school is probably relatively easy because you remember most things you've learned in the past and have little or no trouble assimilating new knowledge into that framework. But if you have a weak verbal memory, learning probably isn't so easy, because such people have not developed the framework in which to store verbal information.

JIM QUALIFIES HIS USE OF CERTAIN
TERMINOLOGY AND THEN CITES HIS
FOURTH SOURCE.

Unfortunately, our descriptions of semantic aptitude are too general when we say "strong" or "weak." James D. Weinland explains in his book, *How to Improve Your Memory*, that semantic aptitude can be further divided into two major areas: recall and recognition.

JIM GIVES AN EXPLICIT DEFINITION
OF A KEY TERM AND SUPPORTS IT
WITH A CONCRETE EXAMPLE.

Recall is the actual production of entire thoughts pulled at will from our memory banks with little or no cue. If I asked you to recite the Pledge of Allegiance, you probably wouldn't have much trouble—even though it's not written down for you. The point is that you can recite an entire passage that is familiar to you just from hearing its title. This is based upon semantic recall.

JIM USES A CONTRAST DEFINITION TO
DISTINGUISH BETWEEN RECALL AND
SELECTIVE RECALL. HERE HE IS
PROVIDING A PRACTICAL
ILLUSTRATION OF HOW SELECTIVE
RECALL CAN HELP STUDENTS.

Recall is a bit easier when there is a cue. Selective recall is another form of semantic memory, but it needs a larger cue to bring forth stored knowledge. An example of this occurs during a multiple-choice test. You may not always recall the correct answer, but you can sometimes recognize the incorrect answers and thus get the question right through the process of elimination. This type of memory can be extremely helpful when other recall attempts do not work.

BEFORE ENDING THE SPEECH JIM
PROVIDES ONE MORE REASON FOR
LISTENING TO WHAT HE HAS TO SAY
AND EMPHASIZES IT WITH HUMOR.

Now, obviously, since we are all in college, semantic memory is the area in which we want to excel because it helps us to remember facts. While this is important, you should also realize that semantic memory does even more. For example, it helps us to learn, think, read, and remember trivial bits of information, without which we would be unable to play such games as Trivial Pursuit.

JIM'S CONCLUSION PROVIDES A SUMMARY OF WHAT HE HAS SAID AND SOME THOUGHTS ABOUT WHAT WE HAVE LEARNED FROM THE PAST AND STILL NEED TO LEARN IN THE FUTURE.

IN HIS LAST SENTENCE, JIM REEMPHASIZES HIS SPECIFIC PURPOSE.

To the ancient Greeks, memory was an actual place where all human thoughts went—an area controlled by the gods. Remembering was the simple process of retrieving those thoughts from the mysterious region. Today, we have progressed in leaps and bounds in many areas of science, but when we discuss memory, we have not come much further than the Greeks. To be sure, we have managed to differentiate between the three types of memory: sensory, motor skill, and semantic. Yet, this is the major portion of our progress. The research hasn't stopped—scientists are still looking for ways to understand the human brain in order to uncover its mysteries. In addition, they are looking for ways to help us improve our memories. Memory—it is not something we should forget because it affects what we do.

THE STEPS IN DEVELOPING AN INFORMATIVE SPEECH

Although the steps in preparing and developing an informative speech may not always follow the same order or require the same amount of detail and involvement, the following is a typical sequence:

1. Select the topic
2. Research the topic
3. Analyze the audience
4. Determine the specific purpose
5. Organize the speech
6. Develop the supporting materials
7. Practice the delivery
8. Deliver the speech
9. Analyze the effectiveness of the speech

Always remember that each step depends on the other steps and that sometimes you may have to redo a step several times in order to accomplish your specific purpose.

SUMMARY

Information is the act of informing or the condition of being informed; it is the communication of knowledge—knowledge derived from study, experience, or instruction. The ability to present and receive information has become increasingly important in our society over the years. Today it is vital for anyone who wants to be successful. Those who possess information and can communicate it clearly and effectively possess power and command respect.

A fine line based on the speaker's intent distinguishes an informative speech from a persuasive one. The goal of an informative speech is to increase understanding, whereas the goal of a persuasive speech is to change attitudes and behaviors. Information can be presented without any attempt at persuasion, but persuasion cannot be accomplished without attempting to inform.

Your topic for an informative speech should meet two criteria: it should be something that interests you and that you know something about, and it should be something that will interest your audience. You may talk about objects (people, animals, structures, places), processes (how something is put together, works, is done), events (happenings, occasions), and concepts (beliefs, theories, ideas, principles).

To achieve the main goal of increasing knowledge, a speaker must focus on two subgoals: gaining the audience's attention, and increasing the audience's understanding. Listeners are more likely to pay attention to information that is relevant, useful, new, or different. To gain attention, speakers may use *rhetorical questions,* which are questions asked solely to stimulate thinking, but to which no answer is expected. Or they may rely on *information relevance*—relating their information directly to the audience and thus giving them a reason to listen.

A speaker can increase an audience's understanding by systematically organizing the presentation, choosing appropriate language, and providing clear definitions. Two organizational techniques that aid listeners' understanding are planned repetition and advance organizers. *Planned repetition* is the deliberate repeating of a thought, while *advance organizers* are statements that warn the listener that significant information is coming.

Speakers should avoid technical language that might be unfamiliar to the audience. In addition, they should choose words that are concrete rather than abstract and use descriptors to provide even greater clarification. *Concrete words* stand for specific things that can be pointed to, physically experienced, touched, or felt, while *abstract words* refer to ideas, qualities, or relationships. *Descriptors* are words that are used to describe something.

Another way to ensure understanding is to define all terms that the audience may find unfamiliar. Contrasts, synonyms, antonyms, and etymologies can all help to clarify meanings for the listener. A *contrast definition* is used to show or to emphasize differences. A *synonym* is a word, phrase, or concept that has exactly the same or very nearly the same meaning as another word, term, or concept. An *antonym* is a word, phrase, or concept that has the opposite meaning of another word, phrase, or concept. And an *etymology* is a form of definition that traces the origin and development of a word.

Two key steps to developing an effective informative speech are: avoid assumptions and personalize information. Do not assume that your audience is already familiar with your topic and its special terminology. Also, when possible, personalize your speech by providing examples that specifically touch your listeners' needs and interests.

KEY TERMS

Abstract Words: symbols for ideas, qualities, or relationships.

Advance Organizers: statements that preview forthcoming content.

Antonym: a word, phrase, or concept that has the opposite meaning of another word, phrase, or concept.

Concrete Words: symbols for specific things that can be pointed to, physically experienced, touched, or felt.

Contrast Definition: a definition that shows or emphasizes differences.

Descriptors: words used to describe something.

Etymology: a definition that traces the origin and development of a word.

Information: the act of informing or the condition of being informed; communication of knowledge—knowledge derived from study, experience, or instruction.

Information Relevance: relating information to the audience so that they have a reason to listen.

Planned Repetition: the deliberate repetition of thought in order to increase the likelihood that the audience will understand and remember it.

Rhetorical Question: a question that is asked to stimulate thinking, but to which no answer is expected.

Synonym: a word, term, or concept that has virtually the same meaning as another word, term, or concept.

DISCUSSION STARTERS

1. Explain in your own words why information is so important in our society.
2. Why is information powerful?
3. In what ways have you used information to gain power?
4. What are the prerequisites for selecting an informative speech topic?
5. What two or three informative speech topics interest you the most? Why?
6. In planning your informative speech, what should you take into consideration to ensure that you will be as effective as possible?
7. What suggestions that were not included in this chapter would you give to someone preparing an informative speech?

FURTHER READINGS

Dodson, R. J. *A Guide to Speaking in Public.* Salem, Wisc.: Sheffield Publishing Co., 1986.

Fletcher, Leon. *How to Design & Deliver a Speech.* 3rd ed. New York: Harper & Row Publishers, Inc., 1985.

Haskins, William A., and Joseph M. Staudacher. *Successful Public Speaking: A Practical Guide.* Glenview, Ill.: Scott, Foresman and Company, 1987.

Katula, Richard A. *Principles and Patterns of Public Speaking.* Belmont, Calif.: Wadsworth Publishing Co., 1987.

Welsh, James J. *The Speech Writing Guide.* Huntington, N.Y.: Krieger Publishing Co., 1979.

William, Fredrick. *The New Communications.* Belmont, Calif.: Wadsworth Publishing Co., 1984.

NOTES

1. Gilliam, Bonnie Cherp, and Anne Zimmer, *ITV: Promise Into Practice,* (Columbus, Ohio: Department of Education, 1972), p. 36.
2. Elmore, Garland C., "Integrating Video Technology and Organizational Communication," (Paper presented at the Indiana Speech Association Convention, Indianapolis, Indiana, 1981), p. 1.

CHAPTER 11

The Persuasive Speech

After studying this chapter, you should be able to:

1. Define persuasion and its four action goals.
2. Explain what constitutes an appropriate topic for a persuasive speech.
3. Give examples of how questions of fact, value, and policy may serve as the basis of a persuasive speech.
4. Tell why credibility is important in persuasive speaking.
5. Differentiate among appeals to needs, logical appeals, and emotional appeals.
6. Develop a persuasive speech that demonstrates your ability to research, organize, and support your action goal.

If you were to analyze the communication you were involved in during the past week, you would probably discover that you had been in a variety of persuasive situations. In order to prove this point to some doubtful students, a professor asked his entire class to record their communication activities for a period of one week. Here are some sample comments from their reports:

> Called parents for additional money. . . . Discussed who should be elected the next student representative. . . . Asked a person for a date. . . . Discussed with a professor why I had turned a paper in late. . . . Talked about last week's game and how well the team was playing. . . . Asked a fraternity brother for car to go out on date. . . . Returned a pair of running shoes to a sporting goods shop because they were defective. . . . Called my sister to say hello—found out she had the flu and told her she needed to see a doctor. . . . Asked several friends to join our organization. . . . Asked my roommate for a small loan. . . . Tried to talk a police officer out of giving me a traffic ticket. . . . Partied instead of studying for a test. . . . Talked a friend into going to church. . . .

Although not every situation that the students reported involved the use of persuasion, many did, and class members were truly surprised to discover the amount of persuasion they had used.

Like most students, when you think about it, you will find that you, too, are involved in some form of persuasion much of the time. Persuasion is a two-way street: If you are not trying to persuade someone, someone is probably trying to persuade you. For example, you are involved in persuasion every time you ask or you are asked to do or not do something, to give or not give something, to accept or not accept something, and to believe or not believe something. To be more specific, some form of persuasion takes place when you ask your professor to excuse you from an exam, when you coax an employer to hire you, when you ask a friend for a loan, when someone encourages you to see a certain movie or urges you to vote for him or her in the school election, and when you talk yourself into staying home to study even though you'd rather go out with your friends.

Since persuasion is so much a part of our everyday activities, it is important to understand it and its goal. Thus, in this chapter, we will discuss how to select a persuasive speech topic, how to establish credibility, and how to prepare and develop a persuasive speech. Finally, we will discuss some specific hints on how to persuade others effectively.

THE NATURE AND GOAL OF PERSUASIVE SPEAKING

Persuasion is a communication process involving both verbal and nonverbal messages that attempt to reinforce or change listeners' attitudes, beliefs, values, or behavior. Of course, it is possible to change a person's attitudes, beliefs, and values without changing his or her behavior. For example, you may so skillfully argue that your friend should wear a seat belt that

eventually you will win the argument, but despite your friend's new attitude toward seat belts, he or she may still never put one on. Have you used persuasion effectively? This is a debatable question. You have changed someone's attitude but not his or her behavior. Which is more important?

The ultimate goal of all persuasion is action—that is, successful persuasion requires reinforcement or change of behavior. However, getting others to take action and change their behavior is not always easy. Therefore, a speaker may need to settle for a change in attitudes, beliefs, or values, as in the seat belt example. In fact, it is important to realize that a change in attitudes, beliefs, or values, such as the acceptance of the idea of wearing seat belts, is part of the persuasive process and must almost always occur before a change in action or behavior can take place. Not all persuasive speaking will lead to action, nor should persuasive speakers consider themselves failures if they do not obtain behavior change. Especially as a beginner, you should not always expect to obtain a change in action or behavior, but you should be able to get others to listen to what you have to say and to consider your point of view.

Action Goals

When a speaker's main goal is to achieve action, he or she will also seek one of four subgoals: adoption, discontinuance, deterrence, or continuance of the behavior under discussion.[1]

Adoption. **Adoption** is an action goal that asks listeners to demonstrate their acceptance of an attitude, belief, or value by performing the action suggested by the speaker. For example, assume that you had never liked the thought of donating blood, but that one day you saw a television commercial pleading for blood to help the victims of a recent disaster. If, on the next day, you donated blood, you would be displaying adoption. You still might not like the thought of giving blood, but the commercial would have persuaded you to do so. Of course, the fact that you gave blood once does not mean that you will continue to give blood whenever you are asked. That is, your adoption of the persuasive message may be only temporary.

Discontinuance. **Discontinuance** is the opposite of adoption. If your action goal is discontinuance, you want your listeners to stop doing something—running, drinking alcohol, using illegal drugs, paying high tuition, discriminating against others, eating junk food, or avoiding difficult courses.

Deterrence. **Deterrence** is an action goal that asks listeners to demonstrate their acceptance of an attitude, belief, or value by avoiding certain behavior. Sample deterrent messages would be if you don't eat junk food, don't start now; if you don't own a gun, don't buy one; or, if you support busing to promote school integration, don't vote to eliminate the law.

Continuance. **Continuance** is an action goal that asks listeners to demonstrate their acceptance of an attitude, belief, or value by continuing to perform certain behaviors. For example, if you jog, don't stop; keep reading for pleasure; stay involved in extracurricular activities; or, keep buying from your locally owned stores.

Note that the first two action goals, adoption and discontinuance, ask people to change their behavior, while the last two, deterrence and continuance, ask people not to change, but to continue doing what they are already doing.

TOPICS FOR PERSUASIVE SPEECHES

Some themes lend themselves more readily to persuasive speaking than others. Especially adaptable are current and controversial subjects and events. You will increase your likelihood of success if you:

1. Pick a topic that you are interested in, know something about, and are personally concerned about.
2. Select a subject that is *worthwhile* and of potential concern to your audience.
3. Choose a topic for which you can establish an action goal. For example, the notion that smoking is harmful to your health may be a good persuasive theme, but if no one in your audience smokes, could you come up with a strong action goal?

4. Select an issue that is current, but avoid a topic that is common
knowledge or that has been discussed widely, unless you plan
to add a new perspective to it.

Persuasive speeches are most commonly given in situations where there
are two or more opposing viewpoints and the speaker's point of view differs
from that of the audience's. For example, the speaker may want the audience
to support higher tuition because it will lead to better quality instruction,
but most of the audience may believe that tuition is already too high.
Especially when a speaker's goal is adoption or discontinuance, there must
be some difference between the speaker's view and that of the audience, or
there is no need for persuasion. On the other hand, when the speaker's
goal is deterrence or avoidance, the speaker's and the audience's points of
view may be more closely united.

Questions of Fact, Value, and Policy

Persuasive speech topics may center around questions of fact, questions of
value, questions of policy, or any combination of the three.

Questions of Fact.   A **question of fact** asks what is true and what is false.
Some typical questions of fact are: Which building is the tallest in the world?
Which college football player has gained the most yards in a single season?
Which university was the first to be established in the United States? Note
that each of these questions can be answered with a fact that can be verified
in reference books. Because they are cut-and-dried, there can be little debate
about them and they would thus make weak topics for a persuasive speech.

In contrast, persuasive speeches may be built on predictions of future
events that will eventually become matters of fact—for example: Who will
be the next president of the United States? Which college basketball team
will win the national championship next year? Will there be a third world
war in the next five years? Although none of these questions can be
answered with certainty, a persuasive speaker could build an effective case
predicting the answer to each.

Persuasive speeches may also be based on complicated answers to
questions of fact, or justifications for answers that are unclear. For example,
why did so many tragic air disasters occur during the 1980s? Was it because
of drugs? Poor training of air traffic controllers? Overworked controllers?
Outdated equipment? Insufficient rules for the use of air space near airports?
Although no one answer covers the entire situation, a speaker could build
a strong argument to show that one of these factors is the primary cause of
air accidents.

Finally, some persuasive speeches may attempt to answer questions of
fact that are not completely verifiable—for example: Do unidentified flying
objects really exist? Can hypnotism enable a person to relive past lives? Is

there intelligent life in outer space? A speech on the existence of intelligent life in outer space might be planned something like this:

SPECIFIC PURPOSE: To persuade the audience that there is intelligent life in outer space.

MAIN POINTS:
I. There have been numerous signs that there is intelligent life in outer space.
   A. The National Science Foundation in a 1986 report indicates that radio signals are being received from outer space.
   B. Recent sightings of UFOs by military and commercial pilots strongly suggest life in other solar systems.
II. The size of the universe allows sufficient reason to believe that there is some form of intelligent life in outer space.
   A. Scientists suggest that we have only begun to learn about what exists beyond our solar system.
   B. There is an infinite number of solar systems beyond ours, which leaves a strong possibility for other intelligent life.

On the surface, questions of fact may appear more appropriate for an informative speech than for a persuasive one, but if you consider the difficulty of persuading an audience that the world is coming to end, that an earthquake will destroy the western part of the United States, or that the pyramids of Egypt were designed by an intelligence far superior to ours today, you can see that questions of fact can offer rich possibilities for persuasion.

Questions of Value.   A **question of value** asks whether something is good or bad, or desirable or undesirable. Thus, it requires a much more judgmental response than does a question of fact. Some typical questions of value are: Who was the most effective president during the twentieth century? Can the use of outer space for defense be justified? Has religion become too much a part of government? Is public education taking over the role of the parent in teaching our children moral values? The answers to these questions are not based solely on fact, but on what each individual considers to be right or wrong, good or bad, ethical or unethical, acceptable or unacceptable.

It may seem that the answers to questions of value would be based solely on personal opinion and subjectivity rather than on objective evidence, but this is not the case. Effective persuasive speakers will have evidence to support their positions and will be able to justify their opinions. For example, suppose a speaker contends that the social use of drugs is harmful. She might plan her speech as follows:

SPECIFIC PURPOSE: To persuade the audience that the social use of drugs is harmful.

MAIN POINTS:
I. Social use of drugs affects personal relationships.
   A. According to a national survey, social drug users are involved in twice as many divorces as nonusers.

   B. Researchers have shown that the children of social drug users
       are more likely to be loners, have fewer friends, and eventually
       use drugs themselves.
II. Social use of drugs interferes with work.
   A. The rate of absenteeism from work of social drug users is four
       times that of nonusers.
   B. The job turnover rate of social drug users is at least double that
       of nonusers.
   C. Social drug users are 30 percent less productive than nonusers
       doing the same job.

Because values vary so dramatically from one person to the next, a
question of value is not always easy to defend. For example, A may think
that *Top Gun* was a so-so movie and B may think it was great; A may think
that abortion should be illegal and B may think the opposite; or A may
believe that gun control is unreasonable and B may think that it's absolutely
necessary. When it comes to questions of value, one person's judgment is
no better or worse than another's. This is complicated by the fact that
because values are usually rooted in emotionalism rather than reason, it is
often extremely difficult to get people to change their values. Therefore, you
will need to gather a great deal of research and evidence and build a strong
case to support one value over another, even though you know your values
are right, because so are mine.

Questions of Policy.   A **question of policy** goes beyond seeking judgmental
responses to seeking courses of action. Whereas a question of value asks if
something is right or wrong, a question of policy asks if something should
or should not be done. For example: Should we provide aid to farmers in
need? Should the federal government bail out large industries that are in
financial trouble? Should universities allow students to have alcohol in their
dorm rooms? Should we build a defense system in space? Should we allow
sex education in the classroom? Answers to questions of policy involve both
facts and values and are therefore never simple.

Persuasive speakers can defend an existing policy, suggest a new policy
to replace an old one, or create a policy where none exists. If you defend an
existing policy, you are persuading listeners to keep things as they are. If
you want to change an existing policy, you must persuade people that the
old one does not work, but that your new one will. If you hope to create a
new policy, you must persuade your audience that a policy is needed and
that yours is the right one.

When discussing questions of policy, persuasive speakers usually focus
on three considerations: need, plan, and suitability. If you believe that things
are fine as they are, then there is no *need* for change; if you believe that
things are not fine, then you must argue that there is a *need* for change.
When you advocate change, you must provide a *plan*, or solution. The plan
tells the audience what you think should be done. Finally, you must defend
your plan by explaining why it is the best solution for the situation. Examine

how student Mary Trouba used the need, plan, and suitability steps in her persuasive speech:[2]

SPECIFIC PURPOSE: To persuade the audience that radical right-wing hate groups are a danger to society.

NEED:
I. Right-wing religious groups flagrantly violate the American ideas of equality and religious tolerance.
   A. Right-wing hate groups are growing at an alarming rate.
   B. Right-wing hate groups are employing criminal means to achieve their ends.
   C. Right-wing hate groups are building a frightening capacity to inflict moral damage on society.

PLAN:
II. We must enact a twofold solution that includes legal and attitudinal components.
   A. The first step is to take legal action to crack down on paramilitary activity by extremist groups.
   B. The second step is to educate people about these groups.

SUITABILITY:
III. The two-step plan will control these groups and help to reduce their negative impact on society.
   A. Laws can prevent paramilitary groups from forming and thus reduce their criminal activities.
   B. Research has shown that people who are educated about extremist groups are less likely to join them.

PERSUASIVE SPEECH TOPICS: A SAMPLE LIST

Here are some possible topics for persuasive speeches. Of course, this list is by no means exhaustive, and the topics are not necessarily titles of speeches, but may reflect specific purposes or broad areas that need to be narrowed to fit assigned time limits or other requirements set by your instructor.

Increasing Aid to Farmers	The Dumping of Nuclear Waste
Continued Exploration in Space	The Need for Better Teachers
Stopping Vandalism in Our Cities	Improving Our Prisons
The Impact of Videos on Youth	Political Involvement
Having an Internship	Majoring in Communication
Athletes and Winning	Are Unions Outdated?
The Increase in Sexual Assaults	Pornographic Films Are Necessary
Nothing Is Accomplished by War	Teachers' Pay Must Be Higher
Why We Need a Strong Military	Is There Too Much Government?
Should Farm Subsidies Continue?	Are Women Being Hurt in the Job
Should the Speed Laws Be Changed?	Market?

ESTABLISHING CREDIBILITY

The most valuable tool that you, as a persuasive speaker, can possess is **credibility**—that is, believability based on the audience's evaluation of your competence and character. The audience is the ultimate judge of credibility, but there is much you can do to influence their opinion. The key is to firmly establish your competence and credibility right from the beginning of your speech.

Competence

An audience will judge your competence by the amount of knowledge you display. Therefore, the more expertise you show in your subject, the more likely it is that your audience will accept what you have to say. You can establish your expertise by doing the following things:

1. *Relating personal experiences.* One student, in urging action to avoid the chemical pollution of water, described her mother's death as a result of drinking contaminated water. Although her firsthand experiences did not, in themselves, make her an expert environmentalist, they clearly established that she knew something about the dangers of pollution.

2. *Demonstrating your involvement or commitment.* One student chose to speak on the value of internships. Because he had personally participated in the internship program, his audience quickly recognized that he was knowledgeable and committed.

3. *Citing your research.* Quoting information from books, articles, and personal interviews with experts can add weight and objectivity to your arguments. Mentioning sources that are respected by your audience adds to your credibility and indicates that you are well read. One student, who tried to persuade her audience that autopsies are necessary, used the following research to develop her credibility:[3]

> *Scientific American* reported in March of 1983 that despite the fact that cancer and cardiovascular disease are two of the nation's leading killers, each year 90 percent of cancer and cardiovascular disease deaths go uninvestigated.

She went on to cite the following:

> Dr. Robert Anderson, Chief of Pathology at the University of New Mexico's School of Medicine, refers to the lunacy of our present situation: "How do we know how we ought to be operating tomorrow if we don't even know what's going on today? We know more about the cause of death in certain strains of mice than we do about deaths in man."

Each time you cite a valid source, you add to your credibility by demonstrating to your audience that you have done your research and know what you are talking about.

Character

An audience's judgment of your character is based on their perceptions of your trustworthiness and ethics. The best way to establish your character is to be honest and fair.

Trustworthiness.   A speaker's **trustworthiness** is the audience's perception of his or her reliability and dependability. Others attribute trustworthiness to us based on their past experiences with us. For example, they will judge our reliability according to whether we come to class every time it meets. They will evaluate our dependability based on our past record of following through on our promises. People who have had positive experiences with what we have done are more apt to see us as trustworthy.

THINK ABOUT IT

The following appeared in an advertisement promoting a system of horse betting:

> Only Someone Who Could *Positively* 'Produce' would *Dare* Make you Such An Offer! I WILL ***REVEAL*** MY METHOD TO YOU SO YOU CAN EXPECT AN UNHEARD OF *$250.00 A DAY AVERAGE PROFIT* FOR THE NEXT 30 DAYS . . . OR ELSE, YOU PAY ME NOTHING . . . *NOT ONE RED CENT!*

How likely would you be to believe this message if it came from a known mobster? A bookmaker? A stranger? A friend? A religious leader whom you know?

Ethics.   In Chapter 9, we defined **ethics** as an individual's system of moral principles and stated that ethics plays a key role in communication. While this is certainly true of communication in general, it is specifically true of persuasion. Persuasive speakers who are known to be unethical or dishonest are less likely to be successful in obtaining their persuasive purpose than are people who are recognized as ethical and honest. You must earn your reputation as an ethical person through your actions. The best way to establish your ethicalness is to do the following:

1. *Cite sources when information is not your own and cite your sources accurately.* As you develop your speech, be sure you give credit to your sources of information and to ideas that are not your own. Provide the audience with an oral footnote by saying, for example, "The following was taken from . . . " or "The following is a quote from. . . . " Be specific about who and where your information came from.

2. *Avoid falsifying or distorting information in order to make your point.* Never make up information, attribute information to a source that is not responsible for it, take quotes out of context, or distort information to meet your purpose.

3. *Show respect for your audience.* When audience members perceive that you are being respectful—even though they may not agree with your point of view—they are more likely to listen. And when they listen, you at least have a chance of persuading them. Do not try to trick audience members into accepting your point of view or ridicule them for not agreeing with you.

Your audience's evaluation of your credibility will ultimately determine whether they accept or reject your persuasive goals. It is important to remember that credibility is earned and that it depends on others' perceptions. Unfortunately, your credibility as a speaker is not permanent. Rather, it changes from topic to topic, from situation to situation, and from audience to audience. Thus, it is important to establish your credibility each time you speak.

Mini-Exercise

List five well-known individuals whom you believe to be high in credibility and briefly describe what you think makes them credible. Compare your names and opinions with those of your classmates.

Preparing and Developing the Persuasive Speech

Usually in a classroom speech, you will have only one opportunity to coax your audience to accept your persuasive purpose. Therefore, it is important to set your persuasive goals realistically. You will also need to give some special thought to how you research, organize, and support your topic.

Researching Your Topic

Your research for a persuasive speech must be especially thorough. You'll need to gather as much information as possible about your topic because the more you know, the better equipped you will be to defend your position. When doing your research, look primarily for evidence that supports your views. If, in the process, you discover information that contradicts your stand, make note of it and look for material that you can use to refute such information. Such anticipation of possible objections is especially helpful when your position is controversial and when your audience's opinions are likely to be split. If you know the arguments that may be used against you, you will be better able to defend yourself.

Organizing Your Topic

A persuasive speech requires several special decisions that will affect organization.

1. *Should you present one side or both sides of an issue?* The answer to this question depends on your audience. If your listeners basically support your position, then presenting one side may be sufficient. If, on the other hand, their views are divided or opposed to your position, it may be more effective to present both sides. This decision also depends on your audience's knowledge of the topic and their evaluation of your credibility. If audience members are well informed and educated, presenting both sides of the issue may be your best choice. You may also want to present both sides if your credibility is not well established, because then the audience will tend to perceive you as more fair and rational. In addition, presenting both sides of an argument helps to minimize the effect that counterarguments can have on your audience.

2. *When should you present your strongest arguments?* Presenting your strongest arguments at either the beginning or the end of your speech is more effective than presenting them in the middle. A good strategy is to state your strongest arguments early and then repeat them toward the end. Because audience attention is most likely to wander in the middle of a speech, that is a good time to present a lot of personal examples supporting your position.

3. *What is the best way to organize your persuasive speech?* The most effective sequence of presentation depends on your topic, your specific purpose, and your audience. Among the patterns of organization that work well for persuasive speeches are: (1) problem-solution, (2) cause and effect, (3) comparative advantage order, and (4) the motivated sequence. Because the first two were discussed in Chapter 10, we will focus on the second two here.

When using the **comparative advantage order,** a persuasive speaker presents and compares several solutions in order to emphasize the advantages of his or her preferred solution. Like the problem-solution pattern, this approach begins by stating a concern. However, instead of providing only one answer, it offers several with the intention of showing that one is superior. For example:

> Our economy has been fairly stable for the past few years and thus there has been little growth in the interest rates paid on savings accounts. Fortunately, there are several alternatives for investors who seek higher rates of return: (1) government bonds, (2) no-load mutual funds, (3) stocks, or (4) money market step-up accounts. What are the advantages of each of these?

First the speaker would explain all four investments. Then, through examples and evidence, he would proceed to demonstrate that one investment has a clear advantage over the others.

The most appropriate and widely used pattern of organization for the persuasive speech is the **motivated sequence,** which is specifically designed to help the speaker combine sound logic and practical psychology into a single sequence. This method is particularly effective because it follows the human thinking process and motivates listeners to take action. The sequence has five steps: attention, need, satisfaction, visualization, and action.

Step 1: *Attention.* In the first step, the persuader attempts to create an interest and desire in the topic so that the audience will want to listen. This step takes place in the introduction and follows the guidelines for an effective presentation as discussed in Chapter 8. Here the speaker is saying, "Pay attention—this is important to you."

Step 2: *Need.* In the second step, the persuader focuses on the problem by analyzing the things that are wrong and relating them to the audience's interests, wants, or desires. At this point the speaker is saying, "Something is wrong and something must be done about it."

Step 3: *Satisfaction.* In Step 3, the persuader provides a solution or plan of action that will eliminate the problem and thus satisfy the audience's interests, wants, and desires. Here the speaker is saying, "What I have to offer is the way to solve the problem."

Step 4: *Visualization.* At this point the persuader explains in detail how the solution will meet the audience's need. The speaker's main message now becomes, "This is how my plan will work to solve the problem, and if you accept my solution, things will be much better."

Step 5: *Action.* Finally, the persuader asks the audience for a commitment to put the proposed solution to work. He or she closes by asking the audience to do something—"Take action!"

The following abbreviated outline shows how the motivated sequence can be used in a persuasive speech:

SPECIFIC PURPOSE: To persuade my audience to accept the Personalized System of Instruction (PSI) as the best method of teaching.

Introduction

ATTENTION   I. A method of instruction now being used throughout the country makes learning much easier for most students and costs a lot less than traditional methods of instruction.

Body

NEED   II. We need a method of instruction that will increase students' competencies and at the same time reduce the cost of education.

SATISFACTION   III. The only method that appears to accomplish both of these goals is the Personalized System of Instruction, which was created by Dr. Fred Keller.

VISUALIZATION   IV. We can count on PSI to meet our needs because this approach has been shown to boost competency and reduce costs in thousands of schools across the country.

Conclusion

ACTION   V. Tell your teachers and administrators that the PSI method is best
                  for accomplishing the highest student competencies at the lowest
                  cost.

THE MOTIVATED SEQUENCE

Step	Function	Audience Response
1. Attention	Getting attention	I want to listen.
2. Need	Showing the need; describing the problem	Something needs to be done.
3. Satisfaction	Satisfying the need; presenting the solution	This is the thing to do to satisfy the need.
4. Visualization	Visualizing the results	I, myself, can see the satisfaction of doing this.
5. Action	Requesting action	I will do this.

Supporting Your Topic

In persuasive speeches, speakers try not only to prove something, but also to influence their audience through the impressiveness of their supporting materials. Thus, they use their supporting materials as carefully chosen tools to build the kind of appeal that is most likely to sway their listeners. Based on their topic and their audience analysis, persuasive speakers will try to appeal either to their listeners' needs, to their logic, or to their emotions.

Appeals to Needs.   **Appeals to needs** attempt to move people to action by calling on their most basic physical and psychological requirements and desires. Of course, different people have different needs, but most of us want to protect or enhance factors that affect our physical, safety, social, and self-esteem needs.

Physical needs are our most basic physiological requirements, such as the needs for food, water, sleep, sex, and other physical comforts. *Safety needs* pertain to our desires for stability, order, protection from violence, freedom from stress and disease, security, structure, and for law in our lives. *Social needs* relate to our hopes to be loved and to belong—our needs for affection from family and friends, for membership in groups, and for the acceptance and approval of others. Finally, *self-esteem needs* reflect our desires for recognition, respect from others, and self-respect.

Speakers can appeal to any of these needs in order to motivate listeners to take action. For example, a speaker trying to sell individual retirement accounts would aim his or her appeal at our needs for security and stability, while a speaker who hoped to persuade us to lose weight would call on our needs for physical comfort and self-esteem. Our readiness to accept ideas or to take action depends heavily on the speaker's ability to relate his or her message to our needs.

Logical Appeals.   Attempts to move people to action through the use of evidence and proof are called **logical appeals.** When speakers lead their listeners to think "Yes, that's logical" or "That makes sense," they are building their case by calling on their audience's ability to reason. To accomplish this, persuasive speakers use such evidence as statistics, examples, testimony, and any other supporting material that will sway listeners.

In presenting their evidence, persuasive speakers guide their listeners through a carefully planned sequence of thought that clearly leads to the desired conclusion. This train of logic may fall into one of four categories:

1. **Deductive reasoning** is a sequence of thought that moves from general information to a specific conclusion. It presents a general premise and a minor premise that lead to a precise deduction. By using deductive reasoning, one student set up his argument as follows:

GENERAL PREMISE: Heart disease is a major health concern in the Midwest.

MINOR PREMISE: Nebraska is a part of the Midwest.

CONCLUSION: Therefore, heart disease is a major health concern in Nebraska.

Great care must be taken to ensure that the premise is accurate because a faulty generalization will lead to a defective conclusion. For example:

GENERAL PREMISE: All car salespersons are crooks.

MINOR PREMISE: Carolyn is a car salesperson.

CONCLUSION: Therefore, Carolyn is a crook.

The general premise must be both accurate and defensible before deductive reasoning can be used effectively as evidence to support a position.

2. **Inductive reasoning** is the opposite of deductive reasoning—it is a sequence of thought that moves from the specific to the general. An argument based on induction usually progresses from a series of related facts or situations to a general conclusion. A student discussing university teaching evaluations wants her listeners to agree that speech professors at her university are excellent teachers. She therefore leads them through the following sequence of inductive reasoning:

FACTS: a. My speech communication professor is an excellent classroom teacher.
                             b. The speech professor I had last semester was also an excellent classroom teacher.
                             c. My roommate's speech professor is an excellent classroom teacher.
                             d. My roommate has a friend whose speech professor is an excellent classroom teacher.

CONCLUSION: Speech professors at the University of Nebraska are, in general, excellent classroom teachers.

When your facts can be verified and there are sufficient links between your facts that justify your conclusion, inductive reasoning can be an excellent way to persuade an audience of the validity of your argument.

Of course, inductive reasoning can also be misused. For example, how often have you heard or made such general statements as "Football players are intellectually void," "Politicians are crooks," "Farmers are hard working," "College students are elitists," "Single parents are hurting their children," or "The middle class in our country is going broke"? Each of these generalizations is usually based on some past experiences, but the problem is that such experiences are not always sufficient to support the conclusion.

To avoid problems when using inductive reasoning, verify your facts to ensure that they accurately and validly support your conclusion. Also, make sure that your conclusion does not extend beyond the facts you have presented. You will undermine your own case if your conclusion is so general that someone can point out its exceptions.

3. **Causal reasoning** is a sequence of thought that links causes with effects. Thus, it always implies or includes the word *because:* "The earth's temperature is turning colder *because* the ozone layer is thinning as a result of pollution." However, as in any form of reasoning, it is necessary to support the conclusion with evidence. Therefore, in the above example, the speaker would go on to cite some scientific evidence linking pollution and thinning ozone to falling temperatures. The more credible and valid her evidence is, the more defensible her conclusion about the cause-and-effect relationship among pollution, ozone, and temperature will be. Even though other factors may have caused the cooling of the earth's temperature, the speaker's argument can be considered reasonable if she can produce scientific evidence to support her point of view.

4. **Reasoning by analogy** is a sequence of thought that compares similar things or circumstances in order to draw a conclusion. It says, in effect, that what holds true in one case will also hold true in a similar case. Thus, in arguing that American auto manufacturers should change their approach to production, you might provide the following reasoning:

GENERAL PREMISE: American automobile production must improve.

MINOR PREMISE: The Japanese method of auto production has been extremely successful.

CONCLUSION: American auto manufacturers should adopt the Japanese method if they wish to be successful.

Analogy can be a useful reasoning tool when it is used wisely and with appropriate support for its conclusion. The relationship in the analogy must be valid, and the conclusion should be based on the assumption that all other factors are equal. For instance, our example is based on the assumptions that the Japanese method is a good way to manufacture cars and that American manufacturers could be just as successful as the Japanese. On the other hand, if the argument implied that the Japanese method's success could be traced to the workers' pride, dedication, and involvement in the production process itself, then similar factors would have to be applied to the American work force. Thus, to avoid problems in drawing analogies, it is crucial to consider any dissimilarities that may refute your point.

You may wish to base your speech on a single form of reasoning, or you may prefer a combination of types of reasoning. Whatever your choice, you must remember that your argument is only as good as the evidence you use to support it.

Emotional Appeals. Attempts to move people to action by playing on their feelings—for example, by making them feel guilty, unhappy, afraid, happy, proud, sympathetic, or nostalgic, are known as **emotional appeals.** Because emotions are extremely strong motivators, this form of appeal can be highly effective. Note how the following introduction to a persuasive speech appeals to the emotions:

> Until five years ago, Mike Bird lived a normal life as a basketball coach and teacher in my hometown of Springfield, South Dakota. Then he contracted a rare disease which slowly weakened him. His liver was slowly killing him. In January 1982, he and his 11-year-old daughter moved into a Pittsburgh motel room to wait for the only possible cure left. Six months later the cure was found and immediately administered, but it was too late. After two operations, Mike Bird died of complications on September 11, 1982. Possibly, his life could have been saved by earlier administration of the cure. There is a definite problem here, a problem of finding the cure in time.[4]

Emotional appeals can be so powerful that they sway people to do things that might not be logical. Terrorists' kidnapping and killing of innocent people, for example, can by no means be justified through logical thought, but for some people, such actions can be justified through emotional appeal. In fact, persuasive speakers often mix both emotional and logical appeals to achieve the strongest effect.

MINI-EXERCISE

Analyze several advertisements in a national magazine. What appeals did the advertisers use? Did the ads appeal to you? Why? Why not? Were the ads ethical? Why or why not?

HINTS FOR EFFECTIVE PERSUASIVE SPEAKING

Your chances of presenting an effective persuasive speech will be greatly enhanced if you consider the following:

1. Be realistic in setting your persuasive goal and determining what you expect to achieve.
2. Conduct as thorough an audience analysis as possible to help you choose the most appropriate strategy for accomplishing your persuasive goal.
3. In your speech, clearly identify a need so that the audience recognizes that something should be done.
4. Be sure that your solution is consistent with the audience's beliefs, attitudes, values, ethical standards, and experiences.
5. Make sure that your solution is workable and practical so that your audience can actually do or accept what you are asking of them.
6. Build your arguments so that any objections by the audience will be clearly outweighed by the benefits the audience will gain if they accept your proposal.
7. Use only valid and reliable evidence to support your persuasive goal.
8. Remember that people are unlikely to accept your persuasive goal unless they see something in it for themselves. Plan to point out the advantages of what you offer and how those advantages will benefit your listeners.
9. Be ethical and fair in both content and tactics.
10. Practice until you are able to present your speech without having to read it word for word.
11. Deliver your speech with enthusiasm, sincerity, and confidence.

A SAMPLE PERSUASIVE SPEECH WITH COMMENTARY

The Wizard of Oz[5]

SPECIFIC PURPOSE: To persuade the audience that there are many fraudulent products being produced by scientists.

TO GET HER AUDIENCE'S ATTENTION, SUE USES A FAMILIAR STORY THAT LEADS INTO THE CENTRAL IDEA AND PROBLEM.

We all know the classic story of the *Wizard of Oz*. Dorothy and Toto are swept up in a terrible storm and land near Emerald City. They meet the Scarecrow, the Tinman, and the Lion, and the group of newfound friends is taken to the Great Wizard of Oz, who tells them that in order to get what they want, they must defeat the Wicked Witch of the West. After many hardships, Dorothy and friends finally win the battle against the witch. When they return to Emerald City, they find that the Great Wizard is not what he claims to be. The bewildered Dorothy asks the wizard,

"You're nothing but a humbug. Doesn't anyone else know about you?" The Great Wizard replies, "I have been able to fool people for so long that I thought I would never be found out."

SUE LEADS FURTHER INTO THE PROBLEM AND STATES HER PURPOSE. SHE ALSO POINTS OUT THAT THERE IS A NEED TO CHANGE THE WAY IN WHICH THINGS ARE DONE. THIS WOULD HAVE BEEN A GOOD PLACE FOR HER TO ESTABLISH HER CREDIBILITY.

Today, as we walk down that Yellow Brick Road, we shall discover that America has many great wizards who also thought they would never be found out. We shall also discover that these wizards create false hope for happiness while trying to find fame for themselves. The wizards I speak of are scientists and researchers who, through their marvelous creations, attempt to create fraudulent products. Therefore, it is time for us to begin our battle to control fraudulent research in science.

SHE PROVIDES A FORECAST STATEMENT.

To understand the seriousness of this issue, we must examine three variables: the frequency of the fraud, why the fraud is dangerous, and what we can do to control the fraud.

SUE BEGINS TO PROVIDE
INFORMATION TO SUPPORT HER
POSITION. SHE USES SEVERAL
EXAMPLES TO BEGIN HER ARGUMENT.
UNFORTUNATELY, SHE DOES NOT
PROVIDE SOURCES FOR THEM.

Like the Scarecrow, who wanted a brain, we must begin to understand that the temptation of fraud has occurred for centuries. Ptolemy of Alexandria, an early astronomer whose geocentric system of the universe was unchallenged for nearly fifteen hundred years, stole the data from an earlier astronomer. Sir Isaac Newton's theories laid the foundation for modern physics. Newton reported compelling new evidence; unfortunately it was fudged. Gregor Mendel, the father of genetics, buttressed his theories with data that were later recognized as too good to be true. These isolated cases in history were uncovered and their long-term effects were minimal. The same, however, is not true today.

SUE ADDS SOME MORE RECENT
EXAMPLES TO SUPPORT HER
POSITION, BUT ONCE AGAIN SHE FAILS
TO CITE HER SOURCES.

March 29, 1981. Mark Spector, a brilliant young scientist, along with his professor at Cornell University, Effriam Raicker, announced a remarkable new theory in the field of cancer research. Many were sure the young protégé and his professor would win the Nobel Prize. Less than two weeks later those hopes were shattered when it was discovered that the vital data had been cunningly contrived. Their findings were fraudulent.

ANOTHER EXAMPLE. NO SOURCE
CITED.

May 3, 1981. John Darsee, only seven years out of Yale Medical School, had churned out over one hundred publications. He had been recommended for promotion to professorship and given his own lab at Beth Israel Hospital. Then his co-workers caught him labeling a few minutes of data to look like a few weeks' worth. A committee was brought in and discovered that he had falsified nearly all of his work. Darsee's findings were fraudulent.

ANOTHER EXAMPLE. NO SOURCE.

May 30, 1983. Dr. Joseph Calandra, along with Moreno Keplinger, James Plank, and Paul Wright, Industrial Bio-Test Company's four top scientists, were testing the toxicity of trichlorocarbonilide (TCC) on rats. A faulty sprinkler system in the room where the animals were stored caused water problems. Consequently, all the test animals died. The doctors decided that there was no time for an autopsy. The dead rats were simply destroyed and replaced by healthy new ones. This change, however, was never noted by the scientists. The findings of these researchers were all fraudulent.

SUE FINALLY CITES THE SOURCES TO
SUPPORT HER PREVIOUS
STATEMENTS. THESE SOURCES ARE
CRUCIAL BECAUSE THEY PROVIDE
CREDIBILITY TO WHAT SHE HAS BEEN
SAYING. IT WOULD HAVE HELPED,
HOWEVER, IF SHE HAD GIVEN MORE

Furthermore, Frank Golley of the University of Georgia stated in *Science Magazine* that cases such as these are only the tip of the iceberg. Golley estimates that for every major case of fraud that comes to light, one hundred or more go unnoticed. Additionally, the Environmental Protection Agency conducted an audit from 1977 to 1979 of 70

COMPLETE INFORMATION ON HER
SOURCES. SUE IS CONCLUDING HER
ARGUMENT WITH A VISUALIZATION OF
THE VASTNESS OF THE PROBLEM.
SUE IS MAKING A STRONG APPEAL,
BUT IT WOULD HAVE BEEN STRONGER
HAD SHE CITED HER SOURCES.

pesticide-testing laboratories. Results indicate that IBT (a chemical company) alone had approved 123 chemicals for consumer use and nearly half of those were based on invalid testing. IBT is only one of 70 labs. This means that there are possibly hundreds or more chemicals that go unchecked onto the market. This means that there are chemicals, pesticides, and drugs that could be endangering our environment and health. Realize that when a chemical is approved for public use, if questions arise or fraud is discovered later, the chemical is not pulled from the market until the problem has been isolated. This means there are hundreds of potentially harmful chemicals on the market.

SUE IS QUALIFYING HER STATEMENT
TO AVOID OVER-
GENERALIZATION.

Please do not misunderstand my position. I'm not saying that all scientists are immoral, nor am I saying that all science is fraudulent. What I am saying is that, like the Great Wizard, there are hundreds of scientists who are able to fool the public.

SUE BEGINS THE SATISFACTION AND
VISUALIZATION STEPS.

Now it is time for us to stop being so foolish and to find the Lion's courage to seek a solution to this imbalanced equation. Initially, lab directors must assume absolute

SUE CITES A SOURCE TO SUPPORT
HER STATEMENT, BUT SHE COULD
HAVE CITED IT MORE COMPLETELY.

responsibility for the validity of all communicated information. Next, the peer method must become the responsibility of each scientist. Reviews must take place. Each scientist's work should be repeated by another scientist to verify the experiment's validity. In fact, a report by the Association of American Universities concludes that we can significantly reduce scientific fraud through the peer review process. This will help to emphasize quality rather than quantity. The end result will be better products for us, the consumers.

SUE DRAWS A CONCLUSION THAT
LEAVES A VIVID MESSAGE AND TIES
DIRECTLY BACK TO HER
INTRODUCTION.

Finally, we must never forget what we have learned as children from the *Wizard of Oz*. After Dorothy's adventure she realizes that she must return home, because home was where she belonged, and Dorothy believed that home was safe.

ACTION STEP

However, if we cannot stop the wizards and control their marvelous creations, we will truly be able to say, "There's *no* place like home." To stop the fraud, we must take responsibility by demanding that our scientists be held to the highest ethical and professional standards.

SUMMARY   *Persuasion*, because it affects us every day of our lives, is a practical skill to learn. If we are not attempting to persuade others, they are attempting to persuade us. An understanding of persuasion and its strategies can help us to create effective persuasive messages and prepare us to analyze and comprehend the persuasive messages that we receive.

Persuasion is a process involving both verbal and nonverbal messages that attempts to reinforce or change attitudes, beliefs, values, or behavior. The difference between a persuasive and an informative speech depends on the purpose of the speaker: the informative objective is to have listeners understand and learn, whereas the persuasive objective is to change the behavior of the listeners.

There are four action goals in persuasive speaking: (1) *adoption* asks listeners to demonstrate their acceptance of an idea, belief, or value by performing the desired behavior; (2) *discontinuance*, the opposite of adoption, asks an audience to stop doing something; (3) *deterrence* asks an audience to avoid certain behavior, and (4) *continuance* asks the audience to continue certain behavior.

In selecting a persuasive topic you should consider your interest in the subject, its value and concern to your audience, its potential as an action goal, and its currentness. Persuasive speech topics may center around (1) a *question of fact*—what is true and what is false, (2) a *question of value*—whether something is good or bad, or desirable or undesirable, or (3) a *question of policy*—a matter of what actions should be taken.

Credibility—a speaker's believability based on the audience's evaluation of his or her competence and character—is critical to the success of any persuasive speech. Two factors dominate our view of a person's credibility: competence and character. Competence is our perception of a speaker's knowledge, and character is our perception of his or her *trustworthiness*, honesty *(ethics)*, and sincerity.

Preparing and developing a persuasive speech requires special attention to research, organization, and supporting materials. Your research must be particularly thorough and accurate, and your method of organization must be carefully matched to your topic, your specific purpose, and your audience.

Like an informative speech, your persuasive speech may follow a problem-solution or a cause-and-effect sequence.

You may also use a *comparative advantage order* in which you compare several solutions in order to emphasize the advantages of your preferred solution or a *motivated sequence*, which combines sound logic and practical psychology that follows the human thinking process and motivates listeners to take action. The motivated sequence includes five steps: attention, need, satisfaction, visualization, and action.

Persuasive speakers use their supporting materials to build the kind of appeal that is most likely to sway their listeners. An *appeal to needs* attempts to move people to action by calling on their basic physical and psychological requirements and desires. *Logical appeals* use evidence and proof to support the speaker's views. In presenting a logical appeal, a speaker may use (1) *deductive reasoning*—a sequence of thoughts that move from general information to a specific conclusion, (2) *inductive reasoning*—a sequence of thoughts that moves from the specific to the general, (3) *causal reasoning*—a sequence of thought that links causes with effects and implies or includes the word *because*, and (4) *reasoning by analogy*—a sequence of thought that compares similar things or circumstances in order to draw a conclusion.

Finally, emotional appeals attempt to move people to action by playing on their feelings. Emotional appeals, if properly selected, can be a powerful way to sway people to do things that may not necessarily be logical. It is not unusual for persuasive speakers to mix both logical and emotional appeals to achieve the strongest effect.

KEY TERMS

Adoption: an action goal that asks listeners to demonstrate their acceptance of an attitude, belief, or value by performing the behavior suggested by the speaker.

Appeal to Needs: an attempt to move people to action by calling on their most basic physical and psychological requirements and desires.

Causal Reasoning: a sequence of thought that links causes with effects; it either implies or explicitly states the word *because.*

Comparative Advantage Order: a pattern of organization in which a persuasive speaker presents and compares several solutions in order to emphasize the advantages of his or her preferred solution.

Continuance: an action goal that asks listeners to demonstrate their acceptance of an attitude, belief, or value by continuing to perform the behavior suggested by the speaker.

Credibility: a speaker's believability based on the audience's evaluation of his or her competence and character.

Deductive Reasoning: a sequence of thought that moves from general information to a specific conclusion; it consists of a general premise, a minor premise, and a conclusion.

Deterrence: an action goal that asks listeners to demonstrate their acceptance of an attitude, belief, or value by avoiding certain behavior.

Discontinuance: an action goal that asks listeners to stop doing something; the opposite of adoption.

Emotional Appeal: an attempt to move people to action by playing on their feelings.

Ethics: an individual's system of moral principles.

Inductive Reasoning: a sequence of thought that moves from specific facts to a general conclusion.

Logical Appeal: an attempt to move people to action through the use of evidence and proof.

Motivated Sequence: a pattern of organization specifically developed for persuasive speaking that combines logic and practical psychology; it involves five steps: attention, need, satisfaction, visualization, and action.

Persuasion: a communication process involving both verbal and nonverbal messages that attempts to reinforce or change listeners' attitudes, beliefs, values, or behavior.

Question of Fact: A question that asks what is true and what is false.

Question of Policy: A question that asks what actions should be taken.

Question of Value: A question that asks whether something is good or bad, or desirable or undesirable.

Reasoning by Analogy: a sequence of thought that compares similar things or circumstances in order to draw a conclusion; if something is true for one, it must also be true for the other.

Trustworthiness: the audience's perception of a speaker's reliability and dependability.

DISCUSSION
STARTERS

1. In what ways does persuasion affect your daily life?
2. Why is behavioral change the ultimate goal of persuasion?
3. What advice would you give to someone who was assigned to give a persuasive speech and needed to select a topic?
4. How would you determine whether a topic was appropriate for a persuasive speech?
5. What role does credibility play in a persuasive speech?
6. If a person has lost credibility, what can he or she do to regain it?
7. How can you establish your credibility in a classroom persuasive speech assignment?
8. How does the organization of a persuasive speech differ from the organization of other kinds of speeches?
9. Are supporting materials in a persuasive speech used differently from the way they are used in an informative one? Explain your response.

FURTHER
READINGS

Bettinghaus, Erwin, and Michael Coby. *Persuasive Communication*, 4th ed. New York: Holt, Rinehart & Winston, 1987.

Cialdini, Robert. *Influence: How and Why People Agree to Things*. New York: Quill, 1984.

Littlejohn, Stephen W., and David M. Jabusch. *Persuasive Transactions: Principles and Practices*. Glenview, Ill.: Scott, Foresman and Company, 1987.

Ross, Raymond. *Understanding Persuasion: Foundations and Practice*, 2nd ed. Englewood Cliffs, N.J.: Prentice-Hall, Inc., 1985.

Simons, Herbert W. *Persuasion: Understanding, Practice, and Analysis*, 2nd ed. New York: Random House, 1986.

NOTES

1. Adapted from Wallace Fotheringham, *Perspectives on Persuasion*. (Boston: Allyn & Bacon, Inc., 1966), p. 33.
2. Adapted from a speech presented by Mary Trouba, reprinted from *Winning Orations of the Interstate Oratorical Association, 1986*, pp. 69–72. With permission from Interstate Oratorical Association; Mankato State University; Mankato, MN.
3. Taken from a speech presented by Mary Beth Zuerlein, reprinted from *Winning Orations of the Interstate Oratorical Association, 1986*, pp. 72–75. With permission from Interstate Oratorical Association; Mankato State University; Mankato, MN.
4. Speech presented by Phyllis Snethen, reprinted from *Winning Orations of the Interstate Oratorical Association, 1983*, pp. 80–82. With permission from Interstate Oratorical Association; Mankato State University; Mankato, MN.
5. Speech reprinted with permission of Sue Smith, a student at the University of Nebraska-Lincoln, and Dr. Jack Kay, Director of Forensics and Department Chair.

INTERPERSONAL COMMUNICATION

CHAPTER 12

Interpersonal Communication

After studying this chapter, you should be able to:

1. Distinguish between intrapersonal and interpersonal communication.
2. Analyze how needs affect relationships.
3. Discuss four reasons why we develop relationships.
4. Trace the development of a relationship.
5. Explain the role that self-disclosure plays in relationships.
6. Describe how the Johari Window illustrates the process of awareness self-disclosure in interpersonal relationships.
7. Cite three guidelines for self-disclosure.
8. Demonstrate how to improve interpersonal communication.

Relationships! At birth we are brought into a world consisting of relationships—some good and some not so good. Through these relationships we learn to love, to hate, to share, to communicate, and to be ourselves. Therefore, relationships are essential to us in learning who we are, what we mean to others, and how to be ourselves while meeting many of our needs as social beings. The only way to create, continue, and end relationships is through communication.

The following appeared in a newspaper advice column:

Dear Beth:
I'm 18 and was going with a guy who's 28. We had a great relationship and all. Last time I saw him, he said "See you tomorrow." Well, tomorrow came, and he didn't. That was three weeks ago. I really loved him, and I know he loved me. I don't know his phone number or exactly where he lives—*Deserted*

Deserted:
I'm afraid your idea of a great relationship was different from his. It's hard to imagine how you could feel you know a person well enough to have a relationship when you don't even know his number or address. You've been used.

Beth Winship "Teens," *Detroit Free Press*, December 29, 1980, p. 2C.

INTRAPERSONAL COMMUNICATION

In order to communicate well with others, we must first understand how we communicate with ourselves. This process of understanding information within oneself is called **intrapersonal communication.** Although such communication begins and ends within ourselves and no one else need be involved, it affects our other communication and ultimately our relationships with others.

All messages that we create first occur within us. This makes communication a personal event, because we can never divorce ourselves from our interaction with others, no matter how neutral or empathetic we may think we are. We say, "I understand your feelings," to someone, but we can only understand another's feelings after they are filtered through our own feelings and perceptions.

THINK ABOUT IT

"Can we talk?"
Joan Rivers

INTERPERSONAL COMMUNICATION

Interpersonal communication is the informal exchange of information between two or more people. It is interpersonal communication that allows us to establish relationships with others. A **relationship** is an association between at least two people. Relationships may be described in terms of intimacy or kinship—for example, acquaintance, girlfriend, boyfriend, lover, wife, husband, mother, father, child, uncle, cousin. Sometimes relationships are based on roles, such as roommate, neighbor, partner, boss, teacher, minister, or worker. Relationships can also be described in terms of time— for example, "I played basketball with her in high school," "We were engaged at one time," or "They just met her the other day." Finally, relationships may be based on activities or participation in events—"We play softball together," "We go to the same church," "He is in my class," "She works with me," or "We belong to the same fraternity."[1] Through our many different kinds of relationships, we satisfy our social needs.

NEEDS IN RELATIONSHIPS

Each of us has many different physical and emotional needs. The more we understand about our needs and the needs of others, the more effective we can become at interpersonal communication. There are two approaches to examining needs: Abraham Maslow's hierarchy of individual needs and William Schutz's theory of interpersonal needs.

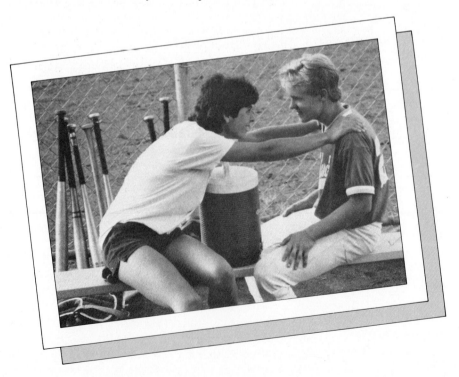

FIGURE 12.1

*Maslow's
Hierarchy of
Needs*

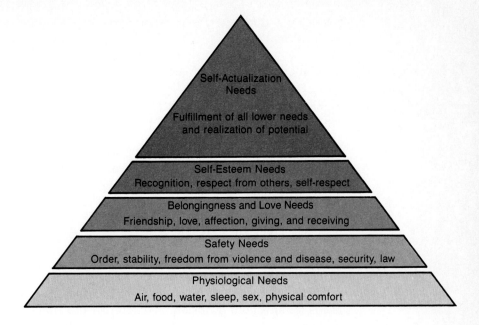

The Hierarchy of Individual Needs

According to Maslow's **hierarchy of individual needs,** human needs can be classified into five categories—physiological, safety, social, self-esteem, and self-actualization—and ranked by order of priority.[2] Because lower-order needs must be satisfied before higher-order needs, Maslow uses a pyramid, as shown in Figure 12.1, to demonstrate how one category builds on to the other.

Physiological Needs.   The first level, physiological needs, includes the most basic biological comforts necessary to maintain life, such as the needs for food, water, sleep, and physical comfort. We must satisfy these basic needs before we can focus on other things.

Safety Needs.   Once we have satisfied our physiological needs, safety needs gain importance. Among these are our needs for stability, order, freedom from violence and disease, and security.

According to Maslow, physiological and safety needs form the basis for most human motivation. People who can satisfy these two lower-order categories can then consider the three higher-order categories.

Need for Belonging and Love.   Our needs for belonging and love include our needs for friendship, acceptance, approval, and the giving and receiving of affection. Such needs are so strong that Maslow considers them to be the foundation for all other higher-order desires. The high priority we place on belonging and love is why interpersonal communication and relationships are important to us.

Need for Self-Esteem.   Maslow defines the next highest need—self-esteem—as the feelings of self-worth and respect we receive from others. Because we judge ourselves by how we believe others see us, our needs for self-esteem strongly motivate us to seek out positive relationships.

Need for Self-Actualization.   The highest-level need, according to Maslow, is for self-actualization. This is our desire for self-fulfillment—our need to live up to our fullest potential. It is simply our need to do our very best given what we have. To be satisfied with who you are and what you can do are achievements that ordinarily require strong interpersonal communication skills and positive relationships.

The Theory of Interpersonal Needs

According to Schutz's **theory of interpersonal needs,** three needs—the needs for affection, inclusion, and control—determine our communication behaviors with others.[3] Because most communication takes place at the interpersonal level, it is essential to recognize the interpersonal needs that we all possess. Although each need can differ from person to person and from situation to situation, understanding these needs can help us in our relationships with others.

The Need for Affection.   Our need for affection is the need we have to feel likable or lovable and is comparable to Maslow's need for belonging and love. Every day we see people striving to fulfill this desire. In Schutz's theory, a person who seems to be liked by everyone and who therefore has adequately fulfilled this need is referred to as "personal." Someone who is unable to fulfill this need is labeled either "underpersonal" or "overpersonal."

Underpersonal people are those who avoid emotional commitments or involvements. If we examine these individuals closely, we often find that they are hiding their true selves because they fear that others may not like them as they are. These people, like all other human beings, have a need for affection, but they have learned to cover it by not letting others get close to them. Some underpersonals find numerous excuses for not getting involved. Others might be friendly to everyone, but they keep their friendships on a superficial level.

Overpersonal individuals are the opposite of underpersonals. They need affection so badly that they often go to extremes to assure themselves of their acceptance by others. They frequently seek approval by being extremely intimate in what they communicate to others. They may even attempt to pay off their friends—for example, by always buying things for others but never letting others buy anything for them. These individuals are also very possessive and may get jealous when others talk to their friends. They may even attempt to block their friends from establishing new friendships by finding fault with every new acquaintance.

People who have fulfilled their needs for affection are classified as personal. They tend to be poised, confident, mature, and able to deal with almost everyone with whom they come in contact. These individuals want to be liked, but they do not consider being liked by everyone essential for happiness. They are easy to talk with and are at ease with themselves.

The Need for Inclusion.   The interpersonal need for inclusion encompasses our needs to feel significant and worthwhile. Schutz describes individuals who have not successfully fulfilled this need as either "undersocial" or "oversocial." Undersocial people do not like being around other people because, like underpersonal individuals, they find communicating with others threatening. They tend to be shy and find initiating conversation with others difficult. Although they are often intelligent, undersocials are loners who prefer to do things by themselves or in large groups where they can hide in the crowd. They typically find it difficult to speak out and generally avoid saying anything for fear of drawing attention to themselves.

The opposite of undersocial is oversocial—that is, people who cannot stop themselves from getting involved and communicating with others. They attempt to dominate conversations, often speak out of turn, and find it hard to keep quiet.

Individuals who have satisfied their needs for inclusion are labeled "social." They are capable of handling situations with or without others, and few, if any, situations make them feel uncomfortable. They have confidence in themselves and are assertive enough to speak when they feel it is necessary to do so.

The Need for Control.   The third need is for control, which is derived from responsibility and leadership. Almost all of us have some need to control others and our own surroundings, but the strength of this need and the way we manifest it determine whether we are abdicrats, autocrats, or democrats.

Individuals who are extremely submissive to others are abdicrats. They have little or no self-confidence, often perceive themselves as incompetent, take few risks, rarely make decisions on their own, and need much reinforcement to see themselves as useful and capable.

Persons who never have enough control are autocrats. These individuals try to dominate others. In a group, they are always willing to make the decisions or, at the least, voice strong opinions about what decision ought to be made. Because they have a strong need for power, they may not care whom they hurt in their search for control. They are also somewhat closed-minded, seeing their own positions as the only correct ones. And they show little, if any, respect for others—much like J. R. Ewing on the television show "Dallas."

Individuals who have their control needs basically satisfied are classified as democrats. They feel comfortable as either leaders or followers, do not exaggerate either the leader's or the follower's role, and are open-minded and willing to accept others' suggestions for the good of the group. These individuals like to get things done, but not at the expense of someone else.

The following review box provides a quick review of Schutz's terms and concepts. If you take a few minutes to examine it, you will see how the needs affect people as they relate self to other, other to self, and self to self.

THE THEORY OF INTERPERSONAL NEEDS

	Self to Other	*Other to Self*	*Self to Self*
Affection (Likability):			
Overpersonal	I don't really like people.	People don't really like me.	I am unlovable.
Underpersonal	I don't like people.	People don't like me.	
Personal	I like people.	People like me.	I am lovable.
Inclusion (Worth):			
Oversocial	I am not really interested in people.	People aren't really interested in me.	I am insignificant.
Undersocial	I am not interested in people.	People are not interested in me.	
Social	I am interested in people.	People are interested in me.	I am significant.
Control (Responsibility):			
Autocrat	I don't trust people.	People don't trust me.	I am incompetent.
Abdicrat	I don't really respect people.	People don't really respect me.	
Democrat	I respect people.	People respect me.	I am responsible.

Adapted from William C. Schutz. *The Interpersonal Underworld*, Palo Alto, Calif.: Science and Behavior, Inc., 1966, p. 19.

REASONS FOR DEVELOPING RELATIONSHIPS

We develop relationships with others for many reasons. Of course, the needs that we have just discussed explain a great deal about why relationships are so important to us, but there are also four more general reasons: avoidance or lessening of loneliness, stimulation, learning about ourselves, and sharing.

THINK ABOUT IT

Man has no choice but to love. For when he does not, he finds his alternatives lie in loneliness, destruction, and despair.

Leo Buscaglia

Avoidance or Lessening of Loneliness

Social relationships are at the core of human life. In a society like ours that promotes the joys of independence, living alone, and being your own best friend, it may seem out of place to speak of loneliness. Yet loneliness is a fact of modern life, as undeniable as the divorce and suicide statistics. Our need to avoid or at least to lessen this feeling causes us to develop relationships.

There is a difference between being alone and being lonely. A person can be alone but not lonely, and a person can be lonely but not alone. Two forms of loneliness, emotional and social, are apparent. Although the symptoms of each differ, the causes appear to be the same: the inability to satisfy the biological need to form relationships.

Emotional loneliness is based on our need for intimacy with a spouse, a lover, or at least a best friend. The symptoms of emotional loneliness include feelings of tension, restlessness, loss of appetite, inability to sleep, and anxiety.

In social loneliness a sense of detachment from others prevails. It is possible to have an emotional relationship with others but still be socially alone. This feeling occurs because meaningful relationships have not developed.

Stimulation

At birth our survival depends largely on others. Without stimulation from other humans, babies tend to withdraw and, in extreme cases, they die. Throughout childhood and adulthood, human interactions are the primary source of our intellectual, physical, and emotional stimulation. Though human contact is not our only form of stimulation, it is the most rewarding and necessary kind. Relationships are formed because of this primary need for stimulation.

Learning About Ourselves

Through contact with others we learn about ourselves. In Chapter 2, we defined self-concept as what we perceive ourselves to be and the mental picture we have of our physical, social, and psychological self. We develop our self-concept based on the wide range of interactions that take place in our lives. The primary contributor to our self-concept is the reactions others have to us. We seek out both supportive and nonsupportive reactions in order to see ourselves in as many different ways as possible and thus gain a better understanding of who we are. The most enduring relationships are those that are supportive and reinforcing in developing our self-concept. Without relationships, we would be uncertain about who we are or how successful we are as individuals.

Sharing

The most obvious reason for needing and establishing relationships with others is to share ourselves in order to maximize the positive and minimize the negative aspects. We need to share our feelings—our successes—to gain rewards or positive reactions, and our sorrows and failures to gain reassurance that we are still all right. Our relationships with others are the main sources of such rewards and reassurances.

THE DEVELOPMENT OF RELATIONSHIPS

A relationship forms any time two people make contact with each other, whether for a moment or for a lifetime. Communication is the single factor that determines the kind of relationship that will develop. How we progress as individuals, survive, develop intimacy, and make sense of our world depends on how we relate to others. The depth and quality of our relationships depend on the kind and amount of communication that exists within them. Each relationship is a process that goes through predictable stages of growth and deterioration that may be viewed as "coming together" and "coming apart."[4]

Coming Together

For most of us, relationships form and develop quite routinely, although the process is easier for some people than it is for others. Initially, people come together because of mutual attraction based on either physical appeal or personality. As you might predict, in our society, we tend to prefer physically attractive people to physically unattractive ones, and we tend to like people who have pleasant personalities rather than unpleasant ones. We are also more attracted to people who seem to like us than we are to those who seem to dislike us.

In addition, we are attracted to individuals who support us and have similar interests, attitudes, likes, and dislikes. In fact, when asked to characterize their ideal friend, people often describe someone who is similar to their perceptions of themselves. For example, those who are religious tend to seek other religious people, those who like sports tend to seek other sports fans, and those who like children tend to seek others who also like children. Of course, opposites sometimes really do attract, but relationships in which there are significant differences in important attitudes or behaviors are often strained and more likely to deteriorate than are those that have no significant disparities.

All relationships, if they are to develop into something more than brief encounters, must go through a number of stages. Although not all deep relationships go through the stages at the same rate or in the same way, the coming together sequence remains the same, progressing from initiating to experimenting, intensifying, integrating, and, ultimately, bonding.

Initiating.   This is the stage when we meet someone and interact with him or her for the first time. The initial interaction may be a brief exchange of words or simple eye contact during which the two parties recognize each other's existence and potential interest to meet and begin conversation. If conversation does not begin, the initiating stage may end and the potential relationship may not progress any further. Whether the interaction continues depends on various assessments that the individuals make—for example, is the other person attractive or unattractive, approachable or unapproachable? The decision to continue depends on whether the other person is open for the encounter—that is, whether she or he is in a hurry, too busy, or too involved with others.

During the initiating stage, we mentally process many impressions that lead to a key decision—"Yes, I do want to meet you," or "No, I am not interested in you." It may take less than 15 seconds to determine whether a relationship is to progress or not. At this stage most of us feel extremely vulnerable and cautious even though there is considerable variance in our initiating behaviors.

Experimenting.   This stage of getting to know the other person requires some risk taking but is mainly an attempt to answer the question "Who is this person?" This phase can be extremely awkward, consisting mainly of small talk: "What's your name?" "Where are you from?" "What's your major?" "Do you know so-and-so?" Such conversation serves several important functions in the development of a relationship: (1) it is a useful process for uncovering similarities and interests that may lead to deeper conversations; (2) it serves as an audition for a continued relationship or a way of increasing the depth of an existing relationship; (3) it is a means of letting the other person know who we are and how he or she can get to know us better; and (4) it provides a common meeting ground with others.

The experimenting stage, although involving some risk, is usually pleasant, relaxed, and uncritical. Involvement and commitment are limited and often remain that way through the duration of the relationship. In fact, most relationships do not go beyond this stage. This is not to imply that such relationships are meaningless or useless. On the contrary, they serve an important function in the human community.

Intensifying. This stage marks an increase in the parties' commitment and involvement in the relationship. Simply put, the two people become close friends.

The commitment is typified by an increased sharing of more personal and private information about oneself and one's family. For example, at this stage, it would not be out of line to share such confidences as "My mother and father are very affectionate people," "I love you," "I am a very sensitive person," "I once cheated on an exam," "My father is having another relationship," "I was promoted," "I drink too heavily," "I don't use drugs," and "I really enjoy sex."

Although a deepening of the relationship occurs at this stage, there is still a sense of caution and testing to gain approval before continuing. In typical male-female relationships we see much testing of commitment—sitting close, for instance, may occur before holding hands, hugging, or kissing. Each movement in the relationship is done to seek approval. The relationship is beginning to mature and the participants are more sensitive to each other's needs.

During this phase many things happen verbally:

1. Forms of address become informal—first name, nickname, or some term of endearment is used.
2. Use of the first person plural becomes more common—"We should do this" or "Let's do this."
3. Private symbols begin to develop, sometimes in the form of a special slang or jargon, or sometimes as conventional language forms that have understood, private meanings.
4. Verbal shortcuts built on a backlog of accumulated and shared assumptions, knowledge, and experiences appear more often. For instance, one party may request that a newspaper be passed by simply saying, "Paper."
5. More direct expressions of commitment may appear—"We really have a good thing going" or "I don't know whom I'd talk to if you weren't around." Sometimes such expressions receive an echo—"I really like you a lot" or "I really like you, too, Elmer."
6. Increasingly, each partner will act as a helper in the other's daily process of understanding what he or she is all about—"In other words, you mean you're . . . " or "But yesterday, you said you were. . . . "

Integrating. At this point the individuals' personalities begin to merge and the relationship conveys a sense of togetherness. Others expect to see the individuals together and when they do not, they often ask about the other person. The relationship has taken on a deep commitment and has become extremely important to those involved. Many assumptions take place between the individuals. For example, sharing is expected and borrowing from the other person usually needs no formal request because it is assumed to be all right.

Although a strong mutual commitment characterizes this stage of a relationship, it does not mean a total giving of oneself to the other. The verbal and nonverbal expressions of the integrating stage take many forms. For example, the individuals see themselves as something special or unique. The sharing of rings, pins, pictures, and other artifacts illustrates not only to themselves, but also to others that they belong to each other. They may wear matching clothing and behave in similar ways or speak of common sharing—our account, our apartment, our stereo.

Bonding

The final stage in a relationship's development and growth is bonding, the public announcement in which the commitment is formally contracted—as when a couple announces that they are going steady, engaged, or getting married. Bonding is the understanding that the commitment has progressed from private knowledge to public knowledge, thus making a breakup of the relationship more difficult.

The relationship at this stage is contractual in nature even though a formal contact, such as a marriage license, is not required. What is required is an agreement between the two parties that the relationship exists and that explicit and implicit agreements hold the relationship together. The commitment implies that the relationship now exists "for better or for worse" and is defined according to established norms, policies, or laws of the culture and society in which it exists.

Coming Apart

In our society there are no guarantees that a formal commitment will create a lasting relationship. When a relationship stops growing and differences begin to emerge, the coming apart process begins. Some relationships may go through some or all of the stages in this process and emerge stronger than before, but when the forces that pull a relationship apart are stronger than the forces that hold it together, the alliance ends. Similar to the coming together process, the coming apart process has five stages—differentiating, circumscribing, stagnating, avoiding, and terminating.

Differentiating. In differentiating, the first stage of coming apart, the differences between the individuals are highlighted and become forces that slow or limit the growth of the relationship.

The pair's communication tends to focus on how each differs from the other and there is less tolerance of these differences. Indeed, differences that were once overlooked or negotiated now become the center of attention, putting stress on the relationship and its existence. Typically, things that were once described as "ours" now become "mine": "This is my apartment," "These are my books," "Those are my records," and "They are my friends."

Conversations often move from mild disagreement to heated anger: "Do I have to do all the work around here? You don't do a darn thing." "Why is it that your so-called friends never clean up after themselves?" "I pay the phone bill, but you're the one who uses it the most." Conflict begins to overshadow the more positive aspects of the relationship and the partners often become cruel to one another.

Circumscribing.   In this stage, information exchange is reduced and some areas of difference are completely avoided because conversation would only lead to a deepening of the conflict. Communication loses some of its personal qualities and becomes increasingly superficial as the relationship becomes more strained. Interactions, in their amount and depth of disclosure, resemble those of the initiating and experimenting stages of coming together—for example: "Have you eaten?" "Did I get any calls today?" and "I saw Joe and he said to say 'hi'." Other common comments during this stage include: "I don't want to talk about it." "Can't you see that I'm busy?" "Why do you keep bringing up the past?" and "Let's just be friends and forget it."

People in the circumscribing stage often put up a good front in public in order to conceal their faltering relationship. For example, driving to a party, a couple may sit in cold silence, staring stonily into space. But once they arrive at their destination, they may suddenly put on their party personalities—smiling, telling jokes, and acting like the life of the party. Finally, of course, when they return to the privacy of their car, they resume their cold behavior.

Stagnating.   At this stage the relationship reaches a standstill. Interaction is usually avoided and care is taken to sidestep controversy. Little hope remains for the relationship once it has deteriorated to this stage, yet one of the partners may still be hoping that it can be revived.

During stagnation, both verbal and nonverbal communication are often more thoroughly thought out than previously, and the partners strategize about what is to be said and not said, making interactions stylized and cold. Both persons are apt to reflect unhappiness and to act as if each is a stranger to the other.

Often the stagnation stage is relatively brief, but when it is extended it is usually because of complications. For example, some people may be seriously distressed by the loss of their relationship even though they know that parting is the right decision. Others may prolong the situation in fear of additional pain, in hopes of getting the relationship back on track, or in an attempt to punish the other person.

Avoiding. Up to this point the participants in the relationship are still seeing each other and may even be sharing the same living quarters. But the fourth stage, the avoiding stage, is marked by physical distancing and eventual separation. Now, the basic message is "I am not interested in being with you anymore." As far as the participants are concerned, the relationship is over and they have no interest in reestablishing it.

At times the interaction in this stage is brief, direct, unfriendly, and even antagonistic—for example, "I really don't care to see you," "Don't call me, we have nothing to discuss," and "I'm busy tonight and, for that matter, I'm going to be busy for quite some time."

Terminating. The last stage in the breaking up of a relationship comes when the individuals take the necessary steps to end it. Termination can occur early—that is, when the relationship has barely begun—or it can occur after many years. In short relationships and in those that did not get beyond the initiating or experimenting stage, the feelings of parting are not complex or lasting. People ending long-term relationships, however, need to prepare for life without the other person.

The interaction during this stage is self-centered and seeks to justify the termination: "What can I do for myself—I've always put more into the relationship than I've gotten out of it," "We just have too many differences that I didn't know existed until now," "I found out that we just weren't meant for each other."

When both individuals know that the relationship is ending, they say goodbye to each other in three ways—in a summary statement, in behaviors signaling the termination or limited contact, and in comments about what the relationship will be like in the future, if there is to be any relationship at all.[5]

Summary statements review the relationship in the past and provide a rationale for its termination: "While our love used to be very special, we both have changed over the years. We are not the same couple that we were when we first met." Ending behaviors reflect new rules of contact: "It would be good for both of us not to see so much of each other," "I wish you would stop coming over all the time." Finally, now that the relationship is over, the participants learn how to deal with each other in the future: "I don't want to see you anymore," "We can get together once in a while, but I only want us to be friends and nothing more."

The processes of coming together and coming apart are complex and continuous as we move in, through, and out of relationships. Most relationships go through the interaction stages systematically and sequentially. At least three reasons explain why this occurs: each stage provides information that allows movement to the next; each stage enables the participants to predict what may or may not occur in the next stage; and each stage must be passed through—skipping one creates risk and uncertainty in the relationship.[6]

THE STAGES OF RELATIONSHIP DEVELOPMENT

Process	Stage	Representative Dialogue
	Initiating	"Hi, how ya doin'?" "Fine. You?"
	Experimenting	"Oh, so you like to ski . . . so do I." "You do?! Great. Where do you go?"
Coming Together	Intensifying	"I . . . I think I love you." "I love you too."
	Integrating	"I feel so much a part of you." "Yeah, we are like one person. What happens to you happens to me."
	Bonding	"I want to be with you always." "Let's get married."
	Differentiating	"I just don't like big social gatherings." "Sometimes I don't understand you. This is one area where I'm certainly not like you at all."
	Circumscribing	"Did you have a good time on your trip?" "What time will dinner be ready?"
Coming Apart	Stagnating	"What's there to talk about?" "Right. I know what you're going to say and you know what I'm going to say."
	Avoiding	"I'm so busy, I just don't know when I'll be able to see you." "If I'm not around when you try, you'll understand."
	Terminating	"I'm leaving you . . . and don't bother trying to contact me." "Don't worry."

Taken from Mark L. Knapp's *Interpersonal Communication and Human Relationships*. Boston:Allyn and Bacon, Inc. 1984, p. 33.

SELF-DISCLOSURE IN RELATIONSHIPS

Relationships are built on interaction. The more sincere, honest, and open the interactions between individuals, the stronger and more lasting their relationship. Much of our interpersonal communication, however, is small talk—talk about the weather, sports, class assignments, a program we saw on television, or a movie we would like to see. Such light conversation usually does not provide a means for us to learn who we are, fulfill our interpersonal needs, or allow for growth in our relationships. Nonetheless, it does maintain an important opening to further interaction.

THINK ABOUT IT

A survey of married couples points to the importance of small talk:

> Small talk may save marriages, according to the findings of two social
> scientists. As reported in the University of California, Berkeley Wellness
> Letter, a survey of 31 married couples (average age, early 40s; average
> length of marriage, 20 years) the communication valued most was not
> evening-long sessions hashing out their differences, but easygoing, pleas-
> ant conversations about everyday events.
>
> Wives, in particular, interpreted this kind of open, informal chatting as
> an indication of mutual affection. Husbands, however, valued empathetic
> listening more than discussions, interpreting it as a sign of affection in
> their wives.
>
> *Chicago Tribune*, February 26, 1987, Section 5, Page 2.

To move from one stage to another in our relationships, we must communicate who we are—we must disclose information about ourselves. **Self-disclosure,** or the voluntary sharing of information about ourselves that another person is not likely to know, can be as simple and unthreatening as telling our name or as complex and threatening as revealing deep, intimate feelings.

When self-disclosure occurs in caring relationships, it usually results in greater self-understanding and self-improvement. Its principal benefit should be personal growth. In addition, our self-disclosure to others encourages them to do the same with us and creates an atmosphere that fosters interpersonal communication and meaningful relationships.

To benefit from disclosure, we must realize that it is an ongoing process that should be incorporated into our daily behavior. Ultimately, disclosure is a prerequisite to personal as well as interpersonal growth.

The Process of Self-Disclosure

One of the best ways to gain understanding of the self-disclosure process is through the **Johari Window.** This graphic model, which depicts the process of awareness in interpersonal relations, was developed to illustrate four kinds of information about a person (see Figure 12.2).[7]

Area I: The Open Area.   The **open area,** or "area of information that is free to self and others," includes information that is readily available to others via observation or willingness to share. For example, when people meet for the first time, they undoubtedly note each other's height, weight, color of skin, and sex. They may freely share their names, hometowns, schools, majors, and courses they are taking.

During the first meeting, individuals usually disclose minimal infor-mation about themselves. Thus, the open area is relatively small, but as

FIGURE 12.2

*The Johari
Window*

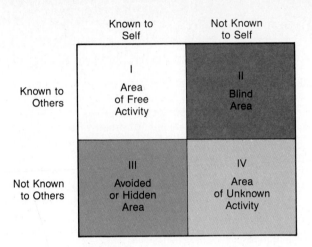

people get to know each other and move through the stages of relationship development, this area becomes much larger, as shown in Figure 12.3.

Area II: The Blind Area.   The **blind area** includes information that others perceive about us, but that we do not recognize or acknowledge about ourselves. For example, instructors who show favoritism to certain students may not realize that their behavior is being interpreted in that way. In fact, when confronted by student evaluations that point out the problem, they often deny such a practice and argue that they treat everyone equally.

Area III: The Hidden Area.   The **hidden area** includes personal and private information about ourselves that we choose not to disclose to others. *Personal* information cannot be known to others unless we choose to disclose it, while *private* information is information that we are even more selective about disclosing. If a relationship is to grow, the hidden area must eventually shrink as its information is shared with the other person.

Area IV: The Unknown Area.   The fourth quadrant in the Johari Window is the **unknown area,** which contains information that is *not known* either to us or to others. For example, can you give artificial respiration to someone if you have never done it before? You may think you can, but you really *don't know* until you actually have the opportunity to do it. Another example might be an event that we subconsciously recall but that we can't be sure actually happened.

The Johari Window clearly illustrates the roles that interaction and sharing play in self-disclosure. Each area expands and contracts to reflect the unique disclosure characteristics of a specific relationship from time to time and from situation to situation. As we interact with others, we present varying window configurations of ourselves and they do the same with us. The amount and kind of disclosure determine the stage of each relationship.

FIGURE 12.3

Johari Window Illustrating Enlargement of Open Area as a Relationship Develops

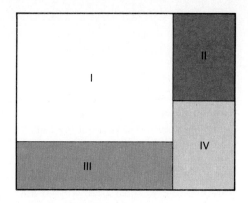

MINI-EXERCISE

Draw Johari Windows that you feel represent you in the following situations:

1. Draw a model that reflects the way in which you relate to people in general.
2. Draw a model that reflects your relationship with someone to whom you are very close—a boyfriend, girlfriend, spouse, or parent.

   How do the windows differ and why do they differ?

Guidelines for Self-Disclosure

The open and honest sharing of our feelings, concerns, and secrets with others is what self-disclosure is all about. This does not mean, however, that we must disclose everything, or that we cannot withhold information if it is likely to hurt us or someone else. The goal is to match the amount and kind of self-disclosure to the situation. Here are a few guidelines that should help you in your self-disclosure.

1. **Use "reasoned self-disclosure."** While open and honest relationships are desirable, it is important to recognize situational constraints. Concern both for oneself and for others should govern each disclosure. For example, even though you know that your best friend once had a serious drinking problem, you may choose not to mention it to your fraternity's membership committee. This does not mean that you are dishonest, but merely that in some situations and with certain individuals, you judge that there is no need to reveal this aspect of your friend's past.

2. **Self-disclosure should be a two-way process.** Relationships built on one-sided exchanges are generally not very enduring, meaningful, or healthy. People are more likely to disclose information when they feel safe and when their openness is positively received. It follows, therefore, that

each party will feel safer if both are involved in the self-disclosure process. Once a feeling of give and take is established, if one person increases self-disclosure, the other person will usually follow suit. In this way, trust builds, self-disclosure continues to increase, and the relationship grows healthier.

3. **Self-disclosure should be appropriate to the situation and to the person to whom it is directed.** When we self-disclose, we run the risk of being rejected. We can somewhat minimize this risk if we carefully match the disclosure to the person and the situation. From the beginning, self-disclosure should be a slow process because rushing can increase vulnerability. In addition, it is safest to disclose only to truly caring people and to be sensitive to both their verbal and their nonverbal cues. Disclosing too much too soon or disclosing to the wrong person can lead to embarrassment, pain, and, sometimes, serious harm.

Ultimately, self-disclosure must be based on personal judgment rather than rigid rules. The key should always be *concern for both self and others*. Self-disclosure is the most sensitive and beautiful form of communication that we can engage in as we develop and maintain lasting relationships. When based on mutual feelings and genuine communication, relationships can't help but grow and mature.

THINK ABOUT IT

Many variables contribute to strong and lasting relationships, but the most important seem to be trust, commitment, dialog, and love.

COMMUNICATING IN RELATIONSHIPS[8]

Establishing supportive and caring relationships is important to our well-being. This process is generally easier when communication is both positive and supportive. In other words, as the old cliché goes, "If you can't say anything nice, don't say anything at all."

Positive and supportive communication occurs in environments that are caring, open, flexible, warm, animated, and receptive. In such environments, communication is constructive and centers on the individuals and their relationship. Here are some descriptions of how people feel when constructive communication is at the center of their relationship:

I feel that I can talk and that there is someone who will listen to
    me.
I feel accepted and supported.
I feel there is a willingness to see my point of view.
I don't feel a need or pressure to change—I am accepted for who I
    am.

I don't feel that I am constantly being judged or evaluated.
I feel that I am trusted.
I feel that I am treated with respect as a person.
I feel that I am treated fairly.
I feel good about myself and about us.
I feel like a responsible person.
I feel that I have control over myself.
I feel that you are interested and care about me.
I don't feel as if I have to justify everything that I do.

Two of the most effective and constructive means of demonstrating care and support for someone are to invite more communication and to listen actively.

Invite More Communication

Many of us listen to others express their feelings and then immediately express our own. This gives the impression that we do not even acknowledge the other person's existence, let alone what he or she has just said. In contrast, skilled and caring communicators usually do not respond immediately with ideas, judgments, or feelings that express their own views. Instead, they invite others to share more of their thoughts by using such noncommittal responses as:

Interesting.	I see.
Uh-huh.	Oh.
You did, huh?	Really?

Or they may be more direct or explicit in asking the other person to continue, saying, for example:

That's interesting. Tell me more.
Tell me about it.
Let's discuss it.
Tell me everything.
I understand. What else happened?

Such invitations to talk can contribute much to the development of a meaningful relationship. The willingness to listen and reserve judgment creates a positive and supportive environment that in effect tells people that they are valuable, that they are loved, and that they have control over their own behavior.

Active Listening

Probably the most effective way to indicate to others that they should continue to communicate is to respond to them by **active listening.** Active listeners analyze and evaluate what another person is saying in an effort to understand the speaker's feelings or the true meaning of the speaker's

message. To check their understanding, they restate the message in their own words and ask the speaker for verification. Active listeners are never judgmental. Neither do they give advice, state opinions, or ask questions in a negative or patronizing tone. They focus only on understanding the speaker's message. Examine the following conversation:

JOHN: I wish I had a different instructor for speech this semester. Sam's instructor doesn't require many speeches, but mine requires one almost every week.

JANE: You feel that you're getting ripped off because of the instructor you have?

JOHN: Yes. Sam gets to go out more often, but I have to stay home to prepare my dumb speeches.

JANE: You'd really like to have Sam's teacher rather than yours, huh?

JOHN: Yes, I don't like giving speeches, plus I hate the time it takes to prepare them.

JANE: So, you hate giving speeches.

JOHN: Yeah! Especially when I have to stay home and Sam gets to go out.

JANE: So, you don't hate it all the time.

JOHN: No, not all the time, but it's that the teacher is so demanding.

JANE: What do you mean demanding?

JOHN: She expects so much of us.

JANE: Is that bad?

JOHN: No, I guess not.

In this short interaction, Jane listened thoughtfully and invited John to voice his feelings and frustrations. She did not try to judge, nor did she agree or disagree. By using active listening she showed that she understood and empathized with John's problem, but she did not try to solve the problem—she left that up to John. Her active listening helped him to understand and deal with his feelings.

Active listening has a number of effects on relationships that should not be ignored:

1. It helps a person overcome the fear of expressing negative feelings.
2. It fosters a relationship of warmth and caring.
3. It helps facilitate problem solving.

Active listening is not easy. Rather, it requires skill and positive attitudes toward the person who is talking. To be an effective active listener, you must:

1. Want to hear what the other person has to say. This means that you are willing to take time to listen.
2. Be receptive to the other person's feelings, whatever they are and no matter how different they may be from your own.
3. Place trust in the other person and avoid being judgmental or evaluative.
4. Recognize that feelings change and that a situation that may seem desperate or insurmountable one day may seem much more manageable the next day.
5. Recognize that the other person is an individual separate from you and that he or she has the same needs for affection, inclusion, and control that you have.

Active listening requires suspension of one's own thoughts and feelings, at least initially, in order to attend to the other person. The use of feedback ensures that meanings are better understood. The more accurately the listener understands the other person, the greater the likelihood that he or she can be of help.

SUMMARY

Interpersonal communication, the informal exchange of information between two or more individuals, cannot exist without *intrapersonal communication,* the process of understanding information within oneself. Interpersonal communication allows *relationships*—which are associations that occur between at least two people—to be established and to grow. Communication allows relationships to develop and satisfy our social needs.

Many needs that we have as humans can be satisfied through communication. Two approaches that attempt to explain needs are Maslow's *hierarchy of individual needs* and Schutz's *theory of interpersonal needs*. Maslow's hierarchy is based on the idea that lower-order physical and safety needs must be satisified before higher-order social, self-esteem, and self-actualization needs can be fulfilled. Each category of need is a stepping stone to the next. Thus, Maslow used a pyramid to illustrate the greater priority of the lower-level needs. According to Schutz, three needs—the needs for affection, inclusion, and control—determine how we communicate with others. People who have satisfied their need for affection are referred to as personal, while those who have been unable to satisfy this need are either underpersonal or overpersonal. People who have satisfied their need for inclusion are called social, while those who have not satisfied that need are classified as either undersocial or oversocial. Individuals who have fulfilled the need for control are democrats, while those who haven't are either abdicrats or autocrats. Both theories explain why relationships are so important to us.

We develop relationships for several key reasons: (1) to avoid or lessen loneliness, (2) to provide stimulation, (3) to learn about ourselves, and (4) to share. Relationships, which occur whenever two people interact, whether for a moment or for a lifetime, go through a series of predictable stages of development and deterioration. The five stages of the coming together phase are initiating, experimenting, intensifying, integrating, and bonding, and the five stages of coming apart are differentiating, circumscribing, stagnating, avoiding, and terminating. All relationships move through at least some of these stages, but not all move through them in the same order or with the same intensity. Superficial relationships go through only the first one or two stages of development and terminate without going through the entire deterioration series. There are three reasons for the complex and continuous process of coming together and coming apart: (1) each stage provides information for the next, (2) each stage helps predict what may or may not occur in the next stage, and (3) each stage must be included. Skipping a stage can be risky, especially when relationships are developing.

Lasting relationships are open, a feature that allows for relatively free *self-disclosure*—the volunteering of information about ourselves to someone who does not know us. The more information people reveal about themselves, the more likely they are to have a relationship that will grow and mature into a healthy and satisfying experience.

The *Johari Window* is a graphic model that depicts the process of awareness and self-disclosure in interpersonal relations. It illustrates four kinds of information about a person: (1) the *open area* represents information that is free to self and others, (2) the *blind area* represents information that others perceive about us but that we ourselves do not know, (3) the *hidden area* represents information about ourselves that we choose not to share with others, and (4) the *unknown area* represents information that is not known either to us or to others. Each of the four areas expands and contracts to reflect self-disclosure as it affects relationships from time to time and from situation to situation.

Because frankness creates vulnerability, each participant must consider situational constraints when deciding what should or should not be disclosed. This is referred to as *reasoned self-disclosure*. Self-disclosure should be built on mutual sharing and should be attempted only when individuals feel safe and believe that their confidences will be received positively. For relationships to grow, there must be self-disclosure.

In a positive and supportive environment, communication between individuals usually reflects caring, openness, flexibility, warmth, animation, and receptivity. The two best ways to develop and maintain relationships are to invite more communication and to be an **active listener**—a person who listens to understand the feelings and meaning of another's message.

KEY TERMS

Active Listening: the process of analyzing and evaluating what another person is saying in an effort to understand the speaker's feelings or the true meaning of the speaker's message.

Blind Area: the quadrant of the Johari Window that represents information others perceive about us, but which we do not recognize or acknowledge about ourselves.

Hidden Area: the quadrant of the Johari Window that represents personal and private information about ourselves that we choose not to disclose to others.

Hierarchy of Individual Needs: a theory developed by Abraham Maslow that ranks physical, safety, social, self-esteem, and self-actualization needs; it states that the lower-order needs must be satisfied before the higher-order needs.

Interpersonal Communication: the informal exchange of information between two or more individuals.

Intrapersonal Communication: the process of understanding information within oneself.

Johari Window: a graphic model that depicts the process of awareness and self-disclosure in interpersonal relations; it also illustrates the proportion of information about oneself that is known and unknown to oneself and others.

Open Area: the quadrant of the Johari Window that represents information that is free to self and others through observation or a willingness to share.

Relationship: an association between at least two people.

Self-Disclosure: the voluntary sharing of information about ourselves that another person is not likely to know.

Theory of Interpersonal Needs: a theory developed by William Schutz that contends that three basic needs—affection, inclusion, and control—determine our communication behaviors with others.

Unknown Area: the quadrant of the Johari Window that represents information not known either to oneself or to others.

DISCUSSION STARTERS

1. What does intrapersonal communication have to do with interpersonal communication? With relationships?

2. What are the similarities and differences between the hierarchy of needs and the theory of interpersonal needs?

3. In what ways do our needs affect our communication?

4. How would you describe an undersocial person? What can you do to help this type of individual?

5. In your opinion, which reason plays the strongest role in people's development of relationships? Explain.

6. What did you agree with and disagree with in the explanation of the stages of relationship development?

7. What is an ideal intimate relationship? An ideal friendship? An ideal business relationship? An ideal student-teacher relationship?

8. Describe what it takes to have a lasting relationship.

9. What happens when a relationship begins to come apart?

10. Why is it so difficult for most of us to self-disclose to those whom we love and who love us?

11. Why is reasoned self-disclosure so important?

12. How would you describe a competent interpersonal communicator?

FURTHER READINGS

Adler, Ronald B., and Neil Towne. *Looking Out, Looking In,* 5th ed. New York: Holt, Rinehart & Winston, 1987.

Beebe, Steven A., and John T. Masterson. *Family Talk: Interpersonal Communication in the Family.* New York: Random House, 1986.

Folger, Joseph P., and Marshall Scott Poole. *Working Through Conflict: A Communication Perspective.* Glenview, Ill.: Scott, Foresman and Company, 1984.

Galvin, Kathleen M., and Bernard J. Brommel. *Family Communication: Cohesion and Change,* 2nd ed. Glenview, Ill.: Scott, Foresman and Company, 1986.

McCroskey, James, Virginia Richmond, and Robert Stewart. *One On One: The Foundations of Interpersonal Communication.* Englewood Cliffs, N.J.: Prentice-Hall, Inc., 1986.

Weaver, Richard L., II. *Understanding Interpersonal Communication,* 4th ed. Glenview, Ill.: Scott, Foresman and Company, 1987.

Wilmot, William W. *Dyadic Communication,* 3rd ed. New York: Random House, 1987.

NOTES

1. Knapp, Mark L., *Interpersonal Communication and Human Relationships,* (Newton, Mass.: Allyn & Bacon, Inc., 1984), p. 30.

2. Maslow, Abraham H., "Hierarchy of Needs," in *Motivation and Personality,* 2nd ed., (New York: Harper & Row, 1970), pp. 35–72.

3. Schutz, William C., *The Interpersonal Underworld,* (Palo Alto, Calif.: Science and Behavior Books, 1966), pp. 13–20.

4. Knapp, *Interpersonal Communication and Human Relationships,* p. 33–41.

5. Knapp, Mark L., R. P. Hart, G. W. Friedrich, et al., "The Rhetoric of Goodbye: Verbal and Nonverbal Correlates of Human Leave-Taking," *Speech Monographs* 40 (1973): 182–198.

6. Knapp, *Interpersonal Communication and Human Relationships,* p. 51.

7. Luft, Joseph, *Group Processes: An Introduction to Group Dynamics,* (Palo Alto, Calif.: The National Press, 1970), pp. 10–14.

8. Ideas for this section came from a Parent Effectiveness Training workshop and from Thomas Gordon, *P. E. T.: Parent Effectiveness Training.* (New York, Peter H. Wyden, Inc., 1970.)

CHAPTER 13

Small Group Communication

After studying this chapter, you should be able to:

1. Distinguish between the personal and task-related purposes of small group communication.

2. Describe three common formats for small group presentations to the public.

3. Define a group.

4. Explain how a group operates as a system.

5. Identify the characteristics that make small group communication unique from other forms of communication.

If you were to list all the times you have participated in group discussions, you would be surprised. Small group activities and meetings are common events in our lives. The family is probably the most predominant small group, but we also participate in work and social groups outside our immediate families. Many of you are members of service or professional groups, such as the Agronomy Club, Geology Club, Theater Club, Association for Computing Machinery, African People's Union, Native American Student Congress, Young Democrats, College Republicans, and Feminist Action Alliance. Even if you do not belong to such formal organizations, anytime you get together with people and talk about issues or problems, you are involved in small group communication. **Small group communication** is the exchange of information among a relatively small number of persons—usually 3 to 13—who share a common purpose, such as doing a job or solving a problem.

Classroom discussion, the most widely used instructional method in our educational system today, is another form of small group communication. Small group communication is so common in business, industry, and government that the average member of middle and higher management (this includes all professions) spends one-fourth to one-third of each working day in such discussions. It should come as no surprise, therefore, that the ability to use effective small group communication to accomplish a group's tasks and establish an atmosphere of cooperation is considered essential to success in virtually every career.

To help you improve your group communication skills, in this chapter we will first consider the purposes and forms of small group presentations. Then we will examine how small groups operate and consider the characteristics that make them a unique context for communication.

THE PURPOSES OF SMALL GROUP COMMUNICATION

Small groups may be used to perform many kinds of tasks and solve many kinds of problems, but all of the purposes that they serve can be grouped into two general categories: personal purposes and group purposes.[1]

Personal Purposes

People's reasons for joining groups fall into four main categories: socialization, catharsis, therapy, and learning.

Socialization. We often engage in small group communication in order to socialize with others—for example, at coffee breaks, parties, or any place people come together to share time and conversation. When we gather in small groups for social purposes, our goals are to strengthen our interpersonal relationships and to promote our own well-being. Such groups fulfill our interpersonal needs for inclusion and affection.

Catharsis.   Small group communication allows us to vent our emotions, including our frustrations, fears, and gripes, as well as our hopes and desires. When we have a chance to let others know how we feel about something, we often feel a catharsis, or release from tension. This purpose is usually accomplished in the supportive atmosphere of bull sessions or family discussions, where self-disclosure is appropriate. Cathartic group communication tends to focus on personal problems rather than interpersonal relationships.

Therapy Group.   Therapeutic small group communication sessions are used primarily to help people alter their attitudes, feelings, or behaviors about some aspect of their personal life. For example, a therapeutic group might include people who have drinking, drug, or other problems, such as coping with the loss of a loved one. Usually, the therapeutic group is led by a trained professional who is well versed in group psychotherapy or counseling.

Learning.   As mentioned in the beginning of the chapter, the most common reason that people join small groups is to learn from one another. Learning occurs in all kinds of settings, but the setting that you are probably most familiar with is the classroom. The underlying assumption of learning groups is that *two heads are usually better than one* and that the sharing of information will lead to collective ideas that will be superior to the ideas of an individual working alone.

Task-Related Purposes

Small group communication is frequently used to accomplish two general tasks—decision making and problem solving.

THINK ABOUT IT

A classic research study demonstrated the value of group decision making. The study focused on a garment factory where managers had always made decisions without seeking input from their workers. The managers had decided to update some of their production techniques, but the workers were resisting the changes.

To get at the problem, an experiment was set up using three different procedures: (1) a *no-participation method*, which was essentially the way things had always been done, in which employees had no voice in planning and change; (2) a *participation-through-representation method*, in which a few employees were involved in the decision-making process; and (3) a *total-participation method*, in which all of the employees were involved. In each case, whether the workers contributed or not, the final decision belonged to management.

The results revealed that:

1. The no-participation group continued to resist changes.
2. Both the participation groups relearned their jobs significantly faster and surpassed the previous average production levels much sooner.
3. The total-participation groups performed slightly better than the participation-through-representation group.

What conclusion can you draw from these results?

Coch, L., and John R. P. French, Jr., "Overcoming Resistance to Change," In D. Cartwright and A. Zander (eds.), *Group Dynamics: Research and Theory,* 2nd ed., Evanston, Ill.: Row Peterson, 1960, pp. 319–341.

Decision Making.   People come together in groups to make decisions—for example, to decide which spring vacation trip to take, where to hold a dance, which play to stage, or which computer is the most practical for student use. Discussing alternatives with others helps people to decide which choice is the best not only for themselves, but for the group as a whole. In addition, when people participate in the decision-making process, they are more likely to accept the final outcome and help carry it out. Most of us resent being told what to do, but we will be more tolerant of a decision—and even feel we have a stake in it—if we help to shape it.

Problem Solving.   Small groups are also an excellent way to solve problems. People form problem-solving groups in almost every imaginable context— in the workplace, in government, in school, and at home. The problems they attempt to solve include how to improve production, how to avoid nuclear war, how to resolve the problem of parking on campus, and how to improve a faltering relationship. Chapter 14 will examine group problem solving and decision making in greater depth.

FORMATS FOR SMALL GROUP PRESENTATIONS

Sometimes small groups are asked to present their findings to an audience. Such presentations may follow a variety of formats. The three that are most commonly used in the classroom are the panel, the forum, and the symposium.

Panel

A **panel** is a group presentation in which members discuss a topic in front of an audience. Such a group usually has a formal leader, and all participants are prepared in advance to discuss the topic. A panel may consist of from 3 to 12 members, but the most practical number of participants is from 3 to 7.

MINI-EXERCISE

The following announcement appeared in a local newspaper:

PTA CANDIDATE FORUM SLATED

The Lincoln Area Council of Parent-Teacher Associations has scheduled a forum for school board candidates at 7:30 p.m. Thursday at the Public Schools Administration Building, 720 S. 22nd St.

Candidates will be asked to discuss their philosophies and beliefs about public education, and to describe the ideal relationship between the Lincoln Board of Education and the superintendent of schools.

After their remarks, candidates will respond to questions from the audience. The meeting is open to the public, and candidates for all four board seats up for election May 5 have been invited.

How would you prepare for this meeting if you were a school board candidate? How would you prepare if you were the president of the PTA? How would you prepare if you were an audience member?

The Lincoln Star, April 18, 1987, p. 7.

Symposium

A **symposium** resembles a panel but, rather than interact, participants each present a speech on one aspect of a topic. A symposium is more formal than a panel and is much more similar to a series of speeches than to interpersonal communication. After all presentations, there is often a question-and-answer session during which participants respond to questions from the audience or from each other.

Forum

A small group presentation that includes the audience's participation is called a **forum.** During a forum, which may follow a speech, a movie, a panel, or a symposium, audience members are encouraged to express their views to one other. Sometimes a forum will be held without a preceding presentation, as in a town hall meeting. People come to the meeting prepared to present their views to a panel, such as an elected board, or to the audience itself.

WHAT IS A GROUP?

A group is not just a number of people who have come together in the same place. To qualify as a group, a collection of people must be related in six ways:

1. *In terms of perceptions.* Do the members make an impression on one another?
2. *In terms of motivation.* Are there rewards for being together?
3. *In terms of goals.* Do the persons working together have a common purpose?
4. *In terms of organization.* Does each person have some assigned role or task?
5. *In terms of interdependency.* Must each person depend on the others for their efforts to be successful?
6. *In terms of interaction.* Is the number of persons small enough so that each person can communicate face to face with every other person.[2]

Thus, for our purposes, a **group** is a collection of individuals who form a system in which members influence one another, derive mutual satisfaction from one another, interact for a common purpose, take on roles, are interdependent, and communicate face to face. If any element is left out, what exists is a collection of independent people—not a group.

People standing at a corner waiting for a bus, for example, meet some of the criteria of a group. They are gathered for a common purpose—

transportation. They may engage in some face-to-face communication, and they may even get some mutual satisfaction from the fact that they do not have to stand alone. But they do not constitute a group according to our definition because they are not interdependent, they normally do not take on roles, and they usually do not interact with a common purpose.

One author defined "groupness"—the necessary property that groups possess but that collections of individuals do not—as follows:

> "Groupness" emerges from the relationship among the people involved, just as "cubeness" emerges from the image of a set of planes, intersects, and angles in specific relationships to each other. One can draw a cube with twelve lines, but only if they are assembled in a definite way. Any other arrangement of the lines gives something other than a cube. Likewise, one can have a collection or set of people without having a group.[3]

The point here is that a group exists as something apart from the individuals who belong to it. Just as twelve lines, when put in the proper relationship, form "cubeness," several individuals, when they develop proper relationships, form a group. And just as the lines that form a cube lose their individual identity, the members of a group lose their individual identities when "groupness" is developed.

THINK ABOUT IT

Small groups can take irrational risks as a result of shared responsibilities. In the mob hangings of the Old West, people who were considered rational and conservative found themselves caught up in a group frenzy when peer pressures took over. The tendency for groups to take actions that a lone, rational individual wouldn't take is called the *risky shift phenomenon.* Can you cite some modern examples of the risky shift phenomenon? Have you ever personally witnessed such an event? How would you explain it?

THE GROUP AS A SYSTEM

When functioning according to our definition, a group is a system that contains four basic parts: input, throughput, output, and feedback.

Input

Input refers to the raw materials in a group—the people and the information used in the interaction. The individuals are inputs because each brings to the group a variety of attributes and qualities, such as personality, age, sex, health, knowledge, attitudes, and values as well as leadership, problem-solving, and communicating abilities.

Throughput

Throughput refers to all the internal processes that occur in a group, whether as a result of what each group member brings or as a result of the group's own development. Throughput involves both verbal and nonverbal communication within the group, how the group thinks as a whole, and how it works toward its common goals. There is always room, however, for disagreement and conflict, especially when it leads to the best decision or solution to a problem. Members should always work for the betterment of the group as a whole, rather than for their own personal gain.

MINI-EXERCISE

To understand a small group, you must understand its structure, the interdependence of its members, and the role each member plays in the group. To illustrate the importance of the group as a system, an exercise called "Cooperative Squares" is often used by speech communication instructors. The object is simple. A group of five people is formed and told to put five separate puzzles together, one for each person. Each completed puzzle must be a square that is the same size as each of the other squares.

The task, however, is more difficult than it appears. The pieces of the puzzles, which are all different sizes and shapes, are randomly placed into five envelopes, and one envelope is given to each group member. After all members have received envelopes, they are given the following rules:

1. You are not allowed to talk to anyone at any time during the exercise.
2. You are not allowed to take a piece of puzzle from any other member.
3. You may receive pieces only when they are given to you.
4. You must have at least one piece of the puzzle in front of you at all times.
5. You may not point or use any nonverbal communication to help the other group members in any way.
6. You are not allowed to violate the rules.

What are the inputs, throughputs, outputs, and feedback in this situation?

Ask your instructor to provide the puzzle pieces. (They are in the *Instructor's Manual*.) Form a group of five students and try to solve the puzzle following the rules. How did the inputs, throughputs, outputs, and feedback affect the group? What did you learn about cooperation and groups? How well did the group members follow the rules?

Output

Output refers to the decisions and solutions reached by a group as a consequence of its interactions. It stems from the input and the throughput, and reflects what the group has or has not accomplished through its interactions. For example, if a dormitory floor committee has been working on ways to reduce noise so that the majority of students can study, the solution to set aside specific hours for quiet becomes the output of the group's interaction.

Feedback

Feedback—earlier defined as the response to a message that the receiver sends to the source—takes on an additional meaning when applied to small group communication. In this context, feedback is the *responses* that link the system together. It provides input for the future of the group as well as a view of its structure, morale, and attitudes—all of which affect the group, its participants, its results, and its continuity. Feedback also allows the group to see if a solution is working and thus provides an evaluation of how things are progressing.

Because feedback is so crucial to a group's well being, a group should constantly assess the results it has produced. For example, the dormitory floor committee would obtain feedback by checking to see if setting specific hours for study reduced the noise and if students are using that time to study. For more information on feedback, review Chapters 1 and 5.

THE CHARACTERISTICS OF SMALL GROUPS

Small groups have a number of characteristics that make them a unique and specialized context for communication. These characteristics, which include a common goal, social facilitation, group personality, cohesiveness, commitment, size, norms, and interdependence, determine who will join the group, how well the group will function, and how the members will interact.

A Common Goal

The driving force that brings people together to form groups is a **common goal**—the desire, for example, to protest a change in dormitory visitation rules, to lobby for more student parking, to provide equal campus access to physically impaired students, or to support a charity. Each of these reasons draws people into groups, even though their approaches to their concerns may differ.

Social Facilitation

In a group, each individual's behavior is affected by the presence of the other members. Each derives energy from the presence of the others that must then be released. This tendency for a person to release energy that would not be released if the individual were acting alone is called **social facilitation.** It can commonly be seen in people's tendencies to compete

with each other in group settings. For example, students' vying for their teacher's attention is a form of social facilitation.

Social facilitation is something akin to running a race with an audience watching as opposed to running a race with no spectators present. The runner will try harder in front of the audience than he or she would if no one were watching. Furthermore, if there were both an audience and other runners, all of the runners would put forth even more effort, which would give the group a sense of energy that is greater than the sum of its parts. Thus, competition can be healthy in a group if it is controlled and carried out in the spirit of cooperation.

Group Personality

When people come together in a group, they form a collective identity that becomes the **group personality.** You have heard comments to illustrate this: fraternity X has all the playboys, fraternity Z the eggheads, sorority Y the snobs, and sorority W the prima donnas.

Each member's personality influences every other member's personality, which, in turn, determines the collective temperament. Of course, there are exceptions. For example, a group that is generally conservative may have some liberal members. Nevertheless, the presence of others can influence each individual so that the separate personalities blend into a single group personality.

Cohesiveness

Cohesiveness is the attraction that group members feel for each other and their willingness to stick together. It is based on each member's need to remain in the group and the group's ability to provide each member with the rewards that make it worthwhile to give time and energy to the group. In a sense, cohesiveness is a form of loyalty.

At times, individuals will stick with a group even when it is not in their best interests to do so. To illustrate cohesiveness, consider the following example. Students are asked to choose one of three solutions to a certain social problem. Usually the class divides fairly equally into three groups. Then, each group is asked to defend its selection and to persuade the instructor that their solution is the best one. As an incentive, students are told that only one of the solutions will be accepted.

As the groups begin to organize, their members make a modest effort to pull together. Each group selects a representative to present its argument. After hearing each representative, the instructor announces that he or she is undecided. Therefore, all groups have one more chance to develop their arguments. The instructor also announces that students who do not like their group's solution are welcome to join another group. No one has ever switched groups, even though some are tempted.

In addition, to raise the stakes, the instructor states that the two losing groups will be assigned a research project over the weekend while the winning group will be exempt from this assignment. In response, the intensity in each group begins to build. Members pull their chairs closer together and talk more forcibly about their solution. They even support each other's views more openly. The common objective has now become quite clear: The students must persuade their instructor that their group's solution is the best one or else they will have to do the research project. As a result, cohesiveness is strengthened.

Cohesiveness is an important characteristic of every group, even when members are joined by chance rather than by choice. Cohesiveness does not mean conformity. Rather, it means that the desire to remain in the group is greater than the desire to leave.

Commitment

Another important characteristic of a group is commitment to the task, to the group, and to the other individuals in the group. **Commitment,** which is closely related to cohesiveness, is the desire of group members to work together to complete their task to the satisfaction of the entire group. Members' commitment to their group stems from their interpersonal attraction, their commonality of attitudes, beliefs, and values, the fulfillment of their interpersonal needs, and the rewards that the group can offer.

Commitment is important to a group's effectiveness and ultimate success. For example, how often have you been in a group where one or two of the members did all the work while the others did little or nothing? And how often have you been in a group whose task really meant something to you? Each of these questions raises the issue of commitment. For a group to be truly effective, all of its members must be committed to the perpetuation of the group and the successful completion of its task.

Group Size

Group size—the number of participants involved in a given small group communication—has important ramifications for the group's effectiveness. Although there is no perfect number of members for a group, there are some indications that certain size groups are more appropriate for certain kinds of tasks. For example, five-member groups are the most effective for dealing with intellectual tasks, coordinating, analyzing, and evaluating information, and making administrative decisions. Many small group textbooks recommend that committees have no fewer than three and no more than nine members.

A group that is too small may limit the ideas and information that are generated, while a group that is too large may limit the contribution that each person can make to the discussion. As a group increases in size, the number of possible interactions increases dramatically, as shown in Table 13.1.

An important consideration in deciding group size is that the larger the group, the greater the variety of skills and information possessed by its members. On the other hand, the advantages gained when a group has more than seven members seem to be outweighed by potential disadvantages. For example, ten opinions are superior to five, and twenty opinions are superior to ten, but having twice as many opinions can create twice as

TABLE 13.1   *Potential Interactions in Groups*

Number in Group	Interactions Possible
2	2
3	9
4	28
5	75
6	186
7	441
8	1056

much potential for conflict and make consensus at least twice as difficult to reach.

When deciding on the most effective size for a group, remember the following points:

1. Large groups reduce the time and amount of individual interaction.
2. Large groups provide a greater opportunity for aggressive members to assert their dominance. As a result, less assertive members may feel isolated and may withdraw from the group altogether.
3. Large groups make it difficult to follow a set agenda. It is very easy for someone in a large group to switch topics or introduce subjects that are not related to the group's original priorities.

Norms

Norms are the expected and shared ways in which group members behave. Both informal and formal guidelines determine which behaviors are acceptable and which are not. In most group situations, the norms are informal and unwritten. In your speech class, for example, certain behaviors are expected of you. At a minimum, it is assumed that you will read your assignments, respect others' rights to speak, do your own work, and be on time for class. There may also be written rules, such as specific dates for the completion of assignments, attendance requirements, and guidelines for achieving specific grades.

For a group to function effectively, its members must agree on how things are to be done. Therefore, groups, no matter what their size or task, establish norms. This is done for a variety of reasons, but the strongest one is that shared ways of behaving enable members to attain group goals and to satisfy interpersonal needs. If there were no guidelines for behavior, most groups would be ineffective and disorganized.

Norms also help to give a group structure. If members know what is expected of them, they are more likely to act accordingly and to function more efficiently. Sometimes the norms are as simple as getting the task done or as involved as participating in complex rituals and ceremonies that must be respected if a member is to remain in the group.

In more formal situations, to increase efficiency and order, many groups use preestablished rules to guide their interaction. *Robert's Rules of Order* is the most widely used authority on conducting social, business, and government meetings (See appendix at the end of this chapter.) Such formal rules specify the roles of members, how meetings should be conducted, and how topics for discussion should be introduced, discussed, and accepted or rejected by the group's members. When it is important to maintain formal order, a group may appoint a parliamentarian to ensure that its rules are correctly interpreted and followed.

Interdependence

Probably the most essential characteristic of a small group is **interdependence**—the mutual dependence of group members on one another. Interdependence is reflected in all the other group characteristics, for without it, there would be no group. To a large extent, interdependence is built on each member's willingness to subordinate his or her individual desires and goals in order to accomplish the group's goal. An example is the class assignment in which a group of students are expected to produce a joint project. Invariably, at least one member is not motivated, will not conform, or is not committed to the task and thus tries to avoid doing his or her share of the work. Usually, these projects are evaluated so that all group members receive the same grade. Since each individual's grade depends on the others' contributions, either the group will have to pressure the nonperforming member to produce his or her share, or each member will have to work harder to make up for the nonperformer's failure.

Groups function best and are most satisfying for their members when each individual recognizes and respects the crucial role that interdependence plays in group processes. Such members can appreciate that the group's success is based on each member's cooperation and willingness to work toward a common goal.

MINI-EXERCISE

In your opinion, is each of the following an advantage or a disadvantage of small group communication? Justify your responses.
1. Two heads are frequently better than one.
2. Small group communication requires interpersonal communication skill.
3. Working in a small group limits individual responsibility.
4. People are more likely to carry out decisions that they have helped to make.
5. Group decision making and problem solving takes time.
6. Working in a group can help to satisfy social needs.
7. Membership in a group can change individual attitudes and behavior.

SUMMARY *Small group communication* is the exchange of information that occurs among a relatively small number of persons—usually 3 to 13—who share a common purpose such as doing a job or solving a problem. Small group communication serves a wide range of purposes that can be grouped into two categories: personal purposes and task-related purposes. Personal purposes include socialization, catharsis, therapy, and learning, while task-related purposes include decision making and problem solving.

There are three formats in which most public small group communication occurs: (1) the *panel*, in which group members discuss a topic or issue before an audience; (2) the *symposium*, which resembles a panel but in which each member gives an individual speech about some aspect of the topic; and (3) the *forum*, a presentation that includes audience participation.

A *group* is a collection of individuals who form a system in which the members influence one another, derive mutual satisfaction from one another, interact for a common purpose, take on roles, are interdependent, and communicate face to face. The small group is a system made up of *input* (raw materials), *throughput* (internal processes), *output* (decisions and solutions), and *feedback* (responses that link). It is a process in which the components of the system are interdependent, each affecting the other.

Several characteristics make the small group a unique context for communication. They are: a *common goal* (a driving force), *social facilitation* (a release of energy), *group personality* (a collective identity), *cohesiveness* (attraction), *commitment* (the desire to work together), *group size* (the number of participants), *norms* (expected and shared behavior), and *interdependence* (mutual dependence).

KEY TERMS

Cohesiveness: the attraction that group members feel for each other and their willingness to stick together; a form of loyalty.

Commitment: the desire of group members to work together to get their task completed to the satisfaction of the entire group.

Common goal: the driving force that brings people together to form groups.

Feedback: the response to a message that the receiver sends to the source; in a small group, the responses that link the system together.

Forum: a small group presentation that includes audience participation.

Group: a collection of individuals who form a system in which members influence one another, derive mutual satisfaction from one another, interact for a common purpose, take on roles, are interdependent, and communicate face to face.

Group Personality: the collective identity that members of a group form when they come together.

Group Size: the number of participants involved in a given small group communication.

Input: the raw materials in a group—the people and the information used in the interaction.

Interdependence: the mutual dependence of group members on one another.

Norms: the expected and shared ways in which group members behave as determined by formal and informal guidelines.

Output: the decisions and solutions reached by the group.

Panel: a group presentation in which members discuss a topic in front of an audience.

Small Group Communication: the exchange of information among a relatively small number of persons—usually 3 to 13—who share a common purpose, such as doing a job or solving a problem.

Social Facilitation: the tendency for a person to release energy that would not be released if the individual were acting alone.

Symposium: a group presentation that resembles a panel but, rather than inter-act, participants each present a speech on one aspect of the topic.

Throughput: all the internal processes that occur in a group, whether as a result of what each group member brings or as a result of the group's own development.

DISCUSSION STARTERS

1. Why is it important to have good group communication skills?

2. What are the relationships between personal and task-related purposes in small group communication?

3. What are some personal goals that would not permit you to accept conflicting group goals under any circumstances?

4. What makes a group?

5. How does a group operate as a system?

6. Which group characteristic do you think is the most important? Why?

7. Describe a group in which you have participated that you believe illustrates the characteristic of cohesiveness.

8. What are the effects of group size?

9. Describe at least two norms that are operating in your class.

10. What role does small group communication play in your daily activities?

11. Do the advantages of groups outweigh the disadvantages? Explain.

FURTHER READINGS

Barker, Larry, Sharon Kibler, Kathy Wahlers, et al. *Groups in Process: An Introduction to Small Group Communication,* 3rd ed. Englewood Cliffs, N.J.: Prentice-Hall, Inc., 1987.

Beebe, Steven A., and John T. Masterson. *Communicating in Small Groups: Principles and Practices,* 2nd ed. Glenview, Ill.: Scott, Foresman and Company, 1986.

Brilhart, John K. *Effective Group Discussion,* 5th ed. Dubuque, Iowa: Wm. C. Brown Publishers, 1986.

Gouran, Dennis S. *Making Decisions in Groups: Choices and Consequences.* Glenview, Ill.: Scott, Foresman and Company, 1982.

Johnson, David W., and Frank P. Johnson. *Joining Together: Group Theory and Group Skills,* 2nd ed. Englewood Cliffs, N.J.: Prentice-Hall, Inc., 1982.

Snell, Frank. *How to Win the Meeting.* New York: Hawthorn Books, 1979.

Verderber, Rudolph F. *Working Together: Fundamentals of Group Decision Making.* Belmont, Calif.: Wadsworth Publishing Co., 1984.

NOTES

1. Harnack, R. Victor, Thorrel B. Fest, and Barbara Schindler Jones, *Group Discussion Theory and Technique,* 2nd ed., (Englewood Cliffs, N.J.: Prentice-Hall, Inc., 1977), pp. 25–28.

2. Shaw, M. E., *Group Dynamics: The Psychology of Small Group Behavior,* 2nd ed., (New York: McGraw Hill, 1976), pp. 6–10.

3. Brilhart, John. *Effective Group Discussion,* 3rd ed., (Dubuque, Iowa: Wm. C. Brown Publishers, 1978), p. 21.

APPENDIX 13 Parliamentary Procedure for Handling Motions

Classification of motions	Types of motions and their purposes	Order of handling	Must be seconded	Can be discussed	Can be amended	Vote required [1]	Can be reconsidered
Main motion	(To present a proposal to the assembly)	Cannot be made while any other motion is pending	Yes	Yes	Yes	Majority	Yes
Subsidiary motions [2]	To postpone indefinitely (to kill a motion)	Has precedence over above motion	Yes	Yes	No	Majority	Affirmative vote only
	To amend (to modify a motion)	Has precedence over above motions	Yes	When motion is debatable	Yes	Majority	Yes
	To refer (a motion) to committee	Has precedence over above motions	Yes	Yes	Yes	Majority	Until committee takes up subject
	To postpone (discussion of a motion) to a certain time	Has precedence over above motions	Yes	Yes	Yes	Majority	Yes
	To limit discussion (of a motion)	Has precedence over above motions	Yes	No	Yes	Two-thirds	Yes
	Previous question (to take a vote on the pending motion)	Has precedence over above motions	Yes	No	No	Two-thirds	No
	To table (to lay a motion aside until later)	Has precedence over above motions	Yes	No	No	Majority	No
Incidental motions [3]	To suspend the rules (to change the order of business temporarily)	Has precedence over a pending motion when its purpose relates to the motion	Yes	No	No	Two-thirds	No
	To close nominations [4]	[4]	Yes	No	Yes	Two-thirds	No
	To request leave to withdraw or modify a motion [5]	Has precedence over motion to which it pertains and other motions applied to it	No	No	No	Majority [5]	Negative vote only
	To rise to a point of order (to enforce the rules) [6]	Has precedence over pending motion out of which it arises	No	No	No	Chair decides [7]	No
	To appeal from the decision of the chair (to reverse chair's ruling) [6]	Is in order only when made immediately after chair announces ruling	Yes	When ruling was on debatable motion	No	Majority [1]	Yes
	To divide the question (to consider a motion by parts)	Has precedence over motion to which it pertains and motion to postpone indefinitely	[8]	No	Yes	Majority [8]	No
	To object to consideration of a question	In order only when a main motion is first introduced	No	No	No	Two-thirds	Negative vote only
	To divide the assembly (to take a standing vote)	Has precedence after question has been put	No	No	No	Chair decides	No

APPENDIX 13 (cont'd)

Privileged motions						
To call for the orders of the day (to keep meeting to order of business) [6, 9]	Has precedence over above motions	No	No	No	No vote required	No
To raise a question of privilege (to point out noise, etc.) [6]	Has precedence over above motions	No	No	No	Chair decides [7]	No
To recess [10]	Has precedence over above motions	Yes	No [10]	Yes	Majority	No
To adjourn [11]	Has precedence over above motions	Yes	No [11]	No [11]	Majority	No
To fix the time to which to adjourn (to set next meeting time) [12]	Has precedence over above motions	Yes	No [12]	Yes	Majority	Yes
Unclassified motions						
To take from the table (to bring up tabled motion for consideration)	Cannot be made while another motion is pending	Yes	No	No	Majority	No
To reconsider (to reverse vote on previously decided motion) [13]	Can be made while another motion is pending [13]	Yes	When motion to be reconsidered is debatable	No	Majority	No
To rescind (to repeal decision on a motion) [14]	Cannot be made while another motion is pending	Yes	Yes	Yes	Majority or two-thirds [14]	Negative vote only

1. A tied vote is always lost except on an appeal from the decision of the chair. The vote is taken on the ruling, not the appeal, and a tie sustains the ruling.
2. Subsidiary motions are applied to a motion before the assembly for the purpose of disposing of it properly.
3. Incidental motions are incidental to the conduct of business. Most of them arise out of a pending motion and must be decided before the pending motion is decided.
4. The chair opens nominations with "Nominations are now in order." A member may move to close nominations, or the chair may declare nominations closed if there is no response to his/her inquiry, "Are there any further nominations?"
5. When the motion is before the assembly, the mover requests permission to withdraw or modify it, and if there is no objection from anyone, the chair announces that the motion is withdrawn or modified. If anyone objects, the chair puts the request to a vote.
6. A member may interrupt a speaker to rise to a point of order or of appeal, to call for orders of the day, or to raise a question of privilege.
7. Chair's ruling stands unless appealed and reversed.
8. If propositions or resolutions relate to independent subjects, they must be divided on the request of a single member. The request to divide the question may be made when another member has the floor. If they relate to the same subject but each part can stand alone, they may be divided only on a regular motion and vote.

9. The regular order of business may be changed by a motion to suspend the rules.
10. The motion to recess is not privileged if made at a time when no other motion is pending. When not privileged, it can be discussed. When privileged, it cannot be discussed, but can be amended as to length of recess.
11. The motion to adjourn is not privileged if qualified or if adoption would dissolve the assembly. When not privileged, it can be discussed and amended.
12. The motion to fix the time to which to adjourn is not privileged if no other motion is pending or if the assembly has scheduled another meeting on the same or following day. When not privileged, it can be discussed.
13. A motion to reconsider may be made only by one who voted on the prevailing side. It must be made during the meeting at which the vote to be reconsidered was taken, or on the succeeding day of the same session. If reconsideration is moved while another motion is pending, discussion on it is delayed until discussion is completed on the pending motion; then it has precedence over all new motions of equal rank.
14. It is impossible to rescind any action that has been taken as a result of a motion, but the unexecuted part may be rescinded. Adoption of the motion to rescind requires only a majority vote when notice is given at a previous meeting; it requires a two-thirds vote when no notice is given and the motion to rescind is voted on immediately.

CHAPTER 14

Participating in Small Groups

After studying this chapter, you should be able to:

1. Distinguish between the terms *leadership* and *leader.*

2. Define the three styles of leadership.

3. Explain the effects that leadership styles have on small groups.

4. Identify the responsibilities of a leader.

5. Specify the responsibilities of a small group participant.

6. Distinguish between constructive and counterproductive group contributions.

7. Outline the steps in problem solving and decision making.

8. Develop criteria for evaluating a small group discussion.

The assignment is over and Group X has accomplished its goal. Each member is satisfied not only with the results, but also with the group as a whole. The meetings ran smoothly and very little, if any, time was wasted. On the other hand, Group Y also attained the same goal, but no one seems to be satisfied either with what was achieved or with the group itself. In fact, Group Y's members feel that the assignment was a complete waste of time. How is it possible that two groups could perform the same task and yet produce such different results?

The answer lies in the fact that many variables contribute to a group's success or failure. First, no two groups will produce identical results because no two groups are identical in their makeup. Furthermore, prior success cannot guarantee that a group will always be successful in every problem or situation that it confronts. Nonetheless, group members' understanding of some key factors can increase a group's chances of success. Thus, to help you become a more effective group member, this chapter explores the four crucial aspects of small group communication: leadership, member participation, methods of group problem solving and decision making, and evaluation.

LEADERSHIP

Leadership, which plays a significant part in the success of every small group, is any behavior that helps to clarify, guide, or achieve the goals of the group. It is also the ability to exert influence over others. A **leader** is a person who is assigned or selected to guide or provide direction in order to reach the group's goals. In most cases, only one person serves as leader, although sometimes two or more persons may share the responsibility. Leadership is a role that can only be given by the group, and a leader can lead only with the group's permission.

MINI-EXERCISE

Create a list of five people whom you believe to be leaders. Then, list the qualities that you believe each person possesses as a leader. Does each have the same qualities or are there differences? Is there a quality that is universal among all five? Discuss your answers with your classmates.

Characteristics of Leaders

A leader can be identified as the person who is at the center of a group's attention or the person to whom the group members address their messages. For example, in classrooms, teachers are the leaders and students usually

center their attention on them and address their most important communication to them. Of course, at times, students may address messages to other students or one student may hold the attention of the class, but in neither case does a student actually become the leader of the class.

Another way to identify a leader is by the behaviors that he or she displays in guiding a group to their specific goal. If a person communicates a direction and the group members follow that direction to reach their goal, then that person is demonstrating leadership.

A leader can also be identified by asking the group members themselves. Finally, a leader can be identified by his or her position or title—such as student council president, chairperson of the committee, boss, teacher, captain, father, mother, and so on. But this method of identification requires caution. Even though a title signifies that a person is a leader, it does not mean that he or she has leadership skills. The best way to identify a leader is through behavior. In simple terms, a leader is a person who has the group's permission to lead them.

Leadership Styles

In dealing with their subordinates, most leaders fall into one of two categories.[1] **Task-oriented leaders** gain satisfaction from performing the task, while **relationship-oriented leaders** attempt to obtain a position of prominence and good interpersonal relationships.

Task-oriented leaders are concerned with completing the job or solving the problem. Such leaders do not spend much, if any, time developing relationships unless it will help to get the task completed more quickly. Relationship-oriented leaders, on the other hand, are just the opposite. They emphasize the people rather than the task and tend to be very sensitive to the interpersonal needs of their group's members. Leaders may also be classified as autocratic, democratic, and laissez-faire.[2]

Autocratic Leader.   An **autocratic leader** keeps complete control, makes all decisions for the group, and decides what will be talked about, when it will be talked about, who may speak, and who may not. These people often make decisions that affect the group without consulting its members. They are in charge and "call all the shots." Autocratic leaders are able to tell others what to do because their position gives them the power or because the group allows them to do so.

Democratic Leader.   A **democratic leader** guides and directs the group, but shares control and remains open to all views. This philosophy allows the will of the majority to prevail even when their view may differ from the leader's. Because democratic leaders prefer to guide and suggest rather than prescribe and require, they make a final decision only after consulting all group members. Interaction among group members and democratic leaders is usually quite open and subject only to the constraints established by the group.

Laissez-Faire Leader.   The **laissez-faire leader** gives complete decision-making freedom to the group or to individual members and often becomes a figurehead who remains only minimally involved. This type of leader does not believe in taking charge and may actually feel uncomfortable in such a role. As a result, the group receives little or no direction. Some experts feel that the laissez-faire style of leadership is a contradiction in terms: it implies that a leader is in control without leading at all.

In theory, the differences among the three styles of leadership are clear: the autocratic leader has complete control, the democratic leader shares control, and the laissez-faire leader gives up control to the group. In practice, though, the three styles are not always so clear cut. In fact, most leaders generally operate on a continuum. That is, they do not use the same style all the time, but vary styles to match the situation. Certain circumstances and some group members call for direct control, while others require little or no control. For example, a military leader in combat and a doctor in a medical emergency will undoubtedly be autocratic leaders. Such situations require immediate action, and putting decisions to a vote could create great problems. The democratic leadership style is most often used when a leader is elected. For example, the president of the student government, the president of a fraternity or sorority, the president of an honorary organization, and the chair of a committee would probably use a democratic style. Such a style is most common when the leader is both a representative and a member of the group. Finally, the laissez-faire leadership style is often used when group members do not want a lot of structure—as in, for example, a group discussing an issue in a dorm room or study session. If the group decided that they needed a leader, they would take appropriate action, but in most cases, the group does not desire any assistance and thus remains leaderless.

LEADERSHIP STYLES

Authoritarian	*Democratic*	*Laissez-Faire*
1. Keeps complete control	1. Shares control	1. Gives up control
2. Makes all policy and decisions for the group	2. Involves members in all policy and decision making processes and makes final decision only after consulting with group members	2. Gives total freedom to group members to make policies and decisions and gets involved only when called on
3. Dictates tasks and tells who will work with whom	3. Leaves members free to work with whom they wish and allows group to decide how tasks will be divided	3. Completely avoids participation

The Effects of Leadership Styles

Leaders are not always free to follow the leadership style they prefer. For example, persons who would rather be participative, free-rein leaders might discover that pressures from others, the need to get things done in a certain way, or the desire to save time and energy requires them to be more autocratic than they would like to be. On other occasions, when it is important for members to agree with a decision, leaders are more likely to use a democratic style. Thus, no single leadership style is perfect in all situations.

Research, although not conclusive, suggests that the democratic leadership style is superior to the autocratic style in getting a task done and satisfying group members. Autocratic leaders, on the other hand, are likely to get more done, but member satisfaction is considerably lower. Probably the most significant finding of the research is that autocratic leaders generate more hostility and aggression among group members, whereas democratic leaders produce more originality, more individuality, and more independence. In contrast, groups with laissez-faire leaders accomplished much less, produced work of lower quality, and wasted more time.

Although it is impossible to say exactly when one style will be better than another, common sense tells us that a leader needs to be flexible in order to obtain the best balance of production and satisfaction from a group.

THINK ABOUT IT

Leadership must be viewed as actions that satisfy the needs of a particular group at a particular point in time.[3]

Leading A Group

In most cases a leader's ability to manage determines the success or failure of a group. Granted, not all successes or failures can be traced directly to the person in charge because the participants, the task to be accomplished, and the information available for completing the task also contribute to the outcome. But the role of the leader in small group projects is to get the task done. To do this, he or she must be objective enough to determine how the group is functioning and whether it is progressing toward its goal. This requires detachment from the group—that is, the ability to step back and examine the group from an objective point of view.

All groups have two sets of needs that leaders must help them to accomplish if they are to operate successfully. **Task needs** are related to the content of the discussion and include all behaviors that lead to the completion of the task, including defining and assessing the task, gathering information, studying the problem, and solving the problem. **Maintenance needs** are related to organizing and developing the group so that the group members can realize personal satisfaction from working together. They pertain to such intangibles as atmosphere, structure, role responsibility, praise, and social-emotional control.

To meet these needs, leaders in small groups must carry out a number of functions:

- Initiating—preparing members for the discussion
- Organizing—keeping members on track
- Maintaining effective interaction—spreading participation

- Ensuring member satisfaction—promoting interpersonal relationships
- Facilitating understanding—encouraging effective listening
- Stimulating creativity and critical thinking—encouraging evaluation and improvement

Conducting a Meeting

When a group meets for the first time, the leader usually begins by introducing him- or herself. Then, the leader asks the members to introduce themselves and briefly tell their reasons for joining the group or what they hope to accomplish as a member.

After introductions, and depending on the nature of the group and its assigned task, members may appoint or elect a recording secretary. This person keeps a written account of the meeting's discussion, including a list of the topics and general comments, in order to have a record to refer to if necessary.

To ensure efficiency, procedures must be established and meetings must be conducted according to a well-organized plan. The best way to accomplish this is with an agenda—a list of all topics to be discussed during a meeting. The agenda is usually determined by the leader alone or in consultation with the group before each meeting. Sometimes at the end of one meeting the agenda for the next meeting is determined.

A typical meeting agenda might look like this:

1. Call to order
2. Introduction of new members
3. Reading, correction of, and approval of minutes from previous meeting(s), if any
4. Unfinished business
5. New business
6. Announcements
7. Adjournment

Not all meetings operate in exactly the same way, but a plan and an agenda should make any meeting run smoother.

MEMBER PARTICIPATION

For a group to be successful, all of its members must be actively involved. Just as leaders have certain responsibilities to their groups, so do members. The more members know about their leader's role, the better equipped they will be to perform their own roles. Furthermore, leaders change from time to time, so members should be ready to assume greater authority if it will benefit the group.

Another responsibility of group participants is to know what is on the agenda so that they can come to meetings prepared to contribute. Meaningful input often calls for research, so each participant should be willing to spend time and energy on advance preparation. Probably one of the greatest weaknesses of beginning group participants is their tendency to arrive at meetings unprepared. The group must then either spend time helping them to catch up or do without their contributions. Either way, valuable time, effort, and input are lost.

Enhancing Group Participation

Small group discussions are enhanced when participants show the following traits:

1. An attitude of respect and open-mindedness toward others in the group.
2. A favorable attitude toward flexible, permissive interaction.
3. An awareness of communication barriers and a desire to overcome them.
4. An awareness of the need for understanding group processes.
5. An ability and desire to speak clearly and to the point.
6. An understanding of the need for attentive listening.
7. An ability to think logically and analytically.
8. A desire to cooperate and compromise in order to reach group goals.[4]

Constructive Contributions

Group discussions usually include questions, statements, and exclamations that may be either long or short and focus on one purpose or many. To be productive, all comments should be relevant, related, well timed, sufficiently long, clear, informative, open to evaluation, and provocative.[5]

Relevance. Members' comments should pertain to the topic and goals of the discussion at hand and should deviate only when tension needs to be released. Thus, all contributions should be relevant either to the task or to some interpersonal need.

Relatedness. A comment can be relevant to the topic or to an interpersonal need without being related to the comments that precede or follow it. To relate one thought to another, a speaker might make an explicit transitional statement, such as: "Joe suggested that we change our policy. I agree. Let me provide some additional reasons why we should change" or "Jane indicated that we are in deep financial trouble. That may be so, but before we examine that possibility, we should look at the latest data, which suggest that our membership fees are coming in at a much faster rate than last year." The goal of such comments is to make sure that contributions tie in with what has been said before and what is apt to be said next.

Good Timing.   Because good ideas can come up at any time, it is helpful to record those that are not appropriate at the moment and introduce them when the timing is right. To give more impact to a good idea, introduce it at a favorable time so that it gets full consideration.

Sufficient Length.   Choosing the best length for a comment requires good judgment. The goal is to make sure that whatever you contribute is long enough to make your point. The best advice is to observe the group's reaction to your statements and then act accordingly. Basically, your comments should present your views on a single point, together with your reasons for holding that view and a judgment of its significance. If you think before you speak, you will probably select the most appropriate information and present it more clearly and concisely.

Clarity.   Always remember that meanings are in people and not in words. As a result, you cannot assume that everyone in the group will understand your idea in the same way you do. To avoid misunderstandings, define your terms and provide examples to ensure a common meaning.

Informativeness.   Make sure that your statements are accurate and objective. This requires a good understanding of the topic and prior research. Cite sources of information when appropriate and select sources that are not biased.

Openness to Evaluation.   One of the greatest difficulties group members face is the evaluation of their ideas. Group discussion can lead to the best possible information as well as to the best possible decision, but this will happen only if individuals open their comments to evaluation. At the same time, members must remember that evaluations can only be constructive when they focus on the contribution and not on the person. It is one thing to find fault with some data and it is quite another thing to find fault with the person who introduced the data. To give effective analyses, members should describe or clarify rather than just criticize. While criticism should not be ignored or avoided, it should be based on what is said and not on who said it.

Provocativeness.   Comments should be made not only to bring the group closer to its goal, but also to fuel thought for further contributions. Time is important, and we know that one of the disadvantages of small group discussion is that it takes time, but lack of time should never be the sole reason for closing off discussion if an idea has not been fully discussed and evaluated. Asking questions, challenging ideas, and disagreeing can be valuable contributions if their goal is to make the final group product the best one possible.

Counterproductive Contributions

In most groups, members are eager to make constructive contributions. From time to time, however, you will encounter individuals whose attitudes are not so positive. For the good of the group, it is important to recognize such people and learn how to cope with them. Here are some common counterproductive group behaviors.

Being Aggressive.   Individuals use this tactic to deflate the status of others in order to make themselves look better. The aggressor disapproves of the ideas or values of others, attacks the group as a whole, or declares the problem a waste of time: "Parking on campus stinks and you should know that the administration isn't going to change it, so why should we bother?"

Blocking.   In this role, participants resist, disagree with, and oppose issues beyond reasonableness. They tend to hang onto ideas even after they have been rejected or ruled out by the rest of the group.

Recognition Seeking.   People with this attitude must be the center of attention or they are not happy. They are egotistical and try to gain attention by bragging about themselves or their achievements. They want to be the focus of the discussion and believe that everything must be approved by them before it can possibly be accepted by the group.

Self-Confessing.   Individuals with this trait often contribute irrelevant information about themselves. They frequently use their past experiences as a means of gaining attention: "When I was in high school, the teachers wanted everyone to be involved in student activities. I didn't think they were important then and I certainly don't think they are now."

Acting the Buffoon.   This behavior characterizes the group clown who is constantly joking or participating in other kinds of horseplay. These immature individuals often show a lack of involvement in what the group is trying to accomplish. Basically, they are "goof-offs."

Dominating.   This kind of conduct is found in persons who want to be in charge of everything. They like to control others through manipulation and use flattery, their status, or constant interruptions to do so. They enjoy telling other people what to do, but dislike being told what to do by others.

Help Seeking.   Some people join groups to satisfy their own personal needs. Then they try to get sympathy from other group members by expressing their insecurities or constantly belittling themselves: "I don't know what to do—I guess I'm not much help to this group" or "I really would like to help, but I'm having so much trouble in my other classes that I haven't had time to do my research on this problem."

Withdrawing. Some group members prefer not to participate at all. They choose not to say anything and thus can hardly be considered members of the group. If they are asked for an opinion, they usually say that they do not have one: "John, what do you think about the drinking problem on campus?" "I don't know." Whatever the reason—shyness, boredom, failure to prepare, or lack of interest—the withdrawer does little to contribute to the group's success.[6]

Being able to recognize and handle counterproductive contributions is the responsibility not only of the leader, but of each group member as well. Sometimes the best approach to these situations is to discuss them openly: "John, you sure have been quiet about this problem. What do you think?" "Sally, your comments and jokes seem to indicate that you don't see the issues as very serious. Why?" Sometimes conflict needs to be resolved with a vote by the group. This lets individuals know what the position of the majority is so that discussion can move along.

PROBLEM SOLVING AND DECISION MAKING

Although the goal of some discussions, such as those in classrooms, is to share information, the goal of most is to solve problems and make decisions. For example: How can we raise more money for the band to go on a tour? What can we do about the number of uninvited people who are coming into our dorm? Who should be held responsible for date rape? Each of these questions poses a problem that requires a decision.

When solving problems and making decisions, a group must consider the alternatives and arrive at a joint conclusion. To do this most efficiently, they must take an organized and thorough approach to determining the exact nature of the problem and discussing its many aspects and potential solutions.

Determining the Problem

In many speech communication classroom assignments, the first step is to select a problem or topic for discussion. This is not always easy—after all, the topic has to be both important and interesting to everyone in the group. A good place to start might be areas that need improvement on your own campus: What should be the role of athletics on your campus? Should better protection be provided for students who attend evening classes? What should be the role of students in governing the university? Do library hours adequately serve students' needs?

The surrounding community is also a source for discussion topics: What can be done about public parking in the downtown area? What does the business community do to help college students get jobs? What is the impact of college students on the economies of the surrounding communities?

State, regional, and national issues can provide a broader base for topics: Can the state provide sufficient funding to the university? How does the farm crisis affect the state economy? What should be the role of the federal government in providing loans to students?

Selecting from thousands of topics and problems takes time. However, if the group does its homework, picking one that is agreeable to all members should not be difficult.

After a topic or problem is selected, it should be stated in the form of a question. There are four types of discussion questions: questions of fact, interpretation, value, and policy. A **question of fact** asks whether something is true or false—for example: What is the present cost of tuition? How many students are enrolled in each of the various colleges? A **question of interpretation** asks for the meaning or explanation of something—for example: How does the economy of the state affect tuition? How can athletics contribute to a better education? A **question of value** asks whether something is good or bad, desirable or undesirable—for example: Which college offers the best education for its students? Do coeducational dormitories provide satisfactory living conditions? And a **question of policy** asks what actions should be taken—for example: What restrictions should be placed on alcohol on campus? What role should students have in evaluating instruction on campus?

Questions of fact leave little room for discussion. The answer can usually be found through research, and unless there are discrepancies in the data, no discussion is required. In contrast, questions of interpretation, value, and policy are not easily answered and thus make for good discussions.

When phrasing discussion questions, keep the following guidelines in mind:

1. The wording should reflect the discussion purpose.
2. The wording should focus attention on the real problem.
3. The wording should specify whose behavior is subject to change.
4. The wording should not suggest possible solutions.
5. The wording should avoid loaded language.[7]

Procedures for Discussing the Problem

The second step in group problem solving and decision making is to determine the plan for discussing the topic as it is specified. The agenda for discussing a problem usually includes five very specific steps: (1) definition of the problem, (2) analysis of the problem, (3) suggestions of possible solutions, (4) selection of the best solution, and (5) putting the best solution into operation.[8]

Here is a typical outline of a problem-solving discussion:

I. Definition of the Problem
   A. *Symptoms:* How does the problem show itself, or what are the difficulties, the "hurts"?
   B. *Size:* How large is the problem? Is it increasing or decreasing? What results can be expected if the problem is not solved?
   C. *Goal:* What general state of affairs is desired (in contrast to the present unsatisfactory one)?

II. Analysis of the Problem
   A. *Causes of the problem:* What causes or conditions underlie these difficulties?
   B. *Present efforts to solve the problem:* What is being done now to deal with the problem? In what ways are these efforts unsuccessful? What hints do they provide for further attacks on the problem?
   C. *Requirements of a solution:*
      1. Direction: Where shall we attack the problem?
         a. Would an attack on some outstanding symptom be the most fruitful approach?
         b. Is there a cause that would be worthwhile to attack, a cause with these two essential characteristics:
            (1) Would its removal substantially eliminate or greatly modify the problem?
            (2) Could its removal be accomplished with facilities—personnel, equipment, finances—that are (or can be made) available?
      2. Boundaries: What other values—social customs, laws, institutions—must not be harmed in attempting to solve this problem?

III. Suggestions of Possible Solutions
   A. *One possible solution is . . .*
      1. Nature: What, specifically, *is* the plan?
      2. Strengths: In what ways would this plan effectively fulfill the requirements of a solution, that is, make notable progress in the direction and stay satisfactorily within the boundaries of a solution?
      3. Weaknesses: In what ways would this plan fall short of effectively fulfilling these requirements?
   B. *Another possible solution is . . .*
   C. *Another. . .*
   D. *Another. . . Etc.*

IV. Selection of the Best Solution
   A. *Which solution (or solution with modifications) excels above the others?* In what ways, specifically?
   B. *Does the solution leave any substantial part of the problem unsolved?* If so, why is it still considered the best?
V. Putting the Best Solution into Operation
   A. *What are the major difficulties to be faced?*
   B. *What are possible ways of overcoming them?*
   C. *Which is the best way?*

This approach is widely accepted for more formal problem-solving discussions, such as those you may be required to develop for class. A more informal way of discussing a problem that might be appropriate for other school, work, and social groups you belong to takes the following steps:[9]

1. *Ventilation step:* Here the group members come together and vent their feelings and beliefs about the problem or task.
2. *Clarification step:* After venting their feelings, group members identify the exact problem and try to express it so that all members have the same understanding of it.
3. *Fact-finding step:* The group members collect all the information they can on the problem. The information they find should help them identify the cause(s) of the problem.
4. *Discovery step:* At this stage the group develops possible solutions for the problem under discussion.
5. *Evaluation step:* The group assesses the solutions it has generated. Groups have difficulty in holding off the evaluation process, but it is wise to keep from evaluating too early in the process.
6. *Decision-making step:* The group makes its decision based on its evaluation of what would be the best possible solution.

Sometimes groups find themselves unable to generate new ideas or to be creative in solving a particular aspect of a problem. In such cases, they may find brainstorming helpful. **Brainstorming**—a technique used to generate as many ideas as possible within a limited amount of time—can be used during any phase of the discussion process to produce topics, information, or solutions to problems. Whenever a group stops progressing because it can't generate new ideas, it should consider brainstorming. During the brainstorming session, group members should throw out as many ideas as possible pertaining to their discussion, no matter how farfetched they might seem. The leader should take a laissez-faire approach and let the comments flow freely. Throughout the process, one person should record the ideas for later analysis.

Once the group has freed itself from stale thinking and gained a new perspective, it should continue its discussion as planned.

GUIDELINES FOR PRODUCTIVE BRAINSTORMING

1. Don't criticize any idea.
2. No idea is too wild.
3. Quantity is important.
4. Seize opportunities to improve on or to add to ideas suggested by others.[10]

EVALUATING SMALL GROUP PERFORMANCE

To ensure its success, every group must periodically evaluate itself. Here are some questions that every group leader and every group member should ask:

- Are we using our time efficiently? If not, why not?
- Does everyone have an opportunity to participate?
- Are some people dominating the discussion?
- Are people listening to what others are saying?
- Is each person bringing adequate information and research to the discussion?
- Is the atmosphere free from personal conflict?
- Does the group communication stay within the agenda?
- Are the members happy about what is taking place in the discussions? If not, why not?
- Do we set realistic goals for our meetings?
- Do we get things accomplished? If not, why not?

For an evaluation to produce results, its findings must be shared with the group. A crucial requirement for such sharing is a nonthreatening atmosphere. The leader must be willing to examine what is going on without becoming defensive, and members must be willing to do the same. The group's success is related to each member's willingness to work and cooperate with the others. If the group is not getting its job done, or if its members are unhappy, corrective steps must be taken. Otherwise people will lose interest in the group and it will disintegrate.

MINI-EXERCISE

Develop a set of criteria that could be used to evaluate a small group presenting (1) a panel discussion, (2) a symposium, and (3) a forum. Discuss each set of criteria with your classmates to determine how they would evaluate the same forms of discussion.

SUMMARY   *Leadership* is any behavior that helps to clarify, guide, or achieve the goals of a group, while a *leader* is a person assigned or selected to guide or provide direction in order to reach the group's goal. Leaders may be either *task-oriented*—that is, concerned with completing the job or solving the problem—or *relationship-oriented*—concerned with the individuals who make up the group and their interpersonal needs. Leaders may also be classified as either autocratic, democratic, or laissez-faire. The *autocratic leader* maintains complete control of the group, the *democratic leader* shares control and other responsibilities, and the *laissez-faire leader* gives up almost all the control to the group.

The leader's approach affects the group atmosphere and its effectiveness and efficiency in making decisions. Research indicates that the democratic leadership style is superior to the autocratic style in terms of getting the task done and is more satisfying to group members. Autocratic leaders are able to produce more, but in the process seem to generate more hostility and aggression among group members. Finally, the laissez-faire leader's group tends to accomplish much less, produces work of lower quality, and wastes more time. To be most effective a leader must know how to use all three leadership styles and how to match the appropriate style to the individual situation.

Leaders are responsible for keeping things going, organizing the discussion, promoting interpersonal relationships, facilitating understanding, and stimulating creativity. In addition, they must be able to meet group members' *task needs*—needs related to getting the task completed—and *maintenance needs*—needs related to the personal satisfaction group members gain from working together. The leader is also responsible for setting and carrying out the *agenda*, which is a list of all the topics to be discussed during a meeting.

Member participation is critical to the success of any group. To obtain the best results, participants should possess specific traits: open-mindedness toward others, flexibility, awareness of communication barriers, understanding of the group process, ability to speak clearly and to the point, willingness to listen attentively, capacity to think logically and analytically, and readiness to cooperate and compromise.

Members' comments should be relevant, related, timely, of sufficient length, clear, informative, open to evaluation, and provocative. Certain kinds of behavior can interfere with a group's productivity and effectiveness. These include being aggressive, blocking, recognition seeking, self-confessing, acting the buffoon, dominating, help seeking, and withdrawing. Group members should recognize such behaviors and help the leader to control them.

Problem solving and decision making require a systematic approach if the best conclusions are to be reached. The first step in the process of decision making is to determine the problem or topic, which should then be stated in the form of a question. Questions are of four types: *questions of fact*, which ask whether something is true or false; *questions of interpretation*, which ask for the meaning or understanding of something; *questions of value*, which ask whether something is good or bad, desirable or undesirable; and *questions of policy*, which ask what actions should be taken.

Once the discussion question is clearly formulated, it is time to select a procedure for discussing the problem. There are two common methods of solving problems and making decisions. The first, more formal approach includes five steps: (1) definition of the problem, (2) analysis of the problem, (3) suggestions of possible solutions, (4) selection of the best solution, and (5) putting the best solution into operation. The second, more informal approach includes six steps: (1) ventilation, (2) clarification, (3) fact finding, (4) discovery, (5) evaluation, and (6) decision making.

When a group hits a snag in the problem-solving or decision-making process, *brainstorming* can help them to generate new ideas. The keys to productive brainstorming are openness and creativity.

Evaluation is a key step in ensuring a group's progress and success. For an evaluation to accomplish its purpose, both the leader and all group members must be willing to accept its findings and take the appropriate corrective steps.

KEY TERMS

Agenda: a list of all topics to be discussed during a meeting.

Autocratic Leader: a leader who keeps complete control and makes all the decisions for the group.

Brainstorming: a technique used to generate as many ideas as possible within a limited amount of time.

Democratic Leader: a leader who guides and directs, but shares control and remains open to all views.

Laissez-Faire Leader: a leader who gives complete decision-making freedom to the group or to individual members and often becomes a figurehead who remains only minimally involved.

Leader: a person who is assigned or selected to lead or provide direction in order to reach the group's goals.

Leadership: any behavior that helps to clarify, guide, or achieve a group's goals; the ability to exert influence over others.

Maintenance Needs: needs related to organizing and developing the group so that the members can realize personal satisfaction from working together.

Question of Fact: a question that asks whether something is true or false.

Question of Interpretation: a question that asks for the meaning or explanation of something.

Question of Policy: a question that asks what actions should be taken.

Question of Value: a question that asks whether something is good or bad, desirable or undesirable.

Relationship-Oriented Leaders: leaders who attempt to obtain a position of prominence and good interpersonal relationships.

Task Needs: needs related to the content of the discussion; include all behaviors that lead to the completion of the task.

Task-Oriented Leaders: leaders who gain satisfaction from performing the task.

DISCUSSION
STARTERS

1. Why is leadership so important to the success of small group communication?

2. Are leadership and leader the same? Explain.

3. What is the best way to identify a leader?

4. Which leadership style is the most appropriate for small group discussions? Why?

5. In what ways can leadership affect small group communication?

6. What are the functions of a leader in a small group?

7. What are the responsibilities of a group participant?

8. Explain the differences between constructive and counterproductive contributions by group members.

9. Who is responsible for handling counterproductive contributions?

10. How specifically would you handle a group member who was acting the role of a buffoon?

11. How would you lead withdrawn group members back into a discussion without embarrassing them?

12. How would you organize a discussion on the following topic: What should be the role and responsibility of students in monitoring drug use on campus?

13. Describe a situation in which the use of brainstorming would be appropriate.

14. How would you go about evaluating a small group discussion?

FURTHER
READINGS

Gouran, Dennis S. *Making Decisions in Groups: Choices and Consequences.* Glenview, Ill.: Scott, Foresman and Company, 1982.

Hart, Lois Borland. *Moving Up: Women and Leadership.* New York: American Management Association, 1980.

Kowitz, Albert C., and Thomas J. Knutson. *Decision Making in Small Groups: The Search for Alternatives.* Boston: Allyn & Bacon, 1980.

Scheidel, Thomas M., and Laura Crowell. *Discussing and Deciding: A Desk Book for Group Leaders and Members.* New York: Macmillan, 1979.

Wood, Julia T., Gerald M. Phillips, and Douglas J. Pedersen. *Group Discussion: A Practical Guide to Participation and Leadership,* 2nd ed. New York: Harper & Row Publishers, 1986.

NOTES

1. Fiedler, Fred E., *A Theory of Leadership Effectiveness,* (New York: McGraw-Hill, 1967), pp. 25–32.

2. White, R. K., and R. Lippitt, *Autocracy and Democracy: An Experimental Inquiry,* (New York: Harper & Row, 1960), pp. 26–27.

3. Barker, Larry L., Kathy J. Wahlers, Kittie W. Watson, et al., *Groups in Process: An Introduction to Small Group Communication,* 3rd ed., (Englewood Cliffs, N.J.: Prentice-Hall, Inc., 1987), p. 154.

4. Farwell, M. H., "An Evaluation of a Televised Method of Teaching Good Process," (Unpublished master's thesis, University Park: Pennsylvania State University, 1964).

5. Harnack, R. V., T. B. Fest, and B. S. Jones, *Group Discussion: Theory and Technique,* 2nd ed., (Englewood Cliffs, New Jersey: Prentice-Hall, Inc., 1977), pp. 94–96.

6. Benne, Kenneth D., and Paul Sheats, "Functional Roles of Group Members," *Journal of Social Issues* 4 (1948), pp. 41–49.

7. Harnack, pp. 153–154.

8. Dewey, John, *How We Think*, (Lexington, Mass.: D. C. Heath, 1933).

9. Barnlund, D., and Franklyn S. Haiman, *The Dynamics of Discussion*, (Boston: Houghton Mifflin, 1960), pp. 86–91.

10. Osborn, Alex, *Applied Imagination: Principles and Procedures of Creative Thinking*, (New York: Scribner's Sons, 1953), pp. 300–301.

CHAPTER 15

Interviewing

After studying this chapter, you should be able to:

1. Construct interview questions that will elicit the information you seek.

2. Choose an appropriate recording method and use it correctly.

3. Describe the qualities that employers seek in applicants.

4. Develop a resume that will make a good impression on prospective employers.

5. Research a company to determine its background, products, location, and future.

6. Conduct yourself effectively in an employment interview.

John is seeking information on the recent tuition hike and goes to the president of the university to discover her reasons for the increase and how it is going to benefit the students' education.

For her political science class, Jennifer is doing a research project on the mayor's campaign for reelection, so she decides to get information from the mayor's campaign chairman.

Bill, who is graduating in May, is looking for a public relations position with a major corporation. He has called Mr. Muller, the personnel director of S & S Enterprises, to discuss his chances of being hired.

The students in each of these examples will participate in interviews. John and Jennifer will conduct information interviews, while Bill will have an employment interview. An **interview** is a carefully planned and executed question-and-answer session designed to gather desired information. In Chapters 6 and 7, we discussed the interview as a method of gathering information about an audience or a topic. Our focus was on how to plan and organize an interview when preparing for a speech. In this chapter, we will take that discussion several steps further by presenting specific questions, forms, and recording techniques for information interviews. Then we will take an in-depth look at employment interviews—what you as a job hunter can expect to encounter and how you can prepare to make the best impression.

THE INFORMATION INTERVIEW

The underlying objective of any interview is to obtain reliable and valid information. **Reliability** is the extent to which the same information could be obtained from the same interviewee. If an interviewer asks the same question twice and the interviewee answers similarly both times, the responses would be considered reliable.

Validity, on the other hand, is the extent to which both the interviewer and the interviewee accomplish the purpose of the interview. For the interviewer, this means that each question or statement should lead to a related response. For example, if you ask, "What's it like outside?" and the interviewee answers, "My car doesn't start in cold weather," we have a problem with validity because the interviewee's response has not met your intent in asking the question. For whatever reason, your question, or possibly the way you asked it, did not produce an appropriate response.

Although it is virtually impossible to obtain perfect reliability and validity in all interview situations, you can do much to increase your chances by conscientiously preparing in advance and by being careful not to overgeneralize or misinterpret your subjects' responses.

Preparing an Interview

- Determine the kind of information you are seeking.
- Formulate a clear and concise general objective.
- Select the right person for the interview.
- Organize the interview's opening, body, and closing.
- See Chapter 7 for complete details.

Types of Questions

Asking effective questions, which is the heart of the interview, requires the interviewer to plan carefully. The keys to developing effective questions are (1) knowing the types of questions to ask and (2) phrasing the questions appropriately.

The first step in developing question-asking skills is to identify the various forms of interview questions, their uses, and the kinds of responses each produces. Questions can be classified as either open or closed, primary or secondary, neutral or leading.

Open Questions. **Open questions** usually evoke responses of more than just a few words. They encourage the interviewee to talk. There are two subcategories of open questions. The first is an extremely *vague* and *general* open-ended question that merely specifies a topic or asks the interviewee to tell what he or she knows. Some examples are:

1. Tell me about solar energy.
2. What do you like about the city's new crime prevention program?
3. Tell me about yourself.

The second kind is a more *direct* open-ended question that identifies or limits the topic and asks for a more specific reply. Some examples are:

1. How did your solar equipment perform?
2. What do you think are the main criticisms of the MX missile?
3. Why do you believe Senator Taylor lost the election?

Whether general or direct, the open question is extremely useful because it provides an opportunity for the interviewee to respond freely.

Closed Questions. **Closed questions** usually call for a restricted or short response from the interviewee. Because such questions allow for only a limited number of acceptable, or "right" answers, their responses are often predictable. A yes-no question, also called a **bipolar question,** is an extreme form of closed question, for it allows little or no freedom of expression. Some sample closed questions are:

1. Do you know that the environment is harmful? (bipolar)
2. Was there something else involved in the cost of the new mall? (bipolar)
3. What brand comes to mind when you think of candy?
4. Who is your favorite professor?

Closed questions can be valuable for verifying information, probing a response for more information, or controlling the discussion. They can also be answered quickly and require little effort from the interviewee. On the other hand, closed questions restrict communication and limit the interviewee's opportunities to volunteer information. Beginning interviewers often unknowingly overuse this form of question.

Primary Questions. **Primary questions** introduce new topics or new areas within a topic. They can stand by themselves, and can even be out of context and still make sense to the interviewee. For example:

1. Tell me how the supercomputer will affect our campus.
2. What is your favorite sport?
3. How did you do on your last speech?

Secondary Questions. **Secondary questions** are used to encourage the interviewee to expand on replies that may be incomplete, unresponsive, unclear, or inaccurate. The most commonly used form of secondary questions is the **probing question,** which directs the interviewee's thinking to further explanations of what has been said. In a sense, it is a follow-up question to a superficial or incomplete response and allows further investigation or expansion at a higher level of thinking. Assume, for example, that the interviewer's primary question was "Tell me about yourself" and that the interviewee's response was mainly demographic—that is, she described where she lived as a child, attended school, and lives now. The interviewer might respond with a probing question, such as "That's interesting, but I would like to know more about you and how you get along with people." A probe does not always start with *why* or *how,* although both words are common. In addition, a probe can be brief vocal sounds, such as "oh," or "uh-huh," or short phrases, such as "I see," "Please continue," "Go on," or "Why do you believe that?"

A probing question that is a restatement of something the interviewee said earlier is called a **mirror probe.** For example, if the interviewee said, "I believe Senator Smith is doing a better job because of his experience," a mirror question might be "So you think it's his experience that makes a difference? Why?"

Since a probe is considered a secondary question, it can be introduced at any time during an interview and can be interpreted by the interviewee as an indicator of the interviewer's attentiveness and encouragement to continue speaking. The probe serves two functions: (1) it motivates further communication and (2) it controls the interaction by providing direction.

Neutral Questions. **Neutral questions** avoid implying an expected or desired response. All of the sample questions in the previous sections are neutral questions. Even the sample closed questions allow interviewees to choose their own responses, even if there is only a choice between yes and no.

Leading Questions. The opposite of a neutral question is a **leading question.** Such a question implicitly or explicitly guides the interviewee to an expected or desired response. Look at the following examples of leading and neutral questions:

Leading	*Neutral*
You like speech class, don't you?	Do you like speech class?
The new field house isn't needed, is it?	Do you think we need a new field house?
Isn't the new bookstore easy to use?	Do you think the new bookstore is easy to use?

The use of leading questions can bias the information you receive because interviewees may adapt their responses to match what they think you want to hear. Such questions may also suggest answers to respondents that they would not have thought of on their own. Consequently, if you wish to obtain valid and reliable information, it is crucial to avoid asking leading questions.

MINI-EXERCISE

Identify the following questions as open or closed, primary or secondary, and neutral or leading:

1. What sport do you like best?
2. Do you like the new library building?
3. Tell me about yourself.
4. Your last term paper was researched, wasn't it?
5. Let me see if I have this straight. Did you say that we are going to need more funds for the rally?
6. Go on.
7. You really like speech class, don't you?

Phrasing Questions

The second concern in asking effective questions is *phrasing*. The wording of a question can influence its clarity and reflect its intent. Questions that have too many words or use an illogical word order are considered poorly phrased. Thus, even though the intent of a question may be appropriate and clear in the interviewer's mind, unless that intent is stated effectively, it may not be communicated to the interviewee. A vague question such as "What about the new missile?" gives the interviewee little or no guidance about the kind of information the interviewer is seeking.

Also avoid questions that are too complex. An effective question should contain only one thought or idea. Some examples of overly complex questions are:

1. Why do the ailerons on airplane wings move up and down when the plane is banking laterally in flight?
2. How, when, and why did pollution begin in our city?

Each question could be improved by dividing it into two or more separate questions that are clearer and shorter. Remember that poorly phrased questions hinder the interviewee's thought process and reduce the quality of his or her response.

FORMS OF INTERVIEW QUESTIONS

Open Primary Neutral
Does not limit the response
Introduces a new topic or area
Avoids implying an expected or
    desired response

Open Primary Leading
Does not limit the response
Introduces a new topic or area
Implies an expected or desired
    response

Closed Primary Neutral
Limits the response
Introduces a new topic or area
Avoids implying an expected or
    desired response

Closed Primary Leading
Limits the response
Introduces a new topic or area
Implies an expected or desired
    response

Open Secondary Neutral
Does not limit the response
Follows up and relates to a pre-
    vious response
Avoids implying an expected or
    desired response

Open Secondary Leading
Does not limit the response
Follows up and relates to a pre-
    vious response
Implies an expected or desired
    response

Closed Secondary Neutral
Limits the response
Follows up and relates to a pre-
    vious response
Avoids implying an expected or
    desired response

Closed Secondary Leading
Limits the response
Follows up and relates to a pre-
    vious response
Implies an expected or desired
    response

Mini-Exercise

What's wrong with each of these questions?

1. How does euthanasia affect our society?
2. What are your reactions to the new highway law that is going before Congress?
3. Would you say that the basketball coach is doing a good job or could she do better?
4. What impact do you think the new speed limit of 65 MPH will have on traffic flow and auto accidents in the city, on state highways, and on the interstate?
5. Have you stopped cheating on your taxes?

Methods of Recording Interviews

To ensure that you accurately recall an interview, you will need to record the results. To provide a permanent record, most interviewers use either written notes or a tape recorder. Because your record-keeping skills will greatly affect the outcome of your interview, choose the method that allows you the most freedom to interact with your interviewee.

Taking Notes.   If you decide to take notes, follow these guidelines:

1. At the outset of the interview ask permission to take notes and explain why note taking is necessary. To avoid creating curiosity or concern, show the respondent your notes occasionally, or ask him or her to check them for accuracy.
2. To encourage open and natural communication, try to maintain eye contact. When taking notes, be as inconspicuous as possible and use abbreviations or shorthand to speed the process.
3. To avoid communicating to the respondent what you think is important, do not begin to take notes frantically during or immediately after an answer, but take them throughout the interview.
4. To gain trust, agree to follow any ground rules the interviewee may set up, explain how and when you will use the material, or, if necessary, agree to let him or her see the script of your speech before you deliver it.
5. To assure accurate reporting from your notes, review them as soon after the interview as possible.

Using a Tape Recorder.   If you choose to use a tape recorder, consider the following recommendations:

1. Be thoroughly confident and familiar with the tape recorder so you can minimize the amount of time you spend operating it.
2. Explain the use of the recorder in a forthright and matter-of-fact way.
3. If possible, arrange the physical setting so that the recorder is out of the interviewee's sight.
4. Place the microphone so that it is inconspicuous and out of the direct line of sight as you and the interviewee face each other.
5. Once the interview begins, show no awareness of the recorder's presence.

When you need an accurate record of information and you fully explain this need, your interviewee will probably raise little or no objection to the use of a tape recorder. Here are two ways to explain the need for a tape recorder:

1. I am interested in getting all the details of your story in precisely your own words. Since I can't take shorthand and don't want a third person present, the best way is to let this machine do all the work.
2. I always prefer to record an interview so that the information will be accurate. I transcribe the relevant material on paper so that the tape can be used over again.[1]

In addition, when you are using a tape recorder:

1. Select a machine that operates on batteries and has a built-in microphone.
2. Make sure that everything is operating correctly before the interview.
3. Know exactly how long the tape runs and be prepared to switch quickly to the opposite side or to a new tape at the right time.
4. Practice using the recorder; make sure you have the volume set correctly.

THINK ABOUT IT

Skills! That one word means a lot to your future. The recurring theme among the experts we surveyed is an emphasis on "skills" and "competencies," rather than on specific studies.

Your major alone may not make a decisive difference in your future, but the skills you master and the way you communicate them to others can carry you through a lifetime of careers.[2]

THE EMPLOYMENT INTERVIEW

The purpose of this book is to help you develop the following communication skills: speaking, organizing, researching, persuading, informing, listening, discussing, making decisions, and solving problems, as well as improving your nonverbal, interpersonal, leadership, and language skills. Now it is up to you to show that you have learned these skills and to continue to develop them throughout your education and your lifetime. Because employment interviews are among the most important interpersonal communication events of your life, we have devoted an entire section to them.

Most of you taking this course are probably just beginning your college education. Whether you are a recent high school graduate or someone who has returned to school after pursuing other interests, the following pages on employment interviews will give you important information that will aid you in preparing for your future after graduation. Although graduation and hunting for a full-time job may seem far away, your preparation for them should begin now. You can use the information in this section in interviews for part-time jobs too.

Choosing a career field may be the most important decision you will ever make since an estimated 10,000 days of your lifetime are at stake— that's about how much time the average person spends on the job. According

to some experts, there are 42,000 career options for college students to choose from. However, today's college graduates are finding that the number of job candidates exceeds the number of professional openings available in many career fields. The prediction is that college graduates entering the labor force will exceed the number of job openings during the period from 1978 to 1990 by 3.3 million.[3]

Studying the following pages will not guarantee you the ideal job after graduation, but it should help to improve your chances significantly, especially considering that approximately 150 million employment interviews are conducted in the United States each year. To compete effectively for available jobs requires planning and preparation—now rather than at graduation.

Qualities Employers Seek

Almost every career requires such skills as writing, speaking, reading, listening, decision making, researching, and reasoning, as well as creativity, persuasion, leadership, interpersonal communication, and organization. In addition, there are a number of observable behaviors, such as achievement, aggressiveness, ambition, dependability, discipline, honesty, initiative, motivation, people orientation, persistence, responsibility, self-confidence, self-starting, sensitivity, sincerity, status/power, tenacity, and tough-mindedness, that may be important for specific jobs.[4] The way you acquire these skills and behaviors is, to a great extent, up to you. Without them, no matter how bright and knowledgable you may be, landing a top job is extremely difficult, if not impossible. The most likely way to obtain these abilities and behaviors is through courses, reading, internships, part-time or full-time employment, extracurricular activities, and participation in community functions. Acquiring most of these skills requires training and practice under a qualified instructor.

Knowing what an employer is looking for in a potential employee can help an applicant to prepare for an interview. An interviewer for a major corporation was asked these questions: "What specific skills are you looking for in applicants?" and "How do you identify these skills?" He responded:

> Most important for us in the way of skills is the ability to *communicate*—can people speak clearly? Can they articulate the kind of person they believe themselves to be? In what kinds of work situations do they perform well? What are their strengths and weaknesses? We want to know about the personal qualities of the individual, so I try to ask questions to draw them out and attempt to find out if they have a sense of themselves. What I'm looking for is an ability to verbalize an idea in clear, simple, understandable language. I'm also looking for the ability to listen attentively and then to be able to respond to an idea or thought that has been presented to them. If they do have good communication skills, they will be able to do this logically and succinctly.
>
> I am looking for *creativity*—can they be spontaneous? I will ask some "off-the-wall" questions just to see if this throws them. How do they

respond in these tough situations—can they be creative with their answers? This is very important when they are out in business situations with customers—they will have to respond to very sudden changes and *problem-solving* situations that they are not necessarily familiar with, and I want to know if they can handle them.

What we look for the most are *personal qualities*—assertiveness, self-motivation, drive, ambition, and a competitive instinct. They should be high achievers and want to work hard. I can usually tell about these qualities from how the person presents him- or herself and some of the activities they have engaged in. I pick up things from the *application* and *resume*—how they have written them—and the kinds of things they say— how they present their experiences is often very informative. For example, an assertive person will say "I can do these things" and "I decided on this course of action" whereas a more passive person might say "These are the experiences I have had." All of these things describe the person in some way.[5]

Preparing for an Interview

Preparation for a job interview takes planning and some thought about what will be expected of you as an applicant. Most initial job interviews average only 20 to 30 minutes, a very short amount of time in comparison to the amount of time you've spent earning your college degree. Yet, these are probably the most important minutes you will spend determining your job future. It is surprising how many applicants fail to plan adequately. Instead, they enter the interview saying essentially, "Here I am. Now what?" This gives the impression that they are indifferent—an impression that is seldom dispelled in the course of the interview.

Writing a Resume.   A **resume** is a written document that briefly describes an individual's personal, educational and professional qualifications and experiences. A well-written resume increases a person's chances of making a good impression. On the other hand, a poorly written resume can seriously jeopardize a person's chances, even though he or she may be well qualified.

There are two kinds of resumes: the standard data sheet used by most placement and employment services, as shown in Figure 15.1, and a self-prepared summary, as displayed in Figure 15.2. Because a resume represents an applicant, it is an extremely powerful form of communication and therefore must be accurate, complete, and neat.

The contents and layout of resumes vary as widely as the number of individuals who apply for jobs. A general rule of thumb, and the safest, is to *keep it simple and limit it to one or two pages.* Employers are busy and do not have time to read lengthy, involved reports.

The resume should be typed on bond paper of good quality. Some applicants have their resumes reproduced at local print shops or on word processors to obtain an even more finished look.

FIGURE 15.1

Standard Data Sheet used by a College Placement Center

PERSONAL DATA FORM

Name _____
      Last   First   Middle   Social Security Number

Present Mailing Address _____
      Street / Box   City   State   Zip   (Area Code)   Phone Number

Permanent Address _____
      Street / Box   City   State   Zip   (Area Code)   Phone Number

CAREER OBJECTIVE _____

EDUCATION

University	Major	Degree	Date

Areas Of Concentration And/Or Certification _____

_____

Percent Of College Expenses Earned By: Working _____ Scholarships _____ Other _____
                                                                 (Specify)

Citizen _____ Non-Citizen _____ Type Of Visa _____

EXPERIENCE

Position (Include Student Teaching Experience If Applicable)	Acquired Skills	Dates	Employer/Organization

LOCATION PREFERENCES: Flexible _____ Restricted _____ Location _____

ACTIVITIES, HONORS, AND OTHER INFORMATION:

I hereby authorize the CPPC to release this data sheet and related information including references, to any and all prospective employers and/or institutions of higher learning.

_____   _____
                Signature   Date

Most resumes include sections that present the following information:

- Introductory information
- Career objective
- Educational training
- Work experience
- Extracurricular activities
- References

FIGURE 15.2

*Self-Prepared
Resume*

```
                          Jo Ann Doe
                712 Garfield Street, Apt. 2-A
                    Lincoln, Nebraska 68508
                         402/484-9797

OBJECTIVE
   An administrative assistant position in a federal, state, or
   city government agency where I can utilize my public relations
   skills.

EXPERIENCE
   Assistant Campaign Manager:   Senator Jack Kay, Lincoln, Nebraska
   (July 1985-November 1987).
      Responsible for directing and coordinating all publicity
         activities.
      Arranged and scheduled personal appearances, debates, and
         media releases.
      Purchased, designed, and supervised the development of
         campaign materials.
      Recruited, trained, and supervised community volunteer
         groups.
      Supervised a staff of 16 community volunteers.
   Staff Assistant as an Intern:   United Volunteer Agency, Lincoln,
   Nebraska (December 1984-June 1985).
      Responsible for communicating the scope of Agency programs to
         Lincoln area businesses and community groups.
      Prepared Agency filmstrips, brochures, and news releases.
      Conducted public relations information sessions.
   Legislative Assistant:   Nebraska Legislative Session, Lincoln,
   Nebraska (June 1983-December 1984).
      Responsible for the collection, compilation, and release of
         information briefs and legislative action profiles to
         public news media.
      Typed and edited legislative bills.

EDUCATION
   The University of Nebraska, Lincoln, Nebraska (1983-1987)
      Bachelor of Arts Degree.   Speech Communication and Journalism.
      Grade Point Average: 3.75/4.00.

EDUCATIONAL HIGHLIGHTS
   Outstanding Senior Award, Creative Writing Award.   Speech Club
   Secretary, Phi Delta Kappa Vice-President.

      Related Course Work
         Public Relations and Publicity    Survey of Mass Media
         Social Political Communication     Interviewing
         Public Speaking                    Advertising Principles
         Federal Grant Development          Public Opinion

      Available:  Immediately

      References:  Upon request
```

The *introductory information* section should include the applicant's name, address, and phone number. As an applicant, you are not required to provide information that might be discriminatory. This includes your age, sex, marital status, race, religion, and other data as set forth by the Title VII Equal Employment Opportunity Act of 1972 and other affirmative action laws. The inclusion of such facts in a resume is up to the applicant, but it is generally advised that they be omitted.

Many placement service directors recommend that a brief *career objective* be stated on the resume immediately following the personal data. It should be as specific as possible. For example, a career objective might read:

> My long-term goal is to become a public relations director in either a major corporation or a recognized agency. My immediate goal is to obtain sufficient experience in sales, advertising, or marketing to gain the opportunity to advance as I acquire experience.

Such an objective can help a potential employer to understand the applicant's goals and to assess how the goals can be met by the company.

In the *educational training* section of the resume, the applicant should include a listing of colleges or universities attended, degrees conferred, dates of degrees, majors, minors, and special major subjects. Scholarships should be listed and some statement about grade achievement should be included, although it is not required.

The *work experience* section should include all jobs held, the dates they were held, and the address of each employer. If the applicant has held numerous part-time jobs, then only a few of the most important, recent, and related jobs should be listed. Other job experience can always be discussed at the interview, if it is appropriate to do so.

In the *extracurricular activities* section, the applicant should include all offices held, all organizations—both social and professional—that he or she was involved in, and any athletic participation. This section's purpose is to demonstrate the applicant's outside interests, well-roundedness, and social, leadership, and organizational skills. Such information is less important for experienced or older applicants who have demonstrated similar competencies in other areas.

The *reference* section should simply state that you will provide references upon request (see Figure 15.2). In preparation, you may wish to create a list of persons who are familiar with your work experience and professors in your major field or with whom you have taken several courses. Even though you may not be planning to apply for a job now, it is wise to get to know your professors and to make sure that they get to know you. Find an appropriate time—office hours, perhaps—and reason—discussion of a paper or an assignment—to visit with your professors so that they become acquainted with you. Some students find it intimidating to meet with professors, but if students use common sense and don't overstay their visits, most professors enjoy meeting with them. They will find it easier to write a letter of recommendation for you—and the letter will be more specific—if they know who you are.

Applicants should never place a person's name on a reference list unless they have his or her permission to do so. When asking individuals to be references for you, be prepared to hand them a copy of your resume and to tell them what kind of job you are seeking.

Contacting people to be references or to write letters of recommendation should be done as professionally and efficiently as possible. After all, you are requesting someone to take time to help you. Since most people enjoy helping others, you should never be afraid to ask for a reference.

Mini-Exercise

Create a list of at least three people who could write a letter of recommendation for you. Do not include relatives or personal friends. After each name, describe what you think that individual knows about you as a person, your competencies, and your ability to succeed.

After your resume is completed, you should proofread it carefully for errors and omissions. If you follow these simple steps, your resume should be acceptable.

Searching the Job Market.   Getting a job requires motivation, energy, hard work, and preparation. Even an applicant with superb qualifications faces tremendous competition for the best positions. According to placement service records, the average applicant spends only about five to ten hours a week searching for employment, but the person who is highly motivated will treat the search as if it were a job itself. The more time a person spends searching, the sooner and more likely he or she will find an opening.

Newspaper want ads, professional magazines, placement services, former teachers, and people working in jobs you are interested in can all be good sources of job leads. However, the most productive approach to locating jobs is networking. **Networking** is the systematic contacting of people who can provide information about available jobs or who can actually offer jobs. Relatives, friends, classmates, colleagues, and people at social and professional gatherings are all potential sources of information. If someone does not know of any job openings himself, ask if he knows of anyone who might. Then contact that person. In this way, your network expands from one person to another and you gain information from each new contact. The more people you know, the better your chances of being interviewed and the greater your opportunity for employment.

Researching the Company.   Before arriving for an interview, you should know the full name of the company and how to pronounce the full name of the interviewer. You should also know how old the company is; where its headquarters, plants, offices, or stores are located; what its products or services are; what its economic growth has been; and how its prospects look for the future. Such knowledge demonstrates your initiative and interest to the interviewer and can serve as a springboard for discussions.

MINI-EXERCISE

Go to your college or university placement office and find out what services they offer. What publications and guidance are available? Can they help you research a company? How?

An applicant can find out about virtually any business or professional organization by writing for its annual report or for recruiting materials and by looking through some of the following publications:

Dun and Bradstreet's Middle Market Directory
Dun and Bradstreet's Million Dollar Directory
Encyclopedia of Careers and Vocational Guidance
Moody's Industrial Manual
Occupational Outlook Handbook
Open the Books: How to Research a Corporation
Standard and Poor's Corporation Records

Such resources are standardly available in libraries and placement offices.

Developing Questions for the Interviewer. In preparation for your meeting, you should think about possible questions to ask the interviewer. Sometimes an interviewer may choose to say very little or to stop talking altogether, in which case it becomes your responsibility to carry the conversation by asking questions and continuing to emphasize your qualifications for the job. Whether or not the interviewer stops talking, you should have a list of questions and be prepared to ask them. This does not mean coming to the interview with a written list of questions, but it does mean coming prepared to ask questions—for example; "What are the duties and responsibilities of the job?" "Does the company provide training programs?" "How much traveling is involved in the job?" "What's the next step up from the starting position?" "Will I be able to continue my education?"

You should be prepared to take notes if asked to do so or if certain information needs to be recorded. However, you should not take notes throughout the entire interview.

Other Considerations. As a job applicant, you are expected to show good judgment and common sense about appearance, assertiveness, being on time, and being at the right place. If you plan ahead and follow these simple suggestions you should be able to avoid any serious problems.

The Interview

Much of the responsibility for a successful interview rests with the employer, but this doesn't mean that you should merely relax and let things happen. On the contrary, research suggests that most interviewers make up their minds about a job applicant in the first 30 seconds. Therefore, if you do poorly at the opening, your chances of getting the job are slim, no matter how brilliantly you handle the rest of the interview. It may seem unfair or superficial, but people do judge others on the basis of first impressions, and such impressions can be long lasting.

Frequently Asked Questions.   One expert states that most applicants make two devastating mistakes when they are being questioned. First, they fail to *listen to the question.* Instead, they answer a question that was not asked or give superfluous information. Second, they attempt to answer questions with virtually *no preparation.* Even skillful communicators cannot answer questions spontaneously without reducing their chances for success.

Here are some of the most common questions interviewers ask and some possible responses to them:

1. *"What can you tell me about yourself?"* This is not an invitation to give your life history. The interviewer is looking for clues about your character, qualifications, ambitions, and motivations. The following is a good example of a positive response. "In high school I was involved in competitive sports and I always tried to improve in each sport I participated in. As a college student, I worked in a clothing store part-time and found that I could sell things easily. The sale was important, but for me, it was even more important to make sure that the customer was satisfied. It wasn't long before customers came back to the store and specifically asked for me to help them. I'm very competitive and it means a lot to me to be the best."

2. *"Why do you want to work here?"* This is an obvious question and, if you have done your research on the company, you should be able to give a good reason. Organize your reasons into several short sentences that clearly spell out your interest. For example, "You are a leader in the field of electronics." "Your company is a Fortune 500 company, and your management is very progressive."

3. *"Why should I hire you?"* Once again, you should not be long winded, but you should provide a brief summary of your qualifications. Be positive and show that you are capable of doing the job. "Based on the internships that I have participated in and the related part-time experiences I have had, I can do the job."

4. *"How do you feel about your progress to date?"* Never apologize for what you have done. "I think I did very well in school. In fact, in a number of courses I received the highest exam scores in the class." "As an intern for the X Company, I received some of the highest evaluations that had been given in years." Considering that I played on the university's volleyball team and worked part time, I think you'll agree that I accomplished quite a bit during my four years in school."

5. *"What would you like to be doing five years from how?"* Be realistic— know what you can realistically accomplish. You can find out by talking to others about what they accomplished in their first five years with a particular company. "I hope to be the best I can be at my job and, because many in

this line of work are promoted to area manager, I am planning on that also."

6. *"What is your greatest weakness?"* You should not avoid this question by simply saying that you do not have any. Everyone has weaknesses, so you must be honest. The best approach is to admit your weakness, but show that you are working on it and have a plan to overcome it. If possible, cite a weakness that will work to the company's advantage. "I'm such a perfectionist that I won't stop until a report is written just right." "I'm not very good at detail work, but I have been working on it and I've improved dramatically over the past several years."

7. *"What is your greatest strength?"* This is a real opportunity to "toot your own horn." Do not brag or get too egotistical, but let the employer know that you believe in yourself and that you know your strengths. "I feel that my strongest asset is my ability to stick to things to get them done. I feel a real sense of accomplishment when I finish a job and it turns out just as I'd planned. I've set some high goals for myself. For example, I want to graduate with highest distinction. And even though I had a slow start in my freshman year, I made up for it by doing an honor's thesis."

8. *"What goals have you set and how did you meet them?"* This question examines your ability to plan ahead and meet your plan with specific actions. "Last year, during a magazine drive to raise money for our band trip, I set my goal at raising 20 percent more than I had the year before. I knew the drive was going to begin in September, so I started contacting people in August. I asked each of my customers from last year to give me the names of one or two new people who might also buy a magazine. I not only met my goal, but I also was the top salesperson on the drive."

No matter what question you are asked, answer it honestly and succinctly. Most interviewers are looking for positive statements, clear ideas, persuasiveness, and clear thinking under pressure.

If you should be asked a question that violates the affirmative action laws, you can decline to answer. You might say, "I'm sorry, but I don't find that question relevant to the position being offered and it is against affirmative action laws to ask it." Make sure that you are tactful, but be firm in letting the interviewer know that he or she is doing something illegal.

THINK ABOUT IT

If an interviewer asked you any of the preceding questions, how would you answer them?

Other Considerations. Always maintain eye contact with the interviewer. Show that you are confident by looking straight at the speaker. Eye contact may not get you the job, but lack of eye contact can reduce your chances dramatically. Most interviewers greet the applicant with a handshake. Make sure that your clasp is firm. Being jittery about the interview can result in cold, clammy hands and create a negative impression. Therefore, make sure your hands are warm and dry. When the interviewer asks you to sit down, if you have a choice, take the chair beside the desk rather than the one in front. This helps to eliminate any barriers between you and the interviewer and also makes you a little more equal, for which the interviewer will unconsciously respect you.

Closing the Interview.   Before leaving, try to find out exactly what action will follow the interview, when it will happen, and when you will hear from the interviewer again. Shake hands as you say good-bye and thank the interviewer for spending time with you.

Factors Leading to Rejection

Rejection is very difficult for most of us to accept, but you should never give up. It is not unusual for most job applicants to be rejected a minimum of eight or nine times before finally receiving an offer. Employers from 166 companies were asked "What negative factors most often lead to the rejection of an applicant?" Here are their responses in order of their frequency of mention:

1. Negative personality or poor impression—more specifically, lack of motivation, ambition, maturity, aggressiveness, or enthusiasm.
2. Inability to communicate—poor communication skills.
3. Lack of competence—inadequate training.
4. Low grades—poor grades in major field.
5. Unidentified goals.
6. Unrealistic expectations.
7. Lack of interest in the type of work.
8. Unwillingness to travel to relocate.
9. Poor preparation for the interview.
10. Lack of experience.[6]

SUMMARY

An *interview* is a carefully planned and executed question-and-answer session designed to gather desired information. The objective of any interview should be high *reliability*—the extent to which the same information could be obtained from the same interviewee—and high *validity*—the extent to which both the interviewer and interviewee accomplish the purpose of the interview.

Knowing the basic types of questions helps an interviewer match his or her questions to the kind of information desired. *Open questions* encourage the interviewee to talk, while *closed questions* usually limit or restrict the interviewee's response. The *bipolar question,* because it requires a simple answer of yes or no, is an extreme form of closed question that allows little or no freedom of response.

Primary questions introduce new topics while *secondary questions* encourage the interviewee to expand his or her answers. *Probing questions* are a form of secondary question that directs the interviewee to expand or further explain a response. The *mirror probe,* also a secondary question, restates in question form something that the interviewee said earlier. *Neutral questions* avoid implying an expected response while *leading questions* encourage the interviewee to respond the way an interviewer wants him or her to respond. When phrasing questions, an interviewer should be careful to ensure clarity by avoiding wordiness, vagueness, and unnecessary complexity.

To obtain the most accurate recall, an interview should be recorded. Experienced interviewers either take notes or use a tape recorder—whichever method they find that interferes least with the flow of information.

Choosing a career is one of the most important decisions a person can make, and a successful job interview is a crucial step in achieving that end. Planning and preparation are critical building blocks of a successful employment interview. Applicants must know their strengths and weaknesses and be able to communicate effectively with the interviewer. Getting a job requires motivation, energy, hard work, and research plus knowing where to look and whom to contact in order to obtain the necessary information.

An effective *resume* can pave the way for a productive interview. In judging a resume, employers look for thoughtfulness, creativity, accuracy, and neatness. The two most common kinds of resumes are the standard data sheet used by most placement and employment services, and the self-prepared resume. Both formats summarize basic information about the applicant's career objective, educational training, work experience, extracurricular activities, and references.

To prepare for an interview, an applicant should seek out information about a company's background, location, products or services, growth, and prospects for the future. Based on such data, the applicant can then think about possible questions to ask the interviewer.

The first 30 seconds of an interview are considered the most crucial. As a result, applicants must create a strong positive impression from the moment they meet the interviewer. They should show confidence, maintain eye contact with the interviewer, give a firm handshake, and sit, if given a choice, in the chair at the side of the desk or table rather than in front.

Job applicants who prepare carefully and present themselves well can avoid some of the most common reasons for rejection.

KEY TERMS

Bipolar Question: a yes-no question; an extreme form of closed question that allows little or no freedom of expression.

Closed Question: a question that calls for a restricted or short response.

Interview: a carefully planned and executed question-and-answer session designed to gather desired information.

Leading Question: a question that explicitly or implicitly guides the interviewee to an expected or desired response.

Mirror Probe: a question that is a restatement of something the interviewee said earlier.

Networking: the systematic contacting of people who can provide information about available jobs or about who can actually offer jobs.

Neutral Question: a question that avoids implying an expected or desired response.

Open Question: a question that evokes a response of more than just a few words; it encourages the interviewee to talk.

Primary Question: a question that introduces a new topic or a new area within a topic; it can stand alone, out of context, and still be meaningful.

Probing Question: a question that directs the interviewee's thinking to further explanations of what has already been said.

Reliability: the extent to which the same results could be obtained from the same interviewee.

Resume: a written document that briefly describes a person's personal, educational, and professional qualifications and experiences.

Secondary Question: a question used to encourage the interviewee to expand on replies that may be incomplete, unresponsive, unclear, or inaccurate.

Validity: the extent to which both the interviewer and the interviewee accomplish the purpose of the interview.

DISCUSSION STARTERS

1. What role should reliability and validity play in an interview?
2. What would you tell the beginning interviewer about question formats?
3. If there was one thing that every interviewer should know about recording information, what would it be?
4. Why is the choice of a career field so important?
5. What can people do to increase their chances of getting a job?
6. If you were an employer, what would you look for in a job applicant?
7. If you were to advise fellow students about writing resumes, what would you tell them to do?
8. Why should personal data such as age, sex, marital status, and religion be omitted from a resume?
9. How should you go about getting references? Whom should you ask?
10. What is the best approach to a job search? Why?
11. What should you know about a company before you are interviewed?
12. Why is it important for an applicant to ask questions of the interviewer?
13. What questions does an employer usually ask an applicant?
14. What advice would you give to help someone avoid being rejected?

FURTHER READINGS

Brady, John. *The Craft of Interviewing.* New York: Vintage Books, 1977.

Donaghy, William C. *The Interview: Skills and Applications.* Glenview, Ill.: Scott, Foresman and Company, 1984.

Goyer, Robert S., and Michael Z. Sincoff. *Interviewing Methods.* Dubuque, Iowa: Kendall/Hunt Publishing Company, 1977.

Hunt, Gary, and William Eadle. *Interviewing: A Communication Approach*. New York: Holt, Rinehart & Winston, 1987.

Metzler, Ken. *Creative Interviewing: The Writer's Guide to Gathering Information by Asking Questions*. Englewood Cliffs, New Jersey: Prentice-Hall, Inc., 1977.

Sincoff, Michael Z., and Robert S. Goyer. *Interviewing*. New York: Macmillan, 1984.

Sitzmann, Marion, and Reloy Garcia. *Successful Interviewing: A Practical Guide for the Applicant and Interviewer*. Skokie, Ill.: National Textbook Company, 1977.

Skopec, Eric W. *Situational Interviewing*. New York: Harper & Row Publishers, 1986.

Stewart, Charles J., and William B. Cash. *Interviewing: Principles and Practices*, 5th ed. Dubuque, Iowa: Wm. C. Brown Publishing, 1988.

NOTES

1. Stewart, Charles, and William B. Cash, *Interviewing: Principles and Practices*, 3rd ed., (Dubuque, Iowa: Wm. C. Brown, 1982), pp. 147–149.

2. *Ford's Insider: Continuing Series of College Newspaper Supplements*, (Knoxville, Tenn.: 13–30 Corporation, 1980), p. 14.

3. *Ford's Insider*, p. 4.

4. Stewart, Charles J., and William B. Cash, Jr., *Interviewing Principles and Practices* 4th ed., (Dubuque, Iowa: Wm. C. Brown Publishers, 1985), p. 197.

5. Danielson, Pete, Sales Manager with Xerox Corporation, in an interview at the University of Nebraska-Lincoln, June 1980.

6. *The Endicott Report: Trends in the Employment of College and University Graduates in Business and Industry*, (Evanston, Ill.: The Placement Center, Northwestern University, 1979), p. 8.

GLOSSARY

Abstract Words: symbols for ideas, qualities, and relationships. *(3,10)*

Accenting: the use of nonverbal cues to emphasize or punctuate spoken words. *(4)*

Active Listening: the process of analyzing and evaluating what another person is saying in an effort to understand the speaker's feelings or the true meaning of the speaker's message. *(12)*

Adaptors: nonverbal behaviors that help us to feel at ease in communication situations, such as twisting a ring, scratching, or playing with a pencil. *(4)*

Adoption: an action goal that asks listeners to demonstrate their acceptance of an attitude, belief, or value by performing the behavior suggested by the speaker. *(11)*

Advance Organizers: statements that preview forthcoming content. *(10)*

Affect Displays: nonverbal behaviors that express emotions and feelings. *(3)*

Agenda: a list of all topics to be discussed during a meeting. *(14)*

Alter-adaptors: behaviors learned from our past experiences and from the manipulation of objects, such as putting our hands up to protect our face, moving closer to establish intimacy, and moving toward a door to end a conversation. *(4)*

Analogy: a comparison of two things that are similar in certain essential characteristics. *(7)*

Antonym: a word, phrase, or concept that has the opposite meaning of another word, phrase, or concept. *(10)*

Appeal to Needs: an attempt to move people to action by calling on their most basic physical and psychological requirements and desires. *(11)*

Artifacts: ornaments or adornments that communicate information about a person; they include clothes, perfume, makeup, hairstyle, jewelry, eyeglasses, and cars. *(4)*

Attention: the mental process of focusing on specific stimuli while ignoring or downplaying other stimuli. *(5)*

Attitude: an evaluative disposition, feeling, or position about a person, event, idea, or thing. *(2)*

Audience: a collection of individuals who have come together for a specific reason—to hear a speech. *(6)*

Audience Analysis: the collection and interpretation of data about the basic characteristics, attitudes, values, and beliefs of an audience. *(6)*

Autocratic Leader: a leader who keeps complete control and makes all the decisions for the group. *(13)*

Belief: a conviction or confidence in the truth of something that is based on absolute proof. *(2)*

Bipolar Question: a yes-no question; an extreme form of closed question that allows little or no freedom of expression. *(15)*

Blind Area: the quadrant of the Johari Window that represents information that others perceive about us, but which we do not recognize or acknowledge about ourselves. *(12)*

Body: the main part of an interview that consists of the questions and answers. *(7,8)*

Body Motion: any movement of the face, hands, feet, trunk, or other part of the body that communicates a message. *(4)*

Brainstorming: a technique used to generate as many ideas as possible in a limited amount of time. *(6,13)*

Brief Example: a specific instance that is used to introduce a topic, drive home a point, or create a desired response. *(7)*

Bypassing: the misunderstanding that occurs between a sender and a receiver. *(3)*

Captive Participant: a person who is required to hear a particular speaker or speech. *(6)*

Causal Reasoning: a sequence of thought that links causes with effects; it either implies or explicitly states the word "because." *(11)*

Cause-Effect Pattern: an order of presentation in which the speaker first explains the causes of an event, problem, or issue, and then discusses its consequences. *(8)*

Channel: the route by which messages flow between sources and receivers such as light waves and sound waves. *(1)*

Closed Question: a question that calls for a restricted or short response. *(15)*

Closing: the final portion of the interview process in which the interviewer thanks the interviewee and sums up his or her findings. *(7)*

Closure: the filling in of details by a perceiver so that whatever is perceived appears to be complete. *(2)*

Cohesiveness: the attraction that group members feel for each other and their willingness to stick together; a form of loyalty. *(13)*

Commitment: the desire of group members to work together to get their task completed to the satisfaction of the entire group. *(13)*

Common Goal: the driving force that brings people together to form groups. *(13)*

Communication: the process by which verbal and nonverbal symbols are sent, received, and given meaning. *(1)*

Communication Apprehension: the severest form of speech anxiety—a chronic fear or avoidance of all interactions with others, it can be seen in individuals who either consciously or subconsciously have decided to remain silent. *(9)*

Comparative Advantage Order: a pattern of organization in which a persuader presents and compares several solutions in order to emphasize the advantages of his or her preferred solution. *(11)*

Complementing: nonverbal cues that help to complete, describe, or accent verbal cues. *(4)*

Conclusion: a closing statement that focuses the audience's thoughts on the specific purpose of a speech and brings the most important points together in a condensed and uniform way. *(8)*

Concrete Words: symbols for specific things that can be pointed to, physically experienced, touched, or felt. *(3,10)*

Connotation: the subjective meaning of a word—what a word suggests because of the feelings or associations it evokes. *(3)*

Continuance: an action goal that asks listeners to demonstrate their acceptance of an attitude, belief, or value by continuing to perform the behavior suggested by the speaker. *(11)*

Contrast Definition: a definition that shows or emphasizes differences. *(10)*

Credibility: a speaker's believability based on the audience's evaluation of his or her competence and character. *(11)*

Dating: a form of indexing that helps to sort out events, ideas, places, and people according to time. *(3)*

Deceiving: nonverbal cues used to purposely mislead others by presenting a false appearance or incorrect information. *(4)*

Decoding: the process of translating a message into the thoughts or feelings that were communicated. *(1)*

Deductive Reasoning: a sequence of thought that moves from general information to a specific conclusion; it consists of a general premise, a minor premise, and a conclusion. *(11)*

Definiton by Example: the use of either a spoken or a written example to explain a term or concept. *(7)*

Democratic Leader: a leader who guides and directs, but shares control and remains open to all views. *(14)*

Demographic Analysis: the collection and interpretation of characteristics (age, sex, religion, and so on) about individuals that excludes values, attitudes, and beliefs. *(6)*

Denotation: the core meaning of a word—standard dictionary definition. *(3)*

Descriptive Feedback: means of checking your understanding of another person's nonverbal behavior by describing your interpretation of it. *(4)*

Descriptors: words used to describe something. *(10)*

Deterrence: an action goal that asks listeners to demonstrate their acceptance of an attitude, belief, or value by avoiding certain behavior. *(11)*

Discontinuance: an action goal that asks listeners to stop doing something; the opposite of adoption.   *(11)*

Emblems: nonverbal behaviors/body movements that have a relatively direct translation into words or phrases.   *(4)*

Emotional Appeal: an attempt to move people to action by playing on their feelings.   *(11)*

Empathic Listening: listening that includes understanding and information seeking, but usually excludes critical judgments.   *(5)*

Empathy: intellectual identification with, or vicarious experiencing of, the feelings, thoughts, and attitudes of another person.   *(1)*

Encoding: the process by which the source mentally changes thoughts or feelings into words, sounds, and physical expressions that make up the eventual message to be sent.   *(1)*

Entertainment Speech: a speech whose main function is to provide enjoyment and amusement.   *(6)*

Environment: both the psychological and the physical surroundings in which communication occurs; it encompasses the attitudes, feelings, perceptions, and relationships of the communicators as well as the characteristics of the location in which communication takes place.   *(1,4)*

Ethics: an individual's system of moral principles.   *(11)*

Etymology: a definition that traces the origin and development of a word.   *(10)*

Evaluative Listening: listening to judge or to analyze information.   *(5)*

Example: a simple, representative incident or model that clarifies a point.   *(7)*

Extemporaneous Method: a delivery style in which the speaker carefully prepares the speech in advance, but delivers it with only a few notes and with a high degree of spontaneity.   *(9)*

Eye Contact: the extent to which a speaker looks directly at audience members; associated with facial expression.   *(9)*

Facial Expressions: configurations of the face that can reflect, augment, contradict, or be unrelated to a speaker's vocal delivery.   *(4,9)*

Factual Illustration: tells what has actually happened.   *(7)*

Feedback: the response to a message that the receiver sends to the source.   *(1,3)*

Figurative Analogy: a comparison of things in different categories—for example, a heart and a pump.   *(7)*

Figure and Ground Organization: the ordering of perceptions so that some stimuli are in focus and others become the background.   *(2)*

Force: the intensity and volume level of the voice; an aspect of vocal variety.   *(9)*

Forum: a small group presentation that includes audience participation.   *(13)*

Frozen Evaluation: the tendency to look at events, things, or people as if they never change and to ignore any change that may have taken place.   *(2,3)*

Full Content Outline: an expansion of the main points selected from the preliminary outline; it is a detailed skeleton of a speech with all main and secondary points written in complete sentences.   *(8)*

General Purpose: the overall goal of a speech, which is usually to perform one of three overlapping functions—to inform, to persuade, or to entertain.   *(6)*

Gestures: movements of the head, arms, and hands that help to illustrate, emphasize, or clarify an idea.   *(9)*

Grammar: the rules that govern how words are put together to form phrases and sentences.   *(3)*

Group: a collection of individuals who form a system in which members influence one another, derive mutual satisfaction from one another, interact for a common purpose, take on roles, are interdependent, and communicate face to face.   *(13)*

Group Personality: the collective identity that members of a group form when they come together.   *(13)*

Group Size: the number of participants involved in a given small group communication.   *(13)*

Hearing: the passive, physiological process in which sound is received by the ear.   *(5)*

Hidden Area: the quadrant of the Johari Window that represents personal and private information about ourselves that we choose not to disclose to others.   *(12)*

Hierarchy of Individual Needs: a theory developed by Abraham Maslow that rank orders physical, safety, social, self-esteem, and self-actualization needs; it states that the lower-order needs must be satisfied before the higher-order needs. *(12)*

Hypothetical Illustration: tells what could or probably would happen given a specific set of circumstances. *(7)*

Illustration: an extended example, narrative, case history, or anecdote that is striking and memorable. *(7)*

Illustrators: body movements and facial expressions that accent, reinforce, or emphasize an accompanying verbal message. *(4)*

Impromptu Method: a delivery style in which a speaker delivers a speech without any pre-planning or preparation whatsoever. *(9)*

Indexing: a means of identifying how each person, object, and event is different and unique. *(3)*

Indiscrimination: the neglect of individual differences and the overemphasis of similarities. *(3)*

Inductive Reasoning: a sequence of thought that moves from specific facts to a general conclusion. *(11)*

Inference Confusion: the tendency of people to go beyond their observations to draw incorrect conclusions that they assume are correct. *(3)*

Information: the act of informing or the condition of being informed; communication of knowledge—knowledge derived from study, experience, or instruction. *(10)*

Information Relevance: relating information to the audience so that they have a reason to listen. *(10)*

Informative Speech: a speech that enhances an audience's knowledge and understanding by explaining what something means, how something works, or how something is done. *(6)*

Input: the raw materials in a group—the people and the information used in the interaction. *(13)*

Intelligibility: a speaker's vocal volume, distinctiveness of sound, clarity of pronunciation, and stress placed on syllables, words, and phrases. *(9)*

Intentional Communication: a message that is purposely sent to a specific receiver. *(1)*

Interaction: an exchange of communication in which communicators take turns sending and receiving messages. *(1)*

Interdependence: the mutual dependence of group members on one another. *(13)*

Internal Summary: a short review statement that should be given at the end of each main point. *(8)*

International Phonetic Alphabet (IPA): an alphabet of sounds devised to provide a consistent and universal system for transcribing speech sounds of all languages. *(3)*

Interpersonal Communication: the informal exchange of information between two or more individuals. *(12)*

Interpretation: the assigning of meaning to stimuli. *(2)*

Interview: a carefully planned and executed question-and-answer session designed to gather desired information. *(7,15)*

Intrapersonal Communication: the process of understanding information within oneself. *(12)*

Introduction: an opening statement that orients the audience to the subject and motivates them to listen. *(8)*

Johari Window: a graphic model that depicts the process of awareness and self-disclosure in interpersonal relations; it also illustrates the proportion of information about oneself that is known and unknown to oneself and others. *(12)*

Laissez-Faire Leader: a leader who gives complete decision-making freedom to the group or to individual members and often becomes a figurehead who remains only minimally involved. *(14)*

Language: a structured system of signs, sounds, gestures, and marks used and understood to express ideas and feelings among people within a community or nation, within the same geographical area, or within the same cultural tradition. *(3)*

Leader: a person who is assigned or selected to lead or provide direction in order to reach the group's goals. *(14)*

Leadership: any behavior that helps to clarify, guide, or achieve a group's goals; the ability to exert influence over others. *(14)*

Leading Question: a question that either explicitly or implicitly guides the interviewee to an expected or desired response. *(15)*

Listening: the active process of receiving aural stimuli by selecting, attending, understanding, and remembering. *(5)*

Listening for Enjoyment: listening purely for pleasure, personal satisfaction, or appreciation. *(5)*

Listening for Information: listening to gain comprehension. *(5)*

Literal Analogy: a comparison of members of the same category—for example, two churches, two businesses, or two states. *(7)*

Logical Appeal: an attempt to move people to action through the use of evidence and proof. *(11)*

Logical Definition: the most common form of definition used by speakers that usually contains two parts: a term's dictionary definition and the characteristics that distinguish the term from other members of the same category. *(7)*

Main Points: the principal subdivisions of a speech. *(8)*

Maintenance Needs: needs related to organizing and developing the group so that the members can realize personal satisfaction from working together. *(14)*

Manuscript Method: a delivery style in which a speaker writes the speech in its entirety and then reads it word for word. *(9)*

Mean: a statistic often referred to as the average, it is obtained by adding all the scores in a set of scores and dividing by the number of scores in the set. *(7)*

Median: the middle score in a series of numbers; half the scores are above the median and half are below it. *(7)*

Memorized Method: a delivery style in which a speaker memorizes a speech in its entirety, usually from a word-for-word script. *(9)*

Message: the stimulus that is produced by the source. *(1)*

Mirror Probe: a question that is a restatement of something the interviewee said earlier. *(15)*

Mode: the most frequent score in a series of numbers. *(7)*

Moderately Scheduled Interview: an interview format in which the interviewer has listed the basic questions or topics to be discussed with possible probes included under each question or topic. *(7)*

Motivated Sequence: a pattern of organization specifically developed for persuasive speaking that combines logic and practical psychology; it involves five steps: attention, need, satisfaction, visualization, and action. *(11)*

Networking: the systematic contacting of people who can provide information about available jobs or about who can actually offer jobs. *(15)*

Neutral Question: a question that avoids implying an expected or desired response. *(15)*

Noise: anything that distorts, interferes with, or changes the meaning of an intended message. *(1)*

Nonscheduled Interview: an interview format in which the interviewer follows a central objective or a list of possible topics and subtopics; there is no formalized order of questions and there are no anticipated responses. *(7)*

Nonverbal Communication: information that is conveyed without words. *(4)*

Norms: the expected and shared ways in which group members behave as determined by formal and informal guidelines. *(13)*

Object-adaptors: nonverbal behaviors that involve the use of an object or prop, such as a pencil, a paper clip, or keys, for something other than its intended purpose. *(4)*

Observation: an audience research method in which the speaker watches audience members and notes their behaviors and characteristics. *(6)*

Open Area: the quadrant of the Johari Window that represents information that is free to self and others through observation or a willingness to share. *(12)*

Open Question: a question that evokes a response of more than just a few words; it encourages the interviewee to talk. *(15)*

Opening: the introduction to an interview in which the interviewer explains the purpose of the interview, establishes rapport, and provides background information if needed. *(7)*

Operational Definition: a definition that explains how an object or concept works; some operational definitions merely illustrate the steps that make up a process. *(7)*

Organization: the categorizing of stimuli in our environment in order to make sense of them. *(2)*

Organizing: the arranging of ideas or elements into a systematic and meaningful whole. *(8)*

Outlining: a standardized approach to arranging written materials into a logical sequence, often referred to as the blueprint or skeleton of a speech. *(8)*

Output: the decisions and solutions reached by the group. *(13)*

Panel: a group presentation in which members discuss a topic in front of an audience. *(13)*

Paralanguage: the way we vocalize, or say, the words we speak. *(4)*

Pendulum Effect: the secalating conflict that results from the use of either-or terms to describe and defend our perceptions of reality. *(3)*

Perception: the process of sensing, selecting, organizing, interpreting, and evaluating information in order to give it personal meaning. *(2)*

Perceptual Set: a predetermined view of events, things, or people based on past experiences. *(2)*

Persuasion: a communication process involving both verbal and nonverbal messages that attempts to reinforce or change listeners' attitudes, beliefs, values, or behavior. *(11)*

Persuasive Speech: a speech that attempts to change listeners' attitudes or behavior by advocating or trying to gain acceptance for the speaker's point of view. *(6)*

Phoneme: the smallest distinctive and functional unit of sound in a language. *(3)*

Pitch: how low or high the voice is on a tonal scale; an aspect of vocal variety. *(9)*

Planned Repetition: the deliberate repetition of a thought in order to increase the likelihood that the audience will understand and remember it. *(10)*

Polarization: the tendency to view things in terms of extremes—either good or bad, black or white, etc. *(3)*

Preliminary Outline: a list of all the main points that may be used in a speech. *(8)*

Presentational Outline: a condensation of the full-content outline that eases delivery by minimizing detail and listing key words and phrases in place of full sentences. *(8)*

Primary Question: a question that introduces a new topic or new area within a topic; it can stand alone, out of context, and still be meaningful. *(15)*

Probing Question: a question that directs the interviewee's thinking to further explanations of what has already been said. *(15)*

Problem-Solution Pattern: an order of presentation that first discusses a problem and then suggests solutions. *(8)*

Process: a continuous series of actions that is constantly changing, with no beginning or end. *(1)*

Proxemics: the study of how we use space and the distance we place between ourselves and others when communicating. *(4)*

Proximity: the grouping of stimuli perceived to be either physically or psychologically close to one another. *(2)*

Psychological Analysis: the collection and interpretation of data about audience members' values, attitudes, and beliefs. *(6)*

Public Speaking: the presentation of a speech, usually prepared in advance, during which the speaker is the central focus of an audience's attention. *(6)*

Question of Fact: a question that asks whether something is true or false. *(11,14)*

Question of Interpretation: a question that asks for the meaning or explanation of something. *(14)*

Question of Policy: a question that asks what actions should be taken. *(11,14)*

Question of Value: a question that asks whether something is good or bad, desirable or undesirable. *(11,14)*

Questionnaire: a set of written questions that is distributed to respondents to gather desired information. *(6)*

Random Sampling: a method of selecting a small number of interviewees from a larger group so that every individual has an equal chance of being selected. *(6)*

Range: the highest and lowest numbers in a series of numbers. *(7)*

Rate: the speed at which a speaker speaks, normally between 125 words and 150 words per minute; an aspect of vocal variety. *(9)*

Reasoning by Analogy: a sequence of thought that compares similar things or circumstances in order to draw a conclusion; if something is true for one, it must also be true for the other. *(11)*

Receiver: an individual who analyzes and interprets a message. *(1)*

Regulating: the use of nonverbal cues to control the flow of conversation. *(4)*

Regulators: nonverbal behaviors that control, monitor, or maintain the back-and-forth interaction between speakers and listeners. *(4)*

Relationship: an association between at least two people. *(12)*

Relationship-Oriented Leaders: leaders who attempt to obtain a position of prominence and good interpersonal relationships. *(14)*

Reliability: the extent to which the same results could be obtained from the same interviewee. *(15)*

Remembering: recalling something by an act of memory—thinking of something again. *(5)*

Repeating: the use of nonverbal cues to repeat what was expressed verbally. *(4)*

Restatement: expression of the same idea using different words; it includes the use of summaries, synonyms, rephrasing, and repetition. *(7)*

Resume: a written document that briefly describes a person's personal, educational, and professional qualifications and experiences. *(15)*

Rhetorical Question: a question that is asked to stimulate thinking, but to which no answer is expected. *(10)*

Secondary Question: a question used to encourage the interviewee to expand on replies that may be incomplete, unresponsive, unclear, or inaccurate. *(15)*

Selecting: the process of choosing what we are going to listen to. *(5)*

Selection: the sorting of one stimulus from another. *(2)*

Selective Attention: the process of focusing on a specific stimuli while ignoring or downplaying other stimuli. *(2)*

Selective Retention: the processing, storage, and retrieval of information that we have already selected, organized, and interpreted. *(2)*

Self-adaptors: nonverbal behaviors that are generally not directed at others but, rather, serve some personal need, such as scratching oneself, smoothing one's hair, and straightening one's clothes. *(4)*

Self-Concept: a person's mental picture of his or her physical, social, and psychological self. *(2)*

Self-Disclosure: the voluntary sharing of information about ourselves that another person is not likely to know. *(12)*

Self-Esteem: our feelings and attitudes toward ourselves. *(2)*

Self-Fulfilling Prophecy: the carrying out of expectations. *(2)*

Self-Image: the mental picture we have of ourselves or the person we perceive ourselves to be. *(2)*

Self-Inventory: an analysis of one's own interests used in choosing a speech topic. *(6)*

Semantics: the study of meaning, or the association of words with ideas, feelings, and contexts. *(3)*

Signposts: words, phrases, or short statements that indicate to an audience the direction a speaker will take next. *(8)*

Similarity: the grouping of elements that resemble one another in size, shape, color, or other traits. *(2)*

Small Group Communication: the exchange of information among a relatively small number of persons—usually 3 to 13—who share a common purpose, such as doing a job or solving a problem. *(13)*

Social Facilitation: the tendency for a person to release energy that would not be released if the individual were acting alone. *(13)*

Source: the creator of messages. *(1)*

Spatial Pattern: an order of presentation in which the content of a speech is organized according to relationships in space. *(8)*

Specific Purpose: a single phrase that defines precisely what is to be accomplished in a speech. *(6)*

Speech Anxiety: the fear of speaking before an audience. *(9)*

Speech Communication: a humanistic and scientific field of study, research, and application. Its focus is upon how, why, and with what effects people communicate through spoken language and associated nonverbal messages. *(1)*

Statistics: numerical data that show relationships between and among phenomena (variables, observations, collections) or that summarize and interpret many instances. *(7)*

Stereotype: a relatively fixed mental picture of some class or group that is attributed to an individual member of that group without regard to his or her unique characteristics and qualities. *(3)*

Stimulus: something that incites or quickens action, feeling, or thought. *(2)*

Substituting: the use of nonverbal messages in place of verbal messages when speaking is impossible, undesirable, or inappropriate. *(4)*

Survey Interview: a carefully planned and executed person-to-person question-and-answer session during which the speaker tries to discover specific information that will help in the preparation of a speech. *(6)*

Symposium: a group presentation that resembles a panel but, rather than interact, participants each present a speech on one aspect of the topic. *(13)*

Synonym: a word, term, or concept that is the same or very nearly the same in meaning as another word, term, or concept. *(10)*

System: a combination of parts interdependently acting to form a whole. *(1)*

Task Needs: needs related to the content of the discussion; include all behaviors that lead to the completion of the task. *(14)*

Task-Oriented Leaders: leaders who gain satisfaction from performing a task. *(14)*

Territoriality: the need to identify certain areas of space as our own. *(4)*

Testimony: the opinions or conclusions of recognized witnesses or authorities. *(7)*

Theory of Interpersonal Needs: a theory developed by William Schutz which contends that three basic needs—affection, inclusion, and control—determine our communication behaviors with others. *(12)*

Throughput: all the internal processes that occur in a group, whether as a result of what each group member brings or as a result of the group's own development. *(13)*

Time Sequence (Chronological) Pattern: an order of presentation that begins at a particular point in time and continues either forward or backward. *(8)*

Topical Pattern: an order of presentation in which the main topic is divided into a series of related subtopics. *(8)*

Transaction: an exchange of communication between people that is a simultaneous, shared event; that is, both encoding and decoding go on at the same time. *(1)*

Transitions: phrases and words used to link ideas. *(8)*

Trustworthiness: the audience's perception of a speaker's reliability and dependability. *(11)*

Understanding: the assigning of meaning to the stimuli that we have selected and attended to. *(5)*

Unintentional Communication: a message that is not intended to be sent or is not intended for the person who receives it. *(1)*

Unknown Area: the quadrant of the Johari Window that represents information not known either to oneself or to others. *(12)*

Validity: the extent to which both the interviewer and the interviewee accomplish the purpose of the interview. *(15)*

Value: a broad-based, relatively long-lasting ideal that guides our behavior. *(2)*

Verbal Communication: the use of words to convey a message. *(4)*

Visual Aids: all materials and equipment, such as key words, diagrams, models, real objects, photographs, tables, charts, and graphs, that speakers may use to supplement their words. *(9)*

Vocal Quality: the overall impression a speaker's voice makes on his or her listeners. *(9)*

Vocal Variety: the combination of rate, force, and pitch variations that adds to a speaker's overall vocal quality. *(9)*

Voluntary Participant: a person who chooses to hear a particular speaker or speech. *(6)*

Words: symbols that stand for the objects and concepts that they name. *(3)*

Index